Java Concurrent Programming:

A Quantitative Approach

Henry H. Liu

$\mathcal{P}$ **PerfMath**

The right of Henry H. Liu to be identified as author of this book has been asserted by him in accordance with the Copyright, Designs and Patens Act 1988.

The contents in this book have been included for their instructional value. They have been tested with care but are not guaranteed for any particular purpose. Neither the publisher nor author shall be liable for any loss of profit or any other commercial damages, including but not limited to special, incidental, consequential, or other damages.

ISBN-13: 978-1514849873

ISBN-10: 1514849879

10 9 8 7 6 5 4 3 2 1

10142015

To My Family

Table of Contents

List of Programs

Table of Figures

Preface

WHY THIS BOOK

As we all know, Java is one of the most popular programming languages for developing applications, especially enterprise applications. (For the latest statistics about the popularity of the programing languages, refer to Figure P.1 on the next page.) Whether you are already using Java to develop exciting cloud computing or big data or traditional enterprise applications or planning to enter these areas as a beginner or an experienced Java developer, having a systematic understanding of the power and flexibility that the modern Java concurrent programming frameworks offer is important. Applications in these areas require high performance and scalability, driving unprecedented high demands for skills in Java concurrent programming.

However, Java concurrent programming is one of the most challenging areas in terms of complexity and unpredictability. Certainly, no books can be so helpful to turn anybody into an expert overnight, but the approach to acquiring a new skill (programming or anything else) certainly matters. My observation is that there are far more books in teaching general programming in Java than in teaching concurrent programming in Java. Even though there are a few texts teaching concurrent programming in Java, they are either outdated or not sufficiently systematic, coherent and comprehensive. This text attempts to fill these gaps by taking a new approach that emphasizes more on understanding how various Java concurrent programming models, collections, synchronizers and frameworks are actually implemented internally. The text is also accompanied by many carefully-crafted examples.

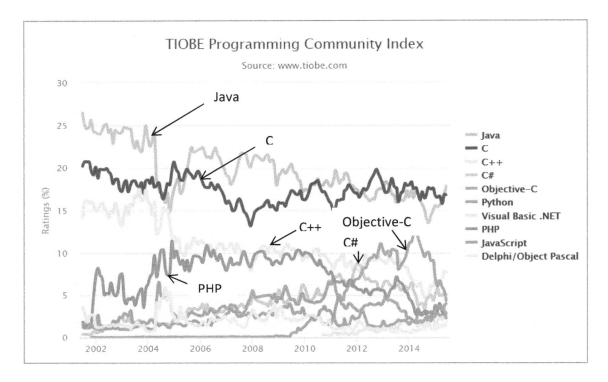

Figure P.1 Statistics on popularity of programming languages

Of course, programming is both science and art, which means that one can get started as quickly as possible, but it may take many years of experience to master it. Having said that, it's not this book's objective to teach those who are already masters in this field. Instead, I hope that this book can provide an easier entry into Java concurrent programming for those who are passionate about programming, especially motivated and determined to develop high-performance and scalable Java software.

WHOM THIS BOOK IS FOR

Obviously, this text is for those who are interested in learning Java concurrent programming. The text is based on how various classes are actually implemented internally. I took this approach in order to minimize the possibilities of any kind of misperceptions and misunderstandings. Besides, a great additional benefit out of this approach is that it gives all of us an opportunity to see and appreciate how those masters coded all of those classes that we use every day for our Java concurrent programming activities. Therefore, I am confident that this book will not only enhance your Java concurrent programming skills specifically but also Java programming skills *in general*.

HOW THIS BOOK IS ORGANIZED

This book consists of the following chapters:

- **Chapter 1 Multithreaded Programming in Java**: This chapter starts with the most basic concept of what a Java thread is about, and then helps you understand how to create a thread, how to use the traditional implicit monitor locks to synchronize a method or a block of code, and how inter-thread communications work. It also covers the concepts of livelock, starvation and deadlock and how to detect them effectively.
- **Chapter 2 Java Thread ExecutorService Framework:** This chapter focuses on understanding the ExecutorService framework, which is the most commonly used framework for many real Java applications to manage the lifecycle of the threads that perform various tasks concurrently.
- **Chapter 3 The Java Collections Framework**: This chapter is dedicated to the unsynchronized collections that are used in many real Java applications. These collections are covered not only because they are important but also because their synchronized counterparts are built on them.
- **Chapter 4 Atomic Operations**: This chapter introduces the atomic operations provided at the lowest level, including the Unsafe class and the atomic classes for synchronizing single variables.
- **Chapter 5 Locks**: This chapter introduces the finer-grade locks that are explicit and flexible, including the ReentrantLock and ReentrantReadWriteLock classes.
- **Chapter 6 Synchronizers**: This chapter covers all common types of synchronizers such as semaphores, cyclic barriers, countdown latches, exchangers and phasers. The entire Java concurrent programming framework would be incomplete without these synchronizers.
- **Chapter 7 Synchronized Collections**: This chapter focuses on various built-in thread-safe lists, queues, sets and maps. These synchronized collections are well-tested and should be used as much as possible as it's hard to build an application without using proper data structures, especially using synchronized data structures if the application will be run in multithreaded environment.
- **Chapter 8 Parallel Programming Using the Fork-Join Framework**: This chapter introduces the Fork-Join framework for solving large dataset related challenging computational tasks in the realm of parallel programming. This framework is becoming more and more relevant with the advent of new areas such as cloud computing, big data analytics, and so on.
- **Appendix A Algorithm Analysis**: This appendix gives an introductory review of algorithm analysis to help you understand the performance characteristics of various operations associated with those collections. This is an important skill to have for being able to choose proper data structures among many of them to solve a particular problem.
- **Appendix B The Bridge Exercise**: This appendix provides a reference implementation for the classic bridge exercise.

My recommendation is that you start with *Appendix A Algorithm Analysis*, and then follow the sequence of all chapters, which, from my perspectives, is the most logical way of learning Java concurrent programming.

SOFTWARE AND HARDWARE

I hope that you do not just read the text but also try to understand all code snippets and examples as well. In order to work on those examples, you need a PC and install a version of JDK 7, preferably with the

Eclipse IDE as well. You can download all examples from this book's website, import them into your IDE, examine them and run them.

HOW TO USE THIS BOOK

To achieve the maximum effectiveness and efficiency, the suggested way to use this book is:

1. Try to understand the concepts first at the high level, for example, why a class or data structure is needed and what problems it helps solve.
2. Try to understand the partial implementation of a class by tracing it with the help of the text or on your own. It will not only help you become a master of solving concurrency challenges but also a master of programming in Java in general.
3. For the many examples presented in the text, don't just read them. Instead, import them on to your system and get your hands dirty with them by even modifying them and running them yourself.

You can find colored images (when color is important) at this book's companion website at http://www.perfmath.com/jcp/colored_images.pdf. The book also contains exercises at the end of each chapter to help you check and solidify what you have learnt after completing a chapter.

TYPOGRAPHIC CONVENTIONS

Times New Roman indicates normal text blocks.

Italic indicates *emphasis*, *definitions*, *email addresses*, and *URLs* in general.

`Courier New` font indicates code listings, scripts, and all other types of programming segments.

`Courier` indicates programming elements outside a program or script as well as everything related to executing a program or script such as commands, file names, directoy paths, entries on an HTML form, etc.

HOW TO REACH THE AUTHOR

All errors in the text are the author's responsibility. You are welcome to email the typos, errors and bugs you found as well as any questions and comments you may have to me at *henry_h_liu@perfmath.com*. Your valuable feedback will be greatly appreciated.

THE BOOK'S WEB SITE

For downloads and updates, please visit the book's website at http://www.perfmath.com.

Henry H. Liu, PH. D.

Palo Alto, California

Summer, 2015

Acknowledgements

First, I would really like to thank the self-publishing vendors I have chosen for making this book available to you. This is the most cost-effective and efficient approach for both you as my audience and myself as author. Computer and software technologies evolve so fast that a more timely publishing approach is beneficial for all of us. In addition, my gratitude extends to my wife Sarah and our son William, as I could have not been able to complete this book without their support and patience.

I would also like to thank my audience for valuable feedback and comments, which I have taken whole-heartedly and included every time this book was updated. I am particularly grateful to those master-level programmers who implemented various classes that make Java concurrent programming not only very useful but also enjoyable. The text heavily depends on their well-documented implementations of various classes to explain as accurately as possible how those frameworks work. I do not feel I have the privilege to mention their names here, but we all know whom they are.

1 Multithreaded Programming in Java

As we all know, software programs execute in processes and threads. The difference between a process and a thread is that a process has its own self-contained execution environment, including a private memory area, while a thread is often called a lightweight process as it *shares* the containing process's resources, such as memory and open files. A thread resides within its parent thread or process.

Threads are as important as processes, as they allow more than one task to be executed *concurrently* within a process, which enhances a system's overall throughput – regardless of whether the system has one processor or multi-processors or multi-cores. Even if a system has only one processor, most OS supports a feature called *time slicing*, which allows various processes and threads take turn to execute, giving a user an illusion that multiple tasks were being executed concurrently.

Prior to our journey to exploring multithreaded programming in Java, I'd like to scope out the perspectives of concurrent programming upfront. This will help us understand where our battlefields will be and how we know we are successful with our concurrent programming efforts.

1.1 PERSPECTIVES OF CONCURRENT PROGRAMMING

Perhaps we should ask why we need to exploit concurrent programming in the first place after all. The answer is that it's all *performance-driven*. Let's start with a performance law next.

Assume that we have a task that takes two stages to complete sequentially, as shown in Figure 1.1. What is the total system throughput, given throughput X_1 for stage 1 and throughput X_2 for stage 2?

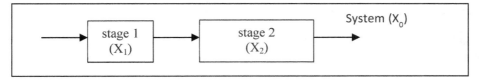

Figure 1.1 A job consisting of two consecutive stages

It turns out that the total system throughput, X_0, can be expressed as follows [*Java Performance and Scalability: A Quantitative Approach*, Henry H. Liu, CreateSpace, 2013]:

$$X_0 = \frac{X_1 \times X_2}{X_1 + X_2} \qquad (1.1)$$

where $X_1 = N/\Delta T_1$ (stage 1) is the stage 1 throughput and $X_2 = N/\Delta T_2$ is the stage 2 throughput. Here, N is the total number of transactions to be processed by the two stages sequentially, while ΔT_1 and ΔT_2 are the durations taken at stages 1 and 2, respectively. Equation (1.1) sets the performance law for sequential programs. It can be extended to the case of n sequential stages as follows:

$$X_0 = \frac{\prod_{i=1}^{n} X_i}{\sum_{i=1}^{n} X_i} \qquad (1.2)$$

However, it's sufficient to limit n to $n = 2$ to make our point clear here: This formula reveals the key to understanding the performance bottleneck of a system. Suppose stage 2 is the bottleneck, namely, stage 2's throughput is much lower than that of stage 1, or:

$$X_2 \ll X_1 \qquad (1.3)$$

Equation (1.1) can now be approximated as:

$$X_0 \cong X_2 \qquad (1.4)$$

The above formula states that in order to improve the total system throughput, optimization efforts have to focus on stage 2. In addition to many potential optimization and tuning opportunities, let's see how we can improve the performance of stage 2 using *concurrency*, which is the main theme of this text.

Let's further simplify the matter by assuming that:

1. Stage 1 is *sequential* and cannot be made to run concurrently or in parallel.
2. Let's assume that the total wall-clock, elapsed time is $\Delta T = \Delta T_1 + \Delta T_2$, X_1 and X_2 can be re-formatted as

$$X_1 = \frac{N/\Delta T}{\Delta T1/\Delta T} = \frac{X_0}{s} \qquad (1.5a)$$

$$X_2 = \frac{N/\Delta T}{\Delta T2/\Delta T} = = \frac{1/\Delta T}{(\Delta T - \Delta T1)/\Delta T} = \frac{X_0}{1-s} \qquad (1.5b)$$

Here, we assume that the total portion of the sequential stage is $s = \Delta T_1/\Delta T$, the portion of the time spent in stage 1; thus the portion of stage 2 that can run concurrently is $1 - s$, which would be $(1 - s)/m$ if executed by m threads concurrently. Substituting X_1 and X_2 expressed in Equations (1.5a) and (1.5b) into Equation (1.1) gives:

$$p = \frac{1}{s + \frac{1-s}{m}} \qquad (1.6)$$

Equation (1.6) is called Amdahl's law, which represents the speedup (p) if the portion that can run concurrently is run concurrently by m threads. Let's use the following two extreme examples to illustrate the implications of Equation (1.6), assuming $m = 10$:

1. $s = 0.1$ (10%). This case means that 90% of the process can be run concurrently. With $m = 10$, $p \approx 5.3$, which implies that by running the portion that can be run concurrently with 10 threads, the maximum speedup would be 5.3 times, not 10 times.
2. $s = 0.9$ (90%). This case means that 10% of the process can be run concurrently. With $m = 10$, $p \approx 1.1$, which implies that by running the portion that can be run concurrently with 10 threads, the maximum speedup would be 10% only.

The above examples confirm an important principle that whether sequential or concurrent, the evaluation of software system performance must be *quantitative*. We do not need to follow all principles of metrologies, but a basic rule is that all performance optimization initiatives and efforts must be based on well-designed and executed measurements. For example, it's meaningless is to make 10% of the process run concurrently and achieve 10% gain only while ignoring the 90% of it, as shown by the second case described above.

However, it's important to recognize and acknowledge that pursuing the performance of concurrent programs is different from pursuing the performance of sequential programs. For concurrent programs, we are mainly concerned with two things:

1. **Thread-safety**. This concern means that the three properties of *mutual exclusion, deadlock-free*, and *starvation-free* are all preserved, or *"nothing bad ever happens,"* as vaguely stated in some texts. However, it's not so easy to guarantee thread-safety as threads do not follow repeatable sequences of executions unless coordinated properly. Whenever threads need to be coordinated properly to produce desired results, it's a thread-safety concern.
2. **Liveness failures**. Liveness means that concurrent operations execute and produce deterministic results as if they were sequential, or *"something good eventually happens,"* as vaguely stated in some texts. Therefore, a liveness failure is a reflection that expected outcome did not occur. As you will see, liveness failures may occur in a variety of forms, such as *livelock, starvation, deadlock*, and so on.

Next, we give a historical overview of concurrent algorithms for two purposes:

- To help re-enforce the thread-safety and liveness concerns as stated above.
- To help reflect on some brilliant ideas about composing concurrent algorithms during the earlier days of computers when no hardware-level and/or OS-level synchronization primitives were available to help ease concurrent programming. I hope that after this overview, you would appreciate more how fortunate we are with massive support of Java concurrent constructs that will be detailed throughout the remainder of this text.

We will cover three most representative concurrent algorithms, developed by Dekker, Peterson and Lamport, respectively. Instead of dragging you into the drudgery of rigorous, formal proofs, we will focus more on the ideas and concepts behind those algorithms.

1.2   A HISTORICAL OVERVIEW OF CONCURRENT ALGORITHMS

It's significantly harder to write concurrent programs than to write sequential programs, as there is only one pre-determined execution path with a sequential program, while there could be many execution paths with execution steps from multiple processes or threads intermingled un-deterministically, which may result in un-predictable and/or un-desirable results. Dijkstra recognized the difficulty with concurrent programming in 1960's and contributed significantly in helping shape the field and provide some solutions, especially through the concept of semaphores, as will be covered later in this text.

Essentially, a concurrent algorithm is deemed *correct* if it can be proved that it preserves the following three properties:

1. **Mutual exclusion**: The two processes may not be in their respective critical sections simultaneously.
2. **Deadlock-free**: The two processes may never block each other without letting the other party ever enter its critical section.
3. **Starvation-free**: Any one process may never take exclusive control over execution and not give chances for the other party to enter its critical section.

The first concurrent algorithm was offered by Dekker, which is *correct,* but kind of *ad-hoc*. About 14 years later, Peterson solved the same problem in a simplest, more elegant way, which *"puts an end to the myth of concurrent programming control ...,"* in his own words in his two-page seminal paper with well-deserved provocativeness. Finally, in 1970's, Lamport published his famous Bakery algorithm, which laid the foundation for today's fault-tolerance implementations in clustered computing. Retrospectively, those episodes are very inspiring and enjoyable.

Next, let's start with Dekker's algorithm, which is often used as a prelude to Peterson's algorithm, which is one of the center themes of this section. We conclude this section with Lamport's Bakery algorithm, which is an important milestone not only for concurrent programming but also for high-availability or fault-tolerance systems we build today.

1.2.1 Dekker's Algorithm

Dekker's algorithm was documented in Dijkstra's 1968 lecture notes, titled *Co-operating sequential processes* (https://www.cs.utexas.edu/users/EWD/transcriptions/EWD01xx/EWD123.html). The original algorithm was described using convoluted *if-then* and *goto* statements, which are not intuitive and hard to reason about. However, it does satisfy the three properties of a correct concurrent algorithm as stated previously.

Dekker's algorithm, as shown in Listing 1.1, can be understood as follows:

- Line 1: Repeat while true;
- Line 2: I intend to enter my critical section;
- Line 3: I wait while she intends to enter;
- Line 4: If it's her turn;
- Line 5: I back off;

- Line 6: I spin wait while it's her turn;
- Line 7: She is done so I intend to enter;
- Line 8: Exit the turn-loop;
- Line 9: Exit the intend-loop;
-         /* Critical Section */
- Line 10: Give turn to her;
- Line 11: I do not intend to enter my CS for now.

The two while-loops, expressed at lines 3 and 6, respectively, set up a polite manner to wait as long as the other party intends to enter the CS (line 3) and the turn favors the other party (line 6), which help guarantee mutual exclusion and deadlock-free. Lines 10 – 11 guarantee the property of deadlock-free by setting the turn to the other party and signaling that he/she has just exited his/her critical section.

It's clear that Dekker's algorithm looks a bit *ad-hoc*. About 13 years later, Peterson solved the same problem in a much simpler and elegant manner, as is discussed in the next section.

Listing 1.1 Dekker's algorithm

```
    /* (c1, c2 = 0 or 1; turn = 1 or 2) */
```

```
/* process P1 */              |    /* process P2 */
1   while (true) {            |    1   while (true) {
2      c1 = 1;                |    2      c2 = 1;
3      while (c2 == 1) {      |    3      while (c1 == 1) {
4         if (turn == 2) {    |    4         if (turn == 1) {
5            c1 = 0;          |    5            c2 = 0;
6            while (turn == 2) {}  |  6            while (turn == 1) {}
7            c1 = 1;          |    7            c2 = 1;
8         }                   |    8         }
9      }                      |    9      }
       /* the Critical Section */  |       /* the Critical Section */
10     turn = 2;             |    10     turn = 1;
11     c1 = 0;              |    11     c2 = 0;
       /* Non-Critical Section */  |       /* Non-Critical Section */
12  }                        |    12  }
```

1.2.2 Peterson's Algorithm

14 years later in 1981, Peterson came up with a concurrent algorithm that is much simpler and more elegant than Dekker's algorithm. If you are really interested in studying concurrent algorithms, I strongly suggest that you read his original paper, titled *Myths About The Mutual Exclusion Problem*, published in *Information Processing Letters*, Vol. 12, No. 3, pp 115 – 116 (only two pages), 1981.

Listing 1.2 shows Peterson's algorithm, which I have tried to make as close to its original presentation as possible. It can be understood as follows:

- Line 1: Expresses the intention to enter;
- Line 2: Sets the turn favorable to me;
- Line 3: Sets up a busy wait to wait until neither she wants to enter nor it is her turn, or in other words, wait while she wants to enter and it is her turn. Note the logical operator precedence of NOT (3), == (9), and OR (14), where the numbers in brackets are the precedence in C++ assigned to each of those logical operators. The line under line 3 is the equivalent busy-wait loop that is closer to what we would have in real programming languages.
- Line 4: Signals the current state of having just exited the critical section.

A significant difference between Dekker's algorithm and Peterson's algorithm is that the former has two loops while the latter has only one as shown at line 3 in Listing 1.3. Instead of giving you my version of understanding of how his algorithm guarantees the mutual exclusion, deadlock-free and starvation-free properties, I'd like to quote one of his paragraphs as follows:

"Since the more complex algorithms naturally require more complex proofs, one wonders whether the prevalent attitude on 'formal' correctness arguments is based on poorly structured algorithms. Perhaps good parallel algorithms are not really that hard to understand. In any case, this solution puts an end to the myth that the two process mutual exclusion problem requires complex solutions with complex proofs. (Dijkstra has recently devised a more formal proof of mutual exclusion for this algorithm [7] which, to this author, seems unnaturally complex for such a simple algorithm.)"

Next, we discuss the Bakery algorithm devised by Lamport.

Listing 1.2 Peterson's algorithm

```
    /* (Q1, Q2 = true or false; TURN = 1 or 2) */

----------------------------------------------------------------------------------------
/* trying protocol for P1 */      |     /* trying protocol for P2 */
1   Q1 = true;                    |     1   Q2 = true;
2   TURN = 1;                     |     2   TURN = 2;
3   wait until not Q2 or TURN == 2; |   3   wait until not Q1 or TURN == 1;
    // while (Q2 && TURN != 2) {}  |        // while (Q1 && TURN != 1) {}
    /* critical section */        |         /* critical section */
    /* exit protocol for P1 */    |         /* exit protocol for P2 */
4   Q1 = false;                   |     4   Q2 = false;
----------------------------------------------------------------------------------------
```

1.2.3 The Bakery Algorithm

Prior to the Bakery algorithm by Lamport, Knuth [*Additional comments on a problem in concurrent programming control. Comm. Acm 9, 5 (May 1966), 321-322*], deBruijn [*Additional comments on a problem in concurrent programming control. Comm. Acm 10, 3 (Mar. 1967), 137-138*], Eisenberg and

McGuire [*Further comments on Dijkstra's concurrent programming control problem. Comm. Acm* 15, 11 (Nov. 1972), 999] published their solutions to the concurrent programming problem laid out initially and solved by Dijkstra [*Solution of a problem in concurrent programming control. Comm. Acm* 8, 9 (Sept. 1965), 569] and later solved by Dijkstra using semaphores [*The structure of THE multiprogramming system. Comm. Acm* 11, 5 (May 1968), 341-346]. All these solutions, including the semaphore-based solution, assume that all computers share a same memory location. If this shared memory fails, the entire system halts.

Lamport's Bakery algorithm assumes N processors, each containing its own memory unit. A processor may read from any other processor's memory, but it need only write into its memory, which is a typical "*shared read, exclusive write*" pattern. In the case that if a read and a write operation to a single memory location occur simultaneously, only the write operation must be performed correctly, while the read operation may return any arbitrary value, which is remarkable.

The essence of the Bakery algorithm is that a processor is allowed to fail at any time without bringing down the entire system. It is assumed that when a processor fails, it immediately goes to its noncritical section and halts. The failed processor's memory may return arbitrary values but eventually will return a value of zero.

Unlike the previous algorithms, the Bakery algorithm also guarantees the fairness of first-come-first-served. When a processor wants to enter its critical section, it first executes a loop-free block of code, that is, a fixed number of steps. It is then guaranteed to enter its critical section prior to any other processor that later comes for service.

The algorithm mimics how a bakery works. A customer receives a number when entering the shop. The holder of the lowest number is the next one to be served. The processors are named 1, ..., N, each of which chooses its own number. If two processors choose the same number, then the one with the lowest ID (or name) goes first.

Listing 1.3(a) shows the Bakery algorithm in its original form as published by Lamport. It starts with two integer arrays, choosing[1:N] and number[1:N]. The elements of choosing[i] and number[i] are in processor i's memory, and are initially zero. The range of number[i] is unbounded. The expression

(number[j], j) < (numbet[i], i) means number[j] < number[i], or j < i if number[j] = number[i].

The processor i is allowed to fail at any time, and then restarted in its non-critical section with choosing[i] = number[i] = 0. However, if a processor keeps failing and restarting, it may deadlock the system.

Listing 1.3(a) The Bakery Algorithm (original form)

```
1    integer array choosing[1:N], number[1:N];
2    begin integer j;
3      L1: choosing[i] := 1;
4          number[i] := 1 + maximum(number[1],...,number[N]);
5          choosing[i] := 0;
6          for j = 1 step 1 until N do
7            begin
8                L2: if choosing[j] !=0 then goto L2;
```

```
9                L3: if number[j] != 0 and (number[j], j) < (number[i], i)
                     then goto L3;
10          end;
11          critical section
12          number[i] = 0;
13          noncritical section;
14          goto L1;
15 end
```

Listing 1.3(b) shows the same Bakery algorithm in a revised form to make it easier to understand. There are two important states for processor *i*:

- *In the door way* when choosing[i] is set to 1 at line 4
- *In the bakery* from when choosing[i] is set to 0 at line 6 until it either fails or leaves the critical section prior to line 11.

Listing 1.3(c) shows a Java implementation of the Bakery algorithm, adapted from an article available online at https://en.wikipedia.org/wiki/Lamport%27s_bakery_algorithm. Note that Java initializes all elements of an int array to zero and all members of a Boolean array to false by default. Lines 7–30 and 32–34 show the lock and unlock methods for thread i, respectively.

The key to understanding the Bakery algorithm lies with the two while-loops displayed at lines 8 and 9, respectively. Line 8 means that processor *i* should wait while processor j is still in the door way choosing its number, while line 9 means that while in the bakery, processor *i* should continue waiting while there exist processes with lower numbers or lower ID's if numbers are equal.

It's interesting to note the arrangement that each thread only writes its own storage, and only reads are shared. Since the algorithm is not built on top of some lower level *atomic* operations, such as compare-and-swap (CAS), as we will discuss later, it can be used to implement mutual exclusion on memory that lacks synchronization primitives provided at the hardware or OS level, e.g., a storage shared among a cluster of computers. Thus, Lamport's Bakery algorithm is not only interesting academically but also practically.

You can refer to Lamport's original paper for the proofs of all three properties of *mutual exclusion*, *deadlock-free* and *starvation-free*. Next, we discuss the evolution of Java concurrency support.

Listing 1.3(b) The Bakery Algorithm (revised form)

```
1   integer array choosing[1:N], number[1:N];
2   integer j;
3   while (true) {
      /* doorway */
4     choosing[i] = 1;
5     number[i] = 1 + maximum(number[1],...,number[N]);
      /* bakery */
6     choosing[i] = 0;
7     for (int j = 1; j < N; j++) {
8       while(choosing[j] != 0) {};
9       while(number[j] != 0 && (number[j], j) < (number[i], i)) {}
10    };
```

```
       /* critical section */
11     number[i] = 0;
       /* noncritical section */
12  }
```

Listing 1.3(c) Bakery.java

```
1   public class Bakery {
2     int threads = 10;
3
4     int[] number = new int[threads];
5     boolean[] choosing = new boolean[threads];
6
7     public void lock(int i)
8     {
9       choosing[i] = true;
10      int max = 0;
11      for (int n : number) {
12        if (n > max) {
13          max = n;
14        }
15      } // find max in the array
16      number[i] = 1 + max;
17      choosing[i] = false;
18      for (int j = 0; j < number.length; ++j) {
19        if (j != i) {
20          while (choosing[j]) {
21            Thread.yield();
22          }
23          while (number[j] != 0
24              && (number[j] < number[i] ||
                    (number[i] == number[j] && j < i))) {
25            Thread.yield();
26          }
27        }
28      }
29      /* critical section */
30    }
31
32    public void unlock(int i) {
33      number[i] = 0;
34    }
35  }
```

1.3   EVOLUTION OF JAVA CONCURRENCY SUPPORT

As one of the most popular, modern programming languages, the Java platform began with providing basic concurrency support in the Java programming language itself and its class libraries since its earliest version of JDK 1.0, mostly through the *synchronized* keyword and the *volatile* keyword, as will be discussed later. Java 5 enhanced the concurrency support by providing high-level concurrency API in the `java.util.concurrent` package, making Java concurrent programming more flexible with the following new features:

- Lock objects for finer-granularity mutual exclusion control
- Executor interface for much-needed thread pool management for large scale applications
- Concurrent collections for managing large collections of data with reduced need for synchronization
- Atomic variables for minimizing the need for synchronization at the application level

Java 7 further introduced a new thread pool named Fork-Join pool, which was designed for computations that can be broken into smaller pieces and processed recursively. The Fork-Join pool spreads split sub-tasks among multiple CPU cores transparently, which greatly simplifies concurrent programming while enhancing the performance and scalability of an application.

Finally, I'd like to mention that Java 8 added new extensions for more powerful parallel-processing support with features such as `CompletableFuture` and `streams`, which will be covered in future versions of this book.

1.4 JAVA THREADS

A Java thread is a single unit of execution on its own for executing a designated computing task. A Java thread can be defined by implementing an interface named `Runnable` or by extending a class named `Thread`, which implements `Runnable`. However, the challenging is not with how to create a Java thread, but with how to coordinate threads so that they don't stampede on each other and end up with un-deterministic results.

Next, let's review some of the issues that might arise with Java concurrent programming.

1.4.1 Potential Issues with Java Concurrency

The following issues may arise associated with Java multithreaded programming:

- **Thread Interference.** Each thread has its own prescribed set of operations to carry out. Interference occurs when operations that run in different threads but act on the same data interleave. Depending on how the sequences of steps overlap, the results may be un-deterministic.
- **Memory Inconsistency Errors**. It's imperative that all threads have consistent views of the state of a *shared* resource or data structure or object in general. However, depending on how multiple threads are coordinated, memory inconsistency errors may occur, causing undesirable data corruption issues.
- **Context Switching Overhead**. Whenever execution moves to a different thread, the context of the current thread must be switched, causing context switching overhead that eventually limits the scalability of a system. This is more of a scalability issue than a multi-threading *correctness* issue.

To some extent, memory inconsistency errors are a consequence of thread interference not coordinated properly. Memory inconsistency errors can be avoided by establishing a *happens-before* relationship, which guarantees that memory write by one thread is visible to a read by another thread if the write operation *happens-before* the read operation. Various mechanisms, such as described below, exist in the earlier versions of Java to help enforce happens-before relationships:

- **Synchronization**: Synchronization uses an internal entity known as the intrinsic lock or monitor lock or simply *monitor* to help both enforce exclusive access to an object's state and establish happens-before relationships that are essential to guarantee the visibility of the modified state from one thread to all others. In Java, every object has a built-in monitor associated with it. By convention, a thread that needs exclusive and consistent access to an object's fields has to acquire the object's intrinsic lock before accessing them, and then release the intrinsic lock when it's done with them. A thread is said to own the intrinsic lock between the time when it has acquired the lock and the time before it releases the lock. As long as a thread owns an intrinsic lock, no other thread can acquire the same lock. The other thread will block when it attempts to acquire the lock. When a thread releases an intrinsic lock, a happens-before relationship is established between that action and any subsequent acquisition of the same lock.
- **The volatile keyword**: The Java programming language has the *volatile* keyword, which can be applied to a field to guarantee that there is a global ordering on the reads and writes to a volatile variable. There are two implications associated with a volatile variable: (1) the compiler should not apply optimizations to a volatile variable, and (2) a thread should fetch a volatile variable's value from memory instead of from cache for every access. In Java 5 or later, volatile reads and writes establish a *happens-before* relationship, much like acquiring and releasing a mutex. However, it may not work as intended in some situations; therefore, exercise caution when you use a volatile variable with your application.
- **Thread.start()**: Causes the thread to begin execution; the Java Virtual Machine calls the `run` method of the thread.
- **Thread.sleep(long millis)**: Causes the currently executing thread to sleep (temporarily cease execution) for the specified number of milliseconds.
- **Thread.join()**: The calling thread waits until the called thread terminates.

We will dive into the above mechanisms in detail throughout the remainder of this text. For the time being, you can get a glimpse of why the above issues arise by understanding the various states that a Java thread might be in at any given point of time, which is the subject of the next section.

1.4.2 All Possible States for a Java Thread

Figure 1.2 shows the various states that a thread might be in at any given point of time, such as:

- **NEW**: Created but not started to run yet.
- **RUNNABLE**: Currently executing or waiting in the run queue for its turn to execute when it gains access to the CPU. The thread is either ready to be scheduled to run or running.
- **BLOCKED**: Suspended for waiting to acquire a monitor lock.
- **WAITING**: Suspended *indefinitely* caused when the non-timeout versions of `Object.wait()` or `Thread.join()` or `LockSupport.park()` (to be covered later) are called. Will be woken up when another thread calls `notify()`/`notifyAll()`.
- **TIMED_WAITING**: Suspended for a specified period, for example, caused when the following methods are called:
  - `sleep(sleepTime)`
  - `wait(timeout)`
  - `join(timeout)`

    ° `LockSupport.parkNanos()`
    ° `LockSupport.parkUntil()`

- **TERMINATED**: Reached the end of its life and exited.

It's important to remember that a thread can be in only one state at a given point in time. In addition, those states are Java virtual machine states rather than any operating system thread states.

Next, we describe common situations, such as livelock, starvation and deadlock, to avoid when designing and coding concurrent programs.

☜**Note: BLOCKED versus WAITING.** It might be obvious what the states of NEW, RUNNABLE and TERMINATED mean. However, there is a subtle difference between BLOCKED and WAITING: BLOCKED means waiting synchronously to acquire a lock, while WAITING means that the thread has gone into asleep and will wake up when notified asynchronously or timeout expires.

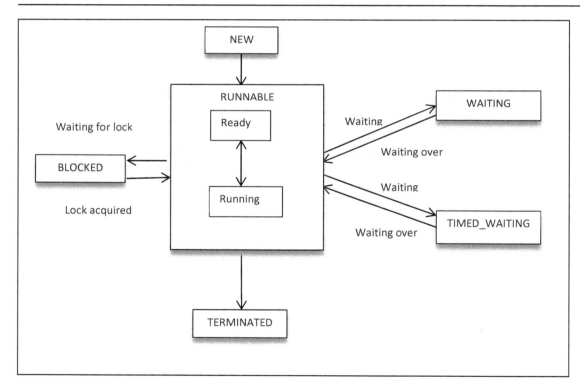

Figure 1.2 Possible states of a thread

1.4.3 Livelock, Starvation and Deadlock

Livelock, starvation and *deadlock* are important concepts to be aware of for current programming. They differ in that:

- **Livelock**: Both threads are attempting to access the same resource at the same time to get their work done but unable to make progress. The situation is similar to two persons facing each other and moving to the same direction to yield to the other party.
- **Starvation**: Describes a situation where one thread grabs and uses the resource solely, making one or more threads have no chance to gain regular access to the shared resource and be unable to make progress. In this case, only one thread – the greedy thread – can make progress. One should avoid starvation as much as possible.
- **Deadlock**: Describes a situation where two or more threads are *blocked* forever, waiting for each other to release the resource.

We will show examples of livelock, starvation and deadlock later in this chapter. Next, we describe how to create a Java thread.

1.5 CREATING A THREAD

In Java, you can create a thread by one of the following two ways:

- implementing the Runnable interface
- extending the Thread class

The Runnable interface is incredibly simple. It is as simple as shown in Listing 1.4, with only one public method named run, which has no arguments and does not return a result.

Listing 1.4 Runnable.java

```
36  package java.lang;
37  public interface Runnable {
38      public void run();
39  }
```

As is seen, if you need to create a class with potentially many instances for executing certain tasks, all you need to do is to create a class that implements the Runnable interface, with the intended tasks coded in the run() method. This interface is meant to be a common construct for objects to execute code while they are active until they are stopped. Runnable is lightweight and is particularly suitable for defining computational tasks, as will be demonstrated throughout this text.

Listing 1.5 shows the Thread class definition, extracted from its actual implementation as of JDK 1.7u75 – the last update of JDK 7 as of this writing. The entire implementation is 2058 lines long, including comments, which is too lengthy to be fully listed here. Even with this partial listing, we can see:

- Lines 3 – 17: What classes the Thread class depends on, such as Reference, ReferenceQueue, AccessController, Map, HashMap, ConcurrentHashMap, LockSupport, Interruptible, and so on.
- Line 19: The Thread class implements the Runnable interface.
- Lines 21 – 23: Fields such as name, priority, and threadQ, and so on.

- Lines 26 – 30: Fields such as `threadLocals`, `stackSize`, `tid` for Thread ID, `threadStatus`, and so on.
- Lines 32 – 34: How the `synchronized` keyword is used to guard incrementing the `threadSeqNumber` field.
- Line 36: How the `volatile` keyword is used to guard the `blocker` variable of type `Interruptible`.
- Lines 37 – 43: How the `synchronized` and `volatile` keywords are used together to synchronize the `blockerOn` method.
- Lines 47 – 61: The `sleep( ... )` method and `init ( ... )` method
- Lines 64 – 69: Some private helper methods related to operations such as `setPriority`, `stop`, `suspend`, `resume`, `interrupt`, and `setNativeName`.

Note that the purpose here is not to help you get some immediate and deep understanding of how the Java `Thread` class is actually coded. Instead, even with this partial list, you could get a glimpse of many of the multithreading concepts wired into the Java `Thread` class implementation.

Listing 1.5 Thread.java (partial)

```
1    package java.lang;
2
3    import java.lang.ref.Reference;
4    import java.lang.ref.ReferenceQueue;
5    import java.lang.ref.WeakReference;
6    import java.security.AccessController;
7    import java.security.AccessControlContext;
8    import java.security.PrivilegedAction;
9    import java.util.Map;
10   import java.util.HashMap;
11   import java.util.concurrent.ConcurrentHashMap;
12   import java.util.concurrent.ConcurrentMap;
13   import java.util.concurrent.locks.LockSupport;
14   import sun.nio.ch.Interruptible;
15   import sun.reflect.CallerSensitive;
16   import sun.reflect.Reflection;
17   import sun.security.util.SecurityConstants;
18
19   public class Thread implements Runnable {
20
21       private char        name[];
22       private int         priority;
23       private Thread      threadQ;
24       private long        eetop;
25
26       ThreadLocal.ThreadLocalMap threadLocals = null;
27       ThreadLocal.ThreadLocalMap inheritableThreadLocals = null;
28       private long stackSize;
29       private long tid; // Thread ID
30       private volatile int threadStatus = 0;
31
32       private static synchronized long nextThreadID() {
```

```
33              return ++threadSeqNumber;
34          }
35
36      private volatile Interruptible blocker;
37      private final Object blockerLock = new Object();
38
39      void blockedOn(Interruptible b) {
40          synchronized (blockerLock) {
41              blocker = b;
42          }
43      }
44
45      public static native Thread currentThread();
46
47      public static void sleep(long millis, int nanos)
48      throws InterruptedException { // ...}
49
50      private void init(ThreadGroup g, Runnable target, String name,
51                          long stackSize, AccessControlContext acc) {
52          if (name == null) {
53              throw new NullPointerException("name cannot be null");
54          }
55
56          this.name = name.toCharArray();
57
58          Thread parent = currentThread();
59          SecurityManager security = System.getSecurityManager();
60          // ...
61      }
62
63      /* Some private helper methods */
64      private native void setPriority0(int newPriority);
65      private native void stop0(Object o);
66      private native void suspend0();
67      private native void resume0();
68      private native void interrupt0();
69      private native void setNativeName(String name);
70      // other methods are omitted
71  }
```

A thread is an isolated execution unit in a program. Every thread has a priority. Threads with higher priorities are executed in preference to threads with lower priorities. In addition, a thread may be marked as a daemon. The Java Virtual Machine allows an application to have multiple threads to run concurrently. When a Java Virtual Machine starts up, there is usually a single non-daemon thread. The Java Virtual Machine continues to execute threads until either of the following occurs:

- The exit method of the class Runtime has been called and the security manager has permitted the exit operation to take place.
- All non-daemon threads have exited, either by returning from the call to the run method or by throwing an exception that propagates beyond the run method.

Before showing some actual examples of creating Java threads, I'd like to call your attention to the two more methods of the Thread class, start() and run(), as shown in Listings 1.6 and 1.7. The start() method starts up a thread while the run() method initiates the thread to execute the tasks defined in the run() method immediately. It's interesting to see from line 1 of Listing 1.6 that the start() method of a thread itself is synchronized.

Listing 1.6 The start method of the Thread class

```
1     public synchronized void start() {
2         if (threadStatus != 0)
3             throw new IllegalThreadStateException();
4
5         /* Notify the group that this thread is about to be started
6          * so that it can be added to the group's list of threads
7          * and the group's unstarted count can be decremented. */
8         group.add(this);
9
10        boolean started = false;
11        try {
12            start0();
13            started = true;
14        } finally {
15            try {
16                if (!started) {
17                    group.threadStartFailed(this);
18                }
19            } catch (Throwable ignore) {
20                /* do nothing */
21            }
22        }
23    }
24
25    private native void start0();
```

Listing 1.7 The run method of the Thread class

```
26    public void run() {
27        if (target != null) {
28            target.run();
29        }
30    }
```

Regarding the run() method of the Thread class as shown in Listing 1.7, if the thread was constructed using a separate Runnable object, then that Runnable object's run method is called; otherwise, the run method does nothing and returns. Refer to Figure 1.3, taken from the JDK7u75 source project imported onto my Eclipse IDE, for other fields and methods for the Thread class. Note the symbol next to each entry, such as *S* for static, *E* for enum, *I* for interface, *V* for volatile, *C* for constructor, *F* for final, and *N* for native. You can learn a lot just by going through all entries by their names, which are indicative of what they are meant for. For example, look under the enum State for BLOCKED, NEW,

RUNNABLE, TERMNINATED, TIMED_WAITING and WAITING, which correspond to the Java thread states shown in Figure 1.2.

▲ ⬚ Thread.java
  ▲ Ⓟ Thread
    ▲ Ⓖ Caches
      subclassAudits
      subclassAuditsQueue
    ▲ Ⓔ State
      BLOCKED
      NEW
      RUNNABLE
      TERMINATED
      TIMED_WAITING
      WAITING
   ▷ Ⓞ UncaughtExceptionHandler
   ▷ Ⓖ WeakClassKey
   defaultUncaughtExceptionHandler
   EMPTY_STACK_TRACE
   MAX_PRIORITY
   MIN_PRIORITY
   NORM_PRIORITY
   SUBCLASS_IMPLEMENTATION_PERMISSION
   threadInitNumber
   threadSeqNumber
   {...}
   activeCount() : int
  ▷ auditSubclass(Class) : boolean
   currentThread() : Thread
   dumpStack() : void
   dumpThreads(Thread[]) : StackTraceElement[
   enumerate(Thread[]) : int
   getAllStackTraces() : Map<Thread, StackTrace
   getDefaultUncaughtExceptionHandler() : Unc
   getThreads() : Thread[]

holdsLock(Object) : boolean
interrupted() : boolean
isCCLOverridden(Class) : boolean
nextThreadID() : long
nextThreadNum() : int
processQueue(ReferenceQueue<Class<?>>, C
registerNatives() : void
setDefaultUncaughtExceptionHandler(Uncaugl
sleep(long) : void
sleep(long, int) : void
yield() : void
blocker
blockerLock
contextClassLoader
daemon
eetop
group
inheritableThreadLocals
inheritedAccessControlContext
name
nativeParkEventPointer
parkBlocker
priority
single_step
stackSize
stillborn
target
threadLocals
threadQ
threadStatus
tid
uncaughtExceptionHandler

(a)   (b)

(c)   (d)

Figure 1.3 Fields and methods for the Thread class

From Figure 1.3, you can also notice what constructors are available for creating a Thread object. Here is a summary of all seven constructors:

1. **Thread()**: Allocates a new, anonymous Thread object.
2. **Thread(Runnable target)**: Allocates a new, anonymous Thread object from a Runnable target.
3. **Thread(Runnable target, String name)**: Allocates a new Thread object with a Runnable target and with a given name.

4. **Thread(ThreadGroup group, Runnable target)**: Allocates a new Thread object with a given ThreadGroup and a given Runnable target.

5. **Thread(ThreadGroup group, Runnable target, String name)**: Allocates a new Thread object with a given ThreadGroup, a given Runnable target and a given name.

6. **Thread(ThreadGroup group, Runnable target, String name, long stackSize)**: Allocates a new Thread object with a given ThreadGroup, a given Runnable target, a given name, and a specified stack size.

7. **Thread(ThreadGroup group, String name)**: Allocates a new Thread object with a given ThreadGroup and a given name.

Notice the arguments you can pass into a constructor, essentially as a combination of the parameters such as a Runnable object, a name, and a ThreadGroup object, etc. This will become clear after we show the creating thread examples next. The option 3 with a given Runnable target and a given name is the most common one, though, as demonstrated in the next section.

Next, we show how to create threads by implementing the Runnable interface or by extending the Thread class.

Note: When to use Runnable or Thread. In most cases, the Runnable interface should be used if you are only planning to override the run() method and no other Thread methods. This is important because classes should not be subclassed unless the programmer intends to modify or enhance the fundamental behavior of the class.

1.5.1 Implements Runnable

Listing 1.8(a) shows how a new thread can be defined by *implementing* the Runnable interface. It follows the below procedure:

1. Line 2: Declares a thread variable t.

2. Lines 4 – 9: Define a constructor, within which, a Thread object is instantiated using the Thread class's constructor of Thread (Runnable target, String name) as introduced in the preceding section. Here the Runnable target is the instance itself as designated as "this" and the name is "New Thread." Then, at line 8, the start() method is called to start the thread.

3. Lines 12 -22: Define the run method, which contains a for-loop that loops three times to print a message after sleeping for one second each time. The for-loop is wrapped in a try-catch block to capture InterruptedException.

This example shows how one can create a simple Java thread by implementing the Runnable interface. Next, we describe the driver class.

Listing 1.8(a) NewThread.java

```
1   class NewThread implements Runnable {
2     Thread t;
3
```

```
4    NewThread() {
5       // Create a new thread
6       t = new Thread(this, "New Thread");
7       System.out.println("Child thread: " + t);
8       t.start(); // Start the thread in the constructor
9    }
10
11   // The run method for the new thread
12   public void run() {
13      try {
14         for (int i = 3; i > 0; i--) {
15            System.out.println("Child Thread: " + i);
16            Thread.sleep(1000);
17         }
18      } catch (InterruptedException e) {
19         System.out.println("Child interrupted.");
20      }
21      System.out.println("Exiting child thread.");
22   }
23 }
```

Listing 1.8(b) is a regular Java class for testing the NewThread class as shown in Listing 1.8(a). At line 3, it simply creates a NewThread object without calling its start method, which is already coded in the constructor of the NewThread class as shown at line 8 in Listing 1.8(a). Then, lines 5 – 12 set up a for-loop that loops five times, each of which prints a message and then sleeps for one second prior to the next iteration.

When the MainThread object is executed, it starts up a NewThread object at line 3 and then moves on to execute its own code – mostly the for-loop from line 6 to 9. Now, as we have set up two threads to take turns to get access to CPUs and execute (which would do time-slicing as we described previously), we should explore how they would go each time the MainThread class is run. Figure 1.4 shows the result: The left screenshot and the right screenshot show the sequences of executions interleaved between the main and the child thread out of two separate runs, respectively. As you see, the sequences are different between the first and second runs: The first run had the sequence of 5, 3, 4, 2, 1, 3, ... while the second run had the sequence of 5, 3, 4, 2, 3, 1, ..., with the sub-sequence of 1, 3 swapped between the main and child threads during the second run. This simple example demonstrates exactly the problems that may arise with multithreaded programming: One cannot assume that multiple threads would execute by following a deterministic sequence; and therefore their operations must be coordinated properly to achieve predictable results every time they are executed.

Next, we demonstrate how to create a thread by extending the Thread class.

Listing 1.8(b) MainThread.java

```
1    class MainThread {
2       public static void main(String args[]) {
3          new NewThread(); // create a new thread
4
5          try {
```

```
6              for (int i = 5; i > 0; i--) {
7                  System.out.println("Main Thread: " + i);
8                  Thread.sleep(1000);
9              }
10         } catch (InterruptedException e) {
11             System.out.println("Main thread interrupted.");
12         }
13         System.out.println("Main thread exiting.");
14     }
15 }
```

```
Child thread: Thread[New Thread,5,main]
Main Thread: 5
Child Thread: 3
Main Thread: 4
Child Thread: 2
Child Thread: 1
Main Thread: 3
Exiting child thread.
Main Thread: 2
Main Thread: 1
Main thread exiting.
```
```
Child thread: Thread[New Thread,5,main]
Main Thread: 5
Child Thread: 3
Main Thread: 4
Child Thread: 2
Main Thread: 3
Child Thread: 1
Exiting child thread.
Main Thread: 2
Main Thread: 1
Main thread exiting.
```

Figure 1.4 Main and child threads with un-deterministic sequence of executions

1.5.2 Extends Thread

Listing 1.9(a) shows how a new thread can be defined by *extending* the Thread class. It follows the below procedure:

1. Lines 2 - 7: Since it extends the Thread class instead of implementing the Runnable interface, it does not need to declare a thread variable t, as was the case with the preceding example shown in Listing 1.8(a). Instead, it starts with defining a constructor straightforwardly, within which, the super method is called with a thread name, and then the start() method is called to start the thread.
2. Lines 10 – 20: Define the run method, which is identical to the preceding example that it contains a for-loop that loops three times to print a message after sleeping for one second each time. The for-loop is wrapped in a try-catch block to capture InterruptedException associated with the sleep method.

This example shows how one can create a simple Java thread by extending the Thread class. Next, we describe the driver class.

Listing 1.9(a) ExtendedThread.java

```
1   public class ExtendedThread extends Thread {
2       ExtendedThread () {
3           // Create a new thread
4           super("ExtendedThread");
5           System.out.println("Child thread: " + this);
6           start(); // Start the thread in the constructor
```

```
7     }
8
9     // The run method for the new thread.
10    public void run() {
11       try {
12          for (int i = 3; i > 0; i--) {
13             System.out.println("Child Thread: " + i);
14             Thread.sleep(1000);
15          }
16       } catch (InterruptedException e) {
17          System.out.println("Child interrupted.");
18       }
19       System.out.println("Exiting child thread.");
20    }
21 }
```

Listing 1.9(b) is a regular Java class, named MainThread2, for testing the ExtendedThread class as shown in Listing 1.9(a). At line 3, it simply creates an ExtendedThread object without calling its start method, which is already coded in the constructor of the ExtendedThread class as shown at line 6 in Listing 1.9(a). Then, lines 5 – 12 set up a for-loop that loops five times, each of which prints a message and then sleeps for one second prior to the next iteration.

When the MainThread2 is executed, it starts up an ExtendedThread object at line 3 and then moves on to execute its own code – mostly the for-loop from line 6 to 9. Similar to the preceding example, as we have set up two threads to take turns to get access to CPUs and execute, we explore how they would go each time when MainThread2 is run. Figure 1.5 shows the result: This time, it took four runs in my environment in order to see a different sequence of executions between the main and the child threads from start to finish. Once again, this simple example demonstrates that one cannot assume that multiple threads would execute by following a deterministic sequence, and therefore their operations must be coordinated properly to achieve predictable results every time they are executed.

I hope you have been convinced that threads need to be coordinated properly for their operations to yield predictable results no matter how many times when they are executed. The next section demonstrates how that can be done by synchronizing the operations of multiple threads by using the synchronized keyword made available since Java 1.

Listing 1.9(b) MainThread2.java

```
1  class MaindThread2 {
2     public static void main(String args[]) {
3        new ExtendedThread(); // create a new thread
4
5        try {
6           for (int i = 5; i > 0; i--) {
7              System.out.println("Main Thread: " + i);
8              Thread.sleep(1000);
9           }
10       } catch (InterruptedException e) {
11          System.out.println("Main thread interrupted.");
```

```
12        }
13        System.out.println("Main thread exiting.");
14    }
15 }
```

```
Child thread: Thread[ExtendedThread,5,main]
Main Thread: 5
Child Thread: 3
Main Thread: 4
Child Thread: 2
Main Thread: 3
Child Thread: 1
Exiting child thread.
Main Thread: 2
Main Thread: 1
Main thread exiting.
```

```
Child thread: Thread[ExtendedThread,5,main]
Main Thread: 5
Child Thread: 3
Main Thread: 4
Child Thread: 2
Main Thread: 3
Child Thread: 1
Exiting child thread.
Main Thread: 2
Main Thread: 1
Main thread exiting.
```

```
Child thread: Thread[ExtendedThread,5,main]
Main Thread: 5
Child Thread: 3
Main Thread: 4
Child Thread: 2
Main Thread: 3
Child Thread: 1
Main Thread: 2
Exiting child thread.
Main Thread: 1
Main thread exiting.
```

```
Child thread: Thread[ExtendedThread,5,main]
Main Thread: 5
Child Thread: 3
Main Thread: 4
Child Thread: 2
Main Thread: 3
Child Thread: 1
Exiting child thread.
Main Thread: 2
Main Thread: 1
Main thread exiting.
```

Figure 1.5 Sequences interleaved between the main and child threads out of four runs: one is different from the other three

1.6 SYNCHRONIZATION

As you've seen from lines 32 – 43 from Listing 1.5, as copied over here as shown below, one can synchronize a method (lines 32 – 34) or a block of code (lines 40 – 42) by applying the synchronized keyword. In both cases, there is an implicit lock associated with every Java object; and when a method or a block is synchronized, that implicit monitor lock will work behind the scene. In this section, we use two examples to demonstrate these two different synchronization approaches.

```
32    private static synchronized long nextThreadID() {
33        return ++threadSeqNumber;
34    }
35
36    private volatile Interruptible blocker;
37    private final Object blockerLock = new Object();
38
39    void blockedOn(Interruptible b) {
40        synchronized (blockerLock) {
41            blocker = b;
42        }
43    }
```

1.6.1 Synchronized Methods

This section provides an example to demonstrate how multiple Java threads that share a resource can be coordinated by using the `synchronized` keyword available since Java 1. The example consists of three classes as shown in Listings 1.10(a), (b) and (c), respectively. The function of each class is described as follows:

- **Messager.java** [Listing 1.10(a)]. This is a regular Java class, meaning that it does not implement the `Runnable` interface or extend the `Thread` class. It simply outputs a given message flanked by a left arrow bracket and a right arrow bracket. The `sendMessage(String msg)` method has a `Thread.sleep (1000)` statement, which puts the thread into sleep for one second each time when it's called. Keep in mind that each thread will have its own copy of the `Messager` object instance, so some chaotic behavior might occur to those `Messager` object instances if they were not synchronized.
- **MessageThread.java** [Listing 1.10(b)]. This is a Java thread class that implements the `Runnable` interface. As expected, it implements the `run()` method, within which the target `Messager` object's `sendMessage` method is called with a given message.
- **SynchTest0.java** [Listing 1.10(c)]. This is the driver class that tests the above two classes. It creates a `Messager` object instance, which will be passed to three threads of type `MessageThread`, with a message passed in together for each thread to send.

As shown in Listing 1.10(c), the three threads are supposed to send the messages of "Java", "Concurrent" and "Programming", respectively, with each message to be flanked by "<" and ">", respectively, as well. However, without synchronizing the `Messager` object, as indicated by line 2 commented out in Listing 1.10(a), the output of running the SynchTest0 class as shown in Listing 1.10(c) would look like the following:

```
<Java<Concurrent<Programming>
>
>
```

Now, after un-commenting line 2 and commenting out line 3 in `Messager.java` shown in Listing 1.10(a), the output of running the same `SynchTest0.java` class would look like the following:

```
<Java>
<Programming>
<Concurrent>
```

or

```
<Concurrent>
<Java>
<Programming>
```

Namely, each message is flanked properly, although the sequence of the messages may differ, which is acceptable as long as the integrity of each thread is preserved.

Next, we demonstrate how to use synchronized blocks or statements to achieve the same purpose.

Listing 1.10(a) Messager.java

```
1   public class Messager {
```

```
2    //synchronized void sendMessage (String msg) {
3    void sendMessage (String msg) {
4        System.out.print("<" + msg);
5        try {
6            Thread.sleep(1000);
7        } catch (InterruptedException e) {
8            System.out.println("Interrupted: " + e.getStackTrace());
9        }
10       System.out.println(">");
11   }
12 }
```

Listing 1.10(b) MessageThread.java

```
1  class MessageThread implements Runnable {
2    String msg;
3    Messager target;
4    Thread t;
5
6    public MessageThread(Messager targ, String s) {
7        target = targ;
8        msg = s;
9        t = new Thread(this);
10       t.start();
11   }
12
13   public void run() {
14       target.sendMessage (msg);
15   }
16 }
```

Listing 1.10(c) SynchTest0.java

```
1  public class SynchTest0 {
2    public static void main(String args[]) {
3        Messager target = new Messager();
4        MessageThread messager1 = new MessageThread(target, "Java");
5        MessageThread messager2 = new MessageThread(target, "Concurrent");
6        MessageThread messager3 = new MessageThread(target, "Programming");
7
8        // wait for threads to end by calling the join () method
9        try {
10           messager1.t.join();
11           messager2.t.join();
12           messager3.t.join();
13       } catch (InterruptedException e) {
14           System.out.println("Interrupted");
15       }
16   }
17 }
```

1.6.2 Synchronized Blocks

In order to show how to synchronize a block of code rather than a method, I simply copied the three classes introduced in the preceding section and renamed them from `Messager.java` to `Messager1.java`, from `MessageThread.java` to `MessageThread1.java`, and `SynchTest0.java` to `SynchTest1.java`, as shown in Listings 1.11(a), (b) and (c), respectively. Unlike the previous version, notice that the shared `Messager1.java` class has no `synchronized` keyword applied to its `sendMessage` method. Instead, the `synchronized` keyword is applied to the `target` object in the `run` method of the `MessageThread1.java` class, which surrounds the statement of `target.sendMessage (msg)` as shown from lines 14 – 16 in Listing 1.11(b) `MessageThread1.java`.

If you run `SynchTest1.java` class as shown in Listing 1.11 (c), you should get an output similar to the following:

```
<Java>
<Programming>
<Concurrent>
```

Namely, each message was flanked by "<" and ">" as expected. As you see, we can apply synchronization either at the shared resource level or at the thread level. From the programming point of view, synchronizing a method is simpler than synchronizing a block; and in many cases, the two approaches might be equivalent in terms of performance. However, when it comes to the scope of locking, synchronizing a block should be considered first, as noted below.

◄Note: **Synchronizing methods versus synchronizing blocks: which one should be used?** One should in general favor synchronizing blocks over synchronizing methods, as the former generally reduces scope of lock, which is beneficial for performance. Put it another way, it's always a better choice to lock only a critical section of code rather than an entire method. With a synchronized method, the lock is acquired by the thread when it enters the method and released when it leaves the method, whereas with a synchronized block, the thread acquires the lock only when it enters the synchronized block and releases the lock as soon as it leaves the synchronized block.

In addition, one can synchronize different blocks using different lock objects within a method, if necessary, which is unachievable when an entire method is synchronized. Therefore, synchronizing a block provides extra finer granularity when needed.

Listing 1.11(a) Messager1.java

```
1   public class Messager1 {
2     void sendMessage (String msg) {
3       System.out.print("<" + msg);
4       try {
5         Thread.sleep(1000);
6       } catch (InterruptedException e) {
7         System.out.println("Interrupted: " + e.getStackTrace());
```

```
8          }
9          System.out.println(">");
10     }
11  }
```

Listing 1.11(b) MessageThread1.java

```
1   class MessageThread1 implements Runnable {
2       String msg;
3       Messager1 target;
4       Thread t;
5
6       public MessageThread1(Messager1 targ, String s) {
7           target = targ;
8           msg = s;
9           t = new Thread(this);
10          t.start();
11      }
12
13      public void run() {
14          synchronized (target) { // synchronized block
15              target.sendMessage(msg);
16          }
17      }
18  }
```

Listing 1.11(c) SynchTest1.java

```
1   public class SynchTest1 {
2       public static void main(String args[]) {
3           Messager1 target = new Messager1();
4           MessageThread1 messager1 = new MessageThread1(target, "Java");
5           MessageThread1 messager2 = new MessageThread1(target, "Concurrent");
6           MessageThread1 messager3 = new MessageThread1(target, "Programming");
7
8           // wait for threads to end by calling the join () method
9           try {
10              messager1.t.join();
11              messager2.t.join();
12              messager3.t.join();
13          } catch (InterruptedException e) {
14              System.out.println("Interrupted");
15          }
16      }
17  }
```

1.7 INTER-THREAD COMMUNICATIONS

As we emphasized earlier, executions of threads often have to be coordinated in order to achieve deterministic results. In order to program coordination among threads, some kind of inter-thread communication mechanisms are called for. This section explores some options for coordinating threads, from very primitive ones such as busy-wait or busy-spin, to advanced ones such as wait(), notify() (which wakes up only one thread) and notifyAll() (which wakes up all threads – more efficient if many threads are waiting for the same lock).

Let's begin with explaining the concept of busy-wait or busy-spin next.

1.7.1 Busy Wait / Busy Spin

Busy wait or busy spin means the same thing: A process or a thread runs in an infinite loop, checking repeatedly if a certain condition has become true; and if the condition that it is waiting for becomes true, it gets out of the infinite loop and continues. For example, the following code snippet does busy wait:

```
1   private boolean happened;
2   // ...
3   while (!happened) {} // busy wait here - waste of CPU time
4   System.out.println ("It has just happened!");
5   // do something else
```

Apparently, the above "do nothing" loop deprives other threads of access to CPUs and thus wastes valuable CPU times. In general, busy-wait is considered an anti-pattern and should be avoided as much as possible.

It's possible to alleviate the CPU wasting impact that a busy-wait incurs by letting the running thread sleep for a fixed period between consecutive condition-checking operations. For example, we can modify line 3 in the above code snippet into the following:

```
3   while (!happened) {Thread.sleep (100);}
```

, which puts the running thread to sleep for 100 milliseconds before the next iteration starts. If the sleep time is significantly longer than the time for checking the state of the condition variable, the running thread will spend most of its time asleep and wastes very little CPU time.

However, an alternative like putting the running thread to sleep for a fixed period still is not a very flexible and elegant solution to the busy-wait problem. Since its earlier versions, Java has provided formal constructs for coordinating inter-thread communications. In the next section, we describe how such constructs can help coordinate thread executions effectively and efficiently.

1.7.2 A Simple Buffer Accessed by a Single Thread

Let's start with the simplest case: a simple buffer to be accessed by a single thread only. As shown in Listing 1.12(a), this SimpleBuffer has two fields, a constructor and two methods as explained below:

- An integer array named buffer to be used as an integer number container
- An integer field named currIndex, which designates the current array element available for storing a new element
- A constructor for allocating memory for the array with a given capacity as well as for initializing the currIndex field to zero

- A method named put(int i) that stores the given value of i at the currently available array element. Note the post-increment operation in currIndex++ at line 13 that bumps the current index to the next available array element in one statement.
- A method named get() that retrieves the latest array element located at the end of the array. This is similar to a last-in-first-out (LIFO) data structure like a Stack, but that's not important for the time being. Eventually, we'll change it into a first-in-first-out (FIFO) data structure like a Queue as will be discussed later. In addition, note the pre-decrement operation in --currIndex at line 17 that moves the index pointer back to the position that contains the last value stored in the buffer.

Next, we describe a single-threaded program that accesses this simple buffer.

Listing 1.12(a) SimpleBuffer.java

```
1    package jcp.ch1.buffer.v0;
2
3    public class SimpleBuffer {
4       private final int[] buffer;
5       private int currIndex;
6
7       SimpleBuffer(int capacity) {
8          this.buffer = new int[capacity];
9          this.currIndex = 0;
10      }
11
12      final void put(int i) {
13         buffer[currIndex++] = i;
14      }
15
16      final int get() {
17         return buffer[--currIndex];
18      }
19   }
```

Listing 1.12(b) shows a SimpleBufferTest Java class that does the following:

- Lines 6 - 7: Initialize the capacity parameter for the buffer to 10 and create a SimpleBuffer object with that capacity accordingly.
- Lines 10 – 13: Fill the buffer up to the capacity as specified above by calling the simpleBuffer object's put method.
- Lines 15 – 18: Get (remove and return) the element of the integer array buffer one by one in the LIFO order by calling the simpleBuffer object's get method.

Running this simple example would result in the following output:

SimpleBuffer: put 0 1 2 3 4 5 6 7 8 9
SimpleBuffer: get 9 8 7 6 5 4 3 2 1 0
done

As you see, nothing surprises us when the above buffer is accessed by a single thread. Next, we'll see immediately what would happen if the above simple buffer were accessed by two threads concurrently.

Listing 1.12(b) SimpleBufferTest.java

```
1   package jcp.ch1.buffer.v0;
2
3   public class SimpleBufferTest {
4     public static void main(String args[]) {
5
6        int capacity = 10;
7        SimpleBuffer simpleBuffer = new SimpleBuffer(capacity);
8
9        System.out.print("SimpleBuffer: put");
10       for (int i = 0; i < capacity; i++) {
11          simpleBuffer.put(i);
12          System.out.print(" " + i);
13       }
14
15       System.out.print("\nSimpleBuffer: get");
16       for (int i = 0; i < capacity; i++) {
17          System.out.print(" " + simpleBuffer.get());
18       }
19       System.out.print("\ndone");
20    }
21  }
```

1.7.3 The Simple Buffer Accessed by Two Threads: Busy-Wait with no Conditional Check (OOB)

For the same simple buffer as shown in Listing 1.12(a), let's set up two threads to access it concurrently: one named Producer.java as shown in Listing 1.13(a) for filling the buffer by calling its put method and the other named Consumer.java as shown in Listing 1.13(b) for consuming the buffer by calling its get method. Take a moment and examine how the constructor for each class is coded: First, the simpleBuffer field is initialized with the simpleBuffer object passed-in, and then a new thread is created with its start method called.

As you see from the following two listings, the run method of the Producer class, shown from lines 14 – 16 in Listing 1.13(a), uses an infinite while-loop to keep filling the buffer by calling its put method. On the other hand, the run method of the Consumer class, shown from lines 11 – 14 in Listing 1.13(b), uses an infinite while-loop to keep emptying the buffer by calling its get method.

Listing 1.13(a) Producer.java

```
1   package jcp.ch1.buffer.v1;
2
3   class Producer implements Runnable {
4     SimpleBuffer simpleBuffer;
5
6     Producer(SimpleBuffer simpleBuffer) {
7        this.simpleBuffer = simpleBuffer;
```

```
8          new Thread(this, "Producer").start();
9      }
10
11     public void run() {
12         int i = 0;
13
14         while (true) {
15             simpleBuffer.put(i++);
16         }
17     }
18 }
```

Listing 1.13(b) Consumer.java

```
1  package jcp.ch1.buffer.v1;
2
3  public class Consumer implements Runnable {
4      SimpleBuffer simpleBuffer;
5
6      Consumer(SimpleBuffer simpleBuffer) {
7          this.simpleBuffer = simpleBuffer;
8          new Thread(this, "Consumer").start();
9      }
10
11     public void run() {
12         while (true) {
13             simpleBuffer.get();
14         }
15     }
16 }
```

Listing 1.13(c) shows the test driver. It creates a 10-element SimpleBuffer object and passes it to the Producer and Consumer threads. We do not have to call the start method for each thread in the test driver, as it's already coded into the constructor of each thread class. Now, if you just ran the test driver with the SimpleBuffer class as shown in Listing 1.12(a) with no modifications, you would quickly get an *OutOfBounds* (OOB) exception or ArrayIndexOutOfBoundsException as shown below:

```
Exception in thread "Producer" Exception in thread "Consumer" java.lang.ArrayIndexOutOfBoundsException: 10
    at jcp.ch1.buffer.v1.SimpleBuffer.put(SimpleBuffer.java:13)
    at jcp.ch1.buffer.v1.Producer.run(Producer.java:15)
    at java.lang.Thread.run(Thread.java:744)
java.lang.ArrayIndexOutOfBoundsException: 10
    at jcp.ch1.buffer.v1.SimpleBuffer.get(SimpleBuffer.java:17)
    at jcp.ch1.buffer.v1.Consumer.run(Consumer.java:13)
    at java.lang.Thread.run(Thread.java:744)
```

That's because the SimpleBuffer class shown in Listing 1.12(a) does not check full and empty conditions: A buffer should array not be attempted for filling when it's *full* and it should not be attempted for retrieving when it's *empty*. The next section describes how to add such conditional checks.

Listing 1.13(c) SimpleBufferTest.java

```
1   package jcp.ch1.buffer.v1;
2
3   public class SimpleBufferTest {
4     public static void main(String args[]) {
5       SimpleBuffer simpleBuffer = new SimpleBuffer (10);
6       new Producer(simpleBuffer);
7       new Consumer(simpleBuffer);
8     }
9   }
```

1.7.4 The Simple Buffer Accessed by Two Threads: Busy-Wait with Conditional Check but no Synchronization (Livelock)

Listing 1.13(d) shows a new version of the SimpleBuffer class that checks full and empty conditions. In addition, it uses busy-wait on the above two conditions as shown from lines 13 – 14 for the put method and from lines 22 - 23 for the get method, respectively. Note also that in the put method, we have separated the index post-increment operation out of the buffer filling operation, while in the get method, we have separated the value to be returned from the removing operation as well. The latter is especially necessary, as we need to decrement the current index before returning the value.

So what would happen if we execute the test driver shown in Listing 1.13(c) with the modified SimpleBuffer shown in Listing 1.13(d)? In fact, as shown in Figure 1.6, a livelock situation had occurred. In that case, the consumer was attempting to get the first element indexed at 0 while the producer was attempting to fill the last element indexed at 9; note the colored square at the upper right corner, indicating that the program was still running.

Listing 1.13(d) SimpleBuffer.java

```
1    package jcp.ch1.buffer.v1;
2
3    public class SimpleBuffer {
4      private final int[] buffer;
5      private int currIndex;
6
7      SimpleBuffer(int capacity) {
8        this.buffer = new int[capacity];
9        this.currIndex = 0;
10     }
11
12     final void put(int i) {
13       while (isFull()) {
14       }
15       buffer[currIndex] = i;
16       System.out.println(Thread.currentThread().getName() + ": put " + i
17           + " at " + currIndex);
18       currIndex++;
19     }
20
21     final int get() {
```

```
22          while (isEmpty()) {
23          }
24
25          int value = buffer[--currIndex];
26          System.out.println(Thread.currentThread().getName() + ": get " + value
27              + " at " + currIndex);
28          return value;
29      }
30
31      final boolean isFull() {
32          return currIndex == buffer.length;
33      }
34
35      final boolean isEmpty() {
36          return currIndex == 0;
37      }
38  }
```

```
Console ⊠  Packages  Call Hierarchy
SimpleBufferTest (2) [Java Application] C:\mspc\myapp\Java\jdk1.7.0_45_64bit\b
Consumer: get 137 at 1
Producer: put 138 at 2
Consumer: get 134 at 0
Consumer: get 134 at 0
Producer: put 139 at 1
Producer: put 140 at 1
Producer: put 141 at 2
Producer: put 142 at 3
Producer: put 143 at 4
Producer: put 144 at 5
Producer: put 145 at 6
Producer: put 146 at 7
Producer: put 147 at 8
Producer: put 148 at 9
```

Figure 1.6 Livelock that occurred with the busy-wait/unsynchronized SimpleBuffer example

1.7.5 Detecting Locking Issues

How can we detect a livelock or any locking issues in general? The *jvisualvm* tool can help. This is my favorite Java profiling tool, which comes free and bundled together with every JDK release.

You can start *jvisualvm* up by double-clicking on the *jvisualvm.exe* file in the *bin* directory of a JDK install. Then, select the running Java process you want to profile and click on the *Threads* tab. Figure 1.7 shows the screenshot when the livelock occurred as described above on my Windows 8 laptop while the preceding example was running. Notice the color-coded state for each thread under the *Timeline* tab: *Green* for *Running*, *Purple* for *Sleeping*, *Yellow* for *Wait* and *Red* for *Monitor*. (You can find the colored versions of images from this text's website at http://www.perfmath.com/jcp/colored_images.pdf.) Then, at the lower half of the panel, it clearly shows that the Consumer thread was executing line 22 while the Producer thread was executing line 13 of the SimpleBuffer class shown in Listing 1.13(d), which corresponds to the isFull while-loop in the put method and isEmpty while-loop in the get method, respectively. As you see, this tool can help you pinpoint down exactly where in the Java source code a livelock is happening.

Next, we describe what will happen if we add synchronization to all methods of the SimpleBuffer class shown in Listing 1.13(d).

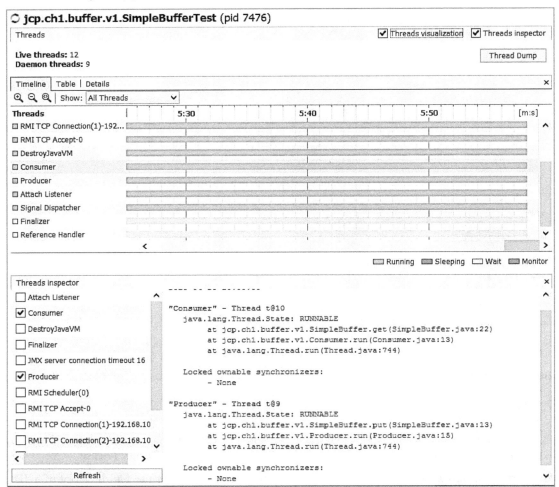

Figure 1.7 The states of the Producer and Consumer threads when a *livelock* occurred

1.7.6 The Simple Buffer Accessed by Two Threads: Busy-Wait with Conditional Check and Synchronization (Starvation)

The previous example shows that the two threads livelocked with a version of the SimpleBuffer class that implements busy-wait and conditional check but no synchronization. What happens if we modify that SimpleBuffer class shown in Listing 1.13(d) to have synchronization added for both the put and get methods. Listing 1.14 shows the modified version of the SimpleBuffer class, with the synchronized keyword added to all four methods of the SimpleBuffer class. The Producer, Consumer and test driver classes are not listed here, as they remain the same.

Listing 1.14 SimpleBuffer.java

```
1    package jcp.ch1.buffer.v2;
2
3    public class SimpleBuffer {
4      private final int[] buffer;
5      private int currIndex;
6
7      SimpleBuffer(int capacity) {
8        this.buffer = new int[capacity];
9        this.currIndex = 0;
10     }
11
12     final synchronized void put(int i) {
13       while (isFull()) {}
14       buffer[currIndex] = i;
15       System.out.println(Thread.currentThread().getName() + ": put " + i
16           + " at " + currIndex);
17       currIndex++;
18     }
19
20     final synchronized int get() {
21       while (isEmpty()) {}
22       int value = buffer[--currIndex];
23       System.out.println(Thread.currentThread().getName() + ": get " + value
24           + " at " + currIndex);
25       return value;
26     }
27
28     final synchronized boolean isFull() {
29       return currIndex == buffer.length;
30     }
31
32     final synchronized boolean isEmpty() {
33       return currIndex == 0;
34     }
35   }
```

Figure 1.8 shows the running state of this example on my Eclipse IDE, indicating that the producer was stuck after filling the last element while the consumer was stuck after retrieving the first element. On the other hand, Figure 1.9 shows the thread states on *jvisualvm*, indicating that the Consumer was running (green color) while the Producer was blocked (red). The lower-half panel further indicates more explicitly that the Consumer was in RUNNABLE state at isEmpty method while the Producer was in BLOCKED state at the put method's isFull method call.

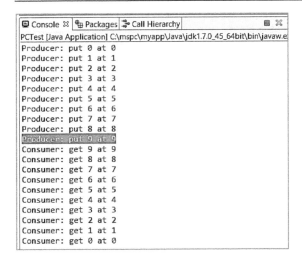

Figure 1.8 The SimpleBuffer starvation situation: The Producer was stuck after filling the last element while the consumer was stuck after retrieving the first element

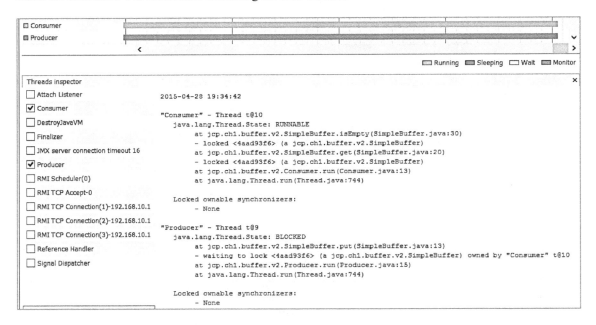

Figure 1.9 Thread states in the starvation situation: One was in RUNNABLE state while the other was in BLOCKED state permanently

Next, we'll see how we can solve the livelock and starvation issues with guarded blocks and asynchronous waiting.

1.7.7 Guarded Blocks with Asynchronous Waiting

Using the SimpleBuffer example, we demonstrated that:

- Busy-wait with no synchronization may result in livelock issues
- Busy-wait with synchronization may result in starvation issues

In this section, we demonstrate that guarded blocks with asynchronous waiting can resolve both the livelock and starvation issues discussed in the preceding sections. Listing 1.15 shows the SimpleBuffer class implemented with guarded blocks. Here, the try-wait-catch blocks in the put and get methods are guarded by their while (isFull()) and while (isEmpty()) loops, respectively. It is imperative to get rid of busy-waits as they do not only waste CPU time but also result in livelock and starvation issues. In addition, it's known that *spurious wakeups* may occur for no reasons, namely, a producer or consumer thread might wake up and only find out that the buffer still is full or empty, in which case, it goes back to sleep again.

Observe the following steps when implementing a guarded block:

1. First, synchronize the method by adding the synchronized keyword.
2. Put the guarded block in a while-loop, which is controlled by a wait condition.
3. Call notify() to wake up the waiting thread only after completing all tasks or before exiting the synchronized method. In other words, do not wake up the waiting thread pre-maturely.

Next, we discuss the result of running this example, following Listing 1.15.

Listing 1.15 SimpleBuffer.java with guarded blocks

```
1    package jcp.ch1.buffer.v3;
2
3    public class SimpleBuffer {
4       private final int[] buffer;
5       private int currIndex;
6
7       SimpleBuffer(int capacity) {
8          this.buffer = new int[capacity];
9          this.currIndex = 0;
10      }
11
12      final synchronized void put(int i) {
13         while (isFull()) {
14            try {
15               wait();
16            } catch (InterruptedException e) {
17               System.out.println("InterrupedException caught: "
18                     + e.getStackTrace());
19            }
20         }
21         buffer[currIndex] = i;
22         System.out.println(Thread.currentThread().getName() + ": put " + i
23               + " at " + currIndex);
```

```
24        currIndex++;
25        notify();
26    }
27
28    final synchronized int get() {
29        while (isEmpty()) {
30          try {
31            wait();
32          } catch (InterruptedException e) {
33            System.out.println("InterrupedException caught: "
34                    + e.getStackTrace());
35          }
36        }
37
38        int value = buffer[--currIndex];
39        System.out.println(Thread.currentThread().getName() + ": get " + value
40                + " at " + currIndex);
41        notify();
42        return value;
43    }
44
45    final synchronized boolean isFull() {
46        return currIndex == buffer.length;
47    }
48
49    final synchronized boolean isEmpty() {
50        return currIndex == 0;
51    }
52  }
```

To verify the above version of the SimpleBuffer implementation, I ran it on my Windows 8 laptop, with the following result obtained on my Eclipse console:

......

Producer: put 39734 at 0
Producer: put 39735 at 1
Producer: put 39736 at 2
Producer: put 39737 at 3
Producer: put 39738 at 4
Producer: put 39739 at 5
Producer: put 39740 at 6
Producer: put 39741 at 7
Producer: put 39742 at 8
Producer: put 39743 at 9
Consumer: get 39743 at 9
Consumer: get 39742 at 8
Consumer: get 39741 at 7
Consumer: get 39740 at 6
Consumer: get 39739 at 5
Consumer: get 39738 at 4

Consumer: get 39737 at 3
Consumer: get 39736 at 2
Consumer: get 39735 at 1
Consumer: get 39734 at 0

......

In addition, Figure 1.10, obtained with the *jvisualvm* tool, shows that the consumer and producer threads blocked and ran alternately. Note that at the time when the screenshot was being taken, the Consumer was waiting for a lock while the Producer was holding several locks.

Figure 1.10 States of the Producer and Consumer threads with the SimpleBuffer class implemented with guarded blocks

However, we still have one more task to accomplish with this SimpleBuffer class: Turning it from a last-in-first-out stack data structure into a first-in-first-out queue data structure, which is the subject of the next section.

1.7.8 Turning the SimpleBuffer Class into a First-In-First-Out Queue-Like Data Structure

As shown in Listing 1.16, to turn the previous SimpleBuffer class into a first-in-first-out, queue-like data structure, the following changes were made:

1. Two fields, head and tail, were added for tracking the head and the tail of the queue. These two fields are also initialized in the constructor, as shown from lines 12 – 13.
2. The guarded blocks, lines 17 – 24 for the put method and lines 37 - 44 for the get method, respectively, were not changed, since they are only tied to the condition of the buffer – whether full or empty.
3. For the put method, line 25 shows that the buffer is filled at the tail. In addition, the tail has to be wrapped to the beginning of the buffer when the buffer is full.
4. For the get method, line 46 shows that the element was taken at the head of the buffer. Similarly, lines 49 – 50 show that when the head reaches the end of the buffer, it has to be wrapped to the beginning of the buffer.

Running this example resulted in the following output on my Eclipse console, which verifies the expected first-in-first-out behavior:

```
......
Producer: put 69023 at 3
Producer: put 69024 at 4
Producer: put 69025 at 5
Producer: put 69026 at 6
Producer: put 69027 at 7
Producer: put 69028 at 8
Producer: put 69029 at 9
Producer: put 69030 at 0
Producer: put 69031 at 1
Producer: put 69032 at 2
Consumer: get 69023 at 3
Consumer: get 69024 at 4
Consumer: get 69025 at 5
Consumer: get 69026 at 6
Consumer: get 69027 at 7
Consumer: get 69028 at 8
Consumer: get 69029 at 9
Consumer: get 69030 at 0
Consumer: get 69031 at 1
Consumer: get 69032 at 2
......
```

Next, we examine a deadlock example, showing how a deadlock may occur with two threads, both waiting for the other party to release its lock.

Listing 1.16 SimpleBuffer.java that acts like a queue

```
1    package jcp.ch1.buffer.v4;
2
3    public class SimpleBuffer {
4      private final int[] buffer;
5      private int currIndex;
6      private int head;
7      private int tail;
8
9      SimpleBuffer(int capacity) {
10       this.buffer = new int[capacity];
11       this.currIndex = 0;
12       this.head = 0;
13       this.tail = 0;
14     }
15
16     final synchronized void put(int i) {
17       while (isFull()) {
18         try {
19           wait();
20         } catch (InterruptedException e) {
21           System.out.println("InterrupedException caught: "
22                 + e.getStackTrace());
23         }
24       }
25       buffer[tail] = i;
26       System.out.println(Thread.currentThread().getName() + ": put " + i
27             + " at " + tail);
28
29       if (++tail == buffer.length)
30         tail = 0;
31
32       currIndex++;
33       notify();
34     }
35
36     final synchronized int get() {
37       while (isEmpty()) {
38         try {
39           wait();
40         } catch (InterruptedException e) {
41           System.out.println("InterrupedException caught: "
42                 + e.getStackTrace());
43         }
44       }
45
46       int value = buffer[head];
47       System.out.println(Thread.currentThread().getName() + ": get " + value
48             + " at " + head);
49       if (++head == buffer.length)
50         head = 0;
51
52       --currIndex;
```

```
53        notify();
54        return value;
55    }
56
57    final synchronized boolean isFull() {
58        return currIndex == buffer.length;
59    }
60
61    final synchronized boolean isEmpty() {
62        return currIndex == 0;
63    }
64 }
```

1.8 DEADLOCK

First, it's important to keep in mind that Java does not prevent deadlocks from happening. It's an application's responsibility to take precaution to prevent deadlocks from happening or to have sound strategies to cope with potential deadlocks when they do occur.

A deadlock occurs when two threads have a circular dependency on a pair of synchronized objects or locks. For example, suppose one thread acquires the lock on object x and another thread acquires the lock on object y. If the thread in x attempts to call a synchronized method on y, it will block as expected. However, if the thread in y attempts to call a synchronized method on x, it would wait forever, as to access x, it would have to release its own lock on y so that the thread x could complete. The next example shows how a circular dependency on locks could potentially happen, leading to a deadlock situation.

1.8.1 A Deadlock Example with a Parent and a Child Thread Calling the callMe Method of two Non-Threaded Objects

Next, we use a simple example to demonstrate how deadlocks may occur. We have two classes: X.java and Y.java as shown in Listings 1.174(a) and (b), respectively. Each of them has a pair of methods, named callMe and hangUp, both of which are synchronized. Within each callMe method, a thread asks the other party to hang up by invoking the other party's hangUp method. At this point, I suggest that you take a few minutes to get familiar with the callMe and hangUp methods for each of the X and Y classes. In particular, note that a sleepTime parameter can be passed to the callMe method of each class so that each object can sleep for a pre-specified amount of time in its callMe method.

Listing 1.17(a) X.java

```
1    package jcp.ch1.deadlock;
2
3    public class X {
4      public synchronized void callMe(Y y, long sleepTime) {
5        String name = Thread.currentThread().getName();
6        System.out.println(name +
7          " entered x thread class's callMe (Y y) method");
```

```
8
9       try {
10        Thread.sleep(sleepTime);
11      } catch (Exception e) {
12        System.out.println("Thread x interrupted");
13      }
14
15      System.out.println(name
16          + " attempting to call x thread class's Y.hangUp () method");
17      y.hangUp();
18    }
19
20    public synchronized void hangUp() {
21      System.out.println("Inside x thread class's X.hangUp ()");
22    }
23  }
```

Listing 1.17(b) Y.java

```
1    package jcp.ch1.deadlock;
2
3    public class Y {
4      public synchronized void callMe(X x, long sleepTime) {
5        String name = Thread.currentThread().getName();
6        System.out.println(name +
7          " entered y thread class callMe (X x) method");
8
9        try {
10         Thread.sleep(sleepTime);
11       } catch (Exception e) {
12         System.out.println("Thread Y interrupted");
13       }
14
15       System.out.println(name
16           + " attempting to call y thread class's X.hangUp () method");
16       x.hangUp();
17     }
18
19     public synchronized void hangUp() {
20       System.out.println("Inside y thread class's Y.hangUp () method");
21     }
22  }
```

Now let's test the above two non-threaded classes in a single-threaded test driver as shown in Listing 1.18(a). In this case, we first create the x and y objects as shown at lines 5 and 6, respectively. Then, we call each object's callMe method at lines 8 and 11, respectively. Since all operations occur within a single thread, we do not expect a deadlock, as is verifiable with the following output obtained by running it on my Eclipse IDE:

main entered x thread class's callMe (Y y) method
main attempting to call x thread class's Y.hangUp () method
Inside y thread class's Y.hangUp () method

Back in Main thread after x.callMe

\---

main entered y thread class callMe (X x) method
main attempting to call y thread class's X.hangUp () method
Inside x thread class's X.hangUp ()
Back in Main thread after y.callMe

Next, let's see what happens when we attempt to use two threads to test it.

Listing 1.18(a) DeadlockDemo0.java

```
1   package jcp.ch1.deadlock;
2
3   public class DeadlockDemo0 {
4     public static void main(String args[]) {
5       X x = new X();
6       Y y = new Y();
7
8       x.callMe(y, 0);
9       System.out.println("Back in Main thread after x.callMe\n---");
10
11      y.callMe(x, 0);
12      System.out.println("Back in Main thread after y.callMe");
13    }
14  }
```

Listing 1.18(b) shows a test driver for the above two non-threaded classes. As with the preceding single-threaded test driver, we create an x object and a y object at lines 4 and 5, respectively. However, the difference is that this test driver is a threaded class as it implements the Runnable interface; so we can create and start a child thread in the parent's constructor from lines 9 – 10 and invoke the x object's callMe method on the y object at line 12. In the run method of the threaded parent object, we invoke the y object's callMe method on x at line 17.

Now let's run the test driver shown in Listing 1.18(b) and see what would happen. As you see, the parent and child threads were deadlocked without being able to proceed, with the following output obtained from my Eclipse IDE's console:

Parent Thread entered x thread class's callMe (Y y) method
Child Thread entered y thread class callMe (X x) method
Child Thread attempting to call y thread class's X.hangUp () method
Parent Thread attempting to call x thread class's Y.hangUp () method

Next, let's see how the jvisualvm tool can help us diagnose this deadlock.

Listing 1.18(b) DeadlockDemo1.java

```
1   package jcp.ch1.deadlock;
2
3   public class DeadlockDemo1 implements Runnable {
4     X x = new X();
```

```
5      Y y = new Y();
6
7      DeadlockDemo1() {
8          Thread.currentThread().setName("Parent Thread");
9          Thread t = new Thread(this, "Child Thread");
10         t.start();
11
12         x.callMe(y, 1000);
13         System.out.println("Back in Parent thread");
14     }
15
16     public void run() {
17         y.callMe(x, 0);
18         System.out.println("Back in Parent thread");
19     }
20
21     public static void main(String args[]) {
22         new DeadlockDemo1();
23     }
24 }
```

1.8.2 Diagnosing Deadlocks Using the jvisualvm Tool

While the two threads were deadlocked, I started up the *jvisualvm* tool and checked the *Monitor* tab as shown in Figure 1.11. Unlike the situation with a livelock, the CPUs were barely breathing when the deadlock occurred.

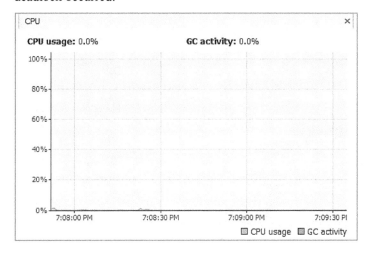

Figure 1.11 Zero CPU usage during the deadlock period

I then switched to the *Threads* tab immediately. As shown in Figure 1.12, both the parent and child threads were in red, indicating that they were waiting for each other to release the locks and deadlocked.

Then, in the lower panel, I checked the *Child* and *Parent* threads and verified further that they were indeed deadlocked with even more verbose test messages describing that:

- Child Thread locked on the Y.callMe method at Y.java's line 16, namely, the x.hangUp() statement.
- Parent Thread locked on the X.callMe method at X.java's line 17, namely, the y.hangUp() statement.

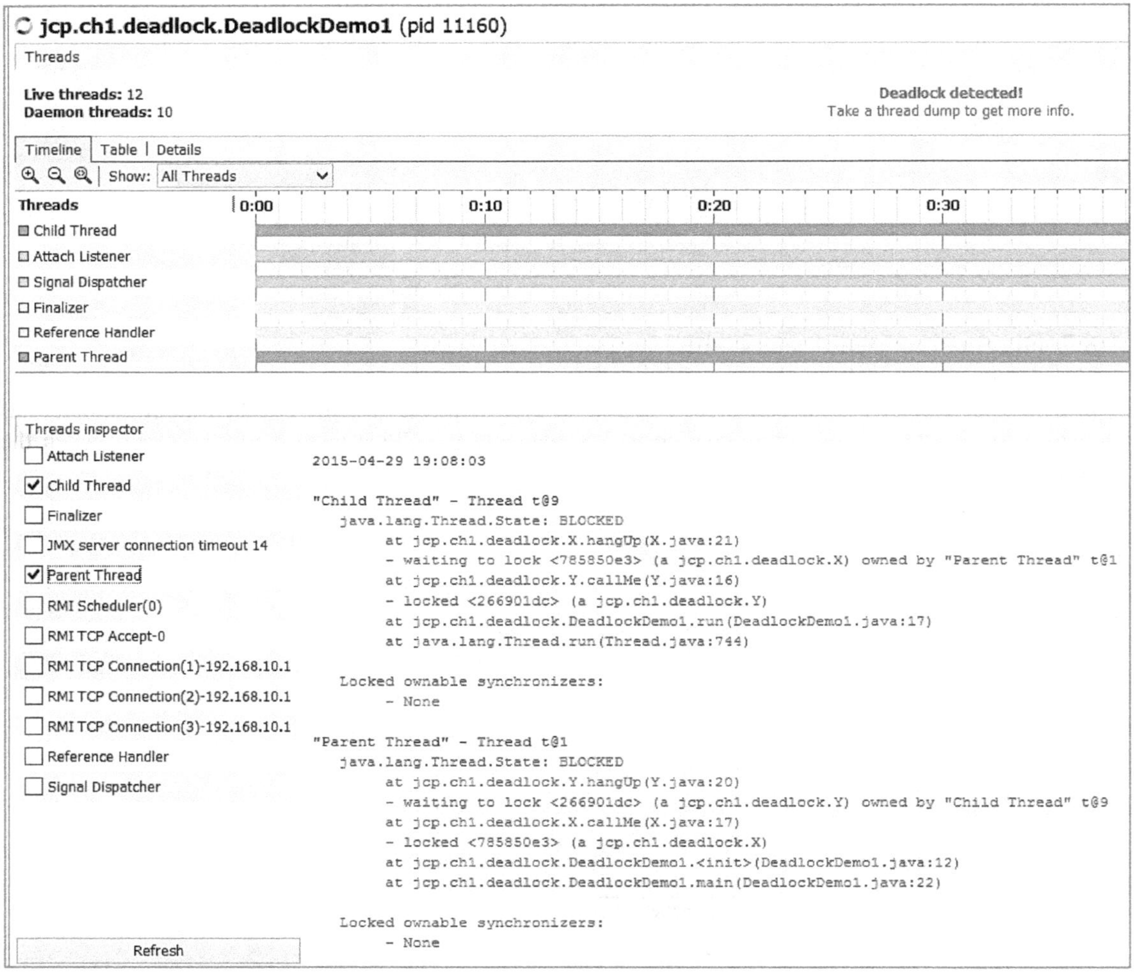

Figure 1.12 A deadlock detected on the jvisualvm tool

In addition, note the alert displayed at the upper right corner in Figure 1.12: "Deadlock detected! Take a thread dump to get more info." I took a thread dump by clicking the button there on the *jvisualvm* tool, with the relevant part shown in Listing 1.19. The first and last segments in Listing 1.19

show similar stack trace information. The middle segment under "Found one Java-level deadlock:" shows a more explicit description of the deadlock between the parent and the child threads that the Child Thread was waiting to lock a monitor held by the Parent Thread, while the Parent Thread was waiting to lock a monitor held by the Child Thread.

This deadlock is obvious and easily detected by the *jvisualvm* tool. However, with real products, debugging deadlock issues is hard for two reasons:

- There might not be an exact execution path for a deadlock to occur, as it may depend on how the CPU schedules its time-slicing from time to time.
- Deadlocks do not necessarily happen only when two threads or two locks get involved. It depends more on a convoluted sequence of events than the number of threads or locks.

Still, tools like *jvisualvm* can help detect deadlocks as we have demonstrated here.

Listing 1.19 Thread dump for the deadlock example (partial)

```
......
"Child Thread" prio=6 tid=0x000000000234d000 nid=0x24ec waiting for monitor entry [0x0000000011fdf000]
   java.lang.Thread.State: BLOCKED (on object monitor)
      at jcp.ch1.deadlock.X.hangUp(X.java:21)
      - waiting to lock <0x00000007ab453ce0> (a jcp.ch1.deadlock.X)
      at jcp.ch1.deadlock.Y.callMe(Y.java:16)
      - locked <0x00000007ab455670> (a jcp.ch1.deadlock.Y)
      at jcp.ch1.deadlock.DeadlockDemo1.run(DeadlockDemo1.java:17)
      at java.lang.Thread.run(Thread.java:744)

   Locked ownable synchronizers:
      - None
......
"Parent Thread" prio=6 tid=0x0000000002253000 nid=0x24dc waiting for monitor entry [0x000000000217f000]
   java.lang.Thread.State: BLOCKED (on object monitor)
      at jcp.ch1.deadlock.Y.hangUp(Y.java:20)
      - waiting to lock <0x00000007ab455670> (a jcp.ch1.deadlock.Y)
      at jcp.ch1.deadlock.X.callMe(X.java:17)
      - locked <0x00000007ab453ce0> (a jcp.ch1.deadlock.X)
      at jcp.ch1.deadlock.DeadlockDemo1.<init>(DeadlockDemo1.java:12)
      at jcp.ch1.deadlock.DeadlockDemo1.main(DeadlockDemo1.java:22)

   Locked ownable synchronizers:
      - None
......
Found one Java-level deadlock:
=============================
"Child Thread":
  waiting to lock monitor 0x000000000f50f278 (object 0x00000007ab453ce0, a jcp.ch1.deadlock.X),
  which is held by "Parent Thread"
"Parent Thread":
  waiting to lock monitor 0x000000000f50dd28 (object 0x00000007ab455670, a jcp.ch1.deadlock.Y),
```

which is held by "Child Thread"

Java stack information for the threads listed above:
==
"Child Thread":
    at jcp.ch1.deadlock.X.hangUp(X.java:21)
    - waiting to lock <0x00000007ab453ce0> (a jcp.ch1.deadlock.X)
    at jcp.ch1.deadlock.Y.callMe(Y.java:16)
    - locked <0x00000007ab455670> (a jcp.ch1.deadlock.Y)
    at jcp.ch1.deadlock.DeadlockDemo1.run(DeadlockDemo1.java:17)
    at java.lang.Thread.run(Thread.java:744)
"Parent Thread":
    at jcp.ch1.deadlock.Y.hangUp(Y.java:20)
    - waiting to lock <0x00000007ab455670> (a jcp.ch1.deadlock.Y)
    at jcp.ch1.deadlock.X.callMe(X.java:17)
    - locked <0x00000007ab453ce0> (a jcp.ch1.deadlock.X)
    at jcp.ch1.deadlock.DeadlockDemo1.<init>(DeadlockDemo1.java:12)
    at jcp.ch1.deadlock.DeadlockDemo1.main(DeadlockDemo1.java:22)

Found 1 deadlock.

1.9 SUSPENDING, RESUMING, AND STOPPING THREADS

Java 1.0 provided methods such as suspend(), resume(), and stop(), to manage thread executions. However, it's important to know that all those methods have been deprecated since Java 2.0 for various reasons, for example:

- The suspend() method is deprecated as it can sometimes cause serious system failures. For example, when a thread has obtained locks on critical data structures and is suspended at some point, those locks may not be relinquished, causing other threads waiting for those resources to be deadlocked.
- The resume() method is deprecated since it is supposed to resume a suspended thread and the suspend() method is deprecated.
- The stop() method is also deprecated since Java 2 for reasons similar to why the suspend() method is deprecated. When a thread is writing to a data structure in the midway while it is stopped, the data structure might be left in a corrupted state. The stop() method causes any lock that the calling thread holds to be released. Thus, the corrupted data might be used by other threads waiting on the same lock.

Since Java 2, it is recommended to depend on Boolean variables, such as a suspendFlag declared within a thread, to control thread suspending and resuming operations. In general, it's not good practice to manage your threads with your own customized code, as there are too many potential execution paths that may lead to system failures. Instead, consider the following:

- Using the *ExecutorService* framework introduced in Java 5 that allows thread pools to be created and managed more transparently.

- Using the *Fork-Join* framework introduced in Java 7 for large-scale, compute-intensive applications, as it will allow applications to scale automatically to make use of the available processors in a modern multi-core system.

The next chapter introduces the ExecutorService framework, while Chapter 8 introduces the Fork-Join framework.

1.10 THE JAVA MEMORY MODEL

In general, Java memory model consists of three parts: locks (implicit or explicit), volatile variables and the *final* keyword. Throughout this text, you will see many such examples. However, the keyword final can be used much more broadly, such as:

1. **Class**: When a class is declared final, it cannot be inherited.
2. **Method**: When a method is declared final, it cannot be overridden.
3. **A variable**: When a variable is declared final, it cannot be modified (or mutated) once initialized. Thus, a "final" object is *immutable*. This is a very important concept, as we know that an immutable object can be read concurrently without having to be locked.

This book focuses on achieving synchronization mostly with the help of locks and sometimes with the volatile modifier.

1.11 THE BRIDGE EXAMPLE

Before concluding this chapter, I'd like to share a Java concurrent programming exercise I once got from a prospective employer prior to an interview arranged later. The description for that exercise is given below. If you are interested in consolidating what you have learnt in this chapter, I suggest that you try to complete this exercise on your own, and then compare with my implementation given in Appendix B.

Programing Exercise

Please write this in Java. The car is the thread and the run method cannot be empty

There is a one-lane bridge on which at most three cars can travel. There is no external coordinator and the cars must make their own decision about crossing the bridge. Assume that all cars play nicely and want to avoid collision. Write a program where the threads (cars) access the bridge (shared resource). Implementation should be fair. If there are cars waiting at both ends, only 3 cars travel from each end in an alternate manner. If there are no cars on the other end, cars can travel until a single car shows up at the other end.'

1.12 SUMMARY

This chapter started with introducing some basic concepts about Java threads, including potential issues with Java concurrency and all possible states for a Java thread. It then focused on how to create Java threads by implementing the Runnable interface or extending the Thread class.

However, the main theme of this chapter is to help you understand how the `synchronized` keyword feature (or the implicit monitor locks) introduced since Java 1.0 can help solve many Java concurrency problems. It's important to understand how threads can be coordinated with methods such as `wait()`, `notify()` and `notifyAll()`, in conjunction with guarded blocks on certain crucial conditions if necessary. Using several different versions of the `SimpleBuffer` example, we demonstrated potential issues caused by busy-waits, such as livelock, starvation, etc. A simple deadlock example was presented to show how a deadlock might happen if a circular dependency exists between two threads waiting for the other party to release a lock first. The *jvisualvm* tool was introduced to demonstrate how a deadlock situation could be accurately pinpointed down with the help of a thread dump, which gives detailed information about the stack trace associated with the deadlocked threads.

I suggest that you study the various versions of the SimpleBuffer example carefully to understand various issues and outcomes as summarized in Table 1.1. I also suggest that you revisit those screenshots taken with *jvisualvm* to characterize patterns of color changes for threads involved, associated with livelock, starvation, deadlock and normal cases.

Table 1.1 Various versions of the SimpleBuffer example

Code Listing	Busy-Wait	Condition check	Synchronized	Outcome	Figure
1.12(a)	yes	no	no	OOB Exception	-
1.13(d)	yes	yes	no	livelock	1.7
1.14	yes	yes	yes	starvation	1.9
1.15	no	yes	yes	OK	1.10

We concluded the chapter by introducing an optional exercise of solving the classical concurrent programming example of having multiple cars crossing a bridge, which can be implemented by just using the synchronized keyword feature introduced since Java 1.0. Appendix B provides a reference for that exercise.

The next chapter focuses on the ExecutorService framework introduced in Java 5. This framework is commonly used in multi-threaded Java applications running in production environments, in the context of dealing with the following concurrent programming problems:

- **Mutual exclusion problems**. Involved memory locations must be accessed by a single thread only, such as the incremental operation (i++).
- **Producer-consumer problems**. Conditional waits must be introduced to block the other party until certain conditions are met.
- **Readers-writers problems**. Readers and writers can be arranged to access a shared data structure concurrently without having to block each other.

It's important to always realize what concurrent programming problems we are trying to solve and how they are solved.

1.13 EXERCISES

Exercise 1.1 What's the difference between a process and a thread?

Exercise 1.2 What's the implication of Equation (1.1), the performance law for sequential programs?

Exercise 1.3 Describe how you can use Equations (1.1) and (1.6) to gauge performance optimization initiatives and efforts for a particular performance issue.

Exercise 1.4 What are the two major concerns with concurrent programs?

Exercise 1.5 What does the term "*happens-before*" mean in the context of concurrent programming? What measures are typically employed to help enforce "*happens-before*" relationships?

Exercise 1.6 Describe the difference between the *synchronized* keyword and the *volatile* keyword.

Exercise 1.7 What does the `Thread.join()` method do?

Exercise 1.8 What's the difference between the thread states of BLOCKED and WAITING/TIMED_WAITING?

Exercise 1.9 Describe when to use the `Runnable` interface or the `Thread` class to create a new thread.

Exercise 1.10 State the criterion for choosing between synchronizing a method and synchronizing a block.

Exercise 1.11 Why is *busy-wait* or *busy-spin* not desirable?

Exercise 1.12 Describe what it means exactly by the term of *livelock* or *starvation* or *deadlock*.

Exercise 1.13 Write a simple deadlock program.

Exercise 1.14 How do you determine if the threads are running normally, or livelocked, or starving, or dead-locked?

Exercise 1.15 With the `SimpleBuffer` examples presented in this chapter, why are array indexes not wrapped around?

2 Java Thread ExecutorService Framework

In Chapter 1, we demonstrated that one can start a new thread in its constructor and that the new thread exits at the end of the execution of its run method. We also mentioned that Java 1 provided us with methods such as suspend(), resume(), and stop() for managing the lifecycle of a thread, but all of them are deprecated now. There are two major reasons why they are deprecated: (1) they often result in system failures; and (2) a newer thread management framework – the Thread Executor Framework, as shown in Figure 2.1, was introduced in Java 5, which automatically manages Java threads as thread pools.

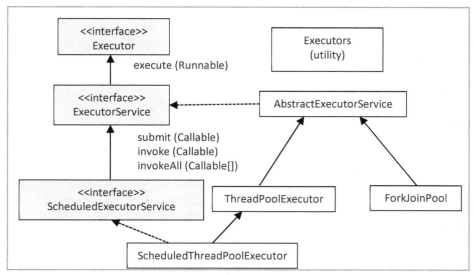

Figure 2.1 The Java thread ExecutorService framework

Since most of the today's multi-threaded Java applications use the ExecutorService framework as shown in Figure 2.1, next, we focus on understanding how this framework works so that you would know how to use it with your own projects. Since the ExecutorService framework depends on two important interfaces named Callable and Future, let's describe these two interfaces first in the next section.

2.1 THE CALLABLE AND FUTURE INTERFACES

You may notice in Figure 2.1 that the methods of submit, invoke and invokeAll take an argument of *Callable*, which is an interface for defining a task that returns a result and may throw an exception. As shown in Listing 2.1, the Callable interface defines a single method named call with no arguments.

Listing 2.1 The Callable interface

```
1    package java.util.concurrent;
2    public interface Callable<V> {
3      public V call() throws Exception;
4    }
```

Both the Callable interface and the Runnable interface are designed for defining classes whose instances are potentially executed as tasks by another thread. However, unlike a Runnable task, a Callable task returns a result and throws a checked exception.

The return type designated as V for the call() method of the Callable interface as shown in Listing 2.1 is designed for returning a Future object as an instance of the Future interface. Put simply, a Future represents the result of an *asynchronous* computation. As shown in Listing 2.2, it defines methods related to canceling a task and getting the result of a task, such as:

- cancel(boolean mayInterruptIfRunning): Attempts to cancel the execution of the task. Note that the task may not be canceled if the task has already completed or has already been cancelled, or could not be cancelled for any other reason. If the task has not started when cancel is called, the task may be cancelled and if successful, the task should never run. If the task has already started, then the mayInterruptIfRunning parameter determines whether the thread executing this task should be interrupted in an attempt to stop the task.
- isCancelled(): Returns true if the task was cancelled before it completed normally.
- boolean isDone(): Returns true if the task completed due to normal termination, an exception, or cancellation.
- V get() throws InterruptedException, ExecutionException: Waits if necessary for the task to complete, and then retrieves its result.
- V get(long timeout, TimeUnit unit) throws InterruptedException, ExecutionException, TimeoutException: The timeout version of the above get() method.

We will see many examples of asynchronous calls with the Future interface defining the results of the calls throughout this text.

Next, we describe the Executor interface.

Listing 2.2 The Future interface

```
1   package java.util.concurrent;
2
3   public interface Future<V> {
4
5       boolean cancel(boolean mayInterruptIfRunning);
6       boolean isCancelled();
7       boolean isDone();
8       V get() throws InterruptedException, ExecutionException;
9       V get(long timeout, TimeUnit unit)
10          throws InterruptedException, ExecutionException, TimeoutException;
11  }
```

2.2   THE EXECUTOR INTERFACE

Notice in Figure 2.1 that we have three interfaces: Executor, ExecutorService and ScheduledExecutorService. In this section, we explain each of these interfaces.

2.2.1 Executor

The top Executor interface is defined with only one method:

void execute (Runnable command)

In the above method, the parameter command represents a task that implements the Runnable interface with a run method containing the details for the task to be executed. It throws a RejectedExecutionException, if the task cannot be accepted for execution or a NullPointerException if the command is null.

The ExecutorService interface to be discussed next is a more extensive interface than the Executor interface, and thus used more commonly.

2.2.2 ExecutorService

The ExecutorService interface extends the Executor interface. Therefore, it makes the Executor's execute(Runnable) method available for use as well by inheritance. In addition, the ExecutorService provides the following two methods for managing termination:

- shutdown(). This method allows previously submitted tasks to execute before being terminated.
- shutdownNow(). This method prevents waiting tasks from starting and attempts to stop currently executing tasks.

An unused ExecutorService should be shutdown to avoid resource leaking. Upon termination, an executor will have no tasks actively executing or awaiting execution, and no new tasks can be submitted.

An ExecutorService has a group of submit methods and a group of invokeAny and invokeAll methods. The submit method's three variations are described as follows:

1. `Future<?> submit (Runnable task)`: Submits a `Runnable` task for execution and returns a `Future` that represents the task. The `Future`'s `get` method will return `null` upon successful completion.

2. `<T> Future<T> submit (Runnable task, T result)`: Submits a `Runnable` task for execution and returns a `Future` that represents the task. The `Future`'s `get` method will return the given result upon successful completion.

3. `<T> Future<T> submit (Callable<T> task)`: Submits a task for execution and returns a `Future` that represents the pending result of the task. The `Future`'s `get` method will return the task's result upon successful completion. If you need to immediately block-waiting for a task, use constructors of the form `result = es.submit (Callable).get()`, where `es` is an `executorService` object.

The `ExecutorService`'s `invokeAll` and `invokeAny` methods are described as follows:

1. `<T> List<Future<T>> invokeAll(Collection<? extends Callable<T>> tasks)` throws `InterruptedException`: Executes the given collection of tasks, returning a list of `Future`s, which holds the status and results of the tasks when all complete. Note that a *completed* task does not necessarily mean *success*, as it could have terminated either normally or by throwing an exception. In addition, the result of this method is undefined if the given collection is modified while this operation is in progress.

2. `<T> List<Future<T>> invokeAll(Collection<? extends Callable<T>> tasks, long timeout, TimeUnit unit)` throws `InterruptedException`: Similar to the above method except that it allows the call to timeout, upon which tasks in progress are cancelled.

3. `<T> List<Future<T>> invokeAny (Collection<? extends Callable<T>> tasks)` throws `InterruptedException, ExecutionException`: Similar to its equivalent `invokeAll` except that it returns if any one task has completed successfully. Upon normal or exceptional return, tasks that have not completed are cancelled.

4. `<T> List<Future<T>> invokeAny(Collection<? extends Callable<T>> tasks, long timeout, TimeUnit unit)` throws `InterruptedException, ExecutionException, TimeoutException`: Similar to the preceding method except that it sets a timeout limit. It throws the `TimeoutException` if the timer expires before any task successfully completes.

Now you have gotten an idea of how an `ExecutorService` works with its `submit` and `invoke` methods. Next, let's take a look at the `ScheduledExecutorService`.

2.2.3 ScheduledExecutorService

The `ScheduledExecutorService` extends `ExecutorService`. Its main function added is to schedule tasks to run after a given delay or periodically.

Since the `ScheduledExecutorService` extends `ExecutorService`, tasks can be submitted using the `Executor.execute(java.lang.Runnable)` method and `ExecutorService` `submit` methods to start execution immediately with zero delay. If you add a delay for kicking off a task, use the `schedule` methods as described below:

- `<V> ScheduledFuture<V> schedule(Callable<V> callable, long delay, TimeUnit unit)`: Schedules a `Callable` task to run after the specified delay.
- `ScheduledFuture<?> schedule(Runnable command, long delay, TimeOut unit)`: Schedules a one-time task to run after the specified delay.
- `ScheduledFuture<?> scheduleAtFixedRate(Runnable command, long initialDelay, long period, TimeUnit unit)`: Schedules a periodic task to run with a delay of `initialDelay` for the first run and a fixed `period` for all subsequent runs, namely, with `period = running time + remaining idle time`. If the execution of a run takes longer than its period, then subsequent execution will start late, with no concurrent overlap between the two adjacent runs.
- `ScheduledFuture<?> scheduleAtFixedDelay(Runnable command, long initialDelay, long delay, TimeUnit unit)`: Schedules a periodic task to run with a delay of `initialDelay` for the first run and a fixed `delay` for all subsequent runs. Here, `FixedDelay` really means `FixedInterval` between the completion of the current run and the commencement of the next.

To summarize, those three interfaces define the methods as shown in Table 2.1.

Table 2.1 Methods from the three ExecutorService interfaces

Interface	Methods
Executor	`execute`
ExecutorService	`submit`, `invokeAny`, and `invokeAll`
ScheduledExecutorService	`schedule`, `scheduleAtFixedRate`, and `scheduleAtFixedDelay`

Next, we discuss Java thread pool classes that implement the above interfaces.

2.3 THE THREAD POOL CLASSES

As shown in Figure 2.1 at the beginning of this chapter, the `Executor` interfaces discussed in the preceding section are implemented by the following four classes (one abstract and other three pool-related):

1. AbstractExecutorService
2. ThreadPoolExecutor
3. ForkJoinPool
4. ScheduledThreadPoolExecutor

The thread pool classes depend heavily on the `RunnableFuture` interface and the `FutureTask` class, which are discussed first next.

2.3.1 The `RunnableFuture` interface and the `FutureTask` class

The `RunnableFuture<V>` interface is defined as follows:

```
public interface RunnableFuture<V> extends Runnable, Future<V> {
  void run();
```

}

As is seen, the RunnableFuture<V> interface extends Runnable and Future<V>, and has only one method of run(). Its purpose is for defining a Runnable that can return a Future. Thus, after the successful execution of its run method, the RunnableFuture's result is accessible via Future's get method.

The FutureTask class implements the RunnableFuture interface, as shown in Figure 2.2. The FutureTask class helps define *cancellable* and *asynchronous* tasks. Listing 2.3 shows the constructors and get method of the FutureTask class. As you see, a FutureTask can be constructed by taking either a callable (line 6) or a runnable and a value object for returning a result (line 12). The get method calls the report method to return the result.

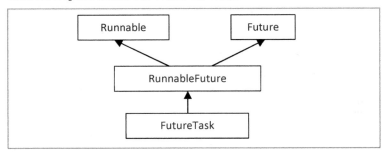

Figure 2.2 The FutureTask class hierarchy

In addition to the inherited run method and the get method, the FutureTask class implements many other methods, such as cancel(...), isCancelled(), done(), isDone(), runAndReset(), set(V v), setException(...), etc., for managing a task, which should be obvious just by looking at the names of those methods.

Next, we discuss the AbstractExecutorService class.

Listing 2.3 FutureTask.java (partial)

```
1    package java.util.concurrent;
2    import java.util.concurrent.locks.LockSupport;
3
4    public class FutureTask<V> implements RunnableFuture<V> {
5
6        public FutureTask(Callable<V> callable) {
7            if (callable == null)
8                throw new NullPointerException();
9            this.callable = callable;
10           this.state = NEW;        // ensure visibility of callable
11       }
12       public FutureTask(Runnable runnable, V result) {
13           this.callable = Executors.callable(runnable, result);
14           this.state = NEW;        // ensure visibility of callable
```

```
15        }
16        public V get() throws InterruptedException, ExecutionException {
17            int s = state;
18            if (s <= COMPLETING)
19                s = awaitDone(false, 0L);
20            return report(s);
21        }
22        // other members omitted
23    }
```

2.3.2 AbstractExecutorService

Here is the declaration of the AbstractExecutorService:

public abstract class AbstractExecutorService extends Object implements ExecutorService

As is seen, AbstractExecutorService is an abstract class, which extends Object and implements ExecutorService. AbstractExecutorService provides default implementations of ExecutorService execution methods, such as all variants of submit, invokeAll, and invokeAny as discussed previously, as shown in Figure 2.3.

```
⊿ 🔠 java.util.concurrent
    ⊿ 🗋 AbstractExecutorService.java
        ⊿ ⓒ AbstractExecutorService
            ▫ doInvokeAny(Collection<? extends Callable<T>>, boolean, long) <T> : T
            ⚲ invokeAll(Collection<? extends Callable<T>>) <T> : List<Future<T>>
            ⚲ invokeAll(Collection<? extends Callable<T>>, long, TimeUnit) <T> : List<Future<T>>
            ⚲ invokeAny(Collection<? extends Callable<T>>) <T> : T
            ⚲ invokeAny(Collection<? extends Callable<T>>, long, TimeUnit) <T> : T
            ◇ newTaskFor(Callable<T>) <T> : RunnableFuture<T>
            ◇ newTaskFor(Runnable, T) <T> : RunnableFuture<T>
            ⚲ submit(Callable<T>) <T> : Future<T>
            ⚲ submit(Runnable) : Future<?>
            ⚲ submit(Runnable, T) <T> : Future<T>
```

Figure 2.3 Methods of the AbstractExecutorService class

After introducing the RunnableFuture interface and the FutureTask class in the preceding section, it is much easier to understand the submit methods for the AbstractExecutorService class shown in Listing 2.4. For example, the first submit method is implemented from lines 11 – 16 as follows:

1. Line 12: First, it checks if the task is null. If it is, it throws a NullPointerException.
2. Line 13: It then creates a future task named ftask, typed RunnableFuture, by creating a newTaskFor object, which has two forms, one defined from lines 3 – 5 for a version with a return value and the other from lines 7 – 9 for a version with no return value.
3. Line 14: It then calls the execute method of ExecutorService to execute the ftask defined prior to it.

4. Line 15: It returns the `ftask` without waiting for the `ftask` to complete, since it's an asynchronous call. The future state of the task can be queried and managed with the `ftask` object.

Next, let's see how the ThreadPoolExecutor class is defined.

Listing 2.4 AbstractExecutorService.java (partial)

```
1   public abstract class AbstractExecutorService implements ExecutorService {
2
3       protected <T> RunnableFuture<T> newTaskFor(Runnable runnable, T value) {
4           return new FutureTask<T>(runnable, value);
5       }
6
7       protected <T> RunnableFuture<T> newTaskFor(Callable<T> callable) {
8           return new FutureTask<T>(callable);
9       }
10
11      public Future<?> submit(Runnable task) {
12          if (task == null) throw new NullPointerException();
13          RunnableFuture<Void> ftask = newTaskFor(task, null);
14          execute(ftask);
15          return ftask;
16      }
17
18      public <T> Future<T> submit(Runnable task, T result) {
19          if (task == null) throw new NullPointerException();
20          RunnableFuture<T> ftask = newTaskFor(task, result);
21          execute(ftask);
22          return ftask;
23      }
24
25      public <T> Future<T> submit(Callable<T> task) {
26          if (task == null) throw new NullPointerException();
27          RunnableFuture<T> ftask = newTaskFor(task);
28          execute(ftask);
29          return ftask;
30      }
31
32      // more omitted
33  }
```

2.3.3 ThreadPoolExecutor

The ThreadPoolExecutor class extends AbstractExecutorService, and thus is an ExecutorService. One of the major benefits of using the ThreadPoolExecutor class is that the submitted tasks would be executed by pooled threads, which would be created and managed automatically without having developers write their own code to accomplish the same.

To help you understand the scope and the capability of the ThreadPoolExecutor class, Listing 2.5 shows partially how it is actually implemented. Let's go through this partial code snippet as follows:

- Lines 1 – 5: Show that this class is defined in the java.util.concurrent package and depends on the AbstractQueuedSynchronizer (AQS), Condition, ReentrantLock, and AtomicInteger classes. We'll discuss more about these classes later.
- Lines 10 – 17: Define the CAPACITY field and various states of RUNNING, SHUTDOWN, STOP, TIDYING and TERMINATED.
- Lines 33 – 38: Define various data structures and fields such as BlockingQueue<Runnable> workQueue, ReentrantLock mainLock, HashSet<Worker> workers, Condition termination, largestPoolSize, and completedTaskCount. We'll discuss BlockingQueue, ReentrantLock, HashSet and Condition later.
- Lines 40 – 49: Define five volatile fields such as ThreadFactory threadFactory, RejectedExecutionHandler handler, long keepAliveTime, int corePoolSize, and int maximumPoolSize.
- Lines 51 – 69: Define a class named Worker, which extends AbstractQueuedSynchronizer and implements Runnable. Note the constructor defined from lines 62 – 65 that uses the ThreadFactory's getThreadFactory().newThread(this) to create a new thread, which shows how a thread is created in production code. Lines 67 – 69 show that ThreadPoolExecutor's run method is implemented with another method: runWorker (this).

Next, we discuss ThreadPoolExecutor's constructors and methods.

Listing 2.5 ThreadPoolExecutor.java (partial)

```
1    package java.util.concurrent;
2    import java.util.concurrent.locks.AbstractQueuedSynchronizer;
3    import java.util.concurrent.locks.Condition;
4    import java.util.concurrent.locks.ReentrantLock;
5    import java.util.concurrent.atomic.AtomicInteger;
6    import java.util.*;
7    public class ThreadPoolExecutor extends AbstractExecutorService {
8    private final AtomicInteger ctl = new AtomicInteger(ctlOf(RUNNING, 0));
9        private static final int COUNT_BITS = Integer.SIZE - 3;
10       private static final int CAPACITY   = (1 << COUNT_BITS) - 1;
11
12       // runState is stored in the high-order bits
13       private static final int RUNNING    = -1 << COUNT_BITS;
14       private static final int SHUTDOWN   =  0 << COUNT_BITS;
15       private static final int STOP       =  1 << COUNT_BITS;
16       private static final int TIDYING    =  2 << COUNT_BITS;
17       private static final int TERMINATED =  3 << COUNT_BITS;
18
19       // omitted some
20
21       private static boolean isRunning(int c) {
22           return c < SHUTDOWN;
23       }
24
```

```
25       /**
26        * Attempt to CAS-increment the workerCount field of ctl.
27        */
28       private boolean compareAndIncrementWorkerCount(int expect) {
29           return ctl.compareAndSet(expect, expect + 1);
30       }
31
32       // omitted some
33       private final BlockingQueue<Runnable> workQueue;
34       private final ReentrantLock mainLock = new ReentrantLock();
35       private final HashSet<Worker> workers = new HashSet<Worker>();
36       private final Condition termination = mainLock.newCondition();
37       private int largestPoolSize;
38       private long completedTaskCount;
39
40       private volatile ThreadFactory threadFactory;
41       private volatile RejectedExecutionHandler handler;
42       private volatile long keepAliveTime;
43       /**
44        * Core pool size is the minimum number of workers to keep alive
45        * (and not allow to time out etc) unless allowCoreThreadTimeOut
46        * is set, in which case the minimum is zero.
47        */
48       private volatile int corePoolSize;
49       private volatile int maximumPoolSize;
50       // omitted some
51       private final class Worker
52           extends AbstractQueuedSynchronizer
53           implements Runnable
54       {
55           /** Thread this worker is running in.  Null if factory fails. */
56           final Thread thread;
57           /** Initial task to run.  Possibly null. */
58           Runnable firstTask;
59           /** Per-thread task counter */
60           volatile long completedTasks;
61
62           Worker(Runnable firstTask) {
63               setState(-1); // inhibit interrupts until runWorker
64               this.firstTask = firstTask;
65               this.thread = getThreadFactory().newThread(this);
66           }
67           public void run() {
68               runWorker(this);
69           }
70   // omitted the rest of it
71 }
```

Figure 2.4 shows the fields of threadFactory, workers, and workQueue as well as the four constructors of the ThreadPoolExecutor class, along with the addWorker and addWorkerFailed methods. Note especially the workQueue for holding tasks before they are executed, which is passed to the three of the four constructors as the parameter typed BlockingQueue. The BlockingQueue is a

Queue that additionally supports operations such as waiting for the queue to become non-empty when retrieving an element and waiting for space to become available in the queue when storing an element. We'll discuss more about it in Section 7.1.1.

- threadFactory
- workers
- workQueue
- ThreadPoolExecutor(int, int, long, TimeUnit, BlockingQueue<Runnable>)
- ThreadPoolExecutor(int, int, long, TimeUnit, BlockingQueue<Runnable>, RejectedExecutionHandler)
- ThreadPoolExecutor(int, int, long, TimeUnit, BlockingQueue<Runnable>, ThreadFactory)
- ThreadPoolExecutor(int, int, long, TimeUnit, BlockingQueue<Runnable>, ThreadFactory, RejectedExecutionHandler)
- addWorker(Runnable, boolean) : boolean
- addWorkerFailed(Worker) : void

Figure 2.4 ThreadPoolExecutor's constructors

Figure 2.5 shows all methods for the TreadPoolExecutor class. It's beneficial to go through the list at least once to get a sense of what operations are supported, which is too lengthy for us to elaborate. Later, we'll have examples showing how some of those methods are used.

- advanceRunState(int) : void
- afterExecute(Runnable, Throwable) : void
- allowCoreThreadTimeOut(boolean) : void
- allowsCoreThreadTimeOut() : boolean
- awaitTermination(long, TimeUnit) : boolean
- beforeExecute(Thread, Runnable) : void
- checkShutdownAccess() : void
- compareAndDecrementWorkerCount(int) : boolean
- compareAndIncrementWorkerCount(int) : boolean
- decrementWorkerCount() : void
- drainQueue() : List<Runnable>
- ensurePrestart() : void
- execute(Runnable) : void
- finalize() : void
- getActiveCount() : int
- getCompletedTaskCount() : long
- getCorePoolSize() : int
- getKeepAliveTime(TimeUnit) : long
- getLargestPoolSize() : int
- getMaximumPoolSize() : int
- getPoolSize() : int
- getQueue() : BlockingQueue<Runnable>
- getRejectedExecutionHandler() : RejectedExecutionHandler
- getTask() : Runnable
- getTaskCount() : long

- getThreadFactory() : ThreadFactory
- interruptIdleWorkers() : void
- interruptIdleWorkers(boolean) : void
- interruptWorkers() : void
- isRunningOrShutdown(boolean) : boolean
- isShutdown() : boolean
- isTerminated() : boolean
- isTerminating() : boolean
- onShutdown() : void
- prestartAllCoreThreads() : int
- prestartCoreThread() : boolean
- processWorkerExit(Worker, boolean) : void
- purge() : void
- reject(Runnable) : void
- remove(Runnable) : boolean
- runWorker(Worker) : void
- setCorePoolSize(int) : void
- setKeepAliveTime(long, TimeUnit) : void
- setMaximumPoolSize(int) : void
- setRejectedExecutionHandler(RejectedExecutionHandler) : void
- setThreadFactory(ThreadFactory) : void
- shutdown() : void
- shutdownNow() : List<Runnable>
- terminated() : void
- toString() : String
- tryTerminate() : void

Figure 2.5 More methods for the ThreadPoolExecutor class

2.3.4 ForkJoinPool

The ForkJoinPool class extends AbstractExecutorService, and thus implements the Executor and ExecutorService interfaces. It is designed for running ForkJoinTasks. It differs from other kinds of ExecutorServices that it supports *work-stealing*, namely, if a thread has finished its job and has no more work to do, it is allowed to "*steal*" work from other threads. The purpose for supporting work-stealing is for better-balancing the entire job as a whole.

Since Chapter 8 focuses on the ForkJoin framework, we spend no more time explaining how ForkJoinPool works here.

2.3.5 ScheduledThreadPoolExecutor

The ScheduledThreadPoolExecutor class extends the ThreadPoolExecutor class and implements ScheduledExecutorService, as shown in Listing 2.6. It has a private class, ScheduledFutureTask<V> as shown from lines 12 − 55, which has three constructors for creating various tasks with different requirements, such as periodic or one-time tasks. Lines 44 − 54 show the implementation of the ScheduledFutureTask's run method, which further invokes the run method of its super class, FutureTask.

In addition to the private class of ScheduledFutureTask, the ScheduledThreadPoolExecutor has another private class, DelayedWorkQueue, which extends AbstractQueue<Runnable> and implements BlockingQueue<Runnable>, as shown from lines 57 − 72 (the body of this class is omitted). This DelayedWorkQueue class is for maintaining delayed tasks. Non-delayed tasks are maintained in a BlockingQueue as shown from lines 74 − 76.

Listing 2.6 ScheduledThreadPoolExecutor.java (partial)

```
1    package java.util.concurrent;
2    import java.util.concurrent.atomic.*;
3    import java.util.concurrent.locks.*;
4    import java.util.*;
5
6    public class ScheduledThreadPoolExecutor
7            extends ThreadPoolExecutor
8            implements ScheduledExecutorService {
9
10       // omitted
11
12       private class ScheduledFutureTask<V>
13               extends FutureTask<V> implements RunnableScheduledFuture<V> {
14
15           // omitted
16
17           ScheduledFutureTask(Runnable r, V result, long ns) {
18               super(r, result);
19               this.time = ns;
20               this.period = 0;
```

```
21                    this.sequenceNumber = sequencer.getAndIncrement();
22                }
23
24            /**
25             * Creates a periodic action with given nano time and period.
26             */
27            ScheduledFutureTask(Runnable r, V result, long ns, long period) {
28                super(r, result);
29                this.time = ns;
30                this.period = period;
31                this.sequenceNumber = sequencer.getAndIncrement();
32            }
33
34            /**
35             * Creates a one-shot action with given nanoTime-based trigger.
36             */
37            ScheduledFutureTask(Callable<V> callable, long ns) {
38                super(callable);
39                this.time = ns;
40                this.period = 0;
41                this.sequenceNumber = sequencer.getAndIncrement();
42            }
43
44            public void run() {
45                boolean periodic = isPeriodic();
46                if (!canRunInCurrentRunState(periodic))
47                    cancel(false);
48                else if (!periodic)
49                    ScheduledFutureTask.super.run();
50                else if (ScheduledFutureTask.super.runAndReset()) {
51                    setNextRunTime();
52                    reExecutePeriodic(outerTask);
53                }
54            }
55        }
56 // omitted
57    static class DelayedWorkQueue extends AbstractQueue<Runnable>
58        implements BlockingQueue<Runnable> {
59
60        /*
61         * A DelayedWorkQueue is based on a heap-based data structure
62         * like those in DelayQueue and PriorityQueue, except that
63         * every ScheduledFutureTask also records its index into the
64         * heap array. This eliminates the need to find a task upon
65         * cancellation, greatly speeding up removal (down from O(n)
66         * to O(log n)), and reducing garbage retention that would
67         * otherwise occur by waiting for the element to rise to top
68         * before clearing...
69         *
70         */
71    // omitted
72        }
```

```
73
74      public BlockingQueue<Runnable> getQueue() {
75          return super.getQueue();
76      }
```

Listing 2.7 shows how a submit method calls a proper schedule method to submit a task. The schedule method takes two parameters: a callable that represents a task, and a delay. Inside the schedule method, the callable parameter and the delay parameter are used to create a ScheduledFutureTask object, which is in turn used with the callable parameter to create a RunnableScheduledFuture thread by calling the decorateTask method. The delayedExecute method is called upon the RunnableScheduledFuture thread to schedule the task asynchronously, after which the thread is returned to the caller as a ScheduledFuture object, which is bubbled back to the submit method as a Future object.

Listing 2.7 One submit method and one schedule method from ScheduledThreadPoolExecutor

```
1       public <T> Future<T> submit(Callable<T> task) {
2           return schedule(task, 0, TimeUnit.NANOSECONDS);
3       }
4       public <V> ScheduledFuture<V> schedule(Callable<V> callable,
5                                                     long delay,
6                                                     TimeUnit unit) {
7           if (callable == null || unit == null)
8               throw new NullPointerException();
9           RunnableScheduledFuture<V> t = decorateTask(callable,
10              new ScheduledFutureTask<V>(callable,
11                                          triggerTime(delay, unit)));
12          delayedExecute(t);
13          return t;
14      }
```

Figure 2.6 shows all schedule and submit methods for the ScheduledThreadPoolExecutor class. It is seen that the submit methods take either a Callable or Runnable parameter and return a Future object; the schedule methods take either a Callable or Runnable as one of their parameters and return a ScheduledFuture object. If you are interested in how a method is actually implemented, you can download the source code from a JDK of your choice and look it up, which is very convenient.

2.4 THE EXECUTORS UTILITY CLASS

In the previous sections, we mentioned that the ExecutorService interface and various thread pool classes, such as ThreadPoolExecutor, ForkJoinPool and ScheduledThreadPoolExecutor, constitute a framework for managing thread pools and executing threaded tasks. In this section, we introduce the Executors utility class, which takes care of tasks, such as creating thread pools, by providing various static factory methods. Figure 2.7 shows all factory methods of the Executors utility class. At this point, a cursory look at each of these methods is helpful.

Next, we demonstrate how some of the members of the Executors utility class are actually implemented.

schedule(Callable<V>, long, TimeUnit) <V> : ScheduledFuture<V>
schedule(Runnable, long, TimeUnit) : ScheduledFuture<?>
scheduleAtFixedRate(Runnable, long, long, TimeUnit) : ScheduledFuture<?>
scheduleWithFixedDelay(Runnable, long, long, TimeUnit) : ScheduledFuture<?>
setContinueExistingPeriodicTasksAfterShutdownPolicy(boolean) : void
setExecuteExistingDelayedTasksAfterShutdownPolicy(boolean) : void
setRemoveOnCancelPolicy(boolean) : void
shutdown() : void
shutdownNow() : List<Runnable>
submit(Callable<T>) <T> : Future<T>
submit(Runnable) : Future<?>
submit(Runnable, T) <T> : Future<T>
triggerTime(long) : long
triggerTime(long, TimeUnit) : long

Figure 2.6 The `schedule` and `submit` methods for `ScheduledThreadPoolExecutor` class

Executors.java
  Executors
    DefaultThreadFactory
    DelegatedExecutorService
    DelegatedScheduledExecutorService
    FinalizableDelegatedExecutorService
    PrivilegedCallable<T>
    PrivilegedCallableUsingCurrentClassLoader<T>
    PrivilegedThreadFactory
    RunnableAdapter<T>
    callable(PrivilegedAction<?>) : Callable<Object>
    callable(PrivilegedExceptionAction<?>) : Callable<Object>
    callable(Runnable) : Callable<Object>
    callable(Runnable, T) <T> : Callable<T>
    defaultThreadFactory() : ThreadFactory
    newCachedThreadPool() : ExecutorService
    newCachedThreadPool(ThreadFactory) : ExecutorService
    newFixedThreadPool(int) : ExecutorService
    newFixedThreadPool(int, ThreadFactory) : ExecutorService
    newScheduledThreadPool(int) : ScheduledExecutorService
    newScheduledThreadPool(int, ThreadFactory) : ScheduledExecutorService
    newSingleThreadExecutor() : ExecutorService
    newSingleThreadExecutor(ThreadFactory) : ExecutorService
    newSingleThreadScheduledExecutor() : ScheduledExecutorService
    newSingleThreadScheduledExecutor(ThreadFactory) : ScheduledExecutorService
    privilegedCallable(Callable<T>) <T> : Callable<T>
    privilegedCallableUsingCurrentClassLoader(Callable<T>) <T> : Callable<T>
    privilegedThreadFactory() : ThreadFactory
    unconfigurableExecutorService(ExecutorService) : ExecutorService
    unconfigurableScheduledExecutorService(ScheduledExecutorService) : ScheduledExecutorService
    Executors()

Figure 2.7 Static factory methods of the `Executors` utility class

2.4.1 The DefaultThreadFactory Inner Class

As shown in Figure 2.7, the first member of the Executors utility class is an inner class named DefaultThreadFactory. Listing 2.8 shows how this class is actually implemented. First, note that it extends the ThreadFactory interface, which is as simple as the following:

```
public interface ThreadFactory {
  Thread newThread(Runnable r);
}
```

Then, it declares a series of fields, such as poolNumber, group, threadNumber, namePrefix, with proper types, especially the type AtomicInteger, which provides a mechanism for efficiently updating the value of a variable without the use of locks, as we will cover later. Besides, the DefaultThreadFactory constructor initializes the group and namePrefix fields with the help of a SecurityManager if used. (Note how the namePrefix is constructed with "pool-" and "-thread-" flanking the poolNumber.) Finally, it creates a new thread with a given Runnable, in addition to the fields of group and namePrefix and an incremented threadNumber. Prior to the newly-created thread is returned, it resets Daemon to false and the thread priority to NORM_PRIORITY, as is obvious from lines 20 - 23.

Listing 2.8 The DefaultThreadFactory Inner Class

```
1    static class DefaultThreadFactory implements ThreadFactory {
2            private static final AtomicInteger poolNumber = new
3                AtomicInteger(1);
4            private final ThreadGroup group;
5            private final AtomicInteger threadNumber = new AtomicInteger(1);
6            private final String namePrefix;
7
8            DefaultThreadFactory() {
9                SecurityManager s = System.getSecurityManager();
10               group = (s != null) ? s.getThreadGroup() :
11                                   Thread.currentThread().getThreadGroup();
12               namePrefix = "pool-" +
13                               poolNumber.getAndIncrement() +
14                           "-thread-";
15           }
16
17           public Thread newThread(Runnable r) {
18               Thread t = new Thread(group, r,
19                   namePrefix + threadNumber.getAndIncrement(),0);
20               if (t.isDaemon())
21                   t.setDaemon(false);
22               if (t.getPriority() != Thread.NORM_PRIORITY)
23                   t.setPriority(Thread.NORM_PRIORITY);
24               return t;
25           }
26       }
```

2.4.2 The newSingleThreadExecutor Method

The Executors utility class has a newSingleThreadExecutor method, which is implemented as shown in Listing 2.9. As you see, it creates a new ThreadPoolExecutor with a pool size of one, no timeout, and a LinkedBlockingQueue for holding Runnables that represent tasks. It is then wrapped in a FinalizableDelegatedExecutorService. You can dive into it more if you want, but it suffices to note in Listing 2.10 that FinalizableDelegatedExecutorService calls shutdown() in its finalize() method so that the developer does not have the responsibility of managing the thread.

The Executor's static factory method, newSingleThreadExecutor, creates an Executor that uses a single worker thread operating off an *unbounded queue*. It's a carefully designed single thread executor so that when the thread terminates due to a failure during execution prior to shutdown, a new thread will take its place to continue executing subsequent tasks if any. Therefore, it's really a single thread *executor*, not just a single *thread* with no ability to recover if something goes wrong. It guarantees that only one task will be active at any given time.

Prior to moving to the Executors' static factory methods for creating methods, I'd like to remind you that you should use this newSingleThreadExecutor method, rather than those shown in Chapter 1 for creating a single thread, when you want to create an application to execute tasks in a single-threaded mode.

Listing 2.9 The newSingleThreadExecutor method

```
1       public static ExecutorService newSingleThreadExecutor() {
2           return new FinalizableDelegatedExecutorService
3               (new ThreadPoolExecutor(1, 1,
4                               0L, TimeUnit.MILLISECONDS,
5                               new LinkedBlockingQueue<Runnable>()));
6       }
```

Listing 2.10 The FinalizableDelegatedExecutorService class

```
1       static class FinalizableDelegatedExecutorService
2           extends DelegatedExecutorService {
3           FinalizableDelegatedExecutorService(ExecutorService executor) {
4               super(executor);
5           }
6           protected void finalize() {
7               super.shutdown();
8           }
9       }
```

2.4.3 The newFixedThreadPool Method

Listing 2.11 shows the actual implementation of the newFixedThreadPool method. It actually returns a new ThreadPoolExecutor object with a given number of threads. (See previous section 2.3.3 for more about the ThreadPoolExecutor class.) It works as follows:

1. It uses a shared unbounded queue, LinkedBlockingQueue, to store the Runnable tasks. We'll cover this data structure later in §7.3.1.
2. At any given point of time, at most nThreads - a fixed number of threads - will be actively processing tasks. If additional tasks are submitted when all threads are active, they will wait in the queue until a thread becomes available.
3. If any thread terminates due to a failure during execution prior to shutdown, a new thread will take place if needed to execute subsequent tasks.
4. A thread in the pool stays until it is explicitly shutdown.

Next, we discuss the newCachedThreadPool method.

Listing 2.11 The newFixedThreadPool method for the Executors utility class

```
1    public static ExecutorService newFixedThreadPool(int nThreads) {
2        return new ThreadPoolExecutor(nThreads, nThreads,
3                                 0L, TimeUnit.MILLISECONDS,
4                                 new LinkedBlockingQueue<Runnable>());
5    }
```

2.4.4 The newCachedThreadPool method

Listing 2.12 shows how the newCachedThreadPool method is implemented. Contrary to the newFixedThreadPool method, it uses a SynchronousQueue instead of a LinkedBlockingQueue to store Runnable tasks. (We'll cover the SynchronousQueue data structure later in §7.1.3.) In addition, it has the following characteristics:

- It reuses previously constructed threads when they become available, and creates additional new threads if needed. The number of threads is not fixed, which starts from zero and can go up to Integer.MAX_VALUE, which is essentially infinite. Since threads in this pool are re-usable, eventually, only a limited number of threads are maintained.
- Threads that have not been used for sixty seconds will be terminated and removed from the cache, thus releasing resources. This makes it possible to scale the pool size up or down automatically.

The newCachedThreadPool helps improve the performance of programs that execute many short-lived asynchronous tasks.

Next, let's see how the ExecutorService framework is used for creating multi-threaded applications.

Listing 2.12 The newCachedThreadPool method for the Executors utility class

```
1    public static ExecutorService newCachedThreadPool() {
2        return new ThreadPoolExecutor(0, Integer.MAX_VALUE,
3                                 60L, TimeUnit.SECONDS,
4                                 new SynchronousQueue<Runnable>());
5    }
```

2.5 SOME EXECUTORSERVICE EXAMPLES

This section presents some examples to demonstrate how the ExecutorService framework works. Specifically, the examples will show:

- execute(Runnable) does not return a result.
- submit(Runnable) returns a Future object representing the status of the Runnable.
- Submit(Callable) returns a Future object representing the result of the Callable.
- invokeAny(Callables) succeeds if any one of the tasks was executed successfully.
- invokeAll(Callables) succeeds if all tasks were executed successfully.

Let's start with our first example showing that the ExecutorService's execute(Runnable) call does not return a result.

2.5.1 The Method execute(Runnable) does not Return a Result

Listing 2.13 shows a SimpleESDemo0 class that does the following:

1. Line 9: Creates an executorService object using the Executors' static factory method newFixedThreadPool with a pool size of five.
2. Lines 12 – 17: Call the executorService's execute method to execute an anonymous task that outputs a message. Note that this call will be asynchronous.
3. Line 19: Calls the shutdown method to shut down the executorService to avoid potential resource leak.

Keep in mind that execute(Runnable) does not return a result. The next example shows that the submit(Runnable) method returns a Future object.

Listing 2.13 SimpleESDemo0.java

```
1   package jcp.ch2.executorservice.example0;
2
3   import java.util.concurrent.ExecutorService;
4   import java.util.concurrent.Executors;
5
6   public class SimpleESDemo0 {
7     public static void main(String args[]) {
8       // 1. Create a newFixedThreadPool using the Executors utility class
9       ExecutorService executorService = Executors.newFixedThreadPool(5);
10
11      // 2. Execute an anonymous thread/task asynchronously
12      executorService.execute(new Runnable() {
13        public void run() {
14          System.out
15              .println("Execute a Runnable with no result returned");
16        }
17      });
18      // 3. shut down executorService to avoid resource leak
19      executorService.shutdown();
20    }
21  }
```

2.5.2 The Method submit (Runnable) Returns a Future Object (Status)

Listing 2.14 shows a SimpleESDemo1 class that does the following:

1. Line 11: Creates an executorService object using the Executors' static factory method newFixedThreadPool with a pool size of five.
2. Lines 14 – 21: Call the executorService's submit method to submit an anonymous task that outputs a message. Line 14 shows that the submit(Runnable) method call returns a Future object.
3. Lines 23 – 31: This is a try-multi-catch block for the future.get() call, which may throw an InterruptedExecption or an ExecutionException. Note that the future.get() call returns null if the task was completed successfully.
4. Line 34: Calls the shutdown method to shut the executorService down to avoid potential resource leak.

Now if you run this example on your Eclipse IDE, you will get a console output like the following:

```
Execute a Runnable with a Future object returned
task was completed successfully
```

However, if you uncomment line 19, namely, making it fail by stopping the thread (a deprecated method for demo purpose only), and run it again, you would get an output similar to the following:

```
Execute a Runnable with a Future object returned
java.util.concurrent.ExecutionException: java.lang.ThreadDeath
    at java.util.concurrent.FutureTask.report(FutureTask.java:122)
    at java.util.concurrent.FutureTask.get(FutureTask.java:188)
    at jcp.ch2.executorservice.example1.SimpleESDemo1.main(SimpleESDemo1.java:24)
Caused by: java.lang.ThreadDeath
    at java.lang.Thread.stop(Thread.java:835)
    at jcp.ch2.executorservice.example1.SimpleESDemo1$1.run(SimpleESDemo1.java:19)
    at java.util.concurrent.Executors$RunnableAdapter.call(Executors.java:471)
    at java.util.concurrent.FutureTask.run(FutureTask.java:262)
    at java.util.concurrent.ThreadPoolExecutor.runWorker(ThreadPoolExecutor.java:1145)
    at java.util.concurrent.ThreadPoolExecutor$Worker.run(ThreadPoolExecutor.java:615)
    at java.lang.Thread.run(Thread.java:744)
```

It is seen that line 19 in Listing 2.14 caused the thread to stop, which caused FutureTask.get to invoke FutureTask.report, which reported the ThreadDeath failure.

The difference between the execute method (previous example) and the submit method (this example) is that the latter allows the status of the submitted task to be queried while the former doesn't. Furthermore, if you need to get the execution result of a task, use submit(Callable) in place of submit(Runnable), as will be illustrated next.

Listing 2.14 SimpleESDemo1.java

```
1    package jcp.ch2.executorservice.example1;
2
```

```
3   import java.util.concurrent.ExecutionException;
4   import java.util.concurrent.ExecutorService;
5   import java.util.concurrent.Executors;
6   import java.util.concurrent.Future;
7
8   public class SimpleESDemo1 {
9     public static void main(String args[]) {
10       // 1. Create a newFixedThreadPool using the Executors utility class
11       ExecutorService executorService = Executors.newFixedThreadPool(5);
12
13       // 2. Execute an anonymous thread/task asynchronously
14       Future future = executorService.submit(new Runnable() {
15         public void run() {
16           System.out.println("Execute a Runnable with " +
17             "a Future object returned");
18
19           //Thread.currentThread().stop();
20         }
21       });
22
23       try {
24         if (future.get() == null) {
25           System.out.println ("task was completed successfully");
26         } else {
27           System.out.println ("task was not completed successfully");
28         }
29       } catch (InterruptedException | ExecutionException e) {
30         e.printStackTrace();
31       }
32
33       // 3. shut down executorService to avoid resource leak
34       executorService.shutdown();
35     }
36 }
```

2.5.3 The Method submit(Callable) Returns a Future Object (Result)

This example shows how the submit(Callable) method of ExecutorService is used to have a task executed asynchronously with a result returned as a Future object, as shown in Listing 2.15. It is constructed as follows:

1. Lines 12 – 13: Define the pool size and task size, with task size larger than pool size.
2. Lines 16 – 17: Create a thread pool by calling Executors.newFixedThreadPool with the given pool size.
3. Line 20: Creates a task array of Future type with the given task size.
4. Line 26: Calls the executorService.submit(Callable) method with a Factorial object that simulates a task.
5. Line 32: Calls the get() method for each Future array element to retrieve the result of the call method of the Factorial class.

6. Line 39: Calls the executorService's shutdown() method to shut down the pool to avoid potential resource leak.

Note the Factorial class defined from lines 43 – 77. It implements the Callable interface and defines the call() method, which returns a string about the factorial computation performed. Executing this example yielded the following result:

```
pool-1-thread-4: count = 4 factorial = 24
pool-1-thread-5: count = 1 factorial = 1
pool-1-thread-1: count = 1 factorial = 1
pool-1-thread-3: count = 2 factorial = 2
pool-1-thread-2: count = 9 factorial = 362880
pool-1-thread-4: count = 3 factorial = 6
future get: count = 1 factorial = 1
future get: count = 9 factorial = 362880
future get: count = 2 factorial = 2
future get: count = 4 factorial = 24
future get: count = 1 factorial = 1
future get: count = 3 factorial = 6
```

As you see, six tasks were executed by five threads, with thread #4 re-used, as expected from a fixed thread pool.

Next, we discuss the use of the invokeAny method.

Listing 2.15 SimpleESDemo2.java

```
1   package jcp.ch2.executorservice.example2;
2
3   import java.util.Random;
4   import java.util.concurrent.Callable;
5   import java.util.concurrent.ExecutionException;
6   import java.util.concurrent.ExecutorService;
7   import java.util.concurrent.Executors;
8   import java.util.concurrent.Future;
9
10  public class SimpleESDemo2 {
11    public static void main(String args[]) {
12      int POOL_SIZE = 5;
13      int TASK_SIZE = POOL_SIZE + 1;
14
15      // 1. Create a newFixedThreadPool using the Executors utility class
16      ExecutorService executorService = Executors
17          .newFixedThreadPool(POOL_SIZE);
18
19      // 2. Create a Future array with the given task size
20      Future<String>[] futures = new Future[TASK_SIZE];
21
22      // 3. Submit anonymous Factorial tasks asynchronously
23      Random random = new Random();
24      for (int i = 0; i < TASK_SIZE; i++) {
```

```
25          int countMax = random.nextInt(10);
26          futures[i] = executorService.submit(new Factorial (i, countMax));
27        }
28
29        // 4. check result
30        try {
31          for (int i = 0; i < TASK_SIZE; i++) {
32            System.out.println("future get: " + futures[i].get());
33          }
34        } catch (InterruptedException | ExecutionException e) {
35          e.printStackTrace();
36        }
37
38        // 5. shut down executorService to avoid resource leak
39        executorService.shutdown();
40      }
41  }
42
43  class Factorial implements Callable<String> {
44      int id;
45      int countMax;
46
47      Factorial(int id, int countMax) {
48        this.id = id;
49        this.countMax = countMax;
50      }
51
52      public String call() throws Exception {
53        return computeFactorial(Thread.currentThread().getName());
54      }
55
56      public String computeFactorial(String name) {
57        int count = -1;
58        int result = 1;
59
60        do {
61          count++;
62          result = factorial(count);
63        } while (count < this.countMax);
64
65        System.out.println(Thread.currentThread().getName() + ": count = "
66              + count + " factorial = " + result);
67        return "count = " + count + " factorial = " + result;
68      }
69
70      public int factorial(int n) {
71        if (n == 0) {
72          return 1;
73        } else {
74          return n * factorial(n - 1);
75        }
76      }
```

77 }

2.5.4 The Method `invokeAny (Callables)` Succeeds if Any One Task Succeeds

This section provides an example to demonstrate how to use the `executorService.invokeAny (Callables)` method to execute a collection of tasks, which succeeds if any one task succeeds. Listing 2.16 shows such an example. It is coded as follows:

1. Line 12: Uses `Executor`'s static factory method to create a `newSingleThreadExecutor` object, which is assigned to `executorService`.
2. Line 14: Creates a `callables HashSet` with a value type of `String` for each `callable`.
3. Lines 16–33: Add three anonymous `callables` to the `callables HashSet`, with each `callable`'s `call` method just returning a `String` for demonstration purpose.
4. Line 37: Calls the `executorService`'s `invokeAny` method with the `callables HashSet` and assigns the returned object to a variable named `result` of `String` type.
5. Line 42: Outputs the result of the `invokeAny(Callables)` call to help verify it works as expected.
6. Line 43: Calls the `executorService`'s `shutdown` method to shut it down.

I ran this example on my Eclipse IDE and got the following output:

result = task 3 succeeded

To help prove that `executorService`'s `invokeAny (Callables)` call succeeds if at least one `callable` succeeds, note the statement of

// Thread.currentThread().stop ();

added to each `callable`'s `call` method at lines 18, 24, and 30, respectively. If you uncomment any two of them, the `executorService`'s `invokeAny(Callables)` call still succeeds. However, if you uncomment all three of them and run the example, here is what you would get:

```
java.util.concurrent.ExecutionException: java.lang.ThreadDeath
    at java.util.concurrent.FutureTask.report(FutureTask.java:122)
    at java.util.concurrent.FutureTask.get(FutureTask.java:188)
    at java.util.concurrent.AbstractExecutorService.doInvokeAny(AbstractExecutorService.java:193)
    at java.util.concurrent.AbstractExecutorService.invokeAny(AbstractExecutorService.java:215)
    at java.util.concurrent.Executors$DelegatedExecutorService.invokeAny(Executors.java:657)
    at jcp.ch2.executorservice.example3.SimpleESDemo3.main(SimpleESDemo3.java:38)
Caused by: java.lang.ThreadDeath
    at java.lang.Thread.stop(Thread.java:835)
    at jcp.ch2.executorservice.example3.SimpleESDemo3$2.call(SimpleESDemo3.java:25)
    at jcp.ch2.executorservice.example3.SimpleESDemo3$2.call(SimpleESDemo3.java:1)
    at java.util.concurrent.FutureTask.run(FutureTask.java:262)
    at java.util.concurrent.Executors$RunnableAdapter.call(Executors.java:471)
    at java.util.concurrent.FutureTask.run(FutureTask.java:262)
    at java.util.concurrent.ThreadPoolExecutor.runWorker(ThreadPoolExecutor.java:1145)
    at java.util.concurrent.ThreadPoolExecutor$Worker.run(ThreadPoolExecutor.java:615)
    at java.lang.Thread.run(Thread.java:744)
```

result =

Next, we discuss the executorService's invokeAll(Callables) method.

Listing 2.16 SimpleESDemo3.java

```
1    package jcp.ch2.executorservice.example3;
2
3    import java.util.HashSet;
4    import java.util.Set;
5    import java.util.concurrent.Callable;
6    import java.util.concurrent.ExecutionException;
7    import java.util.concurrent.ExecutorService;
8    import java.util.concurrent.Executors;
9
10   public class SimpleESDemo3 {
11     public static void main(String args[]) {
12       ExecutorService executorService = Executors.newSingleThreadExecutor();
13
14       Set<Callable<String>> callables = new HashSet<Callable<String>>();
15
16       callables.add(new Callable<String>() {
17         public String call() throws Exception {
18           //Thread.currentThread().stop();
19           return "task 1 succeeded";
20         }
21       });
22       callables.add(new Callable<String>() {
23         public String call() throws Exception {
24           //Thread.currentThread().stop();
25           return "task 2 succeeded";
26         }
27       });
28       callables.add(new Callable<String>() {
29         public String call() throws Exception {
30           //Thread.currentThread().stop();
31           return "task 3 succeeded";
32         }
33       });
34
35       String result = "";
36       try {
37         result = executorService.invokeAny(callables);
38       } catch (InterruptedException | ExecutionException e) {
39         e.printStackTrace();
40       }
41
42       System.out.println("result = " + result);
43       executorService.shutdown();
44     }
45   }
```

2.5.5 The Method `invokeAll (Callables)` Succeeds if All Callables Succeed

This section provides an example to demonstrate how to use the `executorService.invokeAll (Callables)` method to execute a collection of tasks, which succeeds if all tasks succeed. Listing 2.17 shows such an example. It is coded as follows:

1. Line 14: Uses the `Executor`'s static factory method to create a `newSingleThreadExecutor` object, which is assigned to `executorService`.
2. Line 16: Creates a `callables` HashSet with a value type of `String` for each `callable`.
3. Lines 18–33: Add three anonymous `callables` to the `callables` HashSet, with each `callable`'s `call` method just returning a `String` for demonstration purpose.
4. Line 38: Calls the `executorService`'s `invokeAll` method with the `callables` HashSet and assigns the returned result to a `futures` List, with each `future` holding a `String`.
5. Lines 40–42: Output the result of the `invokeAll (Callables)` call to help verify that it works as expected. Note that this is a `for`-loop that iterates through each `future` of the `futures` list.
6. Line 47: Calls the `executorService`'s `shutdown` method to shut it down.

I ran this example on my Eclipse IDE and got the following output:

```
future.get = task 3 succeeded
future.get = task 1 succeeded
future.get = task 2 succeeded
```

To help prove that `executorService`'s `invokeAll(Callables)` call succeeds only if all `callables` succeed, note the statement of

```
// Thread.currentThread().stop ();
```

added to the third `callable`'s `call` method at line 30. If you uncomment that line out, the `executorService`'s `invokeAll(Callables)` call will fail, as shown below, obtained by running this example on my Eclipse IDE:

```
java.util.concurrent.ExecutionException: java.lang.ThreadDeath
    at java.util.concurrent.FutureTask.report(FutureTask.java:122)
    at java.util.concurrent.FutureTask.get(FutureTask.java:188)
    at jcp.ch2.executorservice.example4.SimpleESDemo4.main(SimpleESDemo4.java:40)
Caused by: java.lang.ThreadDeath
    at java.lang.Thread.stop(Thread.java:835)
    at jcp.ch2.executorservice.example4.SimpleESDemo4$3.call(SimpleESDemo4.java:30)
    at jcp.ch2.executorservice.example4.SimpleESDemo4$3.call(SimpleESDemo4.java:1)
    at java.util.concurrent.FutureTask.run(FutureTask.java:262)
    at java.util.concurrent.ThreadPoolExecutor.runWorker(ThreadPoolExecutor.java:1145)
    at java.util.concurrent.ThreadPoolExecutor$Worker.run(ThreadPoolExecutor.java:615)
    at java.lang.Thread.run(Thread.java:744)
```

This concludes our coverage of the Java thread `ExecutorService` Framework.

Listing 2.17 SimpleESDemo4.java

```
1    package jcp.ch2.executorservice.example4;
2
3    import java.util.HashSet;
4    import java.util.List;
5    import java.util.Set;
6    import java.util.concurrent.Callable;
7    import java.util.concurrent.ExecutionException;
8    import java.util.concurrent.ExecutorService;
9    import java.util.concurrent.Executors;
10   import java.util.concurrent.Future;
11
12   public class SimpleESDemo4 {
13     public static void main(String args[]) {
14        ExecutorService executorService = Executors.newSingleThreadExecutor();
15
16        Set<Callable<String>> callables = new HashSet<Callable<String>>();
17
18        callables.add(new Callable<String>() {
19          public String call() throws Exception {
20             return "task 1 succeeded";
21          }
22        });
23        callables.add(new Callable<String>() {
24          public String call() throws Exception {
25             return "task 2 succeeded";
26          }
27        });
28        callables.add(new Callable<String>() {
29          public String call() throws Exception {
30             //Thread.currentThread().stop();
31             return "task 3 succeeded";
32          }
33        });
34
35        String result = "";
36        try {
37          List<Future<String>> futures =
38             executorService.invokeAll(callables);
39
40          for(Future<String> future : futures){
41             System.out.println("future.get = " + future.get());
42          }
43        } catch (InterruptedException | ExecutionException e) {
44          e.printStackTrace();
45        }
46
47        executorService.shutdown();
48     }
49   }
```

2.6 SUMMARY

This chapter introduced the Java thread `ExecutorService` framework. We first covered the following interfaces:

- `Executor`
- `ExecutorService`
- `ScheduledExecutorService`

We then examined the classes that implement those interfaces, including:

- `AbstractExecutorService`
- `ThreadPoolExecutor`
- `ForkJoinPool`
- `ScheduledThreadPoolExecutor`

Next, we focused on the `Executors` utility class, whose static factory methods are used for creating thread pools, including:

- `newSingleThreadExecutor()`: For creating a single, recoverable thread to execute one or more tasks.
- `newFixedThreadPool(POOL_SIZE)`: For creating a thread pool with a fixed size to execute multiple tasks.
- `newCachedThreadPool()`: For creating a thread pool that can self-adjust its pool size *dynamically* to execute multiple tasks.

The last section provided a few examples to help demonstrate how the `ExecutorService` framework works. Specifically, the examples demonstrated the use of the following methods from an `ExecutorService` object:

- `execute(Runnable)` does not return a result.
- `submit(Runnable)` returns a `Future` object representing the status of the `Runnable`.
- `Submit(Callable)` returns a `Future` object representing the result of the `Callable`.
- `invokeAny(Callables)` succeeds if any one of the tasks was executed successfully.
- `invokeAll(Callables)` succeeds if all tasks were executed successfully.

Whether creating an executor thread pool or a single thread executor, you should use this framework, rather than creating separate threads as shown in Chapter 1. Listing 2.15 is a good example to remember for the general procedure of using the `ExecutorService` framework, regardless of which method you call: `execute`, `submit`, `invokeAny` or `invokeAll`. If you use a `Callable` task, remember that the `Future`'s `get()` method waits until the result is available.

The next chapter covers the Java Collections Framework.

2.7 EXERCISES

Exercise 2.1 Describe the differences between the `execute` method and the `submit` method of an `ExecutorService` object.

Exercise 2.2 Describe how you would use the `ThreadFactory` method to create a new thread. What's the benefit of doing so?

Exercise 2.3 Do you use a single thread or a fixed thread pool or a cached thread pool to execute invokeAny and invokeAll methods?

Exercise 2.4 What's the purpose of the RunnableFuture interface?

Exercise 2.5 Describe the use of the two constructors of the FutureTask class.

Exercise 2.6 Which class will you use for the invokeAny and invokeAll methods?

Exercise 2.7 Which class defines the newFixedThreadPool method and the newCachedThreadPool method? What's the difference between these two methods?

Exercise 2.8 Write a simple multithreaded program that uses the ExecutorService framework to perform a simple task.

Exercise 2.9 After completing all chapters, come back and explain why a newFixedThreadPool uses a LinkedBlockingQueue while a newCachedThreadPool uses a SynchronousQueue to maintain the tasks to be executed.

3   The Java Collections Framework

Java has a package named `java.util` that encompasses a broad range of interfaces and classes that fall into two categories: *common utilities* and the *Collections Framework*. The common utilities in this package takes care of the following tasks:

- Generating pseudorandom numbers
- Managing date and time
- Observing events
- Manipulating sets of bits
- Tokenizing strings
- Handling formatted data

The Collections Framework is carefully designed with a sophisticated hierarchy of interfaces and classes for managing groups of data. Since data structures have always been an inseparable part of concurrent programming, this chapter focuses on understanding the Java Collections Framework.

3.1   COLLECTIONS OVERVIEW

Prior to J2SE 1.2, Java provided several ad hoc classes such as **Dictionary**, **Vector**, **Stack**, and **Properties** as a basic set of data structures for storing and manipulating groups of objects. However, these classes were not designed with extensibility and adaptability taken into account. J2SE provided a more elaborate Collections Framework for storing and manipulating groups of objects, with the following objectives met:

1. **High-performance**. The fundamental collections, such as hash tables, linked lists, trees, and dynamic arrays, and so on, have been made more efficient. These data structures can be used without being re-implemented or enhanced.
2. **Streamlined**. Different types of collections work in a similar manner with similar operations whenever applicable. In addition, they are highly interoperable.
3. **Extensibility**. The framework is built upon a set of standard interfaces, with several standard implementations, such as **LinkedList**, **HashSet**, and **TreeSet**, provided.

4. **Integration of standard arrays**. The standard arrays are made part of the Collections Framework as well.

If you have downloaded the *src.zip* file for a latest JDK, I suggest that you take a cursory look at its `java.util` directory, which should look similar to Figure 3.1. Just by going through the name of each Java file, you could get a glimpse of what classes the Collections Framework contains.

concurrent	FormatFlagsConversionMismatchException.java	NoSuchElementException.java
jar	Formattable.java	Objects.java
logging	FormattableFlags.java	Observable.java
prefs	Formatter.java	Observer.java
regex	FormatterClosedException.java	PriorityQueue.java
spi	GregorianCalendar.java	Properties.java
zip	HashMap.java	PropertyPermission.java
AbstractCollection.java	HashSet.java	PropertyResourceBundle.java
AbstractList.java	Hashtable.java	Queue.java
AbstractMap.java	IdentityHashMap.java	Random.java
AbstractQueue.java	IllegalFormatCodePointException.java	RandomAccess.java
AbstractSequentialList.java	IllegalFormatConversionException.java	RegularEnumSet.java
AbstractSet.java	IllegalFormatException.java	ResourceBundle.java
ArrayDeque.java	IllegalFormatFlagsException.java	Scanner.java
ArrayList.java	IllegalFormatPrecisionException.java	ServiceConfigurationError.java
Arrays.java	IllegalFormatWidthException.java	ServiceLoader.java
BitSet.java	IllformedLocaleException.java	Set.java
Calendar.java	InputMismatchException.java	SimpleTimeZone.java
Collection.java	InvalidPropertiesFormatException.java	SortedMap.java
Collections.java	Iterator.java	SortedSet.java
ComparableTimSort.java	JapaneseImperialCalendar.java	Stack.java
Comparator.java	JumboEnumSet.java	StringTokenizer.java
ConcurrentModificationException.java	LinkedHashMap.java	Timer.java
Currency.java	LinkedHashSet.java	TimerTask.java
Date.java	LinkedList.java	TimeZone.java
Deque.java	List.java	TimSort.java
Dictionary.java	ListIterator.java	TooManyListenersException.java
DualPivotQuicksort.java	ListResourceBundle.java	TreeMap.java
DuplicateFormatFlagsException.java	Locale.java	TreeSet.java
EmptyStackException.java	LocaleISOData.java	UnknownFormatConversionException.java
Enumeration.java	Map.java	UnknownFormatFlagsException.java
EnumMap.java	MissingFormatArgumentException.java	UUID.java
EnumSet.java	MissingFormatWidthException.java	Vector.java
EventListener.java	MissingResourceException.java	WeakHashMap.java
EventListenerProxy.java	NavigableMap.java	XMLUtils.java
EventObject.java	NavigableSet.java	

Figure 3.1 java.util package

Some additional features about the Collections Framework:

- **Algorithms**. In addition to collections, the `java.util` package has a `Collections` class, which has many common algorithms defined as static methods. You can apply any of the algorithms to any collection for intended operations such as sorting.
- **The iterator interface**. In order to help facilitate the use of the Collections Framework, an *iterator* interface is defined to offer a general-purpose, standardized way of accessing the elements of a collection. This interface is implemented by all collections so that you can enumerate the contents of a collection conveniently, if needed.
- **Maps**. The Collections Framework defines a few map interfaces and classes. Maps are provided for storing key-value pairs. Strictly speaking, maps are *not* collections. However, you can obtain a collection-view of a map so that you can process the contents of a map as a collection when needed. This is possible, as keys and values of a map can be considered *collections*. Later, you'll learn how to use `Map`'s `Entry` interface and `entrySet` method to return a `Set` that contains the entries in the map.

Finally, JDK 5 introduced more changes to the Collections Framework, making it more versatile and flexible. The new features introduced in JDK 5 include *generics*, *autoboxing*/*unboxing* and the for-each style *for*-loop, as described below:

- **Generics**. All collections are generic now so that many of the methods of collections take generic type parameters, which is essentially a type safety feature. Before this change, all collections stored Object type references so that any collection could store any type of objects. If different types of objects are stored in a collection, runtime type mismatch errors may occur. With generics, one specifies explicitly the type of objects to be stored, thus preventing runtime type mismatch errors potentially.
- **Autoboxing/unboxing**. A collection can store only references, not primitive values, such as `int`, `double`, and so on. Prior to JDK 5, type wrappers and explicit type casts were needed. With JDK 5's autoboxing/unboxing features, such nuances are taken care of automatically.
- **The for-each style for-loop**. JDK 5 retrofitted the Collections Framework so that the `Iterable` interface is implemented by all collections. This has made it possible for cycling through the elements of a collection by using a for-each style for-loop, rather than manually constructing a for-loop as we used to. We'll see some examples later about how to use the for-each style for-loop to visit all elements of a collection.

Next, we cover various collection interfaces and classes.

3.2 THE COLLECTION INTERFACES

The Java collection interfaces are defined in the `java.util` package. Figure 3.2 illustrates the interfaces defined by the Collections Framework. Before we dive into various collection interfaces, let's discuss the `Iterable` and `Iterator` interfaces first next.

3.2.1 The Iterable and Iterator Interfaces

As you see in Figure 3.2, the top-most interface is named `Iterable`, which is defined in the `java.lang` package as shown in Listing 3.1. Implementing this interface allows an object to be used in a for-each loop for cycling through its elements of type `T`, since it has only one line in its body: a statement that returns an iterator over a set of elements of type T, as shown at line 6. The `Iterator` interface is defined in the `java.util` package, as shown in Listing 3.2. It has the following methods:

- **hasNext()**: Returns `true` if the iteration has more elements.
- **next()**: Returns the next element in the iteration. Since it throws `NoSuchElementException` if the iteration has no more elements, it typically is used with the `hasNext()` method.
- **remove()**: Removes the last element from the underlying collection, if called.

Next, let's discuss the Collection interface.

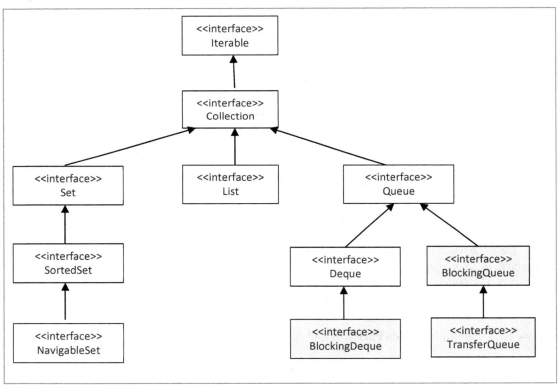

Figure 3.2 The interfaces defined by the Collections Framework

Listing 3.1 The Iterable interface

```
1    package java.lang;
2
3    import java.util.Iterator;
4
```

```
5    public interface Iterable<T> {
6        Iterator<T> iterator();
7    }
```

Listing 3.2 The Iterator interface

```
1    package java.util;
2
3    public interface Iterator<E> {
4        boolean hasNext();
5        E next();
6        void remove();
7    }
```

3.2.2 The Collection Interface

Listing 3.3 shows how the Collection interface is defined. It extends the Iterable interface to enable a collection to be cycled through within a for-each style for-loop, since only classes that implement Iterable can be cycled through in a for-each for–loop.

Listing 3.3 Collection.java

```
1    package java.util;
2
3    public interface Collection<E> extends Iterable<E> {
4        // 1. Query Operations
5        int size();
6        boolean isEmpty();
7        boolean contains(Object o);
8        Iterator<E> iterator();
9
10       // 2. Converting to an array
11       Object[] toArray();
12       <T> T[] toArray(T[] a);
13
14       // 3. Modification Operations
15       boolean add(E e);
16       boolean remove(Object o);
17
18       // 4. Bulk Operations
19       boolean containsAll(Collection<?> c);
20       boolean addAll(Collection<? extends E> c);
21       boolean removeAll(Collection<?> c);
22       boolean retainAll(Collection<?> c);
23       void clear();
24       // 5. Comparison and Hashing
25       boolean equals(Object o);
26       int hashCode();
27   }
```

As noted in Listing 3.3, the methods of the `Collection` interface are divided into the following five categories:

- **Query operations**. This category includes `size()` for returning the number of elements in the collection, `isEmpty()` for checking whether the collection is empty, and `contains(Object o)` for checking whether the collection contains a specific object.
- **Converting to an array**. The `toArray()` methods return an array that contains the elements stored in the invoking collection. The first form, parameter-less, returns an array of type `Object`, while the second form returns an array of elements that have the same type as specified by the typed parameter.
- **Modification operations**. The `add(E e)` method adds a new element to the collection, while the `remove(Object o)` method removes an element from the collection.
- **Bulk operations**. This category of methods operate on more than one element. The `containsAll (Collection<?> c)` method checks if the collection contains all elements stored in c, the `addAll (Collection<? extends E> c)` method adds all elements of c to the collection, the `removeAll (Collection<?> c)` method removes all elements as specified in c, while the `retailAll (Collection<?> c)` method retains all elements as specified in c. The `clear()` method empties the collection.
- **Comparison and hashing**. The `equals(Object o)` method compares the collection with the specified object for equality.

Next, we discuss the `Set` interface.

3.2.3 The Set Interface

`Set` is a kind of collection that allows no duplicate items. The Java `Set` collection is designed for this purpose, namely, for holding unique elements. It is defined as follows:

```
public interface Set<E> extends Collection<E> {
    // methods from Collection
}
```

Here, E specifies the type of objects the set will hold. The Java `Set` interface has no methods added except those extended from the `Collection` interface as shown in Listing 3.3. However, since it does not allow duplicate items, its `add` method returns `false` if an attempt is made to add a duplicate item.

A `Set` does not only contain no duplicate objects but also maintain no order for the items it contains. The `SortedSet` interface provides a mechanism for sorting the items a set contains, as discussed next.

3.2.4 The SortedSet Interface

The `SortedSet` interface extends `Set` with one additional feature that it maintains objects in ascending order. In addition to the methods extended from `Set/Collection`, it has five new methods of its own, as shown in Listing 3.4(a). Each of those methods is described as follows:

- **Comparator<? super E> comparator()**: Returns the comparator of the invoking sorted set, or `null` if the natural ordering is used for the set. The term *natural ordering* means that the objects can be ordered *naturally*, for example, Strings alphabetically, Dates chronologically, numerical types in ascending order, etc. Natural ordering is made possible by making corresponding types implement the Comparable interface, which specifies how ordering should be imposed for a given type that can be ordered naturally. Many types cannot be ordered naturally, though. For example, how would you compare two countries, by population, by land area or even by GDP? In such cases, the object types must implement the Comparable interface, which has a compareTo() method as shown below. This method returns "0" for "equal" or "< 0" for "smaller than" or "> 0" for "larger than." Refer to a Java programming book if you are interested in knowing how the Comparable interface can be implemented exactly.

```
public interface Comparable<T> {
    public int compareTo(T o);
}
```

- **SortedSet<E> subSet(E fromElement, E toElement)**: Returns a SortedSet that starts from the fromElement and ends prior to the toElement, with toElement excluded.
- **SortedSet<E> headSet(E toElement)**: A special case of the subSet method with fromElement = headElement.
- **SortedSet<E> tailSet(E fromElement)**: Returns the second part of the sorted set, starting from the fromElement through the tailElement.
- **E first()**: Returns the first element in the invoking sorted set.
- **E last()**: Returns the last element in the invoking sorted set.

Note that when you return a subSet or a headSet or a tailSet, their elements are still referenced by the invoking sorted set, which means that if an element is modified in a sub-set, the effect will be reflected in the invoking set as well.

Listing 3.4(a) The SortedSet interface

```
1    public interface SortedSet<E> extends Set<E> {
2      Comparator<? super E> comparator();
3      SortedSet<E> subSet(E fromElement, E toElement);
4      SortedSet<E> headSet(E toElement);
5      SortedSet<E> tailSet(E fromElement);
6      E first();
7      E last();
8    }
```

3.2.5 The NavigableSet Interface

The NavigableSet interface defines more methods to give more flexibility for accessing a SortedSet, as shown in Listing 3.4(b). The lower(E e) and higher(E e) methods return the largest element that is smaller or larger than e, respectively; or in other words, the closest element that is lower or higher than e. The floor(E e) method returns the largest element that is smaller than e (or immediately below), while the ceiling(E e) method returns the smallest element that is larger than e (or immediately above). The pollFirst()/pollLast() method returns the first/last element while removing it in the invoking set. The other methods, such as subSet, headSet, and tailSet, provide one extra Boolean parameter for specifying whether a from- or a to-element should be inclusive. The descendingIterator() method returns an iterator over the elements in the set, in descending order, while the descendingSet() method returns a reverse order view of the elements contained in the set.

Next, we discuss the List interface.

Listing 3.4(b) The NavigableSet interface

```
1   public interface NavigableSet<E> extends SortedSet<E> {
2       E lower(E e);
3       E higher(E e);
4       E floor(E e);
5       E ceiling(E e);
6       E pollFirst();
7       E pollLast();
8       Iterator<E> iterator();
9       NavigableSet<E> descendingSet();
10      Iterator<E> descendingIterator();
11      NavigableSet<E> subSet(E fromElement, boolean fromInclusive,
12                             E toElement,   boolean toInclusive);
13      NavigableSet<E> headSet(E toElement, boolean inclusive);
14      NavigableSet<E> tailSet(E fromElement, boolean inclusive);
15      SortedSet<E> subSet(E fromElement, E toElement);
16      SortedSet<E> headSet(E toElement);
17      SortedSet<E> tailSet(E fromElement);
18  }
```

3.2.6 The List Interface

A list stores a sequence of items. Therefore, a list object represents an ordered (but not necessarily a sorted) collection. Unlike a Set, a List can contain duplicate items.

In addition to the methods inherited from the Collection interface, Java List interface has ten of its own methods, as shown in Listing 3.5. Most of these methods provide index-based access to a list, such as:

- indexOf(Object o): For getting the index of an object in the list
- lastIndexOf(Object o): For getting the index of the last object if duplicate items exist
- get(int index): For getting the item at the specified index
- add(int index, E element): For inserting an element at the specified index
- addAll(int index, Collection<? extends E> c): For inserting all elements contained in c at the specified index, with all existing elements starting from the specified index shifted back
- remove(int index): For removing and returning the element at the specified index in the list
- set(int index, E element): For replacing the element at the specified index and returning the original element
- subList(int fromIndex, int toIndex): For returning references to a sub list of the elements ranging from fromIndex to (toIndex − 1), with the element at toIndex is not included

The remaining two methods, listIterator() and listIterator(int index), return an iterator to the start of the invoking list or to the element at the specified index of the list (whole or partial). A list iterator for lists allows the programmer to traverse the list in either direction, modify the list during iteration, and obtain the iterator's current position in the list, as discussed next.

Listing 3.5 List interface

```
1   public interface List<E> extends Collection<E> {
2       int indexOf(Object o);
3       int lastIndexOf(Object o);
4       E get(int index);
5       void add(int index, E element);
6       boolean addAll(int index, Collection<? extends E> c);
7       E remove(int index);
8       E set(int index, E element);
9       List<E> subList(int fromIndex, int toIndex);
10      ListIterator<E> listIterator();
11      ListIterator<E> listIterator(int index);
12  }
```

3.2.7 The ListIterator Interface

As shown in Listing 3.6, the Java ListIterator interface has nine methods that facilitate traversing and modifying a list. The pair of methods, hasNext() and next(), can be used to probe whether there is a next element, and retrieves it if it does. On the other hand, the pair of methods, hasPrevious() and previous(), can be used to probe whether there is a previous element, and retrieves it if it does. The nextIndex() and previousIndex() methods help obtain the next index and previous index without moving the cursor.

The remaining three methods, add, set and remove, facilitate the operations for modifying a list. The add(E e) method inserts the specified element into the list immediately before the element that would be returned by next(), if any, and after the element that would be returned by previous(), if any. The set(E e) method replaces the last element returned by next() or previous() with the specified element. This call can be made only if neither remove() nor add(E) have been called after the last call to next or previous. Finally, the remove() method removes from the list the last element returned by next() or previous(). This call can only be made once per call to next or previous. It can be made only if add(E e) has not been called after the last call to next() or previous().

Next, we discuss the Queue interface.

Listing 3.6 ListIterator interface

```
1   public interface ListIterator<E> extends Iterator<E> {
2       boolean hasNext();
3       E next();
4       boolean hasPrevious();
5       E previous();
6       int nextIndex();
7       int previousIndex();
8       void add(E e);
```

```
9     void set(E e);
10    void remove();
11  }
```

3.2.8 The Queue Interface

A simple queue conceptually is a first-in, first-out (FIFO) list. However, in computer science, queues do not necessarily order elements by following the FIFO rule. For example, priority queues order elements according to a supplied comparator, or the elements' natural ordering. In addition, FILO queues (or stacks) order the elements in a first-in, last-out (FILO) manner.

This section discusses simple, FIFO queues, which add new elements at the tail. A FIFO queue's methods are designed around the FIFO characteristic of the collection, as shown in Listing 3.7. These methods can be used for all common operations on a queue as follows:

- add(E e): Inserts the specified element into the queue at the end if the operation does not violate capacity restrictions. It returns true upon success and throws an IllegalStateException if no space is currently available.
- offer(E e): Inserts the specified element into the queue at the end if the operation does not violate capacity restrictions. Unlike the add(E e) method, which throws an IllegalStateException if no space is currently available, it returns false if no space is currently available.
- remove(): Retrieves and removes the head of the queue. It throws a NoSuchElementException if the queue is empty.
- poll(): Retrieves and removes the head of the queue. Unlike the remove() method, which throws a NoSuchElementException if the queue is empty, it returns null if the queue is empty.
- element(): Retrieves, but does not remove, the head of the queue. It throws an exception if the queue is empty.
- peek(): Retrieves, but does not remove, the head of the queue. Unlike the element() method, which throws an exception if the queue is empty, it returns null if the queue is empty.

Listing 3.7 The Queue interface

```
1   public interface Queue<E> extends Collection<E> {
2     boolean add(E e);
3     boolean offer(E e);
4     E remove();
5     E poll();
6     E element();
7     E peek();
8   }
```

Note that this simple Queue interface does not define blocking queue methods, which are common in concurrent programming. Blocking queue methods wait for elements to appear or for space to become available. They are defined in the BlockingQueue interface, which extends this simple Queue interface. We will cover BlockingQueue later.

Another special note is that simple `Queue` implementations generally do not allow insertion of `null` elements, as `null` is also used as a special return value by the `poll` method to indicate that the queue contains no elements.

Next, we discuss the `Deque` interface.

3.2.9 The Deque Interface

A deque is a linear collection that supports insertion and removal operations at both ends. Thus, it acts like a double-ended queue. Listing 3.8 shows the `Deque` interface. As is seen, its methods are classified into three categories:

1. **First/last methods**. These methods operate on the first and last elements of the deque. As you already learnt in the preceding section, add/remove/get versions throw exceptions, while offer/poll/peek versions return `false` if the operations fail. In addition, like `Queue`s, `Deque`s allow duplicate elements, so `removeFirstOccurrence(Object o)` and `removeLastOccurrence(Object o)` methods are provided for removing first/last occurrences if duplicates do exist.
2. **Queue methods**. These methods reflect the fact that a deque can act like a FIFO *Queue*.
3. **Stack methods**. These methods reflect the fact that a deque can act like a FILO *Stack*. If you once used the deprecated, legacy `Stack` collection, these methods of `push`, `pop`, `remove`, and `contains` should look familiar to you. (If you write new code, favor `Deque` over `Stack`.)

Note that using the methods suffixed with *First/Last* alone can simulate a queue or a stack. For example, you can use the `addLast` method to mimic a `Queue`'s `add` method to add an element at the end, or use the `addFirst` method to mimic a `Stack`'s `push` method, and so on.

If you refer back to Figure 3.2, you would note that three other interfaces, `BlockingDeque`, `BlockingQueue`, and `TransferQueue`, are shown as well. These interfaces belong to the `java.util.concurrent` package, and we will cover them in Chapter 7.

The next section covers the collection classes that implement the interfaces discussed in this section.

Listing 3.8 The Deque interface

```
1   public interface Deque<E> extends Queue<E> {
2       // first/last methods
3       void addFirst(E e);
4       void addLast(E e);
5       boolean offerFirst(E e);
6       boolean offerLast(E e);
7       E removeFirst();
8       E removeLast();
9       E pollFirst();
10      E pollLast();
11      E getFirst();
12      E getLast();
13      E peekFirst();
```

```
14   E peekLast();
15   boolean removeFirstOccurrence(Object o);
16   boolean removeLastOccurrence(Object o);
17   // queue methods
18   boolean add(E e);
19   boolean offer(E e);
20   E remove();
21   E poll();
22   E element();
23   E peek();
24   // stack methods
25   void push(E e);
26   E pop();
27   boolean remove(Object o);
28   boolean contains(Object o);
29 }
```

3.3   THE SET COLLECTION CLASSES

Figure 3.3 shows the Set class hierarchy. First, note that the AbstractSet class extends the AbstractCollection class and implements the Set interface, both of which implement the Collection interface. Then, we have the HashSet class that extends the AbstractSet class, and the LinkedHashSet class that extends the HashSet class. Finally, note the TreeSet class that extends the AbstractSet class and implements the NavigableSet → SortedSet → Set interfaces.

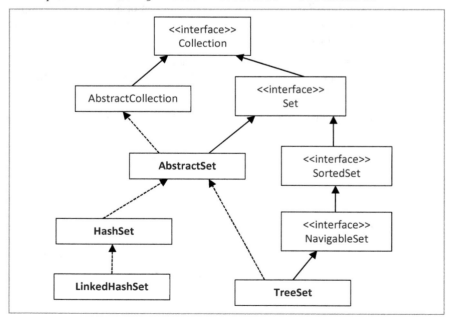

Figure 3.3 The Set collection classes

In the `Set` collection class hierarchy as shown in Figure 3.3, the `AbstractSet` class defines a common set of operations for `HashSet`, `LinkedHashSet` and `TreeSet`. The `HashSet` and `LinkedHashSet` classes are based on a storage technique termed *hashing*, which uses the hash code of an object as the key to uniquely identify an object. The major difference between `HashSet` and `LinkedHashSet` is that `HashSet` does not maintain insertion-order while `LinkedHashSet` maintains insertion-order. On the other hand, `TreeSet` creates a `Set` collection based on a tree for storage. In a `TreeSet`, objects are stored in sorted, ascending order, which makes access and retrieval operations very fast. Thus, `TreeSet` is an excellent choice for storing large amounts of stored information that can be searched rapidly.

Next, we discuss each of those `Set` classes. We start with the `AbstractSet` class first.

3.3.1 The AbstractSet Class

Listing 3.9 shows how the `AbstractSet` class is implemented in Java. As is seen, the `AbstractSet` class provides the comparison and hashing mechanism for all Set-based classes. The full source code is provided here so that you can observe how some of the methods of the Collection interfaces we introduced in the previous sections are used to implement the methods of a collection class. The `AbstractSet`'s methods include:

1. The `equals(Object o)` method. This method uses the `size()` method of the target collection instance as one of the conditions to check if the invoking collection equals the target collection. It also uses the `containsAll(c)` method as another condition to check if the invoking collection equals the target collection. The method returns `false` if the `ClassCastException` or `NullPointerException` is thrown.
2. The `hashCode()` method. This method returns the hash code of the set. It uses the `iterator()` method of the set to calculate the `hashCode` of the set by cascading the `hashCode` of all objects stored in the set. Note the use of the `hasNext()` and `next()` methods of the `iterator` interface in the `while`-loop.
3. The `removeAll(Collection<?> c)` method. This method removes all elements contained in collection `c`, which is passed in as a parameter. Depending on whether the source set is larger than the target set, it feeds the `remove(...)` method with every element in the source or target set to remove the contained elements in the source set.

This example also provides an opportunity for learning master-level coding skills exhibited in these methods.

Next, we discuss the `HashSet` class.

Listing 3.9 The AbstractSet class

```
1    package java.util;
2
3    public abstract class AbstractSet<E> extends AbstractCollection<E>
     implements Set<E> {
4        protected AbstractSet() {
5        }
6
```

```
7        // Comparison and hashing
8
9        public boolean equals(Object o) {
10           if (o == this)
11               return true;
12
13           if (!(o instanceof Set))
14               return false;
15           Collection c = (Collection) o;
16           if (c.size() != size())
17               return false;
18           try {
19               return containsAll(c);
20           } catch (ClassCastException unused)   {
21               return false;
22           } catch (NullPointerException unused) {
23               return false;
24           }
25       }
26
27       public int hashCode() {
28           int h = 0;
29           Iterator<E> i = iterator();
30           while (i.hasNext()) {
31               E obj = i.next();
32               if (obj != null)
33                   h += obj.hashCode();
34           }
35           return h;
36       }
37
38       public boolean removeAll(Collection<?> c) {
39           boolean modified = false;
40
41           if (size() > c.size()) {
42               for (Iterator<?> i = c.iterator(); i.hasNext(); )
43                   modified |= remove(i.next());
44           } else {
45               for (Iterator<?> i = iterator(); i.hasNext(); ) {
46                   if (c.contains(i.next())) {
47                       i.remove();
48                       modified = true;
49                   }
50               }
51           }
52           return modified;
53       }
54  }
```

3.3.2 The HashSet Class

Listing 3.10 shows partially how the HashSet class is implemented in Java. As you see at line 8, the HashSet is implemented with a HashMap internally by taking its *key-part* only. It has five constructors that allow various HashSet collection instances to be created, from parameter-less to taking some parameters, such as a given collection, or a given initialCapacity/loadFactor, etc. Its methods, such as iterator(), size(), isEmpty(), contains(Object o), add(E e), remove(Object o), and clear(), etc., are all wrappers of their counterparts in HashMap. We'll cover HashMap in a later section.

Listing 3.10 The HashSet class

```
1   package java.util;
2   public class HashSet<E>
3       extends AbstractSet<E>
4       implements Set<E>, Cloneable, java.io.Serializable
5   {
6       static final long serialVersionUID = -5024744406713321676L;
7
8       private transient HashMap<E,Object> map;
9
10      // Dummy value to associate with an Object in the backing Map
11      private static final Object PRESENT = new Object();
12
13      public HashSet() {
14          map = new HashMap<>();
15      }
16
17      public HashSet(Collection<? extends E> c) {
18          map = new HashMap<>(Math.max((int) (c.size()/.75f) + 1, 16));
19          addAll(c);
20      }
21
22      public HashSet(int initialCapacity, float loadFactor) {
23          map = new HashMap<>(initialCapacity, loadFactor);
24      }
25
26      public HashSet(int initialCapacity) {
27          map = new HashMap<>(initialCapacity);
28      }
29
30      HashSet(int initialCapacity, float loadFactor, boolean dummy) {
31          map = new LinkedHashMap<>(initialCapacity, loadFactor);
32      }
33
34      public Iterator<E> iterator() {
35          return map.keySet().iterator();
36      }
37
38      public int size() {
39          return map.size();
40      }
41
```

```
42      public boolean isEmpty() {
43          return map.isEmpty();
44      }
45
46      public boolean contains(Object o) {
47          return map.containsKey(o);
48      }
49
50      public boolean add(E e) {
51          return map.put(e, PRESENT)==null;
52      }
53
54      public boolean remove(Object o) {
55          return map.remove(o)==PRESENT;
56      }
57
58      public void clear() {
59          map.clear();
60      }
61
62      public Object clone() {
63          //omitted
64      }
65
66      private void writeObject(java.io.ObjectOutputStream s)
67       // omitted
68      }
69
70      private void readObject(java.io.ObjectInputStream s)
71          throws java.io.IOException, ClassNotFoundException {
72          // omitted
73      }
74  }
```

Listing 3.11 shows a simple HashSet demo. It creates a hash set by using the parameter-less HashSet constructor, and then adds the Strings of "This is a HashSet demo" using the add method. If you execute this program, you may get an output like the following:

[demo, This , HashSet , a, is]

As you see, the insertion order is not preserved, as expected from a HashSet. The LinkedHashSet class preserves the insertion-order, as will be illustrated next.

Listing 3.11 HashSetDemo.java

```
1   package jcp.ch3.set;
2   import java.util.*;
3
4   public class HashSetDemo {
5     public static void main (String args[]) {
6         // create a hash set
7         HashSet<String> hs = new HashSet<String> ();
```

```
8
9          // add elements
10         hs.add ("This ");
11         hs.add ("is ");
12         hs.add (" a");
13         hs.add (" HashSet ");
14         hs.add ("demo");
15         System.out.println (hs);
16     }
17 }
```

3.3.3 The LinkedHashSet Class

Listing 3.12 shows how the LinkedHashSet class is implemented in Java. It looks incredibly simple – just four constructors. You might wonder how LinkedHashSet actually makes itself behave like a linked list, as it extends HashSet, which is not a list and does not preserve insertion-order. The answer is hidden in the fifth constructor of the HashSet class, shown from lines 30 -- 32 in Listing 3.10, which is copied below:

```
30    HashSet(int initialCapacity, float loadFactor, boolean dummy) {
31        map = new LinkedHashMap<>(initialCapacity, loadFactor);
32    }
```

Unlike the other four constructors of HashSet, this constructor is not declared public, which makes it accessible at the package level by default in Java. In addition, this constructor uses a LinkedHashMap, rather than a HashMap, to create a Set instance. As we will discuss later, LinkedHashMap is based on a hash table and linked list implementation of the Map interface, with predictable iteration order. It differs from HashMap in that it maintains a doubly-linked list running through all of its entries. All four constructors of LinkedHashSet use LinkedHashMap to construct an instance of LinkedHashSet, which makes it doubly-linked-list capable.

Listing 3.12 LinkedHashSet.java

```
1   package java.util;
2
3   public class LinkedHashSet<E>
4       extends HashSet<E>
5       implements Set<E>, Cloneable, java.io.Serializable {
6
7       private static final long serialVersionUID = -2851667679971038690L;
8
9       public LinkedHashSet(int initialCapacity, float loadFactor) {
10          super(initialCapacity, loadFactor, true);
11      }
12
13      public LinkedHashSet(int initialCapacity) {
14          super(initialCapacity, .75f, true);
15      }
16
```

```
17    public LinkedHashSet() {
18        super(16, .75f, true);
19    }
20
21    public LinkedHashSet(Collection<? extends E> c) {
22        super(Math.max(2*c.size(), 11), .75f, true);
23        addAll(c);
24    }
25  }
```

Listing 3.13 shows a LinkedHashSet example, retrofitted from the previous HashSet demo. If you execute this example, you would get the following output predictably:

[This , is , a, HashSet , demo]
[This , is , a, HashSet , demo]

Namely, the insertion-order is preserved, as expected from a LinkedHashSet.

Next, we discuss TreeSet.

Listing 3.13 LinkedHashSetDemo.java

```
1    package jcp.ch3.set;
2    import java.util.*;
3
4    public class LinkedHashSetDemo {
5      public static void main (String args[]) {
6          // create a hash set
7          HashSet<String> lhs = new LinkedHashSet<String> ();
8
9          // add elements
10         lhs.add ("This ");
11         lhs.add ("is ");
12         lhs.add (" a");
13         lhs.add (" HashSet ");
14         lhs.add ("demo");
15         System.out.println (lhs);
16         System.out.println (lhs.toString ());
17     }
18  }
```

3.3.4 The TreeSet Class

Listing 3.14 shows partially how TreeSet is implemented in Java. As you see, TreeSet extends AbstractSet and implements NavigableSet interface. However, internally, TreeSet is backed by a MavigableMap for its storage, as shown at line 7. Lines 15 – 17 define the package-level constructor for the TreeSet class. Similar to TreeSet that implements NavigableSet interface, TreeMap implements NavigableMap interface. This is why we see TreeSet's no-arg constructor defined from lines 19 – 21 and the comparator-based constructor defined from lines 23 – 25 use a TreeMap to construct a TreeSet instance. Lines 32 – 34 define a TreeSet constructor based on a given collection c.

Since `TreeSet` uses `TreeMap` as its backing store and `TreeMap` implements `NavigableMap`, the elements of a tree set instance are ordered using natural ordering, or by a `Comparator` provided at set creation time, depending on which constructor is used. `TreeSet` implements its methods defined by the `Collection` and `NavigableSet` interfaces as well as the `AbstractSet` class by operating on its `NavigableMap` backing store, as illustrated by the `subSet` method defined from lines 37 − 41.

A couple of special notes about `TreeSet`:

- Performance-wise, this `TreeSet` implementation provides guaranteed *log(n)* time cost for its basic operations, such as `add`, `remove` and `contains`.

- Concurrency-wise, this `TreeSet` implementation is not synchronized. If multiple threads access a tree set concurrently, and at least one of the threads mutates the set, the set must be synchronized externally, which is typically accomplished by synchronizing on some object that encapsulates the set.

If a tree set cannot be synchronized externally on some object, the set can be "wrapped" using the `Collections.synchronizedSortedSet` method, which should be done at creation time in order to prevent accidental unsynchronized access to the set:

```
SortedSet s = Collections.synchronizedSortedSet(new TreeSet(...));
```

In the above case, the iterators returned by `TreeSet`'s iterator method are *fail-fast*, which means that if the set is modified at any time after the iterator is created, in any way except through the iterator's own `remove` method, the iterator will throw a `ConcurrentModificationException`. Thus, when concurrent modification occurs, the iterator fails quickly and cleanly, rather than risking arbitrary, non-deterministic behavior at an undetermined time in the future.

Note: About fail-fast. Note that the fail-fast behavior of an iterator cannot be guaranteed, as in general, it is impossible to make any hard guarantees in the presence of unsynchronized concurrent modification. Fail-fast iterators are designed to throw `ConcurrentModificationException` on a best-effort basis. Therefore, the fail-fast behavior of iterators should be used only to detect bugs and one should not depend on this exception for guaranteeing its correctness for concurrency.

Listing 3.14 TreeSet.java

```
1    public class TreeSet<E> extends AbstractSet<E>
2        implements NavigableSet<E>, Cloneable, java.io.Serializable
3    {
4        /**
5         * The backing map.
6         */
7        private transient NavigableMap<E,Object> m;
8
9        // Dummy value to associate with an Object in the backing Map
10       private static final Object PRESENT = new Object();
11
```

```
12      /**
13       * Constructs a set backed by the specified navigable map.
14       */
15      TreeSet(NavigableMap<E,Object> m) {
16          this.m = m;
17      }
18
19      public TreeSet() {
20          this(new TreeMap<E,Object>());
21      }
22
23      public TreeSet(Comparator<? super E> comparator) {
24          this(new TreeMap<>(comparator));
25      }
26
27      public TreeSet(Collection<? extends E> c) {
28          this();
29          addAll(c);
30      }
31
32      public TreeSet(SortedSet<E> s) {
33          this(s.comparator());
34          addAll(s);
35      }
36
37      public NavigableSet<E> subSet(E fromElement, boolean fromInclusive,
38                                    E toElement,   boolean toInclusive) {
39          return new TreeSet<>(m.subMap(fromElement, fromInclusive,
40                                        toElement,   toInclusive));
41      }
42      // other methods omitted
43  }
```

Listing 3.15 shows a TreeSet demo program. The letters 'a' through 'f' are inserted onto the tree set, and then printed out twice: first the entire set and then the subset from b to e with e excluded by design. Executing this program would produce the following output:

[a, b, c, d, e, f]
[b, c, d]

In the above output, the first line represents the entire set. Since TreeSet stores its elements in a tree structure, the elements are sorted in natural order, namely, alphabetically. The second line represents the sub set that starts with 'b' and ends with 'd', as specified in the subSet method call at line 17.

Next, we discuss the List collection class.

Listing 3.15 TreeSetDemo.java

```
1   package jcp.ch3.set;
2   import java.util.*;
3
4   public class TreeSetDemo {
```

```
5    public static void main (String args[]) {
6        // create a tree set
7        TreeSet<String> ts = new TreeSet<String> ();
8
9        // add elements
10       ts.add ("f");
11       ts.add ("a");
12       ts.add ("e");
13       ts.add ("c");
14       ts.add ("b");
15       ts.add ("d");
16       System.out.println (ts);
17       System.out.println (ts.subSet ("b", "e"));
18   }
19 }
```

3.4   THE LIST COLLECTION CLASSES

Figure 3.4 shows the List class hierarchy. First, note the ArrayList class that extends the AbstractList class and implements the List and RandomAccess interfaces. Then, note that the AbstractList class extends the AbstractCollection class and implements the List interface, both of which implement the Collection interface. Finally, note the AbstractSequentialList class that extends the AbstractList class, and the LinkedList class that extends the AbstractSequentialList class. Note that LinkedList also implements the Deque and Queue interfaces.

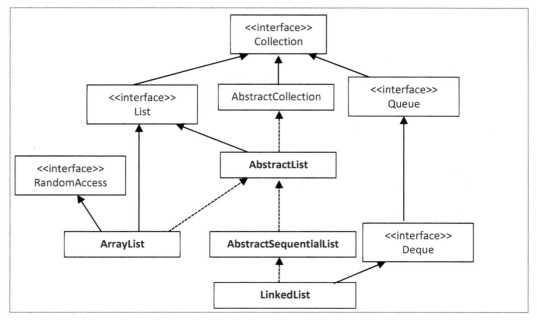

Figure 3.4 The List collection classes

Next, we discuss each of those List classes. We start with the AbstractList class first.

3.4.1 The AbstractList Class

The AbstractList class provides default implementations for some of the methods it inherits from the List interface and AbstractCollection class. Listing 3.16 shows partially how the AbstractList class is implemented in Java. As you see, it either provides no implementation (e. g., line 12 for the get method), or throws UnsupportedOperationException (e. g., lines 14 – 20 for the set and add methods), or provides a default implementation (e. g., lines 22 – 34 for the indexOf method). Since this is only a skeleton class, we move on next to discussing the RandomAccess interface prior to discussing the ArrayList class.

Listing 3.16 AbastractList.java (partial)

```
1    package java.util;
2
3    public abstract class AbstractList<E> extends AbstractCollection<E>
     implements List<E> {
4        protected AbstractList() {
5        }
6
7        public boolean add(E e) {
8            add(size(), e);
9            return true;
10       }
11
12       abstract public E get(int index);
13
14       public E set(int index, E element) {
15           throw new UnsupportedOperationException();
16       }
17
18       public void add(int index, E element) {
19           throw new UnsupportedOperationException();
20       }
21
22       public int indexOf(Object o) {
23           ListIterator<E> it = listIterator();
24           if (o==null) {
25               while (it.hasNext())
26                   if (it.next()==null)
27                       return it.previousIndex();
28           } else {
29               while (it.hasNext())
30                   if (o.equals(it.next()))
31                       return it.previousIndex();
32           }
33           return -1;
34       }
```

```
35      // other methods omitted
36  }
```

3.4.2 The RandomAccess Interface

Since the ArrayList class implements the RandomAccess interface, we need to discuss the RandomAccess interface prior to discussing the ArrayList class.

The RandomAccess.java file only contains the following contents for the RandomAccess class:

```
package java.util;
public interface RandomAccess {
}
```

So, what's the use of an interface if it has no members and why does the ArrayList class implement such an interface that has no members? It is used as a mechanism for signaling that the collection class that implements it supports efficient random access to its elements, usually O (1) or constant time. To be more specific, the RandomAccess interface is a marker interface. As the programmer can use instanceof to determine at runtime if a class implements an interface, by implementing the RandomAccess interface, it's possible to allow generic algorithms to alter their behavior to provide good performance when applied to either random or sequential access lists of large collections.

◀Note: **Random versus Sequential Access**. The algorithms for manipulating random access lists, such as ArrayList, may produce quadratic access time when applied to sequential access lists, such as LinkedList. Thus, a generic list algorithm should check whether the given list is an instanceof the RandomAccess interface to avoid poor performance if it were applied to a sequential access list, and then alter its behavior for better performance.

In addition, the distinction between random and sequential access might be fuzzy. For example, some List implementations provide asymptotically linear access times if the list collection gets large, but actually constant access times in practice. Therefore, such a List implementation should generally implement the RandomAccess interface. In general, a List implementation should implement the RandomAccess interface if, for typical instances of the class, the following loop (random access):

```
for (int i=0, n=list.size(); i < n; i++)
    list.get(i);    // random access
```

runs faster than this loop (sequential access):

```
for (Iterator i=list.iterator(); i.hasNext(); )
    i.next();    // sequential access
```

Next, we discuss the ArrayList class.

3.4.3 The ArrayList Class

Java `ArrayList` is a variable-length array of object references. Unlike standard arrays of fixed length, an `ArrayList` can dynamically increase or decrease in size. When the default size is exceeded, the `ArrayList` collection is automatically enlarged. When objects are removed, the `ArrayList` collection can be shrunk.

Listing 3.17 shows partially the `ArrayList` collection implemented in Java, with the following implementation details:

- Line 6 shows the default capacity of 10 to start with. Any empty `ArrayList` will be expanded to the `DEFAULT_CAPACITY` when the first element is added.
- Line 13 shows the array buffer named `elementData` for holding the elements of an `ArrayList`
- Lines 17 -- 23 define an `ArrayList` constructor with a given initial capacity
- Lines 25 – 28 define the no-arg default constructor
- Lines 30 – 37 define a constructor with a given collection
- Lines 39 – 49 define the `grow` method for dynamically increasing the size of an `ArrayList`
- Lines 51 – 55 define the `add` method with a given element. Line 53 shows that the given element is appended to the `ArrayList` at the end.
- Lines 57 – 65 define the `add` method at a given index. Lines 61 – 62 make the space at the given index available by shifting the array right using the `System.arraycopy` method, while line 63 adds the new element at the specified index.

Of course, `ArrayList` has a lot more methods than illustrated here. The above implementation details are given to help you gain some insight into how `ArrayList` is actually implemented internally. You can refer to the source code of `ArrayList.java` for how its common operations, such as add/get/remove/set, are implemented. A special note here: The `set` operation is actually equivalent to the `update` operation, as shown by its implementation below: It first does `rangeCheck` to make sure the index is still in range; then, it retrieves the value of the existing element, replaces the element with the new element, and returns the old value of the element.

```java
public E set(int index, E element) {
    rangeCheck(index);

    E oldValue = elementData(index);
    elementData[index] = element;
    return oldValue;
}
```

Listing 3.17 ArrayList.java (partial)

```java
1   package java.util;
2
3   public class ArrayList<E> extends AbstractList<E>
4           implements List<E>, RandomAccess, Cloneable, java.io.Serializable
5   {
6       private static final int DEFAULT_CAPACITY = 10;
7
8       /**
9        * Shared empty array instance used for empty instances.
```

```
10       */
11      private static final Object[] EMPTY_ELEMENTDATA = {};
12
13      private transient Object[] elementData;
14
15      private int size;
16
17      public ArrayList(int initialCapacity) {
18          super();
19          if (initialCapacity < 0)
20              throw new IllegalArgumentException("Illegal Capacity: "+
21                                                  initialCapacity);
22          this.elementData = new Object[initialCapacity];
23      }
24
25      public ArrayList() {
26          super();
27          this.elementData = EMPTY_ELEMENTDATA;
28      }
29
30      public ArrayList(Collection<? extends E> c) {
31          elementData = c.toArray();
32          size = elementData.length;
33          // c.toArray might (incorrectly) not return Object[] (see 6260652)
34          if (elementData.getClass() != Object[].class)
35              elementData = Arrays.copyOf(elementData, size,
36                  Object[].class);
37      }
38
39      private void grow(int minCapacity) {
40          // overflow-conscious code
41          int oldCapacity = elementData.length;
42          int newCapacity = oldCapacity + (oldCapacity >> 1);
43          if (newCapacity - minCapacity < 0)
44              newCapacity = minCapacity;
45          if (newCapacity - MAX_ARRAY_SIZE > 0)
46              newCapacity = hugeCapacity(minCapacity);
47          // minCapacity is usually close to size, so this is a win:
48          elementData = Arrays.copyOf(elementData, newCapacity);
49      }
50
51      public boolean add(E e) {
52          ensureCapacityInternal(size + 1);  // Increments modCount!!
53          elementData[size++] = e;
54          return true;
55      }
56
57      public void add(int index, E element) {
58          rangeCheckForAdd(index);
59
60          ensureCapacityInternal(size + 1);  // Increments modCount!!
61          System.arraycopy(elementData, index, elementData, index + 1,
```

```
62                            size - index);
63           elementData[index] = element;
64           size++;
65       }
66       // other methods omitted
67  }
```

Listing 3.18 shows an `ArrayListDemo` program, while Listing 3.19 shows the output of running this program (for convenience, the output results are numbered). The demo program is explained as follows:

- Line 7 creates an empty `ArrayList`.
- Line 8 prints out the initial size of the array list, which is 0 as shown at line 1 in Listing 3.19.
- Lines 11 – 17 add five elements, and then print out the contents of the array list and the size of the array list, as in lines 2 – 3 in Listing 3.19 show.
- Line 18 uses the `indexOf` method to print out the index of a string "simple." Since this string does not exist in the array list, the returned index is -1, as shown at line 4 in Listing 3.19.
- Lines 21 – 23 add a string "simple" at index = 3, and then print out the contents and the size of the array list. Lines 5 -- 6 in Listing 3.19 show the result.
- Lines 26 – 28 add another string of "simple" at index = 5, and then print out the contents and the size of the array list. Lines 7 -- 8 in Listing 3.19 show the result. As you see, the second "simple" string is added after "ArrayList" string. The intention here is to show that lists allow duplicates.
- Lines 31 – 32 show the difference between the `indexOf` and `lastIndexOf` methods: the two methods find the indices of the first and last duplicated elements, respectively. Lines 9 – 10 in Listing 3.19 show the result.
- Finally, lines 34 – 36 remove the "simple" string and then prints out the contents and the size of the array list. Lines 11 – 12 in Listing 3.19 show that the "simple" string has been removed, leaving the size of the array list to 6.

Next, we discuss the `AbstractSequentialList` class.

Listing 3.18 ArrayListDemo.java

```
1   package jcp.ch3.list;
2   import java.util.*;
3
4   public class ArrayListDemo {
5     public static void main (String args[]) {
6       // create an ArrayList collection
7       ArrayList<String> al = new ArrayList ();
8       System.out.println ("Initial size of al: " + al.size());
9
10      // add elements
11      al.add ("This ");
12      al.add ("is ");
13      al.add ("an ");
14      al.add ("ArrayList ");
15      al.add ("demo");
16      System.out.println (al);
17      System.out.println ("Size after adding 5 elements: " + al.size());
```

```
18    System.out.println ("Index for the \"simple \" string: " + al.indexOf
         ("simple "));
19
20    // add an element at index = 3
21    al.add(3, "simple ");
22    System.out.println (al);
23    System.out.println ("Size after adding an element at index = 3: " +
         al.size());
24
25    // add an element at index = 5
26    al.add(5, "simple ");
27    System.out.println (al);
28    System.out.println ("Size after adding an element at index = 5 again:
         " + al.size());
29
30    // indexOf and lastIndexOf
31    System.out.println ("Index for the \"simple \" string: " + al.indexOf
         ("simple "));
32    System.out.println ("Index for the last \"simple \" string: " +
         al.lastIndexOf ("simple "));
33    // remove the "simple" string
34    al.remove("simple ");
35    System.out.println (al);
36    System.out.println ("Size after removing an element: " + al.size());
37    }
38 }
```

Listing 3.19 Output of running the ArrayListDemo.java program

```
1    Initial size of al: 0
2    [This , is , an , ArrayList , demo]
3    Size after adding 5 elements: 5
4    Index for the "simple " string: -1
5    [This , is , an , simple , ArrayList , demo]
6    Size after adding an element at index = 3: 6
7    [This , is , an , simple , ArrayList , simple , demo]
8    Size after adding an element at index = 5 again: 7
9    Index for the "simple " string: 3
10   Index for the last "simple " string: 5
11   [This , is , an , ArrayList , simple , demo]
12   Size after removing an element: 6
```

3.4.4 The AbstractSequentialList Class

Listing 3.20 shows how the AbstractSequentialList class is implemented in Java. The purpose of this class is to provide "random access" to a list that is backed by a "sequential access" data store, such as a LinkedList to be discussed in the next section. It turns "sequential access" to "random access" by implementing the methods of get, set, add and remove on top of the list's list iterator using indexing, as shown in Listing 3.20. Lines 8 – 14 show how the get(int index) method is implemented as such. To save space, the body parts for all other methods are omitted, but they are implemented essentially the same way.

Next, we discuss the LinkedList class.

Listing 3.20 AbstractSequentialList.java

```
1   package java.util;
2
3   public abstract class AbstractSequentialList<E> extends AbstractList<E> {
4
5       protected AbstractSequentialList() {
6       }
7
8       public E get(int index) {
9           try {
10              return listIterator(index).next();
11          } catch (NoSuchElementException exc) {
12              throw new IndexOutOfBoundsException("Index: "+index);
13          }
14      }
15
16      public E set(int index, E element) {
17          // body omitted
18      }
19
20      public void add(int index, E element) {
21          // body omitted
22      }
23
24      public E remove(int index) {
25          // body omitted
26      }
27
28      public boolean addAll(int index, Collection<? extends E> c) {
29          // body omitted
30      }
31
32      public Iterator<E> iterator() {
33          return listIterator();
34      }
35
36      public abstract ListIterator<E> listIterator(int index);
37  }
```

3.4.5 The LinkedList Class

As is shown in Listing 3.21, the LinkedList class extends the AbstractSequentialList class and implements the List and Deque interfaces. A linked list consists of a series of nodes, each of which is defined by a private class, Node, as shown below. This Node class has three fields: item for the content of a node, and next and prev references (or pointers, loosely speaking) pointing to the next and previous nodes, respectively. This shows that a LinkedList is essentially a doubly-linked list, as it implements both the List and Deque interfaces and its nodes have bi-directional pointers.

```
private static class Node<E> {
  E item;
  Node<E> next;
  Node<E> prev;

  Node(Node<E> prev, E element, Node<E> next) {
    this.item = element;
    this.next = next;
    this.prev = prev;
  }
}
```

As is shown in Listing 3.21, LinkedList has two constructors: a no-arg constructor defined from lines 23 – 24 and a non-void constructor defined from lines 26 – 29 that takes an external collection as input for creating a new LinkedList. Since it implements the Deque interface, it has two special members: a first node and a last node, as defined at lines 14 and 21, respectively. As such, it has many methods that operate on the first and last nodes, as discussed below.

The link-oriented methods with LinkedList are non-public as shown from lines 31 – 68 in Listing 3.21, namely, for internal implementation use only. They include:

- linkFirst(E e) for linking e as the first element
- linkLast(E, e) for linking e as the last element
- linkBefore(E e, Node<E> succ) for inserting e before the non-null Node succ
- unlinkFirst(Node<E> f) for unlinking non-null first node f
- unlinkLast(Node<E> l) for unlinking non-null last node l
- unlink(Node<E> x) for unlinking non-null node x

The public methods with LinkedList include:

- **add/offer**: These include add(E e), add(int index, E element), addAll(Collection<? extends E> c), addAll(int index, Collection<? extends E> c), addFirst(E e), addLast(E e), offer(E e), offerFirst(E e), and offerLast(E, e). You might wonder what the difference is between, for example, addFirst(E e) and offerFirst(E e). Their respective implementations make it obvious, as shown below, that is, addFirst is a wrapper of linkFirst, and offerFirst is a wrapper of addFirst except that it returns true if successful.

```
public void addFirst(E e) {
    linkFirst(e);
  }
  public boolean offerFirst(E e) {
    addFirst(e);
    return true;
  }
```

- **get/peek:** These include `get(int index)`, `getFirst()`, `getLast()`, `peek()`, `peekFirst()`, and `peekLast()`. Once again, the difference between `get` and `peek` can be explained by their respective implementations as shown below, that is, `get` throws a `NoSuchElementException` while `peek` returns `null` if the node is null.

```java
public E getFirst() {
    final Node<E> f = first;
    if (f == null)
        throw new NoSuchElementException();
    return f.item;
}
public E peekFirst() {
    final Node<E> f = first;
    return (f == null) ? null : f.item;
}
```

- **remove/poll:** These include `remove()`, `remove(int index)`, `remove(Object o)`, `removeFirst()`, `removeFirstOccurrence(Object o)`, `removeLast()`, `removeLastOccurrence(Object o)`, `poll()`, `pollFirst()`, and `pollLast()`. Once again, the difference between `remove` and `poll` can be explained by their respective implementations as shown below, that is, `remove` throws a `NoSuchElementException` while `poll` returns `null` if the node is null. Note that `remove()` is the same as `removeFirst()` and `poll()` is the same as `pollFirst()`.

```java
public E remove() {
    return removeFirst();
}
public E poll() {
    final Node<E> f = first;
    return (f == null) ? null : unlinkFirst(f);
}
```

- **pop/push:** These two methods mimic the `pop` and `push` operations of the legacy `Stack` class. As shown by the following code snippets, `pop()` is the same as `removeFirst()`, and `push()` is the same as `addFirst()`:

```java
public E pop() {
    return removeFirst();
}
public void push(E e) {
    addFirst(e);
}
```

- **set (int index, E element):** Replaces (or updates) the element at the specified position in this list with the specified element. It actually returns the value of the existing node, as shown below: It first does `rangeCheck` to make sure the index is still in range; then, it retrieves the node at the specified index, stores the value of the existing item, replaces the item of the node with the new element, and returns the old value of the element.

```java
public E set(int index, E element) {
    checkElementIndex(index);
```

```
        Node<E> x = node(index);
        E oldVal = x.item;
        x.item = element;
        return oldVal;
    }
```

Next, we look at an example of using `LinkedList`, following List 3.21.

Listing 3.21 LinkedList.java (partial)

```
1    package java.util;
2
3    public class LinkedList<E>
4        extends AbstractSequentialList<E>
5        implements List<E>, Deque<E>, Cloneable, java.io.Serializable
6    {
7        transient int size = 0;
8
9        /**
10        * Pointer to first node.
11        * Invariant: (first == null && last == null) ||
12        *            (first.prev == null && first.item != null)
13        */
14        transient Node<E> first;
15
16        /**
17        * Pointer to last node.
18        * Invariant: (first == null && last == null) ||
19        *            (last.next == null && last.item != null)
20        */
21        transient Node<E> last;
22
23        public LinkedList() {
24        }
25
26        public LinkedList(Collection<? extends E> c) {
27            this();
28            addAll(c);
29        }
30
31        private void linkFirst(E e) {
32            final Node<E> f = first;
33            final Node<E> newNode = new Node<>(null, e, f);
34            first = newNode;
35            if (f == null)
36                last = newNode;
37            else
38                f.prev = newNode;
39            size++;
40            modCount++;
41        }
```

```
42
43    void linkLast(E e) {
44        final Node<E> l = last;
45        final Node<E> newNode = new Node<>(l, e, null);
46        last = newNode;
47        if (l == null)
48            first = newNode;
49        else
50            l.next = newNode;
51        size++;
52        modCount++;
53    }
54
55    void linkBefore(E e, Node<E> succ) {
56        // body omitted
57    }
58    private E unlinkFirst(Node<E> f) {
59        // body omitted
60    }
61
62    private E unlinkLast(Node<E> l) {
63        // body omitted
64    }
65
66    E unlink(Node<E> x) {
67        // body omitted
68    }
69
70    public E getFirst() {
71        // body omitted
72    }
73
74    public E getLast() {
75        // body omitted
76    }
77
78    public E removeFirst() {
79        // body omitted
80    }
81
82    public E removeLast() {
83        // body omitted
84    }
85
86    public void addFirst(E e) {
87        linkFirst(e);
88    }
89
90    public void addLast(E e) {
91        linkLast(e);
92    }
93
```

```
94        // other methods omitted
95
96   }
```

Listing 3.22 shows a demo of using LinkedList, named LinkedListDemo.java. It was actually based on the previous ArrayListDemo shown in Listing 3.18, with the following changes applied:

- Line 7: Instead of creating an array list, a linked list is created using the no-arg LinkedList constructor.
- Line 21: The set method is called to update the string at index = 3 from "ArrayList" to "LinkedList."

Listing 3.23 shows the output of running this example. As you see, since ArrayList and LinkedList both implement the List interface, they share a common subset of methods inherited from the List interface. However, LinkedList implements the Deque interface, while ArrayList doesn't, which makes a linked list a doubly-linked list. The next section discusses more about the differences between ArrayList and LinkedList.

Listing 3.22 LinkedListDemo.java

```
1    package jcp.ch3.list;
2    import java.util.*;
3
4    public class LinkedListDemo {
5      public static void main (String args[]) {
6        // create a LinkedList collection
7        LinkedList<String> ll = new LinkedList<String> ();
8        System.out.println ("Initill size of ll: " + ll.size());
9
10       // add elements
11       ll.add ("This ");
12       ll.add ("is ");
13       ll.add ("an ");
14       ll.add ("ArrayList ");
15       ll.add ("demo");
16       System.out.println (ll);
17       System.out.println ("Size after adding 5 elements: " + ll.size());
18       System.out.println ("Index for the \"simple \" string: " + ll.indexOf
             ("simple "));
19
20       // update "ArrayList" with "LinkedList"
21       ll.set(3, "LinkedList ");
22
23       // add an element at index = 3
24       ll.add(3, "simple ");
25       System.out.println (ll);
26       System.out.println ("Size after adding an element at index = 3: " +
             ll.size());
27
28       // add an element at index = 5
29       ll.add(5, "simple ");
```

```
30        System.out.println (ll);
31        System.out.println ("Size after adding an element at index = 5 again:
             " + ll.size());
32
33        // indexOf and lastIndexOf
34        System.out.println ("Index for the \"simple \" string: " + ll.indexOf
             ("simple "));
35        System.out.println ("Index for the last \"simple \" string: " +
             ll.lastIndexOf ("simple "));
36        // remove the "simple" string
37        ll.remove("simple ");
38        System.out.println (ll);
39        System.out.println ("Size after removing an element: " + ll.size());
40    }
41 }
```

Listing 3.23 Output of running the LinkedListDemo

```
1  Initill size of ll: 0
2  [This , is , an , ArrayList , demo]
3  Size after adding 5 elements: 5
4  Index for the "simple " string: -1
5  [This , is , an , simple , LinkedList , demo]
6  Size after adding an element at index = 3: 6
7  [This , is , an , simple , LinkedList , simple , demo]
8  Size after adding an element at index = 5 again: 7
9  Index for the "simple " string: 3
10 Index for the last "simple " string: 5
11 [This , is , an , LinkedList , simple , demo]
12 Size after removing an element: 6
```

3.4.6 ArrayList versus LinkedList

As mentioned previously, since ArrayList and LinkedList both implement the List interface, they share a common subset of methods inherited from the List interface. However, LinkedList implements the Deque interface, while ArrayList doesn't, which makes a linked list a doubly-linked list. This is the fundamental difference between ArrayList and LinkedList.

In addition, both ArrayList and LinkedList maintain insertion-order, as we have seen from the previous demo programs for each case.

From the concurrency perspective, both ArrayList and LinkedList are unsynchronized and can be made synchronized explicitly by using Collections.synchronizedList method as discussed previously. The iterator and listIterator returned by both ArrayList and LinkedList are fail-fast, that is, if the list is structurally modified at any time after the iterator is created, in any way except through the iterator's own remove or add methods, the iterator will throw a ConcurrentModificationException.

Memory-wise, `ArrayList` is more efficient than `LinkedList`, though, as `ArrayList` is implemented using an internal array, while `LinkedList` is implemented with a series of nodes that are linked both ways.

Performance-wise, `ArrayList` favors search-intensive operations as it is index-based (or random access), while `LinkedList` favors update-intensive operations as it is more of reference-based (or sequential access). Table 3.1 summarizes the performance comparison between `ArrayList` and `LinkedList`.

Next, we discuss the `Queue` collection classes.

Table 3.1 Performance comparison between ArrayList and LinkedList

Operation	ArrayList	LinkedList
access	random	sequential
search	O (1)	O (n)
update	O (1)	O (n)
insertion	O (n)	O (1)
deletion	O (n)	O (1)

3.5 THE QUEUE COLLECTION CLASSES

Figure 3.5 shows the `Queue` class hierarchy. First, note the `ArrayDeque` class that extends the `AbstractCollection` class and implements the `Queue` interface. Then, note that the `AbstractQueue` class implements the `Queue` interface, which implements the `Collection` interface. Finally, note the `PriorityQueue` class that extends the `AbstractQueue` class. It is important to remember that `Queue` itself is an interface, not a class. For unsynchronized queues, you use either `ArrayDeque`, which mimics the legacy `Stack` class, or `PriortityQueue`, which represents a queue that is prioritized based on the queue's comparator.

This section covers `ArrayDeque`, `AbstractQueue` and `PriorityQueue`. Let's start with `ArrayDeque` first.

3.5.1 The ArrayDeque Class

Listing 3.24 shows how `ArrayDeque` is implemented internally (partial) in Java. As is seen, it extends the `AbstractCollection` class and implements the `Deque` interface. `ArrayDeque` internally maintains an array of `elements` as its back data store, with indexed `head` and `tail` references, as shown from lines 4 – 6 in Listing 3.24. (In contrast, `LinkedList` internally maintains a node structure with `first` and `last` references.) `ArrayDeque` is a special array-based `deque` that:

- Its capacity is the length of the array, which is always a power of two. Array deques have no capacity restrictions; they grow as necessary to support usage.
- All array cells not holding deque elements are always null.

- An array is never allowed to become full, thus avoiding head and tail wrapping around to equal each other.

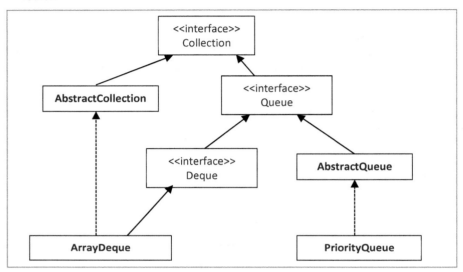

Figure 3.5 The Queue collection classes

To support the above traits, ArrayDeque has the following three private methods as shown from lines 15 – 60:

- allocateElements(int numElements) (lines 15 – 33): Allocates empty array to hold the given number of elements
- doubleCapacity() (lines 35 – 49): Doubles the capacity of the deque, and called when full, i.e., when head and tail have wrapped around to become equal.
- copyElements(T[] a) (lines 51 – 60): Copies the elements from the element array into the specified array, in order (from first to last element in the deque), with the assumption that the array is large enough to hold all elements in the deque.

In terms of constructors, ArrayDeque has three: a no-arg constructor (lines 62 – 64), a constructor with a parameter specifying the number of elements to create (lines 66 - 68), and a constructor with a given collection (lines 70 -73).

One difference between ArrayDeque and LinkedList is that ArrayDeque has no index-based methods exposed externally. Therefore, we only see methods like add/offer, get/peek, remove/poll, with each pair having three versions. For example:

- For the add operation, it has add(E), addFirst(E), and addLast(E).
- For the offer operation, it has offer(E), offerFirst(E), and offerLast(E).
- The get/peek pair and remove/poll pair operations take no parameters.

However, the remove operation has three additional methods that take parameters: remove(Object), removeFirstOccurrence(Object) and removeLastOccurence(Object). In addition, ArrayDeque has pop() and push(E) operations as inherited from Deque to mimic Stack. It does not have a set operation for updating an element mid-way – all operations are performed against the head and tail.

You can study some of these operations, with their implementations given in Listing 3.24. Next, we construct a demo program to illustrate how to use ArrayDeque.

Listing 3.24 ArrayDeque.java (partial)

```
1   public class ArrayDeque<E> extends AbstractCollection<E>
2                               implements Deque<E>, Cloneable, Serializable
3   {
4       private transient E[] elements;
5       private transient int head;
6       private transient int tail;
7
8       /**
9        * The minimum capacity that we'll use for a newly created deque.
10       * Must be a power of 2.
11       */
12      private static final int MIN_INITIAL_CAPACITY = 8;
13
14      // ******  Array allocation and resizing utilities ******
15      private void allocateElements(int numElements) {
16          int initialCapacity = MIN_INITIAL_CAPACITY;
17          // Find the best power of two to hold elements.
18          // Tests "<=" because arrays aren't kept full.
19          if (numElements >= initialCapacity) {
20              initialCapacity = numElements;
21              initialCapacity |= (initialCapacity >>>  1);
22              initialCapacity |= (initialCapacity >>>  2);
23              initialCapacity |= (initialCapacity >>>  4);
24              initialCapacity |= (initialCapacity >>>  8);
25              initialCapacity |= (initialCapacity >>> 16);
26              initialCapacity++;
27
28              if (initialCapacity < 0)   // Too many elements, must back off
29                  initialCapacity >>>= 1;// Good luck allocating 2 ^ 30
30                                         // elements
31          }
32          elements = (E[]) new Object[initialCapacity];
33      }
34
35      private void doubleCapacity() {
36          assert head == tail;
37          int p = head;
38          int n = elements.length;
39          int r = n - p; // number of elements to the right of p
40          int newCapacity = n << 1;
41          if (newCapacity < 0)
```

```
42                 throw new IllegalStateException("Sorry, deque too big");
43            Object[] a = new Object[newCapacity];
44            System.arraycopy(elements, p, a, 0, r);
45            System.arraycopy(elements, 0, a, r, p);
46            elements = (E[])a;
47            head = 0;
48            tail = n;
49        }
50
51        private <T> T[] copyElements(T[] a) {
52            if (head < tail) {
53                System.arraycopy(elements, head, a, 0, size());
54            } else if (head > tail) {
55                int headPortionLen = elements.length - head;
56                System.arraycopy(elements, head, a, 0, headPortionLen);
57                System.arraycopy(elements, 0, a, headPortionLen, tail);
58            }
59            return a;
60        }
61
62        public ArrayDeque() {
63            elements = (E[]) new Object[16];
64        }
65
66        public ArrayDeque(int numElements) {
67            allocateElements(numElements);
68        }
69
70        public ArrayDeque(Collection<? extends E> c) {
71            allocateElements(c.size());
72            addAll(c);
73        }
74
75        // The main insertion and extraction methods are addFirst,
76        // addLast, pollFirst, pollLast. The other methods are defined in
77        // terms of these.
78
79        // Inserts the specified element at the front of this deque.
80        public void addFirst(E e) {
81            if (e == null)
82                throw new NullPointerException();
83            elements[head = (head - 1) & (elements.length - 1)] = e;
84            if (head == tail)
85                doubleCapacity();
86        }
87
88        // Inserts the specified element at the end of this deque.
89        public void addLast(E e) {
90            if (e == null)
91                throw new NullPointerException();
92            elements[tail] = e;
93            if ( (tail = (tail + 1) & (elements.length - 1)) == head)
```

```
94              doubleCapacity();
95       }
96       // other methods omitted
97   }
```

Listing 3.25 shows the `ArrayDequeDemo` program. The sentence of "`This is an ArrayDeque demo`" is broken into five strings, which are pushed into the deque from lines 11--15. Then, the deque is popped in a `while`-loop (lines 20 – 22), yielding the following output:

Initial dq size of adq: 0
[demo, ArrayDeque, an, is, This]
Size after adding 5 elements: 5
Popping the array deque: **demo ArrayDeque an is This**

Note the FILO manner as shown at the last line of the above output.

Listing 3.25 ArrayDequeDemo.java

```
1    package jcp.ch3.queue;
2    import java.util.*;
3
4    public class ArrayDequeDemo {
5      public static void main (String args[]) {
6         // create an ArrayDeque collection
7         ArrayDeque<String> adq = new ArrayDeque ();
8         System.out.println ("Initial dq size of adq: " + adq.size());
9
10        // add elements
11        adq.push ("This");
12        adq.push ("is");
13        adq.push ("an");
14        adq.push ("ArrayDeque");
15        adq.push ("demo");
16        System.out.println (adq);
17        System.out.println ("Size after adding 5 elements: " + adq.size());
18
19        System.out.print ("Popping the array deque: ");
20        while (adq.peek() != null) {
21           System.out.print (adq.pop() + " ");
22        }
23        System.out.println ();
24     }
25   }
```

Some additional comments on `ArrayDeque` are in order here:

- Performance-wise, `ArrayDeque` is likely to be faster than `Stack` when used as a stack, and faster than `LinkedList` when used as a queue. Thus, it is recommended that you use either `ArrayList` or `ArrayDeque` in place of `Stack` or `LinkedList` as a queue. Most `ArrayDeque` operations run in amortized constant time. Exceptions include `remove`, `removeFirstOccurrence`, removeLastOccurrence, contains, iterator.remove, and the bulk operations, all of which run in linear time.

- Concurrency-wise, ArrayDeque is not thread-safe and external synchronization is required, if concurrent access by multiple threads is anticipated.
- ArrayDeque prohibits null elements.
- Similar to other collection classes described previously, the iterators returned by ArrayDeque's iterator method are fail-fast.

Next, we discuss the AbstractQueue class.

3.5.2 The AbstractQueue Class

Listing 3.26 shows how the AbstractQueue class is implemented in Java. As you see, it extends the AbstractCollection class and implements the Queue interface. It is interesting to see that it implements add with offer, remove with poll, element with peek, and clear with poll. It's worthwhile to learn such design and coding skills given the fact that millions of Java developers use Java to develop various kinds of software.

Next, we discuss the PriorityQueue class.

Listing 3.26 AbstractQueue.java (partial)

```
1    package java.util;
2
3    public abstract class AbstractQueue<E>
4        extends AbstractCollection<E>
5        implements Queue<E> {
6
7        protected AbstractQueue() {
8        }
9
10       public boolean add(E e) {
11           if (offer(e))
12               return true;
13           else
14               throw new IllegalStateException("Queue full");
15       }
16
17       public E remove() {
18           E x = poll();
19           if (x != null)
20               return x;
21           else
22               throw new NoSuchElementException();
23       }
24
25       public E element() {
26           E x = peek();
27           if (x != null)
```

```
28              return x;
29          else
30              throw new NoSuchElementException();
31      }
32
33      public void clear() {
34          while (poll() != null)
35              ;
36      }
37
38      public boolean addAll(Collection<? extends E> c) {
39          // body omitted to save space
40      }
41  }
```

3.5.3 The PriorityQueue Class

Listing 3.27 shows (partially) how the PriorityQueue class is implemented in Java. As is seen, it extends the AbstractQueue class. Its data store is an array of queue, as defined at line 4, which can grow infinitely. Thus, a priority queue is essentially an unbounded priority queue.

Listing 3.27 also shows the options for creating a priority queue:

- Line 9: Defines a no-arg constructor
- Line 12: Defines a priority queue with an initial capacity
- Line 15: Defines a priority queue with an initial capacity and a comparator
- Line 20: Defines a priority queue with a given collection
- Line 24: Defines a priority queue with a given priority queue
- Line 28: Defines a priority queue with a given sorted set

Internally, a priority queue is implemented as a priority heap, or more precisely, a balanced binary heap: Given a parent node of queue[n], its two child nodes are queue[2*n+1] and queue[2*(n+1)]. The priority of a priority queue is ordered by comparator, as shown at line 6. Or, if its comparator is null, the priority of a priority queue is ordered by the elements' natural ordering such that for each node n in the heap and each descendant d of n, $n <= d$. Thus, assuming the queue is non-empty, queue[0] always represents the element with the lowest value. The priority is constantly adjusted using internal methods, such as siftDown, siftUp and heapify, as shown in Listing 3.27.

Even though the head of the queue is the least element with respect to the specified ordering, it's possible that multiple elements are tied for the least value, and the head is just one of those elements. In such a situation, ties are broken arbitrarily.

Listing 3.27 PriorityQueue.java (partial)

```
1   public class PriorityQueue<E> extends AbstractQueue<E>
2       implements java.io.Serializable {
3
4       private transient Object[] queue;
5       private int size = 0;
```

```
6        private final Comparator<? super E> comparator;
7        private transient int modCount = 0;
8
9        public PriorityQueue() {
10           // body omitted
11       }
12       public PriorityQueue(int initialCapacity) {
13           // body omitted
14       }
15       public PriorityQueue(int initialCapacity,
16                            Comparator<? super E> comparator) {
17           // body omitted
18       }
19
20       public PriorityQueue(Collection<? extends E> c) {
21           // body omitted
22       }
23
24       public PriorityQueue(PriorityQueue<? extends E> c) {
25           // body omitted
26       }
27
28       public PriorityQueue(SortedSet<? extends E> c) {
29           // body omitted
30       }
31
32       private void siftDown(int k, E x) {
33           if (comparator != null)
34               siftDownUsingComparator(k, x);
35           else
36               siftDownComparable(k, x);
37       }
38
39       private void siftUp(int k, E x) {
40           if (comparator != null)
41               siftUpUsingComparator(k, x);
42           else
43               siftUpComparable(k, x);
44       }
45       private void heapify() {
46           for (int i = (size >>> 1) - 1; i >= 0; i--)
47               siftDown(i, (E) queue[i]);
48       }
49       // other methods omitted
50   }
```

The priority queue has the following methods to facilitate accessing and managing the heap:

- **add(E e)/offer(E e)**: Inserts the specified element into the priority queue.
- **peek()**: Retrieves, but does not remove, the head of the queue, or returns null if this queue is empty.
- **poll()**: Retrieves and removes the head of this queue, or returns null if the queue is empty.

- **remove(Object o)**: Removes a single instance of the specified element from the queue, if it is present.
- **clear()**: Removes all elements in this priority queue.
- **contains(Object o)**: Returns true if the queue contains the specified element.

A few special notes about PriorityQueue:

- Although this class and its iterator implement all of the optional methods of the Collection and Iterator interfaces, the Iterator provided in method iterator is not guaranteed to traverse the elements of the priority queue in any particular order. If you need ordered traversal, consider using Arrays.sort(pq.toArray()).
- The implementation shown in Listing 3.27 is not synchronized. Multiple threads should not access a PriorityQueue instance concurrently if any of the threads modifies the queue. Instead, use the thread-safe PriorityBlockingQueue class to be discussed later.

Performance-wise, this implementation provides constant time for the retrieval methods, such as peek, element, and size, O(log(n)) time for the enqueue and dequeue methods, such as add, offer, poll, and remove, and linear time for the remove(Object) and contains(Object) methods.

Listing 3.28 shows a PriorityQueue demo program. It is constructed as follows:

- Line 7: Defines an integer array as the input for the priority queue.
- Line 9: Creates a priority queue using the no-arg constructor.
- Lines 12 – 14: Print out the initial contents of the priority queue.
- Lines 20 - 21: show the peek() method for getting the highest priority without removing it, and then print the contents of the priority queue after calling the peek() method.
- Lines 23 - 24: show the poll() method for getting the highest priority and removing it, and then print the contents of the priority queue after calling the poll() method.

If you execute this program, you should get the following output:

```
priority input = [2, 9, 1, 3, 1, 8, 7, 0, 5]
original pq = [0, 1, 2, 1, 3, 8, 7, 9, 5] (size = 9)
after peek: 0, pq = [0, 1, 2, 1, 3, 8, 7, 9, 5] (size = 9)
after poll: 0, pq = [1, 1, 2, 5, 3, 8, 7, 9] (size = 8)
```

As you see, after the peek() method call, the first element with priority 0 was not removed and the size of the queue remained to be 9. In addition, the contents of the priority queue were not sorted, as expected. However, after the poll() method call, the first element with priority 0 was removed and the size of the queue reduced to 8.

Next, we discuss the Map interfaces and classes.

Listing 3.28 PriorityQueueDemo.java

```
1    package jcp.ch3.queue;
2    import java.util.*;
3
4    public class PriorityQueueDemo {
5
```

```
6   public static void main(String[] args) {
7      int[] priorities = { 2, 9, 1, 3, 1, 8, 7, 0, 5 };
8      System.out.println("priority input = " + "[2, 9, 1, 3, 1, 8, 7, 0,
          5]");
9      PriorityQueue<Integer> pq = new PriorityQueue<Integer>();
10
11     // add elements to pq using offer() method
12     for (int p : priorities) {
13        pq.offer(p);
14     }
15
16     // print queue and size
17     System.out.println("original pq = " + pq + " (size = " + pq.size()
          + ")");
18
19     // peek the highest priority
20     System.out.println("after peek: " + pq.peek() + ", pq = " + pq +
21         " (size = " + pq.size() + ")");
22
23     // return highest priority and remove it from the queue
24     System.out.println("after poll: " + pq.poll() + ", pq = " + pq +
25         " (size = " + pq.size() + ")");
26  }
27 }
```

3.6 THE MAP INTERFACES

First, conceptually a map is a key-value store that it acts as a container for storing key-value pairs. With a map, for a given key, you can find its value. Keys must be unique, but values may be duplicated.

However, it's important to understand that a map is not a collection. (You can consider a collection a one-dimensional structure and a map a two-dimensional structure.) As such, maps do not implement the Iterable interface and you cannot cycle through them using a for-each style for-loop. In addition, maps do not have iterators as collections do, but you can get a collection-view of a map through the Map.Entry interface so that you can cycle through a map's key-set and value-set using their respective iterators, as will be discussed later.

Figure 3.6 shows the Map interface, along with the classes that implement the Map interface. As you see, Map is the top interface, which is extended by its sub-interface of SortedMap, which is further extended by its sub-interface of NavigableMap. The TreeMap class implements the interface chain of NavigableMap → SortedMap → Map. On the left side, the Map interface is implemented by the AbstractMap class, which forms the top class for HashMap, LinkedHashMap, IdentityHashMap, WeakHashMap, and many others not listed here. In the middle, you also see the HashTable class, which implements the Map interface, but this is a special, legacy map class and we will cover it later.

Next, we discuss Map and its sub-interfaces, following Figure 3.6.

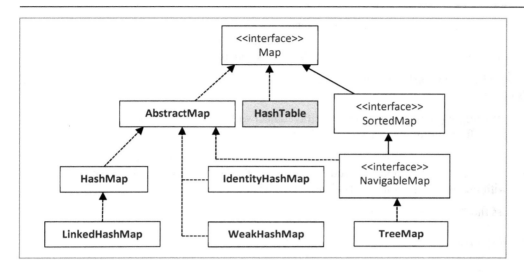

Figure 3.6 The Map interfaces and classes

3.6.1 The Map Interface

Listing 3.29 shows how the Map interface is defined in Java. Let's go through the details as follows:

- **Map parameterization**: Line 3 shows that Map is parameterized with K - a type for key and V – a type for value.
- **Map query operations**: Lines 5 – 8 define methods for map query operations, such as:
  - ○ isEmpty() for checking whether the map contains key-value mappings
  - ○ containsKey(Object key) for checking if the map contains a mapping for the specified key
  - ○ containsValue(Object value) for checking if the map maps one or more keys to the specified value
  - ○ get(Object key) for getting the value to which the specified key is mapped, or null if this map contains no mapping for the key
- **Map modification operations**: Lines 11 and 12 define methods for map modification operations, such as:
  - ○ put(K key, V value) for associating and storing the specified value with the specified key in the map
  - ○ remove(Object key) for removing the mapping for a key from the map if it is present
- **Map bulk operations**: Lines 15 and 16 define methods for map bulk operations, such as:
  - ○ putAll(Map<? extends K, ? extends V> m) for copying all of the mappings from the specified map to the invoking map
  - ○ clear() for removing all mappings from the map
- **Map views**: This segment (lines 19 – 29) defines map views in terms of:

- ° entrySet() for returning a Set view of the mappings contained in this map
- ° keySet() for returning a Set view of the keys contained in the map
- ° values for returning a Collection view of the values contained in the map

- **Map comparison and hashing**: This segment (lines 32 - 33) defines the comparison and hashing methods of:

  - ° equals(Object o) for comparing the specified object with the map for equality
  - ° hashCode() for returning the hash code value for the map

Map also has an embedded interface named Entry, which has five methods of getKey(), getValue(), setValue(V value), equals(Object o) and hashCode(). These methods operate on the entries of the map returned with the entrySet() method call as described above.

Next, we discuss the SortedMap interface.

Listing 3.29 Map.java

```
1   package java.util;
2
3   public interface Map<K,V> {
4       // Query Operations
5       boolean isEmpty();
6       boolean containsKey(Object key);
7       boolean containsValue(Object value);
8       V get(Object key);
9
10      // Modification Operations
11      V put(K key, V value);
12      V remove(Object key);
13
14      // Bulk Operations
15      void putAll(Map<? extends K, ? extends V> m);
16      void clear();
17
18      // Views
19      Set<K> keySet();
20      Collection<V> values();
21      Set<Map.Entry<K, V>> entrySet();
22
23      interface Entry<K,V> {
24          K getKey();
25          V getValue();
26          V setValue(V value);
27          boolean equals(Object o);
28          int hashCode();
29      }
30
31      // Comparison and hashing
32      boolean equals(Object o);
33      int hashCode();
```

```
34
35  }
```

3.6.2 The SortedMap Interface

Listing 3.30 shows how the `SortedMap` interface is defined. As is seen, it extends the `Map` interface. `SortedMap` has the following members:

- `comparator` for sorting the map
- `firstKey()` method for getting the first key of the map
- `lastKey()` method for getting the last key of the map
- `values()` method for getting all values of the map
- `entrySet()` method for getting all entries of the map

In addition, as you see from the last part of Listing 3.30, `SortedMap` has the following methods for manipulating sub-maps:

- `subMap(K fromKey, K toKey)` for returning a sub-map starting from the `fromKey` and ending prior to the `endKey`, namely, the `endKey` entry is excluded.
- `headMap(K toKey)` for returning a sub-map starting from the first key and ending prior to the `endKey`, with the `endKey` entry excluded.
- `tailMap(K fromKey)` for returning a sub-map starting from the `fromKey` entry to the end of the map.

Next, we discuss the `NavigableMap` interface.

Listing 3.30 SortedMap.java

```java
1   public interface SortedMap<K,V> extends Map<K,V> {
2       Comparator<? super K> comparator();
3       K firstKey();
4       K lastKey();
5       Set<K> keySet();
6       Collection<V> values();
7       Set<Map.Entry<K, V>> entrySet();
8
9       SortedMap<K,V> subMap(K fromKey, K toKey);
10      SortedMap<K,V> headMap(K toKey);
11      SortedMap<K,V> tailMap(K fromKey);
12  }
```

3.6.3 The NavigableMap Interface

Similar to the `NavigableSet` interface, the `NavigableMap` interface allows more flexible accesses to the entries and keys of a map. Listing 3.31 shows how the `NavigableMap` interface is defined. It extends the `SortedMap` interface with many navigation-oriented methods designed for returning the closest matches for given search targets, such as:

- The `lowerEntry`/`lowerKey` methods return the smallest entry/key less than the target entry/key

- The higherEntry/higherKey methods return the largest entry/key greater than the target entry/key
- The floorEntry/floorKey methods return the closest entry/key less than or equal to the target entry/key
- The ceilingEntry/ceilingKey methods return the closest entry/key greater than the target entry/key
- The firstEntry/lastEntry methods return the first/last entry of the map
- The pollFirstEntry/pollLastEntry methods return and remove the first/last entry of the map
- The descendingMap/descendingKeySet methods return the map/keySet in descending order
- The navigableKeySet method returns a NavigableSet that contains the keys in the invoking map.

Finally, the submap-related methods are divided into two categories: one returns NavigableMap with Boolean parameters for specifying the inclusiveness while the other returns SortedMap with inclusiveness implied as described in the preceding section about the SortedMap interface.

Next, we discuss various map classes that implement the map interfaces as described above.

Listing 3.31 NavigableMap.java

```
1    package java.util;
2
3    public interface NavigableMap<K,V> extends SortedMap<K,V> {
4
5        Map.Entry<K,V> lowerEntry(K key);
6        K lowerKey(K key);
7
8        Map.Entry<K,V> higherEntry(K key);
9        K higherKey(K key);
10
11       Map.Entry<K,V> floorEntry(K key);
12       K floorKey(K key);
13
14       Map.Entry<K,V> ceilingEntry(K key);
15       K ceilingKey(K key);
16
17       Map.Entry<K,V> firstEntry();
18       Map.Entry<K,V> lastEntry();
19
20       Map.Entry<K,V> pollFirstEntry();
21       Map.Entry<K,V> pollLastEntry();
22
23       NavigableMap<K,V> descendingMap();
24       NavigableSet<K> descendingKeySet();
25       NavigableSet<K> navigableKeySet();
26
27       NavigableMap<K,V> subMap(K fromKey, boolean fromInclusive,
28                                K toKey,   boolean toInclusive);
29
30       NavigableMap<K,V> headMap(K toKey, boolean inclusive);
31       NavigableMap<K,V> tailMap(K fromKey, boolean inclusive);
32       SortedMap<K,V> subMap(K fromKey, K toKey);
```

```
33      SortedMap<K,V> headMap(K toKey);
34      SortedMap<K,V> tailMap(K fromKey);
35  }
```

3.7 THE MAP CLASSES

The previous section covered the Map, SortedMap, and NavigableMap interfaces. This section covers some of the map classes that implement those interfaces, such as:

- AbstractMap: The top class that implements most of the Map interface
- HashMap: Uses a hash table as the data store
- LinkedHashMap: A HashMap with insertion-order preserved
- TreeMap: A HashMap represented as a tree structure for fast search
- IdentityHashMap: A HashMap that uses reference equality when comparing documents
- WeakHashMap: A HashMap that uses a hash table with "weak keys," which allow an element in the map to be garbage-collected when its key is otherwise unreferenced.

Let's begin with the AbstractMap class first next.

3.7.1 The AbstractMap Class

Listing 3.32 shows (partially) the AbstractMap class implemented in Java. As you see at line 4, it implements the Map interface. Most of the methods are implemented by operating on entrySet(), for example, as lines 7 – 9 show for the size() method. Besides, it implements the following two public static classes:

- SimpleEntry<K, V>: Maintains a simple entry with generic parameters of K and V. Its key field is declared final, and thus cannot be mutated. The value of an entry may be changed using the setValue() method, as shown from lines 30 – 33. This class facilitates the process of building custom map implementations.
- SimpleImmutableEntry<K, V>: Maintains a simple *immutable* entry with generic parameters of K and V. Since both key and value attributes are declared final, neither can be mutated. The setValue method throws an UnsupportedOperationException if invoked, as shown from lines 50 – 52. This class may be convenient for methods that return thread-safe snapshots of key-value mappings.

Next, we discuss the HashMap class.

Listing 3.32 AbstractMap.java (partial)

```
1   package java.util;
2   import java.util.Map.Entry;
3
4   public abstract class AbstractMap<K,V> implements Map<K,V> {
5       protected AbstractMap() {
6       }
7       public int size() {
```

```
8           return entrySet().size();
9       }
10      public boolean isEmpty() {
11          return size() == 0;
12      }
13
14      // other methods omitted
15
16      public static class SimpleEntry<K,V>
17          implements Entry<K,V>, java.io.Serializable
18      {
19          private final K key;
20          private V value;
21          public SimpleEntry(K key, V value) {
22              this.key   = key;
23              this.value = value;
24          }
25
26          public SimpleEntry(Entry<? extends K, ? extends V> entry) {
27              this.key   = entry.getKey();
28              this.value = entry.getValue();
29          }
30          public V setValue(V value) {
31              V oldValue = this.value;
32              this.value = value;
33              return oldValue;
34          }
35      }
36
37      public static class SimpleImmutableEntry<K,V>
38          implements Entry<K,V>, java.io.Serializable
39      {
40          private final K key;
41          private final V value;
42          public SimpleImmutableEntry(K key, V value) {
43              this.key   = key;
44              this.value = value;
45          }
46          public SimpleImmutableEntry(Entry<? extends K, ? extends V> entry)
    {
47              this.key   = entry.getKey();
48              this.value = entry.getValue();
49          }
50          public V setValue(V value) {
51              throw new UnsupportedOperationException();
52          }
53      }
54  }
```

3.7.2 The HashMap Class

The HashMap class provides a hash table based implementation of the Map interface. It provides all of the optional map operations, and permits null values and null key. Note that the HashMap class is roughly equivalent to Hashtable, except that it is unsynchronized and permits nulls. The HashMap class does not maintain the order of the map elements.

Listing 3.33 shows (partially) how the HashMap class is implemented in Java. First, note that it extends the AbstractMap class and implements the Map interface. Secondly, note some of its fields such as DEAFULT_LOAD_FACTOR (which is set to 75%), a table that holds the map entries, an private entrySet for providing a base for implementing most of the map operations, and some other fields such as hashSeed, loadFactor, modCount, and so on. HashMap does not have any methods of its own.

The next segment in Listing 3.33, lines 15 – 27, shows all the constructors of HashMap, which give the options for creating hash maps from no arguments to specifying a combination of initialCapacity, loadFactor, and a given map, similar to the constructors of some other collections we covered previously.

Perhaps one of the most interesting parts in Listing 3.33 is how the private EntrySet class is implemented, as shown from lines 38 – 58. An entry set for a HashMap class can be created by invoking the entrySet() public method, which invokes the private entrySet0() method, which in turn creates a new entry set as shown at line 35. After a new entry set is created, its methods of iterator(), contains(Object o), remove(Object o), size() and clear() can be called for desired operations, as shown from lines 39 – 57.

Finally, as an example, lines 60 – 75 show how the getEntry(Object key) method of HashMap is implemented. This method returns the map entry for the given key if found or null if not found. It is coded as follows:

- If the size of the map is zero, it returns null immediately; otherwise, it continues.
- It calculates the hash based on whether the key is null or not.
- The for-loop shown from lines 66 – 73 searches the hash map for the entry for a non-null key. (As shown from lines 82 – 86, HashMap has a static class named Entry, which has four fields of key, value, next and hash. This Entry class for a HashMap is similar to the Node class for a List). Besides, the indexFor (hash, length) method, shown from lines 76 – 80, returns the indexed table entry for a given key's hash code. Thus, the for-loop keeps searching all entries with the same hash and returns the entry if both the hash value and key match.

Next, let's use an example to illustrate how the HashMap class can be used to create a hash map for storing key-value pairs.

Listing 3.33 HashMap.java (partial)

```
1    package java.util;
2    import java.io.*;
3
4    public class HashMap<K,V>
5        extends AbstractMap<K,V>
6        implements Map<K,V>, Cloneable, Serializable
7    {
```

```
8    static final float DEFAULT_LOAD_FACTOR = 0.75f;
9    transient Entry<K,V>[] table = (Entry<K,V>[]) EMPTY_TABLE;
10   private transient Set<Map.Entry<K,V>> entrySet = null;
11   transient int hashSeed = 0;
12   final float loadFactor;
13   transient int modCount;
14
15   public HashMap() {
16      this(DEFAULT_INITIAL_CAPACITY, DEFAULT_LOAD_FACTOR);
17   }
18   public HashMap(int initialCapacity) {
19      this(initialCapacity, DEFAULT_LOAD_FACTOR);
20   }
21
22   public HashMap(int initialCapacity, float loadFactor) {
23       // body omitted
24   }
25   public HashMap(Map<? extends K, ? extends V> m) {
26       // body omitted
27   }
28
29    public Set<Map.Entry<K,V>> entrySet() {
30        return entrySet0();
31    }
32
33    private Set<Map.Entry<K,V>> entrySet0() {
34        Set<Map.Entry<K,V>> es = entrySet;
35        return es != null ? es : (entrySet = new EntrySet());
36    }
37
38    private final class EntrySet extends AbstractSet<Map.Entry<K,V>> {
39        public Iterator<Map.Entry<K,V>> iterator() {
40            return newEntryIterator();
41        }
42        public boolean contains(Object o) {
43            if (!(o instanceof Map.Entry))
44                return false;
45            Map.Entry<K,V> e = (Map.Entry<K,V>) o;
46            Entry<K,V> candidate = getEntry(e.getKey());
47            return candidate != null && candidate.equals(e);
48        }
49        public boolean remove(Object o) {
50            return removeMapping(o) != null;
51        }
52        public int size() {
53            return size;
54        }
55        public void clear() {
56            HashMap.this.clear();
57        }
58    }
59
```

```
60      final Entry<K,V> getEntry(Object key) {
61          if (size == 0) {
62              return null;
63          }
64
65          int hash = (key == null) ? 0 : hash(key);
66          for (Entry<K,V> e = table[indexFor(hash, table.length)];
67               e != null;
68               e = e.next) {
69              Object k;
70              if (e.hash == hash &&
71                  ((k = e.key) == key || (key != null && key.equals(k))))
72                  return e;
73          }
74          return null;
75      }
76  static int indexFor(int h, int length) {
77      // assert Integer.bitCount(length) == 1 :
78      // "length must be a non-zero power of 2";
79      return h & (length-1);
80  }
81
82  static class Entry<K,V> implements Map.Entry<K,V> {
83      final K key;
84      V value;
85      Entry<K,V> next;
86      int hash;
87      // methods omitted
88  }
89
90  // other methods omitted
91  }
```

Listing 3.34 shows the HashMapDemo.java program. It is coded as follows:

1. Line 7: Creates a hash map with the generic type parameters of <String, String> for key and value
2. Lines 10 – 15: Populate the hash map with State/Code key-value pairs by using the put method
3. Line 18: Retrieves the entrySet of the hash map as a Set
4. Lines 21 – 24: Cycle through the key-value pairs using the entry set of the hash map
5. Lines 27 – 28: Get a value by using the HashMap's get(K key) method and print the result

Executing this demo program on my Eclipse IDE resulted in the following output:

California: CA
Washington: WA
Virginia: VA
Massachusetts: MA:
Distric of Columbia: DC
New Jersey: NJ
state abbreviation for California: CA

As you see, the insertion order is not preserved with a HashMap, as expected.

Some special notes about the HashMap class implementation:

- Performance-wise, the HashMap class implementation provides constant-time performance for the basic operations, such as the get and put methods, assuming that the hash function disperses the elements properly among the buckets. Iteration over collection views requires time proportional to the capacity of the HashMap instance (the number of buckets) plus its size (the number of key-value mappings). Thus, it's very important not to set the initial capacity too high, or the load factor too low, if iteration performance is important.
- An instance of HashMap has two parameters that affect its performance: initial capacity and load factor. The capacity is the number of buckets in the hash table, and the initial capacity is simply the capacity at the time the hash table is created. The load factor is a measure of how full the hash table is allowed to get before its capacity is automatically increased. When the number of entries in the hash table exceeds the product of the load factor and the current capacity, the hash table is rehashed, that is, internal data structures are rebuilt, so that the hash table has approximately twice the number of buckets.
- In general, the default load factor (75%) offers a good tradeoff between time and space costs. Higher values decrease the space overhead but increase the lookup cost, reflected in most of the operations of the HashMap class, including the get and put methods. The expected number of entries in the map and its load factor should be taken into account when setting its initial capacity, in order to minimize the number of rehash operations. If the initial capacity is greater than the maximum number of entries divided by the load factor, no rehash operations will ever occur.
- If many mappings are to be stored in a HashMap instance, creating it with a sufficiently large capacity will allow the mappings to be stored more efficiently than letting it perform automatic rehashing as needed to grow the table.
- Concurrency-wise, HashMap is not synchronized. The concept of *fail-fast* as discussed previously applies to HashMap as well.

Next, we discuss the LinkedHashMap class.

Listing 3.34 HashMapDemo.java

```
1   package jcp.ch3.map;
2   import java.util.*;
3
4   public class HashMapDemo {
5     public static void main (String args[]) {
6       // 1. create a hash map
7       HashMap<String, String> hashMap = new HashMap<String, String> ();
8
9       // 2. put key-value pairs to the map
10      hashMap.put("Virginia", "VA");
11      hashMap.put("Washington", "WA");
12      hashMap.put("California", "CA");
13      hashMap.put("Distric of Columbia", "DC");
14      hashMap.put("Massachusetts", "MA");
15      hashMap.put("New Jersey", "NJ");
```

```
16
17      // 3. get map's entrySet
18      Set<Map.Entry<String, String>> set = hashMap.entrySet();
19
20      // 4. Display the entry set
21      for (Map.Entry<String, String> entry : set) {
22         System.out.print (entry.getKey() + ": ");
23         System.out.println (entry.getValue());
24      }
25
26      // 5. get state abbreviation by key
27      String caAbbr = hashMap.get("California");
28      System.out.println ("state abbreviation for California: " + caAbbr);
29   }
30 }
```

3.7.3 The LinkedHashMap Class

Listing 3.35 shows (partially) how the LinkedHashMap class is implemented in Java. As is shown from lines 4 – 6, it extends the HashMap class discussed in the preceding section and implements the Map interface. In contrast to HashMap, LinkedHashMap maintains a doubly-linked list of the entries in the map, in the order in which they were inserted. Therefore, it allows iterating through a collection-view of a LinkedHashMap so that the elements will be returned in the order in which they were inserted. Because it is a doubly-linked list in nature, you can also create a LinkedHashMap that returns its elements in the order in which they were last accessed.

LinkedHashMap has the following fields of its own:

- An Entry variable named header (line 8): The head of the doubly linked list
- A Boolean variable named accessOrder (line 9): true for access-order and false for insertion-order

LinkedHashMap has the following constructors of its own:

- No-arg constructor (lines 11 – 14): It calls HashMap's no-arg constructor and then sets accessOrder to false to convey the intention that access-order will not be maintained.
- Constructor parameterized with initialCapacity (lines 15 – 18): This constructor allows an initial capacity to be specified when the linked hash map is created.
- Constructor parameterized with initialCapacity and loadfactor (lines 19 – 22): This constructor allows a linked hash map to be created with both an initial capacity and a load factor.
- Constructor parameterized with a given map (lines 23 – 26): This constructor allows a linked hash map to be created with a given map.
- Constructor parameterized with initialCapacity, loadFactor and accessOrder (lines 27 – 32): This constructor allows a linked hash map to be created with accessOrder specified as well in addition to initialCapacity and loadFactor.

Lines 34 – 37 show how the init() method is implemented for illustration purpose. Inside the init() method, a new entry of type Entry is created and assigned to the header attribute. This new entry's before and after fields are set to the newly-created header entry.

Lines 39 – 45 show how the `get(Object key)` method is implemented for illustration purpose. Inside this method, it first gets the entry of type `Entry` using the `getEntry` method with the given `key`. Then, it checks if the entry is `null`, and if `null`, it returns `null`; otherwise, it calls the entry's `recordAccess` method with this instance of `LinkedHashMap` and returns the value of the entry.

Above two example methods indicate that they all operate on an entry of type `Entry`. In fact, this `LinkedHashMap` entry is defined from lines 47 – 78 as a private static class. It extends the `HashMap`'s `Entry` class with two fields of type `Entry` added: `before` and `after`. Its only constructor is parameterized with four parameters: `hash`, `key`, `value` and `next` of type `HashMap<K, V>.Entry`. It implements the following four methods:

- **remove()**: Removes the entry from the linked list
- **addBefore(Entry<K,V> existingEntry)**: Inserts the entry before the specified existing entry in the list
- **recordAccess(HashMap<K,V> m)**: This method is invoked by the super class whenever the value of a pre-existing entry is read by `Map.get` or modified by `Map.set`. If the enclosing `Map` is access-ordered, it removes the entry from the end of the list and makes it the new head; otherwise, it does nothing.
- **recordRemoval(HashMap<K,V> m)**: Calls the `remove()` method to remove the entry from the linked list.

In addition, note the method of `removeEldestEntry(Map.Entry)` at the end of Listing 3.35. The method may be overridden to impose a policy for removing stale mappings automatically when new mappings are added to the map.

Next, we use an example to demonstrate the use of a `LinkedHashMap`, following Listing 3.35.

Listing 3.35 LinkedHashMap.java (partial)

```
1    package java.util;
2    import java.io.*;
3
4    public class LinkedHashMap<K,V>
5        extends HashMap<K,V>
6        implements Map<K,V>
7    {
8        private transient Entry<K,V> header;
9        private final boolean accessOrder;
10
11       public LinkedHashMap() {
12           super();
13           accessOrder = false;
14       }
15       public LinkedHashMap(int initialCapacity) {
16           super(initialCapacity);
17           accessOrder = false;
18       }
19        public LinkedHashMap(int initialCapacity, float loadFactor) {
20           super(initialCapacity, loadFactor);
```

```
21          accessOrder = false;
22      }
23      public LinkedHashMap(Map<? extends K, ? extends V> m) {
24          super(m);
25          accessOrder = false;
26      }
27      public LinkedHashMap(int initialCapacity,
28                           float loadFactor,
29                           boolean accessOrder) {
30          super(initialCapacity, loadFactor);
31          this.accessOrder = accessOrder;
32      }
33
34      void init() {
35          header = new Entry<>(-1, null, null, null);
36          header.before = header.after = header;
37      }
38
39      public V get(Object key) {
40          Entry<K,V> e = (Entry<K,V>)getEntry(key);
41          if (e == null)
42              return null;
43          e.recordAccess(this);
44          return e.value;
45      }
46
47      private static class Entry<K,V> extends HashMap.Entry<K,V> {
48          Entry<K,V> before, after;
49
50          Entry(int hash, K key, V value, HashMap.Entry<K,V> next) {
51              super(hash, key, value, next);
52          }
53
54          private void remove() {
55              before.after = after;
56              after.before = before;
57          }
58
59          private void addBefore(Entry<K,V> existingEntry) {
60              after  = existingEntry;
61              before = existingEntry.before;
62              before.after = this;
63              after.before = this;
64          }
65
66          void recordAccess(HashMap<K,V> m) {
67              LinkedHashMap<K,V> lm = (LinkedHashMap<K,V>)m;
68              if (lm.accessOrder) {
69                  lm.modCount++;
70                  remove();
71                  addBefore(lm.header);
72              }
```

```
73              }
74
75              void recordRemoval(HashMap<K,V> m) {
76                  remove();
77              }
78          }
79
80      protected boolean removeEldestEntry(Map.Entry<K,V> eldest) {
81          return false;
82      }
83      // other methods omitted
84  }
```

Listing 3.36 shows the LinkedHashMapDemo.java program. It should look familiar to you that it actually is a version of Listing 3.34 with HashMap replaced with LinkedHashMap. Since it's a linked hash map, its insertion order is preserved as shown by the below console output:

Virginia: VA
Washington: WA
California: CA
Distric of Columbia: DC
Massachusetts: MA
New Jersey: NJ
state abbreviation for California: CA

You can verify that the insertion order has indeed been preserved.

Listing 3.36 LinkedHashMapDemo.java

```
1   package jcp.ch3.map;
2   import java.util.*;
3
4   public class LinkedHashMapDemo {
5     public static void main (String args[]) {
6       // 1. create a hash map
7       LinkedHashMap<String, String> linkedHashMap = new
8          LinkedHashMap<String, String> ();
9
9       // 2. put key-value pairs to the map
10      linkedHashMap.put("Virginia", "VA");
11      linkedHashMap.put("Washington", "WA");
12      linkedHashMap.put("California", "CA");
13      linkedHashMap.put("Distric of Columbia", "DC");
14      linkedHashMap.put("Massachusetts", "MA");
15      linkedHashMap.put("New Jersey", "NJ");
16
17      // 3. get map's entrySet
18      Set<Map.Entry<String, String>> set = linkedHashMap.entrySet();
19
20      // 4. Display the entry set
21      for (Map.Entry<String, String> entry : set) {
```

```
22          System.out.print (entry.getKey() + ": ");
23          System.out.println (entry.getValue());
24      }
25
26      // 5. get state abbreviation by key
27      String caAbbr = linkedHashMap.get("California");
28      System.out.println ("state abbreviation for California: " + caAbbr);
29  }
30 }
```

Some special notes about LinkedHashMap:

- Like HashMap, LinkedHashMap provides constant-time performance for the basic operations (add, contains and remove), assuming the hash function disperses elements properly among the buckets. Performance is likely to be just slightly below that of HashMap, due to the added expense of maintaining the linked list, with one exception: Iteration over the collection-views of a LinkedHashMap requires time proportional to the size of the map, regardless of its capacity. Iteration over a HashMap is likely to be more expensive, requiring time proportional to its capacity.
- Similar to a hash map, a linked hash map has two parameters that affect its performance: initial capacity and load factor. Note, however, that the penalty for choosing an excessively high value for initial capacity is less severe for this class than for HashMap, as iteration times for this class are unaffected by capacity.
- Concurrency-wise, LinkedHashMap is not synchronized. The concept of *fail-fast* as discussed previously applies to LinkedHashMap as well.

Next, we discuss the TreeMap class.

3.7.4 The TreeMap Class

The TreeMap class is implemented as a red-black tree, which is a type of self-balancing binary search tree. The self-balancing property is maintained by painting each node with one of two colors, red or black. When the tree is modified, the new tree is subsequently rearranged and repainted to continue maintaining the coloring properties.

Unlike a hash map or a linked hash map, a tree map is sorted according to the natural ordering of its keys, or by a Comparator provided at map creation time, depending on which constructor is used.

Listing 3.37 shows (partially) how the TreeMap class is implemented. It extends the AbstractMap class and implements the NavigableMap interface. It has a root field of type Entry of its own, which will be discussed after we discuss its constructors next.

Lines 11 – 28 show the four constructors for TreeMap, from no-arg to parameterized with a comparator, or an existing map, or a sorted map.

Perhaps the core part of the TreeMap class is its Entry class, defined with six fields of key, value, left, right, parent and color, as from lines 31 – 36 show. Lines 38 – 42 show the constructor parameterized with key, value, and parent. The implementations of its methods getKey, getValue, equals, hashCode, setValue and toString, are omitted, partially for saving space and partially for their little relevance in this context.

Lines 46 - 64 show how the getEntry(Object key) method is implemented for illustration purpose. This is the version of the getEntry method that applies to tree maps based on natural ordering. The comparator-based version is named getEntryUsingComparator, as lines 48 -- 49 show. The rest of the implementation is straightforward: It uses the typical binary-search algorithm.

Although it's conceptually simple, the implementation of TreeMap is quite large: 2443 lines versus 493 lines for LinkedHashMap. Instead of diving into more implementation details, we show a TreeMap demo program next, following List 3.37.

Listing 3.37 TreeMap.java (partial)

```
1    package java.util;
2    public class TreeMap<K,V>
3        extends AbstractMap<K,V>
4        implements NavigableMap<K,V>, Cloneable, java.io.Serializable
5    {
6    private final Comparator<? super K> comparator;
7
8        private transient Entry<K,V> root = null;
9        private transient int size = 0;
10       private transient int modCount = 0;
11       public TreeMap() {
12           comparator = null;
13       }
14       public TreeMap(Comparator<? super K> comparator) {
15           this.comparator = comparator;
16       }
17       public TreeMap(Map<? extends K, ? extends V> m) {
18           comparator = null;
19           putAll(m);
20       }
21       public TreeMap(SortedMap<K, ? extends V> m) {
22           comparator = m.comparator();
23           try {
24               buildFromSorted(m.size(), m.entrySet().iterator(), null,
                     null);
25           } catch (java.io.IOException cannotHappen) {
26           } catch (ClassNotFoundException cannotHappen) {
27           }
28       }
29
30       static final class Entry<K,V> implements Map.Entry<K,V> {
31           K key;
32           V value;
33           Entry<K,V> left = null;
34           Entry<K,V> right = null;
35           Entry<K,V> parent;
36           boolean color = BLACK;
37
38           Entry(K key, V value, Entry<K,V> parent) {
39               this.key = key;
```

```
40              this.value = value;
41              this.parent = parent;
42          }
43          // methods omitted
44      }
45
46      final Entry<K,V> getEntry(Object key) {
47          // Offload comparator-based version for sake of performance
48          if (comparator != null)
49              return getEntryUsingComparator(key);
50          if (key == null)
51              throw new NullPointerException();
52          Comparable<? super K> k = (Comparable<? super K>) key;
53          Entry<K,V> p = root;
54          while (p != null) {
55              int cmp = k.compareTo(p.key);
56              if (cmp < 0)
57                  p = p.left;
58              else if (cmp > 0)
59                  p = p.right;
60              else
61                  return p;
62          }
63          return null;
64      }
65      // other methods omitted
66  }
```

Listing 3.38 shows the TreeMapDemo.java program. It should look familiar to you that it actually is a version of Listing 3.36 with LinkedHashMap replaced with TreeMap. Since it's a tree map, its sorted access order is preserved as shown by the console output below:

```
California: CA
Distric of Columbia: DC
Massachusetts: MA
New Jersey: NJ
Virginia: VA
Washington: WA
state abbreviation for California: CA
```

You can verify the sorted access order as shown above.

Listing 3.38 TreeMapDemo.java

```
1   package jcp.ch3.map;
2   import java.util.*;
3
4   public class TreeMapDemo {
5     public static void main (String args[]) {
6         // 1. create a tree map
7         TreeMap<String, String> treeMap = new TreeMap<String, String> ();
```

```
8
9        // 2. put key-value pairs to the map
10       treeMap.put("Virginia", "VA");
11       treeMap.put("Washington", "WA");
12       treeMap.put("California", "CA");
13       treeMap.put("Distric of Columbia", "DC");
14       treeMap.put("Massachusetts", "MA");
15       treeMap.put("New Jersey", "NJ");
16
17       // 3. get map's entrySet
18       Set<Map.Entry<String, String>> set = treeMap.entrySet();
19
20       // 4. Display the entry set
21       for (Map.Entry<String, String> entry : set) {
22          System.out.print (entry.getKey() + ": ");
23          System.out.println (entry.getValue()");
24       }
25
26       // 5. get state abbreviation by key
27       String caAbbr = treeMap.get("California");
28       System.out.println ("state abbreviation for California: " + caAbbr);
29    }
30  }
```

Some special notes about TreeMap:

- Performance-wise, the implementation of TreeMap provides guaranteed log(n) time cost for the methods of get, put containsKey and remove operations. Algorithms are adaptations of those in Cormen, Leiserson, and Rivest's classical book titled *Introduction to Algorithms*.
- Concurrency-wise, TreeMap is not synchronized. The concept of *fail-fast* as discussed previously applies to TreeMap as well.

Next, we discuss the IdentityHashMap class.

3.7.5 The IdentityHashMap Class

The IdentityHashMap class uses reference equality when comparing elements. A HashMap defines two keys equal if and only if both keys are null or none of them is null and key1.equals(key2), while an IdentityHashMap considers two keys equal if and only if

key1 == key2

, which is called *reference equality*.

The IdentityHashMap class is not for general use, as is explicitly stated in the Java API documentation. It is included here just for you to become aware of its existence, in case you have a use case that requires such a special kind of reference-equality-enforced hash map.

Next, we discuss the WeakHashMap class.

3.7.6 The WeakHashMap Class

Like the regular HashMap class, the WeakHashMap class extends the AbstractMap class and implements the Map interface. However, unlike the regular HashMap class, the WeakHashMap class uses "weak" keys, which are called that way, because all regular Java references are strong references by default, meaning that if an object is reachable via a chain of strong references (strongly reachable), it is not eligible for garbage collection. On the contrary, elements of a WeakHashMap have their keys typed as WeakReference, providing a mechanism for an entry in a WeakHashMap to be automatically removed when its key is no longer in ordinary use. When a key has been discarded, its corresponding entry in the WeakHashMap is effectively removed from the map and can be garbage-collected.

The WeakHashMap class behaves somewhat differently from other Map implementations. A more detailed coverage is out of the scope of this text. Next, we discuss the algorithms applied to Java collections.

3.8 THE ALGORITHMS APPLIED TO COLLECTIONS

In the java.util package, there is a Collections class that contains many common algorithms, which can be applied to various collections we covered in the previous sections. The consequent huge benefits include reduced programming efforts for developers, reliable high performance for Java-based software applications, interoperability among unrelated APIs, and so on.

The Collections class contains as many as 69 methods as of Java 7. Listing 3.39 shows how one of its methods, addAll, is implemented. As you see, the keyword static is applied to this method (and all others), as all algorithms are generic or stateless.

Listing 3.39 Collections.java (with the addAll method only)

```
1   package java.util;
2   import java.io.Serializable;
3   import java.io.ObjectOutputStream;
4   import java.io.IOException;
5   import java.lang.reflect.Array;
6
7   public class Collections {
8       // Suppresses default constructor, ensuring non-instantiability.
9       private Collections() {
10      }
11
12   public static <T> boolean addAll(Collection<? super T> c, T... elements)
     {
13          boolean result = false;
14          for (T element : elements)
15              result |= c.add(element);
16          return result;
17      }
18   // all other methods omitted
19  }
```

The above method is designed as an algorithm for adding a number of elements to an existing collection named `c` as the first parameter. Since it's a static method, you use the following syntax `Collections.<method>` to invoke it:

Collections.<method> (target, source);

Here, `source` is the input, `target` is the collection for the algorithm to be applied to, and `<method>` represents the algorithm in question. For example, Listing 3.40 shows a demo program that applies the above `addAll` algorithm to an existing `ArrayList` collection. If you execute this program, the output would be as follows:

[This , is , an , ArrayList , demo]
[This , is , an , ArrayList , demo, with , addAll , algorithm , applied]

Namely, the first line represents the original array list, while the second line shows the new array list with four more strings added, as shown at line 19 in Listing 3.40.

Listing 3.40 CollectionsDemo.java

```
1    package jcp.ch3.collections;
2
3    import java.util.ArrayList;
4    import java.util.Collections;
5
6    public class CollectionsDemo {
7      public static void main (String args[]) {
8        // create an ArrayList collection
9        ArrayList<String> al = new ArrayList ();
10
11       // add elements
12       al.add ("This ");
13       al.add ("is ");
14       al.add ("an ");
15       al.add ("ArrayList ");
16       al.add ("demo");
17       System.out.println (al);
18
19       boolean success = Collections.addAll(al, "with ", "addAll ",
             "algorithm ", "applied");
20       if (success) {
21          System.out.println (al);
22       } else {
23          System.out.println ("Collections.addAll failed");
24       }
25     }
26  }
```

The above example shows how you can apply an algorithm implemented in the `Collections` class to a collection. Since it would be too lengthy if we demonstrate every algorithm as above, next, I'll show you what algorithms exist, including the above `addAll` algorithm, and what problems they solve, without accompanying demo programs. If you have not used those algorithms, it should be sufficient just to be aware of them at this point.

Let's start with the algorithms applicable to Collection first.

3.8.1 The Algorithms Applicable to Collections

This class of algorithms is characterized by their target being a generic type of Collection, which applies to all classes that implement the Collection interface. The preceding Listing 3.40 demonstrates one of such examples with the first algorithm named addAll as shown in Table 3.2.

Listing 3.41 shows a simple program, demonstrating how the frequency algorithm is used to count the number of an element in the ArrayList. It is coded as follows:

- Line 8: Creates an ArrayList
- Lines 11 – 17: Add the words of a quote to the ArrayList and print the quote out
- Lines 20 – 21: Use the frequency algorithm to count the occurrence of a specific word and output the count

Not surprisingly, executing this program would yield the following output:

```
[no, bird, soars, too, high, if, he, soars, with, his, own, wings]
Frequency of 'soars' is: 2
```

Listing 3.41 FreqencyDemo.java

```
1   package jcp.ch3.algorithms;
2   import java.util.*;
3
4   public class FrequencyDemo {
5     public static void main(String args[]) {
6
7         // 1. creating an ArrayList
8         List<String> arrayList = new ArrayList<String>();
9
10        // 2. populating the ArrayList
11        arrayList.add("no"); arrayList.add("bird");
12        arrayList.add("soars"); arrayList.add("too");
13        arrayList.add("high"); arrayList.add("if");
14        arrayList.add("he"); arrayList.add("soars");
15        arrayList.add("with"); arrayList.add("his");
16        arrayList.add("own"); arrayList.add("wings");
17        System.out.println(arrayList.toString());
18
19        // 3. getting frequency of 'soars'
20        int freq = Collections.frequency(arrayList, "soars");
21        System.out.println("Frequency of 'soars' is: " + freq);
22     }
23  }
```

Rather than walking you through each of the remaining algorithms listed in Table 3.2, you are suggested to take a look at each of them, focusing on its purpose rather than its syntax or exact algorithm name. The remaining algorithms apply to specific interfaces, such as Set, List, Queue and Map, and their sub-interfaces, as shown in Figure 3.2. Let us move to the algorithms that apply to Set objects next.

Table 3.2 The algorithms applicable to Collections

Method/Algorithm	Description
static <T> boolean addAll(Collection <? super T> c, T... elements)	Inserts the specified elements into the specified Collection c. Returns true if the elements were added and false otherwise.
static <E> Collection<E> checkedCollection(Collection<E> c, Class<E> t)	Returns a runtime type-safe view of a collection. An attempt to insert an incompatible element will cause a ClassCastException.
static boolean disjoint(Collection<?>a, Collection<?>b)	Compares the elements in a to elements in b. Returns true if the two collections contain no common elements, or false if otherwise.
static <T> Enumeration<T> enumeration(Collection<T> c)	Returns an enumeration over c.
static int frequency(Collection<?> c, object obj)	Returns the number of occurrences of obj in c.
static <T> max(Collection<? extends T>c, Comparator<? super T> comp)	Returns the maximum element in c as determined by comp.
static <T extends Object & Comparable<? super T>> T max(Collection<? extends T>c)	Returns the maximum element in c as determined by natural ordering. The collection does not have to be ordered.
static <T> min(Collection<? extends T>c, Comparator<? super T> comp)	Returns the minimum element in c as determined by comp.
static <T extends Object & Comparable<? super T>> T min(Collection<? extends T>c)	Returns the minimum element in c as determined by natural ordering. The collection does not have to be ordered.
static <T> Collection<T> synchronizedCollection(Collection<T> c)	Returns a thread-safe collection backed by c.
Static <T> Collection<T> unmodifiableCollection(Collection <? extends T> c)	Returns an unmodifiable collection backed by c.

3.8.2 The Algorithms Applicable to Sets

Table 3.3 shows the algorithms applicable to the classes that implement the Set interface. For the two algorithms prefixed with checked, the word "*checked*" means type-checking, namely, when an unchecked set is turned into a checked set, adding incompatible elements would result in an exception thrown. Listing 3.42 shows such an example, with the following specifics:

- Line 8 creates a hash set
- Lines 10 – 12 add two strings to the hash set and print the content of the hash set
- Lines 15 -16 add a number 3 and print the modified hash set
- Lines 18 – 19 use the Collections' checkedSet algorithm to turn the unchecked set into a checked set and print the contents of the unchecked set
- Lines 23 – 24 attempt to add the same number of '3' to the checked set and attempt to print the contents of the checked hash set.

Executing this program would yield the following output:

```
Initial unchecked hash set: [One, Two]
Modified unchecked hash set: [3, One, Two]
Initial checked hash set: [3, One, Two]
Exception in thread "main" java.lang.ClassCastException: Attempt to insert class java.lang.Integer element into
collection with element type class java.lang.String
        at java.util.Collections$CheckedCollection.typeCheck(Collections.java:2276)
        at java.util.Collections$CheckedCollection.add(Collections.java:2319)
        at jcp.ch3.algorithms.CheckedSetDemo.main(CheckedSetDemo.java:23)
```

As you see, a ClassCastException had been thrown, as expected. In fact, this algorithm may not be that useful, as if you added the String type to Set at line 8 as follows:

Set**<String>** hashSet = new HashSet**<String>** ();

, you would have caught the exception at line 15 on an IDE like Eclipse. The Java's Generics feature helps detect such issues at compile-time rather than having an exception thrown at runtime.

Listing 3.42 CheckedSetDemo.java

```
1    package jcp.ch3.algorithms;
2    import java.util.*;
3
4    public class CheckedSetDemo {
5
6      public static void main(String a[]) {
7
8        Set hashSet = new HashSet();
9
10       hashSet.add("One");
11       hashSet.add("Two");
12       System.out.println("Initial unchecked hash set: " + hashSet);
13
14       // unchecked allows any type of elements to be added
```

```
15    hashSet.add(3);
16    System.out.println("Modified unchecked hash set: " + hashSet);
17
18    Set checkedHashSet = Collections.checkedSet(hashSet, String.class);
19    System.out.println("Initial checked hash set: " + checkedHashSet);
20
21    // adding incompatible type of elements to a checked collection
22    // throws ClassCastException
23    checkedHashSet.add(3);
24    System.out.println("Modified checked hash set: " + checkedHashSet);
25  }
26 }
```

The remaining two algorithms are designed for returning a thread-safe sorted set and an unmodifiable sorted set, respectively. The transformed sets (both the original and new) share the same sorted sets, though.

Next, we discuss the algorithms applicable to List objects.

Table 3.3 The algorithms applicable to Sets

Method/Algorithm	Description
static <E> Set<E> checkedSet(Set s, Class<E> t)	Returns a runtime type-safe view of a Set s. An attempt to insert an incompatible element will cause a ClassCastException.
static <E> SortedSet<E> checkedSortedSet(SortedSet <E> ss, Class<E> t)	Returns a runtime type-safe view of a SortedSet ss. An attempt to insert an incompatible element will cause a ClassCastException.
static <T> SortedSet <T> synchronizedSortedSet (SortedSet <T> ss)	Returns a thread-safe sorted set backed by ss.
Static <T> SortedSet <T> unmodifiableSortedSet (SortedSet <? extends T> ss)	Returns an unmodifiable sorted set backed by ss.

3.8.3 The Algorithms Applicable to Lists

Table 3.4 shows the algorithms applicable to List objects. As it's too lengthy to walk you through all of them, we use an example named BinarySearchDemo to illustrate how the binarySearch and sort algorithms work. Listing 3.43 shows the example, with the following specifics:

- Line 7 creates an ArrayList
- Lines 10 – 21 add the words of the quote "no bird soars too high if he soars with his own wings." to the ArrayList.

- Lines 22 -24 print the contents of the ArrayList before sorting, search the word 'he' in the list and output it. The intention for this part is to show what would happen if the algorithm is applied to an un-sorted list.
- Lines 27 uses the Collections' sort algorithm to sort the list, which is a prerequisite for the binarySearch algorithm, listed in Table 3.4.
- Lines 28 – 32 print the contents of the sorted list, search the words 'he' and 'soars' using the binarySearch algorithm in question and then output the indices for those two words.

Executing this program would yield the following output:

before sorting: [no, bird, soars, too, high, if, he, soars, with, his, own, wings]
Index of 'he' is: -1
after sorting: [bird, he, high, his, if, no, own, soars, soars, too, wings, with]
Index of 'he' is: 1
Index of 'soars' is: 8

A few notes here:

- As you see from the above output, searching the original, unsorted list for the word 'he' retuned a negative index of -1, which is expected as the binarySearch algorithm returns un-determined results if applied to an unsorted list.
- After sorting, the words are re-positioned in their natural ordering, namely, alphabetically in this case.
- Searching the word 'he' returned an index of 1, which is correct. However, searching for the word 'soars' returned an index of 8, which corresponds to the second 'soars'. This is expected, as the binarySearch algorithm does not guarantee which one would be returned if multiple duplicate elements exist in the list. This is also a good example showing that when you need to use an algorithm introduced here, you may need to study the Java API documentation to learn more about it. The introduction here shows more what algorithms are available, rather than how each of them can be used exactly in practice.

Next, we discuss the algorithms applicable to Queue objects.

Listing 3.43 CheckedSetDemo.java

```
1    package jcp.ch3.algorithms;
2    import java.util.*;
3
4    public class BinarySearchDemo {
5      public static void main(String args[]) {
6          // 1. creating an ArrayList
7          List<String> arrayList = new ArrayList<String>();
8
9          // 2. populating the ArrayList
10         arrayList.add("no");
11         arrayList.add("bird");
12         arrayList.add("soars");
13         arrayList.add("too");
14         arrayList.add("high");
```

```
15    arrayList.add("if");
16    arrayList.add("he");
17    arrayList.add("soars");
18    arrayList.add("with");
19    arrayList.add("his");
20    arrayList.add("own");
21    arrayList.add("wings");
22    System.out.println("before sorting: " + arrayList.toString());
23    int index = Collections.binarySearch(arrayList, "he");
24    System.out.println("Index of 'he' is: " + index);
25
26    // 3. getting the indices of 'he' and 'soars'
27    Collections.sort(arrayList); // must call sort first
28    System.out.println("after sorting: " + arrayList.toString());
29    index = Collections.binarySearch(arrayList, "he");
30    System.out.println("Index of 'he' is: " + index);
31    index = Collections.binarySearch(arrayList, "soars");
32    System.out.println("Index of 'soars' is: " + index);
33    }
34  }
```

Table 3.4 The algorithms applicable to Lists

Method/Algorithm	Description
static <T> int binarySearch(List <? extends T> list, T value, Comparator<? super T> c)	Searches for value in list ordered according to Comparator c. Returns the position of value in list, or a negative number if value is not found.
static <T> int binarySearch(List <? extends Comparable<? super T>> list, T value)	Searches for value in list, ordered *naturally*. Returns the position of value in list, or a negative number if value is not found.
static <T> void copy(List<? super T> list1, list<? extends T> list2)	Copies the elements of list2 to list1.
Static <T> void fill (List<? super T> list, T obj)	Fills list with obj for each of its elements.
static int indexOfSubList(List<?> list, List<?> subList)	Searches list for the first occurrence of subList. Returns the index of the first match, or -1 if no match is found.
static int lastIndexOfSubList(List<?> list, List<?> subList)	Searches list for the last occurrence of subList. Returns the index of the last match, or -1 if no match is found.
static <T> ArrayList<T> list (Enumeration<T> enum)	Returns an ArrayList that contains the elements

	of enum.
static boolean replaceAll(List<T> list, T old, T new)	Replaces of all occurrences of old with new in list. Returns true if at least one replacement occurred, or false otherwise.
static void reverse(List<T> list)	Reverses the sequence in list.
static void rotate (List<T> list, int n)	Rotates list by n places to the right, or left if n is negative.
static void shuffle(List<T> list, Random r)	Shuffles the elements in list by using r as a source of random numbers.
static void shuffle(List<T> list)	Shuffles the elements in list.
static <T> void sort(List<T> list, Comparator<? super T> comp)	Sorts the elements of list as determined by comp.
static <T extends Comparable<? super T>> void sort(List<T> list)	Sorts the elements of list as determined by their natural ordering.
static <T> List<T> synchronizedList(List<T> list)	Returns a thread-safe collection backed by list.
static <T> List<T> unmodifiablelist(List <? extends T> list)	Returns an unmodifiable collection backed by list.

3.8.4 The Algorithms Applicable to Queues

The Collections class has only one algorithm that applies to a Deque, as shown in Table 3.5. This algorithm returns a view of a Deque as a Last-in-first-out (LIFO) Queue, which is essentially a Stack conceptually. Listing 3.44 uses an example to show how this asLifoQueue algorithm works. It is constructed as follows:

- Lines 9 – 13 create and populate an ArrayDeque.
- Lines 14 – 15 print the ArrayQueue and its first element, respectively, to verify that it's a first-in-first-out (FIFO) queue.
- Line 18 calls the Collections' asLifoQueue method with the array deque created above. This statement shows how the algorithm is applied to a deque.
- Lines 23 – 25 test how a new element is added to the queue. Once again, the queue's contents and the first element are printed out, respectively. Note that at this point, the queue still is a FIFO and we should not expect a reversed array deque.

- Lines 28 – 30 test how another new element is added to the queue. Once again, the queue's contents and the first element are printed out, respectively.

Executing this example would yield the following output:

```
Original deque is: [a, b, c, d]
original deque peek: a
Returned queue is: [a, b, c, d]
Returned queue peek: a

Returned queue is: [test1, a, b, c, d]
Returned queue is: test1
Returned queue is: [test2, test1, a, b, c, d]
Returned queue is: test2
```

Now, you see that "test1" and "test2" were "last in, first out," making the queue a LIFO. The key to understanding this algorithm is that the original contents of the deque, "a, b, c, d," were still FIFO, and only the new elements inserted into the queue will behave like a LIFO queue.

Next, we discuss the algorithms that apply to maps.

Listing 3.44 AsLifoQueueDemo.java

```
1    package jcp.ch3.algorithms;
2
3    import java.util.*;
4
5    public class AsLifoQueueDemo {
6      public static void main(String args[]) {
7
8        // 1. create, populate and print the array deque
9        Deque<String> arrayDeque = new ArrayDeque<String>();
10       arrayDeque.add("a");
11       arrayDeque.add("b");
12       arrayDeque.add("c");
13       arrayDeque.add("d");
14       System.out.println("Original deque is: " + arrayDeque);
15       System.out.println("original deque peek: " + arrayDeque.peek());
16
17       // 2. return a view of the array deque as a LIFO queue
18       Queue<String> queue = Collections.asLifoQueue(arrayDeque);
19       System.out.println("Returned queue is: " + queue);
20       System.out.println("Returned queue peek: " + queue.peek() + "\n");
21
22       // 3. test LIFO
23       queue.add("test1");
24       System.out.println("Returned queue is: " + queue);
25       System.out.println("Returned queue is: " + queue.peek());
26
27       // 4. test LIFO again
28       queue.add("test2");
```

```
29        System.out.println("Returned queue is: " + queue);
30        System.out.println("Returned queue is: " + queue.peek());
31    }
32 }
```

Table 3.5 The algorithms applicable to Queues

Method/Algorithm	Description
static <T> Queue<T> asLifoQueue(Deque<T> c)	Returns a last-in, first-out view of c.

3.8.5 The Algorithms Applicable to Maps

The algorithms applicable to maps are mostly related to "checked-," or "synchronized-," or "unmodifiable-," as shown in Table 3.6. It should be obvious what these algorithms are designed for, based on their counterparts for other collections covered in the previous sections, so we would not explain them further.

However, an exception is the public static <E> Set<E> newSetFromMap(Map<E, Boolean> map) algorithm shown in Table 3.6. This method returns a set backed by the specified map. The resulting set displays the same ordering, concurrency, and performance characteristics as the backing map. In essence, this factory method provides a Set implementation corresponding to any Map implementation. However, there is no need to use this method on a Map implementation, such as HashMap or TreeMap, which already has a corresponding Set implementation.

Listing 3.45 shows an example, demonstrating how the newSetFromMap algorithm can be used to create a new set from a map. Note that the specified map must be empty at the time the method is invoked, and should not be accessed directly after this method returns. These conditions could have been ensured if the map were created empty, passed directly to this method, and no reference to the map were retained, as illustrated in the following code fragment:

Set<Object> weakHashSet = Collections.newSetFromMap(new WeakHashMap<Object, Boolean>());

However, we create the weakHashMap at line 7 and pass it to the newSetFromMap algorithm at line 11, so that we can check the contents of the map as a backing store. The rest of it is straightforward: it adds a few strings to the weakHashSet from lines 14 – 16, and prints the contents of the weakHashSet and weakHashMap from lines 19 – 20.

Finally, executing this program would yield the following output:

Initial Map: {}
New Set: [and, Java, C#]
Map: {and=true, Java=true, C#=true}

Next, we discuss the algorithms prefixed with "empty" and "singleton."

Listing 3.45 NewSetFromMapDemo.java

```
1    package jcp.ch3.algorithms;
2    import java.util.*;
3
4    public class NewSetFromMapDemo {
5      public static void main(String args[]) {
6        // 1. create a hash map
7        WeakHashMap<String, Boolean> weakHashMap = new WeakHashMap<String,
             Boolean>();
8        System.out.println("Initial Map: " + weakhashMap);
9
10       // 2. create a new set from map
11       Set<String> weakHashSet = Collections.newSetFromMap(weakHashMap);
12
13       // 3. add entries to set
14       weakHashSet.add("Java");
15       weakHashSet.add("and");
16       weakHashSet.add("C#");
17
18       // 4. set and map values are
19       System.out.println("New Set: " + weakHashSet);
20       System.out.println("Map: " + weakHashMap);
21     }
22   }
```

Table 3.6 The algorithms applicable to Maps

Method/Algorithm	Description
static <K, V> Map<K, V> checkedMap(Map<K, V> c, Class<K>keyT, Class<V> valueT)	Returns a runtime type-safe view of Map. An attempt to insert an incompatible element will cause a ClassCastException.
static <K, V> SortedMap<K, V> checkedSortedMap(SortedMap<K, V> c, Class<K>keyT, Class<V> valueT)	Returns a runtime type-safe view of SortedMap. An attempt to insert an incompatible element will cause a ClassCastException.
static <E> Set<E> newSetFromMap (Map<E, Boolean> m)	Creates and returns a set backed by the map specified by m, which must be empty at the time when this method is called.
static <K, V> Map<K, V> synchronizedMap(Map<K, V> m)	Returns a thread-safe map backed by m.
static <K, V> SortedMap<K, V> synchronizedSortedMap(SortedMap<K, V>sm)	Returns a thread-safe sorted map backed by sm.
static <K, V> Map<K, V> unmodifiableMap(Map <? extends K, ? extends V> m)	Returns an unmodifiable map backed by m.
static <K, V> SortedMap<K, V> unmodifiableSortedMap(SortedMap <? extends K, ?	Returns an unmodifiable sorted map backed by

extends V> sm)	sm.

3.8.6 The emptyXxxx and singletonXxxx Algorithms

The empty-prefixed algorithms shown in Table 3.7 help create immutable, serializable collections or iterators to start with. They are conceptually very simple, so let's use an example next to illustrate their common usage.

We pick the emptyList algorithm for the example, as shown in Listing 3.46. In this example, line 7 creates an emptyList using the Collections.emptyList method. Line 11 attempts to add an element to the empty list, which would result in an exception as shown below:

```
Created an empty immutable list: []
Exception in thread "main" java.lang.UnsupportedOperationException
    at java.util.AbstractList.add(AbstractList.java:148)
    at java.util.AbstractList.add(AbstractList.java:108)
    at jcp.ch3.algorithms.EmptyListDemo.main(EmptyListDemo.java:11)
```

Note that the output indicates where the exception occurred in the code.

Listing 3.46 EmptyListDemo.java

```
1    package jcp.ch3.algorithms;
2    import java.util.*;
3
4    public class EmptyListDemo {
5      public static void main(String args[]) {
6        // 1. create an empty list
7        List<String> emptyList = Collections.emptyList();
8        System.out.println("Created an empty immutable list: " + emptyList);
9
10       // 2. add elements. Expect an exception
11       emptyList.add("x");
12     }
13   }
```

You might wonder why we need an immutable empty list. First, it's bad coding practice to return an empty list using the new operator with a no-arg List constructor, as each time it would create a new empty list object, wasting memory. In such cases, return a shared and immutable empty list, instead, by using the Collections.emptyList() algorithm. Moreover, returning an immutable, shared list is a better choice than returning a null, which may make the client code look messy.

Table 3.7 The emptyXxxx and singletonXxxx algorithms

Method/Algorithm	Description
static <T> Enumeration<T> emptyEnumeration()	Returns an empty enumeration with no elements.

static <T> Iterator<T> emptyIterator()	Returns an empty iterator with no elements.
static <T> List<T> emptyList()	Returns an immutable, empty List object of the inferred type.
static <T> ListIterator<T> emptyListIterator()	Returns an empty list iterator with no elements.
static <T> Map<T> emptyMap()	Returns an immutable, empty Map object of the inferred type.
static <T> Set<T> emptySet()	Returns an immutable, empty Set object of the inferred type.

Table 3.8 shows three algorithms for creating singleton Set, List and Map. In contrast to the empty-prefixed methods listed in Table 3.7, which create zero-element collections and other types of containers, the three methods listed in Table 3.8 create singleton collections or maps that have only one object. These methods are handy when you have a need to create a shared, immutable, serializable set, list or map, saving you time and efforts to create your own in a potentially less optimal way.

Those three algorithms listed in Table 3.8 are simple conceptually. It's also easy to create a demo program to illustrate how they work. Listing 3.47 shows such a demo program. As you see, line 8 creates an object of String type. Line 11 creates a singleton Set by calling Collections' singleton method with the String object created at line 8. Similarly, lines 15 and 16 create a singleton list and map, respectively. Lines 19 – 21 print the singleton set, list and map as stated above, which would look like the following when this program were executed:

```
singleon(Set): [a]
singleonList: [a]
singleonMap: {a=1}
```

Finally, note line 12 commented out in Listing 3.47. If this line were uncommented out, line 12 would result in an exception as shown below:

```
Exception in thread "main" java.lang.UnsupportedOperationException
    at java.util.AbstractCollection.add(AbstractCollection.java:260)
    at jcp.ch3.algorithms.SingletonListDemo.main(SingletonListDemo.java:12)
```

The above output helps verify that the objects created with singleton algorithms are indeed immutable.

Next, we discuss the Arrays class.

Listing 3.47 SingletonDemo.java

```
1    package jcp.ch3.algorithms;
2
3    import java.util.*;
4
5    public class SingletonListDemo {
```

```
6    public static void main(String args[]) {
7        // 1. create a String obj
8        String obj = "a";
9
10       // 2. create a singleton (set)
11       Set<String> set = Collections.singleton (obj);
12       //set.add ("b"); // will throw an exception
13
14       // 3. create a singleton list and map
15       List<String> list = Collections.singletonList(obj);
16       Map<String, Integer> map = Collections.singletonMap(obj, 1);
17
18       // 4. print out
19       System.out.println("singleon(Set): " + set);
20       System.out.println("singleonList: " + list);
21       System.out.println("singleonMap: " + map);
22    }
23  }
```

Table 3.8 The singletonXxxx algorithms

Method/Algorithm	Description
static <T> Set<T> singleton(T obj)	Returns obj as an immutable set. This method offers a simple way for converting a single object into a set.
static <T> List<T> singletonList(T obj)	Returns obj as an immutable list. This method offers a simple way for converting a single object into a list.
static <T> Map<T> singletonMap(T obj)	Returns obj as an immutable map. This method offers a simple way for converting a single object into a map.

3.9   THE ARRAYS CLASS

The java.util package also contains a class named Arrays, which has many methods that operate on various *native* arrays whose elements may be of type of boolean, byte, char, double, float, int, long, short, or Object. The operations on such native type arrays include *search*, *copy*, *fill*, *sort*, and so on. For example, if we want to sort an unsorted array, say, an array of int type, the Arrays class has a method for such a need as shown in Listing 3.48. As you see, line 10 defines a public static void sort method that takes an int array named 'a' as its parameter, so that you can call

Arrays.sort (a);

to get the `int` array 'a' sorted. If you want to search a specific value in the above array, for example, the integer number 99, you can call the `binarySearch` method as denoted from lines 14 – 16, as follows, to get it done:

```
int index = Arrays.binarySearch (a, 99);
```

Here, `index` is the index of the value in the integer array to be searched if found, or -1 if not found.

I could have walked you through all the methods of the `Arrays` class here, but I decided not to do so, as it's more important for you to realize that the `Arrays` class, like many other classes in Java, provides many convenience methods as you can imagine to meet whatever your needs are when dealing with native arrays. Therefore, let's move on to the next section that covers legacy interfaces and classes in the same `java.util` package.

Listing 3.48 Arrays.java

```
1    package java.util;
2
3    import java.lang.reflect.*;
4
5    public class Arrays {
6
7        // Suppresses default constructor, ensuring non-instantiability.
8        private Arrays() {}
9
10       public static void sort(int[] a) {
11             DualPivotQuicksort.sort(a);
12       }
13
14       public static int binarySearch(int[] a, int key) {
15             return binarySearch0(a, 0, a.length, key);
16       }
17
18       // other methods omitted
19   }
```

3.10 LEGACY COLLECTION CLASSES

If you started with programming in Java long time ago, some collection classes such as `Hashtable`, `Vector`, `Stack`, `Dictionary`, and `Properties` may look familiar to you. However, be aware that these collection classes are legacy classes now and considered deprecated. Surprisingly, these classes are all synchronized and thus thread-safe. However, they were provided in earlier Java versions as an ad hoc method of storing objects. The new Java versions (notably since Java 5) provide many newly-designed and implemented, unsynchronized collection classes in the `java.util` package as covered in this chapter, as well as newer, synchronized collections in the `java.util.concurrent` package as will be covered in a later chapter in this text.

Because those collection classes of `Hashtable`, `Vector`, `Stack`, `Dictionary`, and `Properties` are deprecated now, I'd like to save us time by not giving examples here to show how those legacy classes work. Instead, I'd like to encourage you to use the newer collection classes as introduced in this chapter if thread-safety is not a concern for you, or use the new concurrent collection classes to be introduced later if thread-safety is a concern for you. As modern Java applications in the areas of cloud computing and big data demand unprecedented performance and scalability, it's important to choose proper, new collection classes, unsynchronized or synchronized, to meet stringent non-functional requirements for your products.

3.11 SUMMARY

This chapter covered unsynchronized Java collection classes in the `java.util` package. Some of the most commonly used collections and static classes include:

- `HashSet`, `LinkedHashSet`, and `TreeSet`
- `ArrayList` and `LinkedList`
- `ArrayDeque` and `PriorityQueue`
- `HashMap`, `LinkedHashMap` and `TreeMap`
- `Collections` and `Arrays`

Table 3.9 summarizes all collections and their characteristics. I hope that you would practice more by using them to solve real problems for your projects.

Table 3.9 Java unsynchronized collections and their characteristics

Interface	Class	Characteristics
Set	HashSet	Un-ordered, unique entries
Set	LinkedHashSet	Set with insertion order preserved
NavigableSet	TreeSet	Binary tree set for fast search
List	ArrayList	Random access with O(1) for search and update and O (n) for insertion and deletion
List, Deque	LinkedList	Sequential access with O(n) for search and update and O (1) for insertion and deletion
Deque	ArrayDeque	FIFO (queue) or LIFO (stack) data structures
Queue	PriorityQueue	A balanced binary heap. O(1) for `peek`, O(log n) for enqueue and dequeue operations, and O(n) for `remove(Object)` and `contains(Object)`.
Map	HashMap	Unsynchronized hash tables for key-value pairs. Duplicate values are allowed.
Map	LinkedHashMap	Doubly-linked list of map entries
NavigableMap	TreeMap	Self-balancing binary search tree

Although the main theme of this book is about Java concurrent programming, it's equally important to understand unsynchronized collection classes as to understand synchronized collection classes (to be introduced later) for high concurrency use. In fact, synchronized collection classes are based on their unsynchronized counterpart collection classes, and therefore, it's hard to have a good understanding of one without having a good understanding of the other.

Having covered the unsynchronized collection classes comprehensively in this chapter, the remaining chapters continue our coverage of Java concurrent programming with more synchronizers and locking constructs. Let's continue our journey of Java concurrent programming through the remainder of this book.

3.12 EXERCISES

Exercise 3.1 Describe the complete interfaces in the Collections framework.

Exercise 3.2 What is *natural ordering*?

Exercise 3.3 What's the relationship between the `Iterable` and `Iterator` interfaces?

Exercise 3.4 Describe the categories that all collection operations fall into.

Exercise 3.5 What's the relationship between the `SortedSet` interface and the `NavigableSet` interface?

Exercise 3.6 What's the difference between an `Iterator` and a `ListIterator`?

Exercise 3.7 Describe the differences between the add/offer, remove/poll, element/peak methods for a queue.

Exercise 3.8 How does a deque differ from a queue?

Exercise 3.9 Describe how a `HashSet`, a `LinkedHashSet` and a `TreeSet` differ from each other.

Exercise 3.10 What is *fail-fast*?

Exercise 3.11 How do you choose between an `ArrayList` and a `LinkedList`?

Exercise 3.12 What's the purpose of the `RandomAccess` interface?

Exercise 3.13 Write a simple program to demonstrate the use of an `ArrayDeque`.

Exercise 3.14 Write a simple program to demonstrate the use of a `PriorityQueue`.

Exercise 3.15 Describe the differences among a `HashMap`, a `LinkedHashMap` and a `TreeMap`.

Exercise 3.16 Give three examples of algorithms provided by the `Collections` class.

Exercise 3.17 What's the difference between the `Collections` class and the `Arrays` class?

4   Atomic Operations

Chapter 1 introduced the traditional Java multi-thread programming model. As you have learnt, the traditional multi-thread programing model works as follows:

- **Creating new threads**: New threads can be created by implementing the `Runnable` interface or extending the `Thread` class.
- **Synchronization**: Supported by the `synchronized` keyword that can be applied to a method or an object/block.
- **Inter-thread communication**: Supported by methods such as `wait()`, `notify()`, and `notifyAll()`.

The above traditional model had fulfilled the multithread programming needs successfully in earlier days of Java. However, for developing intensively concurrent Java programs, more high-level synchronization features, such as semaphores, thread pools, execution managers, and so on, can provide great help. JDK 5 responded to such new needs by adding many *concurrency utilities*, commonly known as the concurrent API, which is classified into the following three packages:

- **java.util.concurrent.atomic**. This sub-package contains classes for facilitating the use of variables in a concurrent program, through which the value of a variable can be updated without using locks. The underlying mechanism is that the methods in a class execute as a single, non-interruptible operation, with the aid from the OS. The classes included in this sub-package include the `AtomicBoolean`, `AtomicInteger`, `AtomicIntegerArray`, `AtomicReference`, and so on. Refer to Figure 4.1 (a) for all atomic classes contained in this package.
- **java.util.concurrent.locks**. This sub-package contains classes that provide finer-grained control over synchronization by using locks, in contrast to the traditional model based on the `synchronized` keyword. It contains three interfaces (`Lock`, `Condition` and `ReadWriteLock`), three abstract classes (`AbstractOwnableSynchronizer`, `AbstractQueuedSynchronizer`, and `AbstractQueuedLongSynchronizer`), and two lock classes (`ReentrantLock`, and `ReentrantReadWriteLock`), and a lock support class named `LockSupport`. Refer to Figure 4.1 (b) for those locks as mentioned above.
- **java.util.concurrent**. This package includes five *synchronizers* (`Semaphore`, `CountDownLatch`, `CyclicBarrier`, `Exchanger` and `Phaser`), the *ExecutorService* Framework as we covered in Chapter 2, and sixteen *concurrent collections* from `ArrayBlockingQueue` to `TransferQueue`, as shown in Figure 4.2.

(a) (`java.util.concurrent.atomic`)   (b) (`java.util.concurrent.locks`)

Figure 4.1 (a) left: atomic operations; and (b) right: locks

▲ 🐞 java.util.concurrent
  ▷ 🗋 AbstractExecutorService.java
  ▷ 🗋 ArrayBlockingQueue.java
  ▷ 🗋 BlockingDeque.java
  ▷ 🗋 BlockingQueue.java
  ▷ 🗋 BrokenBarrierException.java
  ▷ 🗋 Callable.java
  ▷ 🗋 CancellationException.java
  ▷ 🗋 CompletionService.java
  ▷ 🗋 ConcurrentHashMap.java
  ▷ 🗋 ConcurrentLinkedDeque.java
  ▷ 🗋 ConcurrentLinkedQueue.java
  ▷ 🗋 ConcurrentMap.java
  ▷ 🗋 ConcurrentNavigableMap.java
  ▷ 🗋 ConcurrentSkipListMap.java
  ▷ 🗋 ConcurrentSkipListSet.java
  ▷ 🗋 CopyOnWriteArrayList.java
  ▷ 🗋 CopyOnWriteArraySet.java
  ▷ 🗋 CountDownLatch.java
  ▷ 🗋 CyclicBarrier.java
  ▷ 🗋 Delayed.java
  ▷ 🗋 DelayQueue.java
  ▷ 🗋 Exchanger.java
  ▷ 🗋 ExecutionException.java
  ▷ 🗋 Executor.java
  ▷ 🗋 ExecutorCompletionService.java
  ▷ 🗋 Executors.java
  ▷ 🗋 ExecutorService.java
  ▷ 🗋 ForkJoinPool.java
  ▷ 🗋 ForkJoinTask.java
  ▷ 🗋 ForkJoinWorkerThread.java
  ▷ 🗋 Future.java
  ▷ 🗋 FutureTask.java
  ▷ 🗋 LinkedBlockingDeque.java
  ▷ 🗋 LinkedBlockingQueue.java
  ▷ 🗋 LinkedTransferQueue.java
  ▷ 🗋 package-info.java
  ▷ 🗋 Phaser.java
  ▷ 🗋 PriorityBlockingQueue.java
  ▷ 🗋 RecursiveAction.java
  ▷ 🗋 RecursiveTask.java
  ▷ 🗋 RejectedExecutionException.java
  ▷ 🗋 RejectedExecutionHandler.java
  ▷ 🗋 RunnableFuture.java
  ▷ 🗋 RunnableScheduledFuture.java
  ▷ 🗋 ScheduledExecutorService.java
  ▷ 🗋 ScheduledFuture.java
  ▷ 🗋 ScheduledThreadPoolExecutor.java
  ▷ 🗋 Semaphore.java
  ▷ 🗋 SynchronousQueue.java
  ▷ 🗋 ThreadFactory.java
  ▷ 🗋 ThreadLocalRandom.java
  ▷ 🗋 ThreadPoolExecutor.java
  ▷ 🗋 TimeoutException.java
  ▷ 🗋 TimeUnit.java
  ▷ 🗋 TransferQueue.java

Figure 4.2 Concurrent utilities contained in the `java.util.concurrent` package

The remainder of this text covers atomic operations, synchronizers, locks, concurrent collections, and parallel programming using the Fork-Join framework. Let us start with atomic operations next.

4.1 THE NATIVE UNSAFE CLASS

As mentioned before, atomic operations on single variables are supported through a number of classes such as `AtomicInteger`, etc. However, behind the scene, it's the native class named `Unsafe` that does all the low-level work to help achieve atomicity. Therefore, in order to understand those atomic classes, we need to start with understanding the native `Unsafe` class, which is covered next.

First, the `Unsafe` class is not a Java class. It is a class un-officially documented online at http://www.docjar.com/docs/api/sun/misc/Unsafe.html, in the package of `sun.misc`. You might wonder why it is termed *unsafe*, and why Java actually uses some *unsafe* API to build thread-safe classes.

To understand what the concept of unsafe actually means, let's digress a bit from Java to C#. As is known, to maintain type safety and security, C# does not support pointer arithmetic by default. However, by using the *unsafe* keyword, C# sets an unsafe context in which pointers can be used. As is also known, we need to use pointers as an entry gate for low-level programming. However, Java does not have a keyword equivalent to C#'s unsafe keyword. So, if we need to get into low-level programming in Java, we are forced to use the Java Native Interface (JNI), which requires us to know C, which immediately leads us to code that is tightly coupled to a specific platform. The `sun.misc.Unsafe` class provides an alternative to low-level programming, even though it is discouraged to do so.

From our perspective of Java concurrent programming, perhaps it's not a wise decision to dive too deep into how the `Unsafe` class is implemented internally. It's sufficient for us to take a cursory look at some of its public methods as follows (or at least those in bold if you feel that the list is too boring):

- `public native int addressSize()`: Reports the size in bytes of a native pointer, as stored via `putAddress`. This value will be either 4 or 8.
- `public native Object allocateInstance(Class cls) throws InstantiationException`: Allocates an instance but does not run any constructor.
- `public native long allocateMemory(long bytes)`: Allocates a new block of native memory of the given size in bytes.
- `public native int arrayBaseOffset(Class arrayClass)`: Reports the offset of the first element in the storage allocation of a given array class.
- `public final native boolean` **`compareAndSwapInt`**`(Object o, long offset, int expected, int x)`: Atomically updates an `int` variable to `x` if it is currently holding `expected`.
- `public final native boolean` **`compareAndSwapLong`**`(Object o, long offset, long expected, long x)`: Atomically update a `long` variable to `x` if it is currently holding `expected`.
- `public final native boolean` **`compareAndSwapObject`**`(Object o, long offset, Object expected, Object x)`: Atomically updates an `Object` variable to `x` if it is currently holding `expected`.
- `public void copyMemory(long srcAddress, long destAddress, long bytes)`: Sets all bytes in a given block of memory to a copy of another block.
- `public native void freeMemory(long address)`: Disposes of a block of native memory, as obtained from `allocateMemory` or `reallocateMemory`.

- `public native long getAddress(long address)`: Fetches a native pointer from a given memory address.
- `public native int getInt(Object o, long offset)`: Fetches a value from a given Java variable. More specifically, fetches a field or array element within the given object o at the given offset, or (if o is null) from the memory address whose numerical value is the given offset.
- `public native int getIntVolatile(Object o, long offset)`: Volatile version of getInt(Object, long)
- `public native int getLoadAverage(double[] loadavg, int nelems)`: Gets the load average in the system run queue assigned to the available processors averaged over various periods of time. This method retrieves the given nelem samples and assigns to the elements of the given loadavg array. The system imposes a maximum of 3 samples, representing averages over the last 1, 5, and 15 minutes, respectively.
- `public static Unsafe getUnsafe()`: Provides the caller with the capability of performing unsafe operations. The returned Unsafe object should be carefully guarded by the caller, since it can be used to read and write data at arbitrary memory addresses. It must never be passed to untrusted code. Most methods in this class are very low-level, and correspond to a small number of hardware instructions (on typical machines). Compilers are encouraged to optimize these methods accordingly.
- `public native void monitorEnter(Object o)`: Locks the object. It must get unlocked via monitorExit.
- `public native void monitorExit(Object o)`: Unlocks the object. It must have been locked via monitorEnter.
- `public native int pageSize()`: Reports the size in bytes of a native memory page.
- `public native void park(boolean isAbsolute, long time)`: Blocks the current thread, returning when one of the following conditions occurs:
  - A balancing unpark occurs
  - A balancing unpark has already occurred
  - The thread is interrupted
  - If not absolute and time is not zero, the given time nanoseconds have elapsed
  - If absolute, the given deadline in milliseconds since Epoch has passed
  - Spuriously, i.e., returning for no reason.
- `public native void putAddress(long address, long x)`: Stores a native pointer into a given memory address.
- `public native void putInt(long address, int x)`: Stores a value x into a given address
- `public native void putInt(Object o, long offset, int x)`: Stores a value into a given Java variable. The first two parameters are interpreted exactly as with getInt(Object, long) to refer to a specific Java variable (field or array element). The given value is stored into that variable. The variable must be of the same type as the method parameter x.

I hope the above list gives you a glimpse of what those methods of the Unsafe class do, rather than how they are implemented at low level exactly.

Given the above background information on the Unsafe class, let us examine how the atomic classes in the java.util.concurrent.atomic package is implemented in Java next.

4.2 ATOMICINTEGER

In general, the atomic operations offer a convenient and more efficient alternative to other synchronization mechanisms when only a single variable is involved. For example, when you have a single variable of `int` type to be synchronized, you can use the `AtomicInteger` class to achieve the task.

This section discusses the `AtomicInteger` class. We'll first examine its implementation and then a use case.

4.2.1 Implementation

Listing 4.1 shows how the `AtomicInteger` class is implemented in Java. Here are the specifics about this implementation:

- Line 5 creates an `Unsafe` object to be used for calling `Unsafe.compareAndSwapInt` for updates
- Line 15 declares a volatile `int` field named `value`
- Lines 17 – 22 define two `AtomicInteger` constructors: one is parameterized with an `initialValue`, and the other takes no arguments and will be initialized to zero.
- Lines 24 – 25 define the getter and setter methods for the `value` field.
- Lines 27 – 33 define the `getAndSet` method, which retrieves the current value while setting current value to `newValue`. This method shows how the `comapreAndSet` method of the `Unsafe` class is used to accomplish the task.
- Lines 35 – 37 define the `compareAndSet` method, which is implemented with the `compareAndSwapInt` method of the `Unsafe` class.
- Lines 39 – 46 define the `getAndIncrement` method, while lines 48 – 55 define the `getAndDecrement` method, both of which retrieve the current value, increment/decrement relative to the current value, and use the `compareAndSet` method of the `Unsafe` class to set the new value.
- Lines 57 – 60 show a few other methods, such as `getAndAdd`, `addAndGet`, `incrementAndGet`, `decrementAndGet`. The implementation details are omitted, as they are all similar to the implementations for the `getAndIncrement` and `getAndDecrement` methods.
- Finally, lines 62 – 66 define methods for getting the value in different types, such as `String`, `long`, `float`, and `double`.

Overall, the implementation of the `AtomicInteger` class is straightforward, with low-level details hidden in the methods of `Unsafe` class, such as `comapreAndSet`, `compareAndSwapInt`, etc. Next, let's use an example to demonstrate how a single variable of `int` type can be synchronized with the `AtomicInteger` class.

Listing 4.1 AtomicInteger.java (partial)

```
1   package java.util.concurrent.atomic;
2   import sun.misc.Unsafe;
3
4   public class AtomicInteger extends Number implements java.io.Serializable
    {
5       private static final Unsafe unsafe = Unsafe.getUnsafe();
```

```
6       private static final long valueOffset;
7
8       static {
9         try {
10          valueOffset = unsafe.objectFieldOffset
11              (AtomicInteger.class.getDeclaredField("value"));
12        } catch (Exception ex) { throw new Error(ex); }
13      }
14
15      private volatile int value;
16
17      public AtomicInteger(int initialValue) {
18          value = initialValue;
19      }
20
21      public AtomicInteger() {
22      }
23
24      public final int get() {return value;}
25      public final void set(int newValue) { value = newValue; }
26
27      public final int getAndSet(int newValue) {
28          for (;;) {
29              int current = get();
30              if (compareAndSet(current, newValue))
31                  return current;
32          }
33      }
34
35      public final boolean compareAndSet(int expect, int update) {
36          return unsafe.compareAndSwapInt(this, valueOffset, expect,
                update);
37      }
38
39      public final int getAndIncrement() {
40          for (;;) {
41              int current = get();
42              int next = current + 1;
43              if (compareAndSet(current, next))
44                  return current;
45          }
46      }
47
48      public final int getAndDecrement() {
49          for (;;) {
50              int current = get();
51              int next = current - 1;
52              if (compareAndSet(current, next))
53                  return current;
54          }
55      }
56
```

```
57      public final int getAndAdd(int delta) { // body omitted}
58      public final int addAndGet(int delta) { // body omitted }
59      public final int incrementAndGet() { // body omitted }
60      public final int decrementAndGet() { // body omitted}
61
62      public String toString() {return Integer.toString(get());}
63      public int intValue() {get(); }
64      public long longValue() { return (long)get();}
65      public float floatValue() { return (float)get(); }
66      public double doubleValue() {return (double)get();}
67  }
```

4.2.2 An Example

Listing 4.2 shows a simple program named AtomicIntegerDemo.java to demonstrate the use of the AtomicInteger class. As shown from lines 53 – 72, a class named Permit has a field named permits, simulating the number of permits available for multiple consumers (threads) to grab. Apparently, the variable permits needs to be synchronized for multiple threads to access, which is why we have line 55 defining it as an AtomicInteger variable. The methods of the Permit class simply call the corresponding methods of its AtomicInteger variable of permits.

The next part should be the consumer class that accesses the shared resource class, namely, the Permit class as discussed above. This consumer class is named Drawer, and shown from lines 33 – 50. For simplicity, the Drawer class has only two fields: the id and the shared resource object (permit) set up for it to access. In the run method of the Drawer class, we set it up in a special way that threads with even and odd id's will increment/decrement permits, respectively, so that if the shared resource is accessed by an even number of threads, the value of the permits variable should remain to be the same as its initial value.

The last part is the driver class, which is shown from lines 8 – 30. It is explained as follows:

- Lines 12 – 13 create a permit object and set its permits field to 9. This is for illustrating the use of the set method of the AtomicInteger class only, as we could have used a parameterized constructor for the Permit class to achieve the same.
- Line 16 creates an object as a fixed thread pool with the pool size set to 100.
- Lines 19 to 21 use a for-loop to execute 100 threads, using the executorService object created at line 16.
- Lines 24 – 25 let the executorService thread wait for 5000 milliseconds and then print out the number of permits remaining to verify the result. Note that we have to use a Thread.sleep method to wait for all threads to complete. We'll show a better method using a synchronizer in the next chapter.

Executing this thread would generate the following result, as expected:

Number of permits: 9

Next, we discuss the AtomicIntegerArray class.

Listing 4.2 AtomicIntegerDemo.java

```
1   package jcp.ch4.atomic;
2
3   import java.util.concurrent.atomic.AtomicInteger;
4   import java.util.concurrent.ExecutorService;
5   import java.util.concurrent.Executors;
6
7   // test driver
8   public class AtomicIntegerDemo {
9
10    public static void main(String[] args) throws InterruptedException {
11
12       final Permit permit = new Permit();
13       permit.setPermits (9);
14
15       // 1. Create a newFixedThreadPool using the Executors utility class
16       ExecutorService executorService = Executors.newFixedThreadPool(100);
17
18       // 2. launch 100 drawers
19       for (int i = 0; i < 100; i++) {
20          executorService.execute (new Drawer (i, permit));
21       }
22
23       // 3. wait 5000 ms for all drawers to complete
24       Thread.sleep(5000);
25       System.out.println("Number of permits: " + permit.getPermits());
26
27       // 4. shut down executorService to avoid resource leak
28       executorService.shutdown();
29    }
30  }
31
32  // Thread class: a drawer increments/decrements permits if id is even/odd.
33  class Drawer extends Thread {
34    int id;
35    Permit permit;
36
37    Drawer(int id, Permit permit){
38       this.id = id;
39       this.permit = permit;
40    }
41    public void run() {
42       for (int i = 0; i < 10000; i++) {
43          if ((this.id % 2) == 0) {
44             permit.incrementPermits();
45          } else {
46             permit.decrementPermits();
47          }
48       }
49    }
50  }
51
52  // Shared resource: AtomicInteger synchronizes permits
```

```
53  class Permit {
54
55    private AtomicInteger permits = new AtomicInteger(0);
56
57    public int getPermits() {
58       return permits.get();
59    }
60
61    public void setPermits(int newValue) {
62       permits.set(newValue);
63    }
64
65    public void incrementPermits() {
66       permits.incrementAndGet();
67    }
68
69    public void decrementPermits() {
70       permits.decrementAndGet();
71    }
72  }
```

4.3   ATOMICINTEGERARRAY

The preceding section covered AtomicInteger class, which makes a single variable of int type atomic. The java.util.atomic package also has an AtomicIntegerArray class, which makes every element of an array of int type atomic. Since each element of the array is atomic, the entire array is atomic. Figure 4.3 shows the AtomicIntegerArray class taken on my Eclipse IDE.

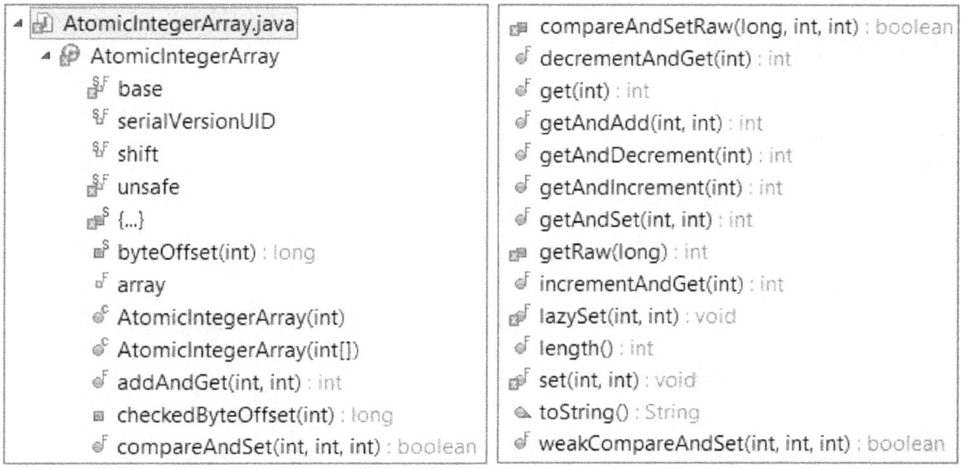

Figure 4.3 The AtomicIntegerArray class on Eclipse IDE

As you see in Figure 4.3, the methods of the `AtomicIntegerArray` class are similar to those for the `AtomicInteger` class, except that most of them are indexed now in order to locate the exact element of the array at the specified index. If you refer back to Listing 4.1, notice the static block defined from lines 8 – 13, which was placed there to be executed during class loading time to initialize the `valueOffset` field. For an integer array, the situation is different: It's the byte address of an element at the specified index that needs to be located before applying an operation. This is reflected in the implementation of the `AtomicIntegerArray` class, as discussed next.

Listing 4.3 shows partially the implementation of the `AtomicIntegerArray` class in Java. As you see, lines 8 – 11 define the four fields of `unsafe`, `base`, `shift`, and `array` for the `AtomicIntegerArray` class. Also, note the static block defined from lines 13 – 18, which initializes the `shift` field during class load time. Look down to line 27 further and notice the `byeOffset(int i)` method, which returns the byte offset for an element at the specified index i. Now, note the following two foundational methods:

- private long **checkedByteOffset**(int i) (lines 20 - 25): This method checks whether an index is in or out of range in the array. If it is out of the range, it throws an `IndexOutOfBoundsException`; otherwise, it returns the `byteOffset` for the given index.
- private int **getRaw**(long offset) (lines 43 - 45): Calls `unsafe.getIntVolatile(array, offset)` to get the value of an element of the given array. It takes an offset, rather than an index, to find the element of the array, which is operated at the low-level.

The above two methods of `checkedByteOffset` and `getRaw` explain how an element of an array is located: The index is given by the programmer at the high level, which is translated into offset to access the element at the low level.

Next, we use an example to demonstrate the use of the `AtomicIntegerArray` class, following Listing 4.3.

Listing 4.3 AtomicIntegerArray.java (partial)

```
1    package java.util.concurrent.atomic;
2    import sun.misc.Unsafe;
3    import java.util.*;
4
5    public class AtomicIntegerArray implements java.io.Serializable {
6        private static final long serialVersionUID = 2862133569453604235L;
7
8        private static final Unsafe unsafe = Unsafe.getUnsafe();
9        private static final int base = unsafe.arrayBaseOffset(int[].class);
10       private static final int shift;
11       private final int[] array;
12
13       static {
14           int scale = unsafe.arrayIndexScale(int[].class);
15           if ((scale & (scale - 1)) != 0)
16               throw new Error("data type scale not a power of two");
17           shift = 31 - Integer.numberOfLeadingZeros(scale);
18       }
19
```

```
20        private long checkedByteOffset(int i) {
21            if (i < 0 || i >= array.length)
22                throw new IndexOutOfBoundsException("index " + i);
23
24            return byteOffset(i);
25        }
26
27        private static long byteOffset(int i) {
28            return ((long) i << shift) + base;
29        }
30
31        public AtomicIntegerArray(int length) {
32            array = new int[length];
33        }
34
35        public AtomicIntegerArray(int[] array) {
36            this.array = array.clone();
37        }
38
39        public final int get(int i) {
40            return getRaw(checkedByteOffset(i));
41        }
42
43        private int getRaw(long offset) {
44            return unsafe.getIntVolatile(array, offset);
45        }
46
47        public final void set(int i, int newValue) {
48            unsafe.putIntVolatile(array, checkedByteOffset(i), newValue);
49        }
50       // other methods omitted
51  }
```

Listing 4.4 shows the AtomicIntegerArrayDemo.java program. It was adapted from the previous AtomicIntegerDemo example, as shown in Listing 4.2. The following changes were introduced:

- The shared resource class PermitArray (lines 61 – 84). Three changes were introduced as follows:

  ○ The constructor (line 63) is given a parameter of 3, indicating that the AtomicIntegerArray has three elements.
  ○ All methods of get, set, increment and decrement are indexed now.
  ○ A new method of length() was added to return the length of the array.

- The Thread class (lines 37 - 58). This class was renamed from Drawer to Drawers to account for the fact that we would be dealing with AtomicIntegerArray, not AtomicInteger.
- The test driver class (lines 8 – 34). Now, we need to initialize all three elements of the permitArray object as shown from lines 13 – 15. Besides, we need to use a for-loop to get the values of the three elements of the permitArray, as shown from lines 27 – 29.

Executing this example would yield the following output, as expected:

# of permits: 9

```
# of permits: 99
# of permits: 999
```

This concludes our coverage of Atomic operations.

Listing 4.4 AtomicIntegerArrayDemo.java

```java
1   package jcp.ch4.atomic;
2
3   import java.util.concurrent.atomic.AtomicIntegerArray;
4   import java.util.concurrent.ExecutorService;
5   import java.util.concurrent.Executors;
6
7   // test driver
8   public class AtomicIntegerArrayDemo {
9
10    public static void main(String[] args) throws InterruptedException {
11
12       final PermitArray permitArray = new PermitArray();
13       permitArray.setPermits (0, 9);
14       permitArray.setPermits (1, 99);
15       permitArray.setPermits (2, 999);
16
17       // 1. Create a newFixedThreadPool using the Executors utility class
18       ExecutorService executorService = Executors.newFixedThreadPool(100);
19
20       // 2. launch 100 drawers
21       for (int i = 0; i < 100; i++) {
22          executorService.execute (new Drawers (i, permitArray));
23       }
24
25       // 3. wait 5000 ms for all drawers to complete
26       Thread.sleep(5000);
27       for (int i = 0; i < 3; i++) {
28          System.out.println("# of permits: " + permitArray.getPermits(i));
29       }
30
31       // 4. shut down executorService to avoid resource leak
32       executorService.shutdown();
33    }
34  }
35
36  // Thread class: a drawer increments/decrements permits if id is even/odd.
37  class Drawers extends Thread {
38    int id;
39    PermitArray permitArray;
40
41    Drawers(int id, PermitArray permitArray){
42       this.id = id;
43       this.permitArray = permitArray;
44    }
```

```
45    public void run() {
46        for (int i = 0; i < 100; i++) {
47            if ((this.id % 2) == 0) {
48                for (int j = 0; j < permitArray.length(); j++) {
49                    permitArray.incrementPermits(j);
50                }
51            } else {
52                for (int j = 0; j < permitArray.length(); j++) {
53                    permitArray.decrementPermits(j);
54                }
55            }
56        }
57    }
58 }
59
60 // Shared resource: AtomicIntegerArray synchronizes permitArray
61 class PermitArray {
62    // AtomicIntegerArray with 3 elements
63    private AtomicIntegerArray permitArray = new AtomicIntegerArray(3);
64
65    public int getPermits(int i) {
66        return permitArray.get(i);
67    }
68
69    public void setPermits(int i, int newValue) {
70        permitArray.set(i, newValue);
71    }
72
73    public void incrementPermits(int i) {
74        permitArray.incrementAndGet(i);
75    }
76
77    public void decrementPermits(int i) {
78        permitArray.decrementAndGet(i);
79    }
80
81    public int length () {
82        return permitArray.length();
83    }
84 }
```

4.4 OTHER ATOMIC CLASSES

This section briefly introduces the other atomic classes in addition to the AtomicInteger and AtomicIntegerArray classes we covered in detail in the previous two sections. Because they work similarly to their counterparts of AtomicInteger and AtomicIntegerArray classes when applicable, we will not dive into their implementations. Instead, we introduce them briefly next.

The remaining atomic classes in addition to the AtomicInteger and AtomicIntegerArray classes include:

- AtomicIntegerFieldUpdater: A reflection-based utility that enables atomic updates to designated volatile int fields of designated classes. This AtomicIntegerFieldUpdater class is designed for use in atomic data structures, in which several fields of the same node are independently subject to atomic updates.
- AtomicLong/AtomicLongArray/AtomicLongFieldUpdater: These classes are similar to AtomicInteger/AtomicIntegerArray/AtomicIntergerFieldUpdater except that the type is for long instead of int.
- AtomicReference<T>/AtomicReferenceArray<E>/AtomicReferenceFieldUpdater<T,V>: These classes are similar to AtomicInteger/AtomicIntegerArray/AtomicIntergerFieldUpdater except that the type is for reference object of type T or type E for array elements instead of type int.
- AtomicBoolean: This class is similar to the AtomicInteger class except that the type is for boolean instead of int.
- AtomicMarkableReference: This class maintains an object reference along with a mark bit that can be updated atomically.
- AtomicStampedReference: This class maintains an object reference along with an integer "stamp" that can be updated atomically.

This concludes our coverage of the Java concurrent utility classes designed for applying atomic operations on single variables of primitive types or object references.

4.5   SUMMARY

In this chapter, we introduced the Java concurrent utility classes that provide atomic operations on single variables or arrays. To help you understand how those classes work, we dived deep into how the AtomicInteger and AtomicIntegerArray classes were implemented using the native Unsafe class. We also provided examples illustrating how these atomic classes can be used. If you have such a need, consider using these classes first, rather than writing your own or using other more heavyweight synchronization classes.

The next chapter discusses the lock classes contained in the package of java.util.concurrent.locks.

4.6   EXERCISES

Exercise 4.1 What's the purpose of the Unsafe class?

Exercise 4.2 Describe the Unsafe's three methods of compareAndSwap(CAS) methods and the park() method.

Exercise 4.3 What's the difference between the AtomicInteger class and the AtomicIntegerArray class?

Exercise 4.4 What other atomic classes does the atomic package include, in addition to the AtomicInteger class and the AtomicIntegerArray class?

5 Locks

A *lock* is an object that offers an alternative to using the *synchronized* keyword to control access to a shared resource. When a thread needs to access a shared resource, it must acquire the lock first. If the shared resource is available and acquiring the lock is successful, the thread must release the lock at the end of its use of the shared resource. On the other hand, if a shared resource is already being used and locked by a thread, the newly-arrived thread must wait for the lock to be released and then try to acquire the lock (as the previous thread did) before it can access the shared resource.

Locks are one of the most central subjects for concurrent programming in Java. This chapter is dedicated to exploring how locks are supported in Java. Specifically, we'll examine the lock-related interfaces and classes implemented in the `java.util.concurrent.locks` package.

As shown in Figure 5.1, the `java.util.concurrent.locks` package contains the following three sets of interfaces and classes:

- **Lock/ReentrantLock**: The `Lock.java` file defines the `Lock` interface, while `ReentrantLock.java` is a class that implements the `Lock` interface. Here, a *reentrant lock* is a lock that can be repeatedly entered by the current thread that holds the lock. The `Lock` interface defines such methods as `lock()`, `lockInterruptibly()`, `newCondition()`, `tryLock()`, `tryLock(long, TimeUnit)`, `unlock()`, where `TimeUnit` is an enumeration that is used to specify the granularity (or resolution) of timing. The class implements these methods and adds some additional methods, as will be discussed later.

- **ReadWriteLock/ReentrantReadWriteLock**: The `ReadWriteLock.java` file defines the `ReadWriteLock` interface, while `ReentrantReadWriteLock.java` defines a class that implements the `ReadWriteLock` interface. A `ReadWriteLock` maintains a pair of associated locks, one for read-only operations and one for writing. The read lock may be held simultaneously by multiple reader threads, so long as there are no writers. The write lock is exclusive. The `ReentrantReadWriteLock` implements the `ReadWriteLock` interface, similar to `ReentrantLock` implementing the `Lock` interface. However, the `ReadWriteLock` interface has only two methods: The `readLock ()` method and `writeLock()` method, both of which having `Lock` return type.

- **Condition/AbstractOwnableSynchronizer(AOS)/AbstractQueuedSynchronizer(AQS)/ AbstractQueuedLongSynchronizer (AQLS)**: Here, `Condition` is an interface, which factors out the `Object` monitor methods (`await`, `awaitUninterruptibly`, `awaitUntil`, `signal` and `signalAll`) into distinct objects to give the effect of having multiple wait-sets per object, by combining them with the use of arbitrary `Lock` implementations. (While a `Lock` replaces the use of synchronized methods and statements, a `Condition` replaces the use of the `Object` monitor methods.) The `AbstractOwnableSynchronizer` (AOS) is an abstract class that defines synchronizers that may be exclusively owned by a thread. The `AbstractQueuedSynchronizer` provides a framework for implementing blocking locks and related synchronizers (semaphores, events, etc.) that rely on first-in-first-out (FIFO) wait queues, while the `AbstractQueuedLongSynchronizer` is a version of `AbstractQueuedSynchronizer` in which synchronization state is maintained as a `long`. Both of `AbstractQueuedSynchronizer` and `AbstractQueuedLongSynchronizer` have an internal class named `ConditionObject`, which implements the `Condition` interface.

The next few sections examine the above Java locking constructs in detail. Let's start with examining the Java `Lock` interface and its implementation classes first in the next section.

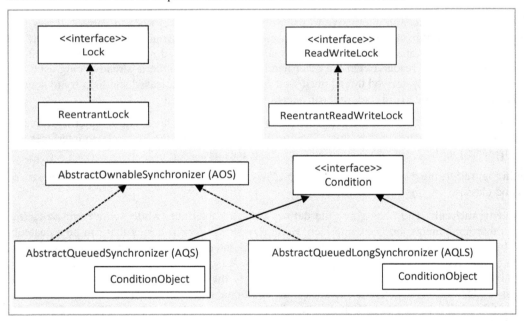

Figure 5.1 Interfaces and classes contained in the `java.util.concurrent.locks` package

5.1 THE JAVA LOCKS

This section examines what methods the Lock interface defines, how they are implemented by the `ReentrantLock` class, and how reentrant locks can be used to control access to shared resources. We start with the `Lock` interface next.

5.1.1 The Lock Interface

As mentioned several times previously, Java locks defined by the Lock interface are explicit locks, in contrast to the implicit locks associated with the synchronized methods or blocks as introduced in Chapter 1. For a synchronized method or statement, the nature of implicitness comes with its presence form as a keyword; so if we want to go from *implicit* to *explicit*, conceptually, we must transit from *keyword* to *class*, which is why we ended up with having a Lock interface and its implementation classes. As soon as we have a class, then we can get as much explicit as we wish, as we can define whatever operations we wish by adding methods.

On the other hand, to some extent, *explicitness* implies *flexibility*. Next, let us look at what kind of flexibilities in terms of locking support we get from the Lock interface, as shown in Listing 5.1, by examining its methods as follows:

- **lock**(): Acquires the lock. If the lock is unavailable, then the current thread is suspended, namely, it becomes disabled for thread scheduling purposes and lies dormant until the lock has been acquired.
- **lockInterruptibly**() throws InterruptedException (*interruptibility*): Acquires the lock if it is available and returns immediately unless the current thread is interrupted. If the lock is unavailable, then the current thread becomes disabled for thread scheduling purposes and lies dormant until one of the two conditions happens:

  ○ The lock is acquired by the current thread;
  ○ Some other thread interrupts the current thread, and interruption of lock acquisition is supported. In this case, an InterruptedException is thrown and the current thread's interrupted status is cleared.

- **tryLock**() (*non-blocking*): Acquires the lock if it is available and returns true immediately. If the lock is not available, then this method will return false immediately. This usage ensures that the lock is unlocked if it was acquired, and doesn't try to unlock if the lock was not acquired, with the following design pattern:

  ```
  Lock lock = ...;
  if (lock.tryLock()) {
    try {
      // access shared resource
    } finally {
      lock.unlock();
    }
  } else {
    // perform alternative actions
  }
  ```

- boolean **tryLock**(long time, TimeUnit unit) throws InterruptedException (*timeout support*): It behaves similarly to the previous no-arg version of tryLock() except that it will wait until it times out, in which case, the value false is returned. If the time is less than or equal to zero, the method will not wait at all.
- **unlock**(): Releases the lock.

- Condition **newCondition**(): Returns a new Condition instance that is bound to this Lock instance. Before waiting on the condition, the lock must be held by the current thread. A call to Condition.await() will atomically release the lock before waiting and re-acquiring the lock before the wait returns.

Therefore, we see that in addition to the basic lock() and unlock () methods, explicit locks as such support interruptibility, non-blocking and timing-out with the three respective methods as stated above. In addition, a Lock class can also provide behavior and semantics, which are quite different from those of the implicit monitor lock, such as guaranteed ordering, non-reentrant usage, and deadlock detection, etc.

Note: **Implicit monitor locks versus explicit locks**. The use of synchronized methods or blocks provides access to the implicit monitor lock associated with every object, but forces all lock acquisition and release to occur in a block-structured way: When multiple locks are acquired, they must be released in the opposite order, and all locks must be released in the same lexical scope in which they were acquired. This should be considered an advantage to some extent. The scoping mechanism for synchronized methods and blocks makes it much easier to program with monitor locks, and helps avoid many common programming errors involving locks. It is recommended to consider using explicit locks in a more flexible way under certain circumstances, though. For example, some algorithms for traversing concurrently accessed data structures require the use of "hand-over-hand" or "chain locking": you acquire the lock of node A, then node B, then release A and acquire C, then release B and acquire D and so on. Implementations of the Lock interface enable the use of such techniques by allowing a lock to be acquired and released in different scopes and in any order.

Next, we discuss how the ReentrantLock class implements the Lock interface.

Listing 5.1 Lock.java

```
1   package java.util.concurrent.locks;
2   import java.util.concurrent.TimeUnit;
3
4   public interface Lock {
5       void lock();
6       void lockInterruptibly() throws InterruptedException;
7       boolean tryLock();
8       boolean tryLock(long time, TimeUnit unit) throws InterruptedException;
9       void unlock();
10      Condition newCondition();
11  }
```

5.1.2 The ReentrantLock Class

Listing 5.2 shows partially how the ReentrantLock class is implemented in Java. Here are some of the implementation specifics:

- The Sync class (lines 6 – 40): This private Sync class serves as the base of synchronization control for this lock. (Note that line 5 declares an instance of this Sync class, which serves as the synchronizer for providing all implementation mechanics.) Line 7 defines an abstract lock() method, which will be implemented by its sub-classes of FairSync and NonfairSync. Its two main methods, nonFiarTryAcquire and tryRelease are defined from lines 8 – 25 and 27 – 38, respectively. These two methods are briefly reviewed as follows:

    ○ **nonfairTryAcquire**(int acquires): Perhaps this is the most interesting method that reveals how locks are acquired with ReentrantLocks. First, the parameter acquires (line 8) represent the # of locks being requested.   Secondly, the getState() method at line 10 (from the AbstractQueuedSynchronizer class) returns the *synchronization state*, which essentially is the lock count. (In other words, the ReentrantLock uses AQS state to represent the number of holds on the lock.) Now, it becomes clear that the condition check of if (c == 0) at line 11 is for checking whether the lock is free or not. If it holds true, it means that the lock is free, and the statements in the block are executed – within another if-block: if persisting the synchronization state to memory is successful, it sets the current thread to be the exclusive owner of the lock and returns true, indicating that the nonfairTryAcquire operation is successful. Otherwise, it goes to the next if-block at line 17, checking if the current thread is the exclusive owner. If it is, it adds the requested number of locks to the AQS's state variable and returns true. If not, it returns false, indicating no lock acquired. In summary, the nonfairTryAcquire works like this: if the lock is free, the current requesting thread gets it and becomes the exclusive owner of the lock; if the lock is not free, only the exclusive owner thread can have more, or in other words, is allowed to re-enter.

    ○ **tryRelease**(int releases) (lines 27 – 38): This method is also quite readable. Line 28 subtracts the releases number of locks to be released from the current number of locks, as getState() returns the number of locks currently being held. The next if-block (lines 29 – 30) essentially says that the non-exclusive-owner thread cannot release the lock. The next if-block (lines 32 – 35) says that if the lock count has reached zero, unset the exclusive owner so that the lock would become truly *free*. That's how this tryRelease method works. Next, we discuss the two sub-classes of the Sync class: NonfairSync and FairSync.

- **NonfairSync** (lines 41 – 52): This class implements the following two methods as explained below:

    ○ lock(): First, it assumes that the lock is free and attempts to set the # of lock to 1. If successful, it sets the current thread to be the exclusive owner and exits. Otherwise, it attempts the AQS's acquire(1) method, which is an operation that acquires in exclusive mode, ignoring interrupts. This acquire(1) method is implemented by invoking at least once tryAcquire, returning on success. Otherwise, the thread is queued, possibly repeatedly blocking and unblocking, invoking tryAcquire until success. This method can be used to implement the method Lock.lock(), as we see here.

    ○ tryAcquire(int acquires): This is simply a wrapper of the nonfairAcquire method from the Sync class that we already discussed as above.

- **FairSync** (lines 54 – 78): This class implements the following two methods as explained below:

- ° lock(): It attempts the AQS's acquire(1) method directly, which is an operation that acquires in exclusive mode, ignoring interrupts, as discussed above.
- ° tryAcquire(int acquires): For this FairSync tryAcquire method, line 63 reveals the secret: it checks if there are queued predecessors, rather than grabbing it without performing such checks, which is non-fair. The rest of it is obvious so we would not spend more time to explain.

The next segment (lines 80 – 85) in Listing 5.2 shows the two constructors of the ReentrantLock: The first no-arg constructor returns NonfairSync by default, and the second constructor allows a parameter to be specified for either NonfairSync or FairSync.

The other methods displayed from lines 87 - 113 are simply wrappers of the sync object's counterparts. The methods displayed from lines 116 – 146 are queue-related, for example, checking the waiting queue length, getting the waiters, and so on. Such methods are obvious and we would not explain further.

Next, we show a program to demonstrate how ReentrantLock can be used for some typical locking operations, following Listing 5.2.

Listing 5.2 ReentrantLock.java (partial)

```
1    package java.util.concurrent.locks;
2    import java.util.*;
3
4    public class ReentrantLock implements Lock, java.io.Serializable {
5        private final Sync sync;
6        abstract static class Sync extends AbstractQueuedSynchronizer {
7            abstract void lock();
8            final boolean nonfairTryAcquire(int acquires) {
9                final Thread current = Thread.currentThread();
10               int c = getState();
11               if (c == 0) {
12                   if (compareAndSetState(0, acquires)) {
13                       setExclusiveOwnerThread(current);
14                       return true;
15                   }
16               }
17               else if (current == getExclusiveOwnerThread()) {
18                   int nextc = c + acquires;
19                   if (nextc < 0) // overflow
20                       throw new Error("Maximum lock count exceeded");
21                   setState(nextc);
22                   return true;
23               }
24               return false;
25           }
26
27           protected final boolean tryRelease(int releases) {
28               int c = getState() - releases;
29               if (Thread.currentThread() != getExclusiveOwnerThread())
30                   throw new IllegalMonitorStateException();
31               boolean free = false;
```

```
32              if (c == 0) {
33                  free = true;
34                  setExclusiveOwnerThread(null);
35              }
36              setState(c);
37              return free;
38          }
39          // other methods omitted
40  }
41      static final class NonfairSync extends Sync {
42          final void lock() {
43              if (compareAndSetState(0, 1))
44                  setExclusiveOwnerThread(Thread.currentThread());
45              else
46                  acquire(1);
47          }
48
49          protected final boolean tryAcquire(int acquires) {
50              return nonfairTryAcquire(acquires);
51          }
52      }
53
54      static final class FairSync extends Sync {
55
56          final void lock() {
57              acquire(1);
58          }
59          protected final boolean tryAcquire(int acquires) {
60              final Thread current = Thread.currentThread();
61              int c = getState();
62              if (c == 0) {
63                  if (!hasQueuedPredecessors() &&
64                      compareAndSetState(0, acquires)) {
65                      setExclusiveOwnerThread(current);
66                      return true;
67                  }
68              }
69              else if (current == getExclusiveOwnerThread()) {
70                  int nextc = c + acquires;
71                  if (nextc < 0)
72                      throw new Error("Maximum lock count exceeded");
73                  setState(nextc);
74                  return true;
75              }
76              return false;
77          }
78      }
79
80      public ReentrantLock() {
81          sync = new NonfairSync();
82      }
83      public ReentrantLock(boolean fair) {
```

```
84              sync = fair ? new FairSync() : new NonfairSync();
85        }
86
87        public void lock() {
88              sync.lock();
89        }
90
91        public void lockInterruptibly() throws InterruptedException {
92              sync.acquireInterruptibly(1);
93        }
94
95        public boolean tryLock() {
96              return sync.nonfairTryAcquire(1);
97        }
98
99        public boolean tryLock(long timeout, TimeUnit unit)
100                 throws InterruptedException {
101             return sync.tryAcquireNanos(1, unit.toNanos(timeout));
102        }
103
104        public void unlock() {
105             sync.release(1);
106        }
107
108        public Condition newCondition() {
109             return sync.newCondition();
110        }
111
112        public final boolean isFair() {
113             return sync instanceof FairSync;
114        }
115
116        public final boolean hasQueuedThreads() {
117             return sync.hasQueuedThreads();
118        }
119
120        public final boolean hasQueuedThread(Thread thread) {
121             return sync.isQueued(thread);
122        }
123
124        public final int getQueueLength() {
125             return sync.getQueueLength();
126        }
127
128        protected Collection<Thread> getQueuedThreads() {
129             return sync.getQueuedThreads();
130        }
131
132        public boolean hasWaiters(Condition condition) {
133             if (condition == null)
134                 throw new NullPointerException();
135             if (!(condition instanceof
```

```
            AbstractQueuedSynchronizer.ConditionObject))
136             throw new IllegalArgumentException("not owner");
137         return
      sync.hasWaiters((AbstractQueuedSynchronizer.ConditionObject)condition);
138     }
139
140     protected Collection<Thread> getWaitingThreads(Condition condition) {
141         if (condition == null)
142             throw new NullPointerException();
143         if (!(condition instanceof AbstractQueuedSynchronizer.
                ConditionObject))
144             throw new IllegalArgumentException("not owner");
145         return sync.getWaitingThreads((AbstractQueuedSynchronizer.
                ConditionObject)condition);
146     }
147 }
```

5.1.3 An Example

Listing 5.3 shows the ReentrantLockDemo.java program. It is composed as follows:

- **The shared resource class**: The Permit class at the end of Listing 5.3 represents the shared resource of a static integer variable named permits, which will be incremented/decremented by multiple threads. Since this resource is not protected at all, each thread will be responsible for acquiring and releasing locks when accessing this resource.
- **The Thread class**: The Drawer class displayed in the middle of Listing 5.3 represents the thread class. In contrast to the AtomicIntegerDemo program shown in Listing 4.2, a reentrant lock, rather than the shared resource object, is passed to the thread. The increment and decrement operations on the shared resource, Permit.permits in this case, is surrounded with the following pattern as described previously:

```
try {
    lock.lock();
    // access the resource
} finally {
    lock.unlock();
}
```

- **The test driver**: The ReentrantLockDemo class serves as the test driver for this example. It is not different from the test driver we used for the previous AtomicIntegerDemo except we need to create a reentrant lock object and pass it to each thread object.

Executing this program would produce the following output, as expected:

Number of permits: 0

Next, we discuss the ReadWriteLock interface.

Listing 5.3 ReentrantLockDemo.java

```
1   package jcp.ch5.locks;
2
3   import java.util.concurrent.locks.*;
4   import java.util.concurrent.ExecutorService;
5   import java.util.concurrent.Executors;
6
7   public class ReentrantLockDemo {
8     public static void main(String[] args) throws InterruptedException {
9       ReentrantLock lock = new ReentrantLock();
10
11      // 1. Create a newFixedThreadPool using the Executors utility class
12      ExecutorService executorService = Executors.newFixedThreadPool(100);
13
14      // 2. launch 100 drawers
15      for (int i = 0; i < 100; i++) {
16        executorService.execute(new Drawer(i, lock));
17      }
18
19      // 3. wait 5000 ms for all drawers to complete
20      Thread.sleep(5000);
21      System.out.println("Number of permits: " + Permit.permits);
22
23      // 4. shut down executorService to avoid resource leak
24      executorService.shutdown();
25    }
26  }
27
28  // Thread class: a drawer increments/decrements permits if id is even/odd.
29  class Drawer extends Thread {
30    int id;
31    ReentrantLock lock;
32
33    Drawer(int id, ReentrantLock lock) {
34      this.id = id;
35      this.lock = lock;
36    }
37
38    public void run() {
39      for (int i = 0; i < 10000; i++) {
40        if ((this.id % 2) == 0) {
41          try {
42            lock.lock();
43            Permit.permits++;
44          } finally {
45            lock.unlock();
46          }
47        } else {
48          try {
49            lock.lock();
50            Permit.permits--;
51          } finally {
52            lock.unlock();
```

```
53              }
54          }
55       }
56     }
57  }
58
59  // Shared resource: number of permits
60  class Permit {
61      static int permits = 0;
62  }
```

5.2   THE JAVA READWRITELOCKS

The ReentrantLocks discussed previously do not make a distinction between read and write operations. Database-centric applications have many read/write operations, which exhibit different characteristics. For example, it's perfectly fine for multiple threads to perform read operations on an unprotected shared resource, as long as no writers attempt to write or modify the resource. However, it may not be a good idea to allow readers performing read options while a writer is modifying the state of the unprotected shared resource. To deal with such delicate issues, Java provides us with a ReadWriteLock interface and a ReentrantReadWriteLock class that implements the ReadWriteLock interface.

This section discusses the ReadWriteLock interface and the ReentrantReadWriteLock implementation class. Let's start with the ReadWriteLock interface first next.

5.2.1 The ReadWriteLock Interface

Listing 5.4 shows the ReadWriteLock interface. As you see, it's incredibly simple that it has only two methods, as explained below:

- Lock **readLock**(): Returns the lock used for reading
- Lock **writeLock**(): Returns the lock used for writing

As is seen from the above listing, a ReadWriteLock maintains a pair of associated locks, one for read operations and one for writing. Once again, the read lock may be held simultaneously by multiple reader threads, so long as there are no writers, while the write lock is exclusive, as we explained previously.

Next, let's examine how the ReentrantReadWriteLock class implements the ReadWriteLock interface.

Listing 5.4 ReadWriteLock.java

```
1   package java.util.concurrent.locks;
2
3   public interface ReadWriteLock {
4       Lock readLock();
5       Lock writeLock();
6   }
```

5.2.2 The ReentrantReadWriteLock Class

Listing 5.5 shows how the ReentrantReadWriteLock class is implemented. Next, let's anatomize this ReentrantReadWriteLock class a bit as follows:

- First, note the inner classes of ReadLock and WriteLock, as indicated from lines 8 – 9, for creating read and write locks. Also, note the two constructors: one no-arg (lines 12 -14) and the other with a fair Boolean parameter for specifying fairness, similar to the constructors we discussed previously for the ReentrantLock class, with the only difference that the readLock and writeLock are created separately, as indicated at lines 18 and 19, respectively.

- Next, starting from line 22, a Sync class is defined, which is similar to the Sync class for the ReentrantLock class, except that a sharedCount field and an exclusiveCount field are declared at lines 27 and 28, respectively. This is a natural outcome of separating readers from writers. Also, note the abstract methods of readerShouldBlock() and writerShouldBlock() displayed at lines 30 and 31, respectively. The following four additional methods are included to help understand how read/write lock acquire/release operations are coded:

  ○ tryRelease(int releases): Lines 32 - 41 show how this operation is coded. This operation can be performed only if the calling thread holds the lock exclusively, as indicated by the if-block from lines 33 – 34.

  ○ tryAcquire(int acquires): Lines 43 – 62 show how this operation is coded. Note that c at line 45 represents the total number of locks, while w at line 46 represents the number of write locks. It works like this: (1) If reader count is nonzero or writer count is nonzero and owner is a different thread, fail; (2) If total count would saturate, fail; (3) Otherwise, this thread is eligible for lock if it is either a reentrant acquire or policy allows it. If so, update state and set owner.

  ○ tryWriteLock(): Lines 64 – 78 show how this operation is operated. To trace how this operation works, you only need to keep in mind that 'c' represents the total number of threads, 'w' represents the number of writer threads, "return true" means "succeeded" and "return false" means "failed." I leave tracing it to you, given so much we have covered so far.

  ○ tryReadLock(): Lines 80 – 107 show how this operation is operated. A few specifics include: (1) lines 84 – 85 mean that if there is another writer holding the lock, fail; (2) If readers have maxed out, fail; (3) Otherwise, update the firstReaderHoldCount and holdCount in the cache and grant the lock.

The remaining segments are about the NonfairSync, FairSync, ReadLock, and WriteLock, which are trivial as they are essentially wrappers.

Next, we present an example to help illustrate how the ReentrantReadWriteLock can be used, following Listing 5.5.

Listing 5.5 ReentrantReadWriteLock.java (partial)

```
1    package java.util.concurrent.locks;
2    import java.util.concurrent.*;
3    import java.util.concurrent.atomic.*;
4    import java.util.*;
5
6    public class ReentrantReadWriteLock
7            implements ReadWriteLock, java.io.Serializable {
```

```
8      private final ReentrantReadWriteLock.ReadLock readerLock;
9      private final ReentrantReadWriteLock.WriteLock writerLock;
10     final Sync sync;
11
12     public ReentrantReadWriteLock() {
13         this(false);
14     }
15
16     public ReentrantReadWriteLock(boolean fair) {
17         sync = fair ? new FairSync() : new NonfairSync();
18         readerLock = new ReadLock(this);
19         writerLock = new WriteLock(this);
20     }
21
22     abstract static class Sync extends AbstractQueuedSynchronizer {
23         static final int SHARED_SHIFT   = 16;
24         static final int SHARED_UNIT    = (1 << SHARED_SHIFT);
25         static final int MAX_COUNT      = (1 << SHARED_SHIFT) - 1;
26         static final int EXCLUSIVE_MASK = (1 << SHARED_SHIFT) - 1;
27         static int sharedCount(int c)    { return c >>> SHARED_SHIFT; }
28         static int exclusiveCount(int c) { return c & EXCLUSIVE_MASK; }
29
30         abstract boolean readerShouldBlock();
31         abstract boolean writerShouldBlock();
32
33         protected final boolean tryRelease(int releases) {
34             if (!isHeldExclusively())
35                 throw new IllegalMonitorStateException();
36             int nextc = getState() - releases;
37             boolean free = exclusiveCount(nextc) == 0;
38             if (free)
39                 setExclusiveOwnerThread(null);
40             setState(nextc);
41             return free;
42         }
43
44         protected final boolean tryAcquire(int acquires) {
45             Thread current = Thread.currentThread();
46             int c = getState();
47             int w = exclusiveCount(c);
48             if (c != 0) {
49                 // (Note: if c != 0 and w == 0 then shared count != 0)
50                 if (w == 0 || current != getExclusiveOwnerThread())
51                     return false;
52                 if (w + exclusiveCount(acquires) > MAX_COUNT)
53                     throw new Error("Maximum lock count exceeded");
54                 // Reentrant acquire
55                 setState(c + acquires);
56                 return true;
57             }
58             if (writerShouldBlock() ||
59                 !compareAndSetState(c, c + acquires))
```

```
59              return false;
60          setExclusiveOwnerThread(current);
61          return true;
62      }
63
64      final boolean tryWriteLock() {
65          Thread current = Thread.currentThread();
66          int c = getState();
67          if (c != 0) {
68              int w = exclusiveCount(c);
69              if (w == 0 || current != getExclusiveOwnerThread())
70                  return false;
71              if (w == MAX_COUNT)
72                  throw new Error("Maximum lock count exceeded");
73          }
74          if (!compareAndSetState(c, c + 1))
75              return false;
76          setExclusiveOwnerThread(current);
77          return true;
78      }
79
80      final boolean tryReadLock() {
81          Thread current = Thread.currentThread();
82          for (;;) {
83              int c = getState();
84              if (exclusiveCount(c) != 0 &&
85                  getExclusiveOwnerThread() != current)
86                  return false;
87              int r = sharedCount(c);
88              if (r == MAX_COUNT)
89                  throw new Error("Maximum lock count exceeded");
90              if (compareAndSetState(c, c + SHARED_UNIT)) {
91                  if (r == 0) {
92                      firstReader = current;
93                      firstReaderHoldCount = 1;
94                  } else if (firstReader == current) {
95                      firstReaderHoldCount++;
96                  } else {
97                      HoldCounter rh = cachedHoldCounter;
98                      if (rh == null || rh.tid != current.getId())
99                          cachedHoldCounter = rh = readHolds.get();
100                     else if (rh.count == 0)
101                         readHolds.set(rh);
102                     rh.count++;
103                 }
104                 return true;
105             }
106         }
107     }
108
109 static final class NonfairSync extends Sync {
110     final boolean writerShouldBlock() {
```

```
111                     return false; // writers can always barge
112             }
113             final boolean readerShouldBlock() {
114                     return apparentlyFirstQueuedIsExclusive();
115             }
116     }
117
118     static final class FairSync extends Sync {
119             final boolean writerShouldBlock() {
120                     return hasQueuedPredecessors();
121             }
122             final boolean readerShouldBlock() {
123                     return hasQueuedPredecessors();
124             }
125     }
126
127     public static class ReadLock implements Lock, java.io.Serializable {
128             private final Sync sync;
129             protected ReadLock(ReentrantReadWriteLock lock) {
130                     sync = lock.sync;
131             }
132
133             public void lock() {
134                     sync.acquireShared(1);
135             }
136
137             public void lockInterruptibly() throws InterruptedException {
138                     sync.acquireSharedInterruptibly(1);
139             }
140
141             public  boolean tryLock() {
142                     return sync.tryReadLock();
143             }
144     }
145
146     public static class WriteLock implements Lock, java.io.Serializable {
147             private final Sync sync;
148             protected WriteLock(ReentrantReadWriteLock lock) {
149                     sync = lock.sync;
150             }
151             public void lock() {
152                     sync.acquire(1);
153             }
154
155             public void lockInterruptibly() throws InterruptedException {
156                     sync.acquireInterruptibly(1);
157             }
158     }
159     // other methods omitted
160 }
```

5.2.3 An Example

Listing 5.6 shows the ReentrantReadWriteLockDemo.java program. To avoid naming collision, the Permit class is renamed to Resource, but the field of permits remains the same, as shown at the end of Listing 5.6. The Thread class is named Worker, which could be a reader or a writer, identifiable by the prefix of the name, as shown in lines 41 and 48, respectively. Lines 42 – 47 show the try-finally block for the reader, while lines 48 – 56 show the try-finally block for the writer. Line 43 shows how a reader acquires a readLock in the try-block by calling the ReentrantReadWriterLock's readLock().lock() method, while line 46 shows how the same readLock is released in the finally-block. Similarly, line 50 shows how a writer acquires a writeLock in the try-block by calling the ReentrantReadWriterLock's writeLock().lock() method, while line 55 shows how the same writeLock is released in the finally-block. The writer does not only modify the shared resource, as shown at line 52, but also reads the resource. The reader and writer use their respective locks similarly except that they use different locks.

The test driver program sets up a ReentrantReadWriteLock to start with, as shown at line 9. Next, it sets up a fixed thread pool using the ExecutorService, as shown in line 12. The for-loop shown from lines 15–19 launches 100 Worker threads, passing each thread a name and the ReentrantReadWriteLock, with each thread's name prefixed with "reader" or "writer" so that they can be identified easily in the run() method of the Worker thread class. I arbitrarily made every one out of ten workers a "writer" with all other nine being "readers," as shown at line 17. Similar to the previous examples, the main thread sleeps for 5000 milliseconds, waiting for all threads to complete, as shown at line 22. Line 23 prints out the final state of the resource to help verify the result. The thread pool is shutdown as shown at line 26 before the main thread exits.

Executing this program would produce the following output:

```
writer-0 writing 0
writer-0 written 1
reader-11 reading 1
reader-1 reading 1
reader-2 reading 1
reader-3 reading 1
reader-13 reading 1
reader-5 reading 1
reader-7 reading 1
reader-4 reading 1
reader-12 reading 1
reader-9 reading 1
reader-14 reading 1
reader-8 reading 1
reader-6 reading 1
writer-10 writing 1
writer-10 written 2
reader-18 reading 2
...
reader-89 reading 9
```

```
writer-90 writing 9
writer-90 written 10
reader-91 reading 10
reader-92 reading 10
reader-93 reading 10
reader-94 reading 10
reader-95 reading 10
reader-96 reading 10
reader-97 reading 10
reader-98 reading 10
reader-99 reading 10
Number of permits: 10
```

As you see, the readers and writers alternate, as expected. Since there are ten writers and each writer increments the permits once, the final number of permits would be 10, as shown at the last line of the above output.

Next, we discuss the Condition class.

Listing 5.6 ReentrantReadWriteLockDemo.java

```
1    package jcp.ch5.locks;
2
3    import java.util.concurrent.locks.*;
4    import java.util.concurrent.ExecutorService;
5    import java.util.concurrent.Executors;
6
7    public class ReentrantReadWriterLockDemo {
8      public static void main(String[] args) throws InterruptedException {
9        ReentrantReadWriteLock rwLock = new ReentrantReadWriteLock();
10
11        // 1. Create a newFixedThreadPool using the Executors utility class
12        ExecutorService executorService = Executors.newFixedThreadPool(100);
13
14        // 2. launch 100 workers
15        for (int i = 0; i < 100; i++) {
16          String name = "reader-" + i;
17          if ((i % 10 == 0)) name = "writer-" + i;
18          executorService.execute(new Worker(name, rwLock));
19        }
20
21        // 3. wait 5000 ms for all drawers to complete
22        Thread.sleep(5000);
23        System.out.println("Number of permits: " + Resource.permits);
24
25        // 4. shut down executorService to avoid resource leak
26        executorService.shutdown();
27      }
28    }
29
```

```
30  // Thread class: a worker reads/writes permits based on name prefix
31  class Worker extends Thread {
32      String id;
33      ReentrantReadWriteLock rwLock;
34
35      Worker(String id, ReentrantReadWriteLock rwLock) {
36          this.id = id;
37          this.rwLock = rwLock;
38      }
39
40      public void run() {
41          if (id.contains ("reader")) {
42              try {
43                  rwLock.readLock().lock();
44                  System.out.println (id + " reading " + Resource.permits);
45              } finally {
46                  rwLock.readLock().unlock();
47              }
48          } else if (id.contains ("writer")){
49              try {
50                  rwLock.writeLock().lock();
51                  System.out.println (id + " writing " + Resource.permits);
52                  Resource.permits++;
53              } finally {
54                  System.out.println (id + " written " + Resource.permits);
55                  rwLock.writeLock().unlock();
56              }
57          } else {
58
59          }
60      }
61  }
62
63  // Shared resource: number of permits
64  class Resource {
65      static int permits = 0;
66  }
```

5.3 THE CONDITION INTERFACE

First, Condition is an interface, with five await methods and two signal methods, as shown in Listing 5.7. For all those five await methods, four of them throw InterruptedException except one of them – awaitUninterruptibly(), which is uninterruptible by design. It is implemented by two classes as an inner class of ConditionObject: AbstractQueuedLongSynchronizer.ConditionObject and AbstractQueuedSynchronizer.ConditionObject, which will be covered in the next section.

The methods of the Condition interface as shown in Listing 5.7 are defined as follows:

- **await()**: Causes the current thread to wait until it is signaled or interrupted. The lock associated with this Condition is atomically released and the current thread becomes suspended until one of the following four events happens:
  - ° Some other thread invokes the signal() method for this Condition and the current thread *happens* to be chosen as the thread to be awakened
  - ° Some other thread invokes the signalAll() method for this Condition
  - ° Some other thread interrupts the current thread
  - ° A "spurious wakeup" occurs

  In all the above cases, before this method can return, the current thread must re-acquire the lock associated with this condition. When the thread returns, it is guaranteed to hold this lock.
- **awaitUninterruptibly()**: Similar to the await() method except it is uninterruptible.
- **awaitNanos(long nanosTimeout)**: Similar to the await() method, except that it has one more wakeup condition of timeout with the specified timeout period. The method returns an estimate of the number of nanoseconds remaining to wait given the supplied nanosTimeout value upon return, or a value ≤ 0 if it timed out. The returned value can be used to determine whether and how long to wait again in cases where the wait returns but an awaited condition has not been met.
- **await(long time, TimeUnit unit)**: Similar to the awaitNanos method except that it specifies the maximum time to wait, and it allows a time unit to be specified. In addition, it returns false if the waiting time expired before returning from the method or true if the waiting time did not expire.
- **awaitUntil(Date deadline)**: Similar to all above await methods except that an absolute deadline, rather than a relative timeout period, is specified.
- **signal()**: Wakes up one waiting thread only. That thread must then re-acquire the lock before returning from await.
- **signalAll()**: Wakes up all waiting thread. All woken-up threads must re-acquire the lock before they can return from await.

Listing 5.7 Condition.java

```
1   package java.util.concurrent.locks;
2   import java.util.concurrent.*;
3   import java.util.Date;
4
5   public interface Condition {
6     void await() throws InterruptedException;
7     void awaitUninterruptibly();
8     long awaitNanos(long nanosTimeout) throws InterruptedException;
9     boolean await(long time, TimeUnit unit) throws InterruptedException;
10    boolean awaitUntil(Date deadline) throws InterruptedException;
11    void signal();
12    void signalAll();
13  }
```

It is important to realize that a Condition replaces the use of the Object monitor methods, such as wait, notify and notifyAll, with the methods as discussed above, just as Locks replace the use of synchronized methods and statements. Conditions are also known as *condition queues* or *condition variables* in various literatures. They provide a means for one thread to suspend execution (to "wait") until signaled by another thread that some state condition may have been met. Because the shared state information is accessed by different threads, it must be protected by a lock of some form; thus, a Condition cannot exist alone and it must be associated with a lock. Just like Object.wait, condition wait atomically releases the associated lock and suspends the current thread.

In practical use, a Condition instance is intrinsically bound to a lock. To obtain a Condition instance for a particular Lock instance, use its newCondition() method. For example, Listing 5.8 shows how a bounded buffer can be implemented with two Condition variables as listed at lines 7 and 8, respectively: one named notFull, representing the *not full* event to wait for, the other named notEmpty, representing the *not empty* event to wait for. Note that line 6 defines a ReentrantLock, which fulfills three tasks: (1) providing the lock() method; (2) providing the unlock() method; and (3) providing the newCondition() method to return a Condition object. Listing 5.8 shows how those two Condition objects are used with the lock() and unlock() methods to implement the put and take methods, as described below:

- In the put method, when the buffer is full (line 16), the notFull condition object's await() method is called to wait for the *not full* event to occur (line 17). When the not full event occurs, new items can be put into the buffer. Eventually (line 23), the notEmpty condition object is signaled in case the producer has been waiting for the buffer to become non-empty.
- In the take method, the opposite occurs. When the buffer becomes empty (line 32), the notEmpty condition object's await() method is called (line 33) to wait for the *not empty* event to occur. When the not empty event occurs, an item can be taken (line 34), after which, the notFull condition object's signal method is called (line 39) in case the consumer is waiting for the buffer to become non-full.

Next, following Listing 5.8, we construct a program to demonstrate the use of the BoundedBuffer class as discussed here.

Listing 5.8 BoundedBuffer.java

```
1    package jcp.ch5.locks;
2
3    import java.util.concurrent.locks.*;
4
5    public class BoundedBuffer {
6      final Lock lock = new ReentrantLock();
7      final Condition notFull = lock.newCondition();
8      final Condition notEmpty = lock.newCondition();
9
10     final Object[] items = new Object[100];
11     int putIndex, takeIndex, count;
12
13     public void put(Object x) throws InterruptedException {
14       lock.lock();
15       try {
16         while (count == items.length)
17           notFull.await();
```

```
18          items[putIndex] = x;
19          //System.out.println ("put " + x + " at " + putIndex);
20          if (++putIndex == items.length)
21             putIndex = 0;
22          ++count;
23          notEmpty.signal();
24       } finally {
25          lock.unlock();
26       }
27    }
28
29    public Object take() throws InterruptedException {
30       lock.lock();
31       try {
32          while (count == 0)
33             notEmpty.await();
34          Object x = items[takeIndex];
35          //System.out.println ("take " + x + " at " + takeIndex);
36          if (++takeIndex == items.length)
37             takeIndex = 0;
38          --count;
39          notFull.signal();
40          return x;
41       } finally {
42          lock.unlock();
43       }
44    }
45 }
```

Listing 5.9 shows the ConditionDemo.java program, which includes the Consumer and Producer classes as well. (Since they are in the same file as the ConditionDemo class, the Consumer and Producer classes cannot be public.) The ConditionDemo class creates a BoundedBuffer object and passes it to the Producer and Consumer objects created by calling their constructors. These two objects perform the put and take operations in their run methods, respectively. Of course, the Consumer and Producer classes are not aware of the condition objects used in the BoundedBuffer class.

Executing the ConditionDemo program on my Eclipse IDE yielded the following results:

```
......
producer put 36414
producer put 36415
producer put 36416
producer put 36417
producer put 36418
producer put 36419
......
consumer got 36412
consumer got 36413
consumer got 36414
consumer got 36415
consumer got 36416
```

consumer got 36417
consumer got 36418
consumer got 36419
......

However, since the `ArrayBlockingQueue` class provides the functionality of a bounded buffer, there is no need to implement a version of a bounded buffer as shown in Listing 5.8.

Next, we discuss the abstract queued synchronizers.

Listing 5.9 ConditionDemo.java

```
1   package jcp.ch5.locks;
2
3   import jcp.ch5.locks.BoundedBuffer;
4
5   public class ConditionDemo {
6     public static void main(String args[]) {
7
8       BoundedBuffer boundedBuffer = new BoundedBuffer ();
9       new Producer(boundedBuffer);
10      new Consumer(boundedBuffer);
11    }
12  }
13
14  class Consumer implements Runnable {
15    private BoundedBuffer boundedBuffer;
16
17    Consumer(BoundedBuffer boundedBuffer) {
18      this.boundedBuffer = boundedBuffer;
19      new Thread(this, "Consumer").start();
20    }
21
22    public void run() {
23      while (true) {
24        try {
25          int number = (Integer) boundedBuffer.take();
26          System.out.println ("consumer got " + number);
27        } catch (InterruptedException ie) {
28          System.out.println ("consumer interrupted");
29        }
30      }
31    }
32  }
33
34  class Producer implements Runnable {
35    BoundedBuffer boundedBuffer;
36
37    Producer(BoundedBuffer boundedBuffer) {
38      this.boundedBuffer = boundedBuffer;
39      new Thread(this, "Producer").start();
```

```
40    }
41
42    public void run() {
43       int i = 0;
44
45       while (true) {
46          try {
47          boundedBuffer.put(i++);
48          System.out.println ("producer put " + i);
49          } catch (InterruptedException ie) {
50             System.out.println ("producer interrupted");
51          }
52       }
53    }
54 }
```

5.4 ABSTRACT QUEUED SYNCHRONIZERS

In addition to reentrant locks, the java.util.concurrent.locks package also contains three abstract queued synchronizer classes: AbstractOwnableSynchronizer, AbstractQueuedSynchronizer and AbstractQueuedLongSynchronizer. Since these classes are very important for implementing synchronizers (Semaphore, CountdownLatch, CyclicBarrier and Phaser, etc.), we cover them here.

Let's begin with the AbstractOwnableSynchronizer class first, which is extended by the AbstractQueuedSynchronizer and AbstractQueuedLongSynchronizer classes.

5.4.1 The AbstractOwnableSynchronizer

The AbstractOwnableSynchronizer class implements a synchronizer that may be exclusively *owned* by a thread. This class provides the basis for creating locks and related synchronizers that may entail a notion of ownership, thus the name *Ownable*.

Listing 5.10 shows the Java implementation of the AbstractOwnableSynchronizer class. As is seen, this very simple class declares an exclusiveOwnerThread field, an empty constructor, together with a set and a get method. Its set method sets the thread that currently owns exclusive access, while its get method returns the thread last set by setExclusiveOwnerThread, or null if never set.

Since the AbstractOwnableSynchronizer class is very simple and needs little explanation, we discuss the AbstractQueuedSynchronizer class next.

Listing 5.10 AbstractOwnableSynchronizer.java

```
1    package java.util.concurrent.locks;
2
3    public abstract class AbstractOwnableSynchronizer
4        implements java.io.Serializable {
5        protected AbstractOwnableSynchronizer() { }
6        private transient Thread exclusiveOwnerThread;
```

```
7     protected final void setExclusiveOwnerThread(Thread t) {
8         exclusiveOwnerThread = t;
9     }
10    protected final Thread getExclusiveOwnerThread() {
11        return exclusiveOwnerThread;
12    }
13 }
```

5.4.2 The AbstractQueuedSynchronizer

The AbstractQueuedSynchronizer class provides a framework for implementing blocking locks and related synchronizers (semaphores, events, etc.) that rely on: (1) first-in-first-out (FIFO) wait queues; and (2) a single atomic int value to represent state. However, its subclasses must define the protected methods that change the synchronization state. It has methods for carrying out all queuing and blocking mechanics.

Listing 5.11 shows (partially) the Java implementation of the AbstractQueuedSynchronizer class. It has two embedded classes: Node (static) and ConditionObject (public). Let's discuss the Node class first next, followed by a discussion on the ConditionObject class as well as some of the methods of the AbstractQueuedSynchronizer class.

The embedded Node class is designed for representing each wait queue node. It is implemented as follows (lines 12 – 49):

- *shared* mode versus *exclusive* mode: Each waiting thread queue node can be in either shared mode or exclusive mode (lines 13 – 14), with *exclusive* being the default mode. When a waiting thread is in exclusive mode, *acquire* attempts by other threads cannot succeed. However, shared mode *acquire* attempts by multiple threads may (but need not) succeed. Usually, implementation subclasses support only one of these modes, but both can come into play, for example, in a ReadWriteLock as discussed previously. Threads waiting in the different modes share the same FIFO queue.
- waitStatus field: This field (line 20) is maintained with the following semantics:
  - ○ CANCELLED: Indicates that the thread is in cancelled state due to timeout or interrupt. A thread with cancelled node never blocks again.
  - ○ SIGNAL: Indicates that the successor's thread needs unparking
  - ○ CONDITION: Indicates that the thread is currently on a condition queue
  - ○ PROPAGATE: Indicates that the next acquireShared should propagate to other nodes
- prev field: Links to the predecessor node that current node/thread relies on for checking waitStatus. Assigned during enqueuing.
- next field: Links to the successor node that the current node/thread unparks upon release. Assigned during enqueuing.
- thread field: The thread that enqueued this node. Initialized on construction and nulled out after use.
- nextWaiter: Links to the next node waiting on a condition queue. Because condition queues are accessed only when holding in exclusive mode, a simple linked queue is needed to hold nodes while they are waiting on conditions.

- `isShared()`: Returns true if the node is waiting in shared mode.
- `predecessor()` : Returns the previous node.
- `Node()`: The no-arg constructor
- `Node(Thread thread, Node mode)`: The constructor parameterized with `thread` and `mode`
- `Node(Thread thread, int waitStatus)`: The constructor parameterized with `thread` and `waitStatus`

Lines 51 – 92 show how the embedded `ConditionObject` class is implemented, as explained below:

- `firstWaiter`: First node of the condition queue (line 52)
- `lastWaiter`: Last node of the condition queue (line 53)
- `await()`: Implements interruptible condition wait (lines 55 – 73), with the following specifics:
  - Lines 56 – 57: If the current thread is interrupted, throw `InterruptedException`
  - Lines 58: Calls the `addConditionWaiter()` method to add the new waiter to the wait queue, and saves the returned node.
  - Line 59: Releases the node and saves the returned state.
  - Line 60: Sets the `interruptMode` to 0 (non-interrupted).
  - Lines 61 – 65: While the node is not on the synchronized queue: (1) Line 62 calls the `LockSupport`'s `park(Object)` method to place the current thread on the waiting queue; and (2) Lines 63 – 64: Break out if interrupted or signaled.
  - Lines 66 – 67: Call the `acquireQueued` method to re-acquire in exclusive uninterruptible mode for the thread already on the queue.
  - Lines 68 - 69: Unlink cancelled waiter nodes from the condition queue.
  - Lines 70–71: Call the `reportInterruptAfterWait` method, which may throw an `InterruptedException`, re-interrupt the current thread, or do nothing, depending on the setting of mode.
- `doSignal(Node first)`: Lines 75 – 82 show how the `doSignal` method is coded to wake up the first node on the condition queue. Note the call to the `transferForSignal` method, which transfers the node from the condition queue to the synchronized queue.
- `signal()`: Lines 84 – 90 show how the `signal` method is coded to move the longest-waiting thread, if one exists, from the queue for this condition to the wait queue for the lock.

Lines 94 – 231 show the fields of `head`, `tail`, and `state` as well as a selected list of methods for the `AbstractQueuedSynchronizer` class. These methods include:

- `enq(Node)`: Inserts the node into the synchronized queue, initializing if necessary, and returns the node's predecessor
- `addWaiter(Node)`: Creates and enqueues the node for the current thread and given mode.
- `parkAndCheckInturrupt()`: A convenience method to park and then check if interrupted. Returns `true` if interrupted.
- `unparkSuccessor()`: Wakes up the node's successor, if one exists.
- `acquireQueued(final Node node, int arg)`: Acquires in exclusive uninterruptible mode for the thread already on the queue. Returns `true` if interrupted while waiting.

- acquire(): Acquires in exclusive mode, ignoring interrupts. Invokes tryAcquire at least once, returning on success. Otherwise, the thread is queued, possibly repeatedly blocking and unblocking, invoking tryAcquire until success.
- release(): Releases in exclusive mode unblocking one or more threads if the call to tryRelease returns true.
- acquireShared(int): Acquires in shared mode, ignoring interrupts.
- hasContended(): Checks whether thread contention has occurred.
- getQueuedThreads(): Returns a collection containing threads that may be waiting to acquire.
- getExclusiveQueuedThreads(): Returns the first (longest-waiting) thread on the queue or null if no threads are currently queued.
- getSharedQueuedThreads(): Returns a collection containing threads that may be waiting in shared mode. This has the same properties as getQueuedThreads except that it only returns those threads waiting due to a shared acquire.

It's too tedious to enumerate how each of the above methods is coded, so I would leave it to you if you are interested in examining how each method is coded exactly. Given what you have learnt, this should not be a too hard task to achieve if you decide to go through the implementation of each of the above methods line by line, as we did with some of the methods of the Node and ConditionObject classes.

Next, we wrap up this chapter with a brief discussion on the AbstractQueuedLongSynchronizer class.

Listing 5.11 AbstractQueuedSynchronizer.java (partial)

```
1   package java.util.concurrent.locks;
2   import java.util.*;
3   import java.util.concurrent.*;
4   import java.util.concurrent.atomic.*;
5   import sun.misc.Unsafe;
6
7   public abstract class AbstractQueuedSynchronizer
8       extends AbstractOwnableSynchronizer
9       implements java.io.Serializable {
10      protected AbstractQueuedSynchronizer() { }
11
12      static final class Node {
13          static final Node SHARED = new Node();
14          static final Node EXCLUSIVE = null;
15
16          static final int CANCELLED =  1;
17          static final int SIGNAL    = -1;
18          static final int CONDITION = -2;
19          static final int PROPAGATE = -3;
20          volatile int waitStatus;
21
22          volatile Node prev;
23          volatile Node next;
24          volatile Thread thread;
25          Node nextWaiter;
26
```

```
27          final boolean isShared() {
28              return nextWaiter == SHARED;
29          }
30          final Node predecessor() throws NullPointerException {
31              Node p = prev;
32              if (p == null)
33                  throw new NullPointerException();
34              else
35                  return p;
36          }
37
38          Node() { // Used to establish initial head or SHARED marker}
39
40          Node(Thread thread, Node mode) {     // Used by addWaiter
41              this.nextWaiter = mode;
42              this.thread = thread;
43          }
44
45          Node(Thread thread, int waitStatus) { // Used by Condition
46              this.waitStatus = waitStatus;
47              this.thread = thread;
48          }
49      }
50
51      public class ConditionObject implements Condition,
            java.io.Serializable {
52          private transient Node firstWaiter;
53          private transient Node lastWaiter;
54
55          public final void await() throws InterruptedException {
56              if (Thread.interrupted())
57                  throw new InterruptedException();
58              Node node = addConditionWaiter();
59              int savedState = fullyRelease(node);
60              int interruptMode = 0;
61              while (!isOnSyncQueue(node)) {
62                  LockSupport.park(this);
63                  if ((interruptMode = checkInterruptWhileWaiting(node))
                      != 0)
64                      break;
65              }
66              if (acquireQueued(node, savedState) && interruptMode
                  != THROW_IE)
67                  interruptMode = REINTERRUPT;
68              if (node.nextWaiter != null) // clean up if cancelled
69                  unlinkCancelledWaiters();
70              if (interruptMode != 0)
71                  reportInterruptAfterWait(interruptMode);
72          }
73      }
74
75          private void doSignal(Node first) {
```

```
 76            do {
 77                if ( (firstWaiter = first.nextWaiter) == null)
 78                    lastWaiter = null;
 79                first.nextWaiter = null;
 80            } while (!transferForSignal(first) &&
 81                    (first = firstWaiter) != null);
 82        }
 83
 84        public final void signal() {
 85            if (!isHeldExclusively())
 86                throw new IllegalMonitorStateException();
 87            Node first = firstWaiter;
 88            if (first != null)
 89                doSignal(first);
 90        }
 91    // other methods omitted
 92    }
 93    // fields and methods for the AbstractQueuedSynchronizer class
 94    private transient volatile Node head;
 95    private transient volatile Node tail;
 96    private volatile int state;
 97
 98    // Queuing utilities
 99    static final long spinForTimeoutThreshold = 1000L;
100    private Node enq(final Node node) {
101        for (;;) {
102            Node t = tail;
103            if (t == null) { // Must initialize
104                if (compareAndSetHead(new Node()))
105                    tail = head;
106            } else {
107                node.prev = t;
108                if (compareAndSetTail(t, node)) {
109                    t.next = node;
110                    return t;
111                }
112            }
113        }
114    }
115
116    private Node addWaiter(Node mode) {
117        Node node = new Node(Thread.currentThread(), mode);
118        // Try the fast path of enq; backup to full enq on failure
119        Node pred = tail;
120        if (pred != null) {
121            node.prev = pred;
122            if (compareAndSetTail(pred, node)) {
123                pred.next = node;
124                return node;
125            }
126        }
127        enq(node);
```

```
128         return node;
129     }
130
131     private final boolean parkAndCheckInterrupt() {
132         LockSupport.park(this);
133         return Thread.interrupted();
134     }
135
136     private void unparkSuccessor(Node node) {
137         int ws = node.waitStatus;
138         if (ws < 0)
139             compareAndSetWaitStatus(node, ws, 0);
140         Node s = node.next;
141         if (s == null || s.waitStatus > 0) {
142             s = null;
143             for (Node t = tail; t != null && t != node; t = t.prev)
144                 if (t.waitStatus <= 0)
145                     s = t;
146         }
147         if (s != null)
148             LockSupport.unpark(s.thread);
149     }
150
151     final boolean acquireQueued(final Node node, int arg) {
152         boolean failed = true;
153         try {
154             boolean interrupted = false;
155             for (;;) {
156                 final Node p = node.predecessor();
157                 if (p == head && tryAcquire(arg)) {
158                     setHead(node);
159                     p.next = null; // help GC
160                     failed = false;
161                     return interrupted;
162                 }
163                 if (shouldParkAfterFailedAcquire(p, node) &&
164                     parkAndCheckInterrupt())
165                     interrupted = true;
166             }
167         } finally {
168             if (failed)
169                 cancelAcquire(node);
170         }
171     }
172     public final void acquire(int arg) {
173         if (!tryAcquire(arg) &&
174             acquireQueued(addWaiter(Node.EXCLUSIVE), arg))
175             selfInterrupt();
176     }
177
178     public final boolean release(int arg) {
179         if (tryRelease(arg)) {
```

```
180                Node h = head;
181                if (h != null && h.waitStatus != 0)
182                    unparkSuccessor(h);
183                return true;
184            }
185        return false;
186    }
187
188    public final void acquireShared(int arg) {
189        if (tryAcquireShared(arg) < 0)
190            doAcquireShared(arg);
191    }
192
193    public final boolean hasContended() {
194        return head != null;
195    }
196
197    // Instrumentation and monitoring methods
198    public final Collection<Thread> getQueuedThreads() {
199        ArrayList<Thread> list = new ArrayList<Thread>();
200        for (Node p = tail; p != null; p = p.prev) {
201            Thread t = p.thread;
202            if (t != null)
203                list.add(t);
204        }
205        return list;
206    }
207
208    public final Collection<Thread> getExclusiveQueuedThreads() {
209        ArrayList<Thread> list = new ArrayList<Thread>();
210        for (Node p = tail; p != null; p = p.prev) {
211            if (!p.isShared()) {
212                Thread t = p.thread;
213                if (t != null)
214                    list.add(t);
215            }
216        }
217        return list;
218    }
219    public final Collection<Thread> getSharedQueuedThreads() {
220        ArrayList<Thread> list = new ArrayList<Thread>();
221        for (Node p = tail; p != null; p = p.prev) {
222            if (p.isShared()) {
223                Thread t = p.thread;
224                if (t != null)
225                    list.add(t);
226            }
227        }
228        return list;
229    }
230    // other methods omitted
231 }
```

5.4.3 The AbstractQueuedLongSynchronizer

The `AbstractQueuedLongSynchronizer` class is a version of `AbstractQueuedSynchronizer`, in which synchronization state is maintained as a `long` as shown in Listing 5.12. This class has exactly the same structure, fields, and methods as `AbstractQueuedSynchronizer` except that all state-related parameters and results are defined as `long` rather than `int`. This class may be useful when creating synchronizers such as multilevel locks and barriers that require 64 bits of state.

This concludes our introduction to the interfaces and classes related to the `Lock` interface in the `java.util.concurrent.locks` package.

Listing 5.12 AbstractQueuedLongSynchronizer.java (partial)

```
1   public abstract class AbstractQueuedLongSynchronizer extends
    AbstractOwnableSynchronizer implements java.io.Serializable {
2       private transient volatile Node head;
3       private transient volatile Node tail;
4       private volatile long state;
5       protected final long getState() {
6           return state;
7       }
8       protected final void setState(long newState) {
9           state = newState;
10      }
11      protected final boolean compareAndSetState(long expect, long update) {
12          return unsafe.compareAndSwapLong(this, stateOffset, expect,
                update);
13      }
14      // other methods omitted
15  }
```

5.5 SUMMARY

This chapter focused on understanding the interfaces and classes contained in the `java.util.concurrent.locks` package. We started with the `Lock` interface, and then examined the `ReentrantLock` class and the `ReentrantReadWriteLock` class. The reentrant locks provide a finer-granularity, explicit locking mechanism than the traditional, implicit monitor locks based on the `synchronized` keyword to lock a method or a block. The reentrant read/write locks further divide locks into shared and exclusive locks, which can help provide finer locking granularities for enhancing the performance and scalability of a multi-thread Java application.

To be complete, we also covered the `Condition` interface, which can be used by reentrant locks to deal with situations that a thread must wait for a certain event to occur or must signal other waiting threads when a certain other event occurs. The `Condition` interface defines methods of `await`, `signal` and `signalAll` for reentrant locks, similar to the methods of `wait`, `notify` and `notifyAll` for the traditional monitor locks.

Finally, we covered abstract queued synchronizers, which have two embedded classes: Node and ConditionObject. The Node class provides the foundation for implementing shared and exclusive queues, while the ConditionObject class provides the foundation for implementing condition queues. The methods of the AbstractQueuedSynchronizer class are explored to illustrate how the Node and ConditionObject classes are used to define abstract queued synchronizers.

The next chapter explores how various more specific synchronizers can be built based on the AQS.

5.6 EXERCISES

Exercise 5.1 What are the pros and cons of using reentrant locks versus using the implicit locks via the *synchronized* keyword?

Exercise 5.2 The ReentrantLock class has three lock methods of lock(), lockInterrutibly() and tryLock(). Describe the differences among these three methods.

Exercise 5.3 How is fairness specified for locks? Is it possible to specify fairness for implicit lock monitors?

Exercise 5.4 The ReentrantLock class has a public method of newCondition(). What can it be used for? How do you achieve the same with an implicit monitor lock?

Exercise 5.5 What is the general pattern for using the lock() method?

Exercise 5.6 What are the benefits of having ReadWriteReentrantLocks?

Exercise 5.7 Does a ReadWriteReentrantLock have the newCondition() method?

Exercise 5.8 Describe the five different methods of the Condition interface.

Exercise 5.9 Compare signal()/signalAll() with notify()/notifyAll() in terms of how waiters are awakened.

Exercise 5.10 Based on the name of the AbstractQueuedSynchronizer (AQS) class, what is your take on what attributes it may have?

Exercise 5.11 How do you control *acquire* attempts with an AQS?

6   Synchronizers

A synchronizer essentially is an object that can be used to coordinate executions of a critical section of code by multiple threads. The previous chapters introduced two kinds of synchronizers: (1) the traditional, implicit monitor locks built into every Java object inherently and exposed with the keyword of synchronized, which can be applied to a method or a block; and (2) the explicit, reentrant locks defined by the Lock interface (sometimes used in conjunction with Condition objects). These two kinds of synchronizers can be used with an arbitrary number of threads. This chapter introduces the synchronizers that are used to control a bounded number of threads for accessing a shared resource or transitioning from one state to another collectively.

Specifically, we cover synchronization classes introduced in Java 5 in the java.util.concurrent package, which implement the general synchronization concepts of *semaphores*, *barriers*, *latches*, *exchangers*, and *phasers*, as briefly introduced below:

- Semaphore: Implemented as the Semaphore class In Java. A Semaphore object *guards* a number of permits. A thread calls the acquire() method of a semaphore object, which blocks until a permit is available, and then takes it, resulting in the number of permits decremented by one. After performing the designated computing task, the thread calls the release() method of the semaphore object, resulting in one permit returned to the semaphore object, which may potentially release an acquirer that is blocked. Semaphores are often used to restrict the number of threads that can access a shared resource.
- Barrier: Implemented as the CyclicBarrier class in Java. A CyclicBarrier object is used to force a set of threads to wait at a predetermined barrier point until all threads have reached that point, before all threads can perform a pre-determined action. The barrier is called *cyclic* because it can be re-used after the waiting threads are released.
- Latch: Implemented as the CountDownLatch class in Java. A CountDownLatch object keeps a count of a specified number of events initialized by the owning thread. The owning thread spawns one or more child threads, which call the countDown() method of the CountDownLatch object at a proper time. The owning thread then calls the await() method of the CountDownLatch object and blocks until the CountDownLatch object's internal counter reaches zero, after which the owning (waiting) thread is released and continues executing the next immediate piece of code.

- Exchanger: Implemented as the Exchanger class in Java. An Exchanger object is designed for exchanging data between threads safely. It has a method named exchange(V buffer) that can be used by two threads to exchange the data contained in the buffer.
- Phaser: Implemented as the Phaser class in Java. It's introduced in Java 7 for a special purpose of letting multiple threads perform various, different tasks that can be considered different *phases* of one job as the whole. Conceptually, it is similar to an assembly line that different workers work on different parts until a final product is formed.

The objective for this chapter is to help you understand clearly which class of synchronizer to use for a given situation. Let's start with the Semaphore synchronizer first next.

6.1 Semaphore

As described in the beginning of this chapter, a semaphore is a classic synchronizer that uses a counter to control access to a shared resource. It conceptually is very simple: If the counter is greater than zero, access is granted; and if the counter is zero, then access is denied. Looking at it another way, a counter may be considered representing a number of *permits* for controlling whether a shared resource should be granted or denied.

Next, we examine how the Semaphore class is implemented in Java.

6.1.1 Semaphore Implementation

The Semaphore class is implemented with about 180 lines of code only. Figure 6.1 shows that a Semaphore object has an instance of the Sync class, which extends the AQS class and is sub-classed by the NonfairSync class and FairSync class.

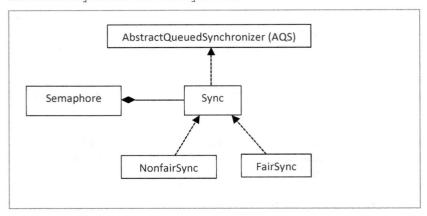

Figure 6.1 A Semaphore object *has* an instance of Sync, which extends AQS and is sub-classed by NonfairSync and FairSync

Listing 6.1 shows partially how the Semaphore class is implemented in Java. As you see, the Semaphore class leverages the AbstractQueuedSynchronizer (AQS) class to maintain of set of permits. What used to be state for AQS is now permits for Semaphore through object containership, as shown at line 8, that a Semaphore object internally is represented as a Sync object. Since the Sync class extends the AQS class, as shown at line 10, a Semaphore object is equipped with a waiting queue for storing the threads that are too unlucky to get a permit when all permits have been exhausted and before one or more permits become available. Furthermore, a Sync object for a Semaphore object could be a Nonfair sync object (lines 60 – 70) or a FairSync object (lines 71- 88).

By examining Listing 6.1 further, we see that:

- The Sync class maintains permits as its state from the AQS class, and its constructor is simply a wrapper of the AQS's setState method (lines 11 – 13). In addition, its getPermits() method is just a wrapper of the AQS's getState() method (lines 15 – 17). The Sync class has a few more methods (nonfairTryAcquireShared(int acquires), tryReleaseShared (int permits), reducePermits (int permits), and drainPermits()), to provide utilities for manipulating permits on behalf of the Semaphore. These methods are elaborated further as follows:

  ° nonfairTryAcquireShared(int acquires): It first gets the current number of permits, and then calculates the *remaining* number of permits if the requested number of permits were granted. Because of the OR (||) operation, the requested number of acquires will be granted through the CAS (compareAndSet...) method call only if remaining is larger than zero. This is why the method name is prefixed with the word "try."
  ° tryReleaseShared(int permits): Similar to the above nonfairTryAcquireShared(int acquires) method, except that it attempts to release the specified number of permits.
  ° reducePermits(int permits): Reduces the number of permits.
  ° drainPermits(): This method zeros the number of permits. However, it does not change the total number of permits available.

- Next, we have the NonfairSync class and FairSync class, both of which extend the Sync class and implement the tryAcquireShared(int permits) method. The difference between the two is that the NonfairSync class just wraps its tryAcquireShared(int permits) method with the Sync's nonfairTryAcquireShared(int permits) method (because that's what it already is), while the FairSync class implements its own tryAcquireShared(int permits) method to make it *fair*, namely, the thread that waited longest would get considered first.
- The Semaphore class has two constructors: The first one (lines 90 – 92) initializes the sync object using an instance of the NonfairSync class with a specified number of permits, while the second one (lines 94 – 96) allows a second parameter (fair) to be specified to indicate whether acquiring permits will be *fair* or *nonfair*.

The remainder of Listing 6.1 shows the acquire and release methods for the Semaphore class. As you see, *release* is much simpler than *acquire*. Similar to the release method, a call to the acquire method acquires one permit a time by default, unless specified explicitly using its parameterized version. In addition, the acquireUninterruptibly methods (no-arg version and parameterized version) allow a waiting thread to ignore interruptions and continue to wait until being signaled by a release call. Obviously, the release method does not need such an option.

◀Note: **Fair versus non-fair Semaphore.** You might wonder whether one should use a fair or non-fair semaphore. Generally, semaphores used to control resource access should be initialized as fair in order to ensure that no thread would incur large latencies due to being starved out from accessing a resource. However, the throughput advantage of the non-fair ordering often outweighs fairness considerations.

Next, we use an example to illustrate the use of Semaphore.

Listing 6.1 Semaphore.java (partial)

```
1    package java.util.concurrent;
2    import java.util.*;
3    import java.util.concurrent.locks.*;
4    import java.util.concurrent.atomic.*;
5
6    public class Semaphore implements java.io.Serializable {
7        /** All mechanics via AbstractQueuedSynchronizer subclass */
8        private final Sync sync;
9
10       abstract static class Sync extends AbstractQueuedSynchronizer {
11           Sync(int permits) {
12               setState(permits);
13           }
14
15           final int getPermits() {
16               return getState();
17           }
18
19           final int nonfairTryAcquireShared(int acquires) {
20               for (;;) {
21                   int available = getState();
22                   int remaining = available - acquires;
23                   if (remaining < 0 ||
24                       compareAndSetState(available, remaining))
25                       return remaining;
26               }
27           }
28
29           protected final boolean tryReleaseShared(int releases) {
30               for (;;) {
31                   int current = getState();
32                   int next = current + releases;
33                   if (next < current) // overflow
34                       throw new Error("Maximum permit count exceeded");
35                   if (compareAndSetState(current, next))
36                       return true;
37               }
38           }
39
```

```
40          final void reducePermits(int reductions) {
41              for (;;) {
42                  int current = getState();
43                  int next = current - reductions;
44                  if (next > current) // underflow
45                      throw new Error("Permit count underflow");
46                  if (compareAndSetState(current, next))
47                      return;
48              }
49          }
50
51          final int drainPermits() {
52              for (;;) {
53                  int current = getState();
54                  if (current == 0 || compareAndSetState(current, 0))
55                      return current;
56              }
57          }
58      }
59
60      static final class NonfairSync extends Sync {
61
62          NonfairSync(int permits) {
63              super(permits);
64          }
65
66          protected int tryAcquireShared(int acquires) {
67              return nonfairTryAcquireShared(acquires);
68          }
69      }
70
71      static final class FairSync extends Sync {
72
73          FairSync(int permits) {
74              super(permits);
75          }
76
77          protected int tryAcquireShared(int acquires) {
78              for (;;) {
79                  if (hasQueuedPredecessors())
80                      return -1;
81                  int available = getState();
82                  int remaining = available - acquires;
83                  if (remaining < 0 ||
84                      compareAndSetState(available, remaining))
85                      return remaining;
86              }
87          }
88      }
89
90      public Semaphore(int permits) {
91          sync = new NonfairSync(permits);
```

```
92       }
93
94       public Semaphore(int permits, boolean fair) {
95           sync = fair ? new FairSync(permits) : new NonfairSync(permits);
96       }
97
98
99       public void acquire() throws InterruptedException {
100          sync.acquireSharedInterruptibly(1);
101      }
102
103      public void acquireUninterruptibly() {
104          sync.acquireShared(1);
105      }
106
107      public boolean tryAcquire() {
108          return sync.nonfairTryAcquireShared(1) >= 0;
109      }
110
111      public boolean tryAcquire(long timeout, TimeUnit unit)
112              throws InterruptedException {
113          return sync.tryAcquireSharedNanos(1, unit.toNanos(timeout));
114      }
115
116      public void release() {
117          sync.releaseShared(1);
118      }
119
120      public void acquire(int permits) throws InterruptedException {
121          if (permits < 0) throw new IllegalArgumentException();
122          sync.acquireSharedInterruptibly(permits);
123      }
124
125      public void acquireUninterruptibly(int permits) {
126          if (permits < 0) throw new IllegalArgumentException();
127          sync.acquireShared(permits);
128      }
129
130      public boolean tryAcquire(int permits) {
131          if (permits < 0) throw new IllegalArgumentException();
132          return sync.nonfairTryAcquireShared(permits) >= 0;
133      }
134
135      public boolean tryAcquire(int permits, long timeout, TimeUnit unit)
136              throws InterruptedException {
137          if (permits < 0) throw new IllegalArgumentException();
138          return sync.tryAcquireSharedNanos(permits, unit.toNanos(timeout));
139      }
140
141      public void release(int permits) {
142          if (permits < 0) throw new IllegalArgumentException();
143          sync.releaseShared(permits);
```

```
144     }
145
146     // other methods omitted
147 }
```

6.1.2 An Example of Using a Binary Semaphore

To use a semaphore to control access to a shared resource, a semaphore object is passed to the threads that access the shared resource. Each thread calls the `acquire` method to get a permit before accessing the resource, and finally calls the `release` method to release the permit. The number of permits assigned to the semaphore object determines how many threads can access the resource at the same time. If only one permit is available, then the semaphore is essentially a *binary* semaphore.

Listing 6.2 shows a binary semaphore example. It has three parts: the driver class (lines 7 − 27), the `Counter` thread class (lines 31 − 58), and the class named `Shared` to simulate a shared resource (lines 61 − 63). It works as follows:

- The driver class creates a binary semaphore object and passes it to an `ExecutorService` pool with three threads.
- The `Counter` thread simulates how the semaphore is used. After calling the semaphore's `acquire()` method, a thread increments/decrements the `count` field of the shared resource five times, depending on whether its id is even or odd. At the end, each thread calls the semaphore's `release()` method to release the permit.

Next, we discuss the execution result of this demo program, following Listing 6.2.

Listing 6.2 SemaphoreDemo.java

```
1    package jcp.ch6.synchronizers;
2
3    import java.util.concurrent.ExecutorService;
4    import java.util.concurrent.Executors;
5    import java.util.concurrent.Semaphore;
6
7    public class SemaphoreDemo {
8      public static void main(String[] args) throws InterruptedException {
9        Semaphore semaphore = new Semaphore(1);
10       int POOL_SIZE = 3;
11       // 1. Create a newFixedThreadPool using the Executors utility class
12       ExecutorService executorService = Executors
13           .newFixedThreadPool(POOL_SIZE);
14
15       // 2. launch 2 counters
16       for (int i = 0; i < POOL_SIZE; i++) {
17         executorService.execute(new Counter(i, semaphore));
18       }
19
20       // 3. wait 5000 ms for all drawers to complete
21       Thread.sleep(5000);
```

```
22       System.out.println("Shared.count = " + Shared.count);
23
24       // 4. shut down executorService to avoid resource leak
25       executorService.shutdown();
26    }
27  }
28
29  // Thread class: Counter increments/decrements count five times if id is
30  // even/odd.
31  class Counter extends Thread {
32    int id;
33    Semaphore semaphore;
34
35    Counter(int id, Semaphore semaphore) {
36      this.id = id;
37      this.semaphore = semaphore;
38    }
39
40    public void run() {
41      try {
42        semaphore.acquire();
43        for (int i = 0; i < 5; i++) {
44          if ((this.id % 2) == 0) {
45            Shared.count++;
46            System.out.println("thread " + id + ": " + Shared.count);
47          } else {
48            Shared.count--;
49            System.out.println("thread " + id + ": " + Shared.count);
50          }
51        }
52      } catch (InterruptedException ie) {
53        System.out.println("interrupted");
54      } finally {
55        semaphore.release();
56      }
57    }
58  }
59
60  // Shared resource:
61  class Shared {
62    static int count = 0;
63  }
```

I ran the above SemaphoreDemo program on my Eclipse IDE and obtained the result as shown in Listing 6.3. As you see, thread 0 incremented the count field of the Shared class five times, followed by five decrements by thread 1, and ended by five increments by thread 2. Because of the binary semaphore, these increment/decrement operations were not intermingled. If the semaphore's acquire() and release() methods were disabled by commenting out lines 42 and 55, you would get intermingled accesses as shown in Listing 6.4, instead.

Next, we discuss an example of a buffer synchronized with semaphores.

Listing 6.3 The result of running the SemaphoreDemo program

```
thread 0: 1
thread 0: 2
thread 0: 3
thread 0: 4
thread 0: 5
thread 1: 4
thread 1: 3
thread 1: 2
thread 1: 1
thread 1: 0
thread 2: 1
thread 2: 2
thread 2: 3
thread 2: 4
thread 2: 5
Shared.count = 5
```

Listing 6.4 The result of running the SemaphoreDemo program with semaphore's acquire() and release() methods commented out

```
thread 0: 1
thread 0: 2
thread 0: 3
thread 0: 4
thread 2: 1
thread 1: 1
thread 1: 5
thread 1: 4
thread 1: 3
thread 2: 6
thread 0: 5
interrupted
thread 2: 3
thread 1: 2
interrupted
thread 2: 4
thread 2: 5
interrupted
Shared.count = 5
```

6.1.3 A Buffer Synchronized with Semaphores

To illustrate some other uses of semaphores, this section presents a buffer class guarded by semaphores. As we know, a buffer class has two operations: put and get. The put method is for producers, while the get method is for consumers. Therefore, we can have two semaphores, one for consumers and the other for producers. In the put method, the Buffer class can arrange an acquire method call for the producer semaphore first. After the buffer is filled, it can arrange a release method call for the consumer semaphore to make the buffer available for a consumer to perform a get operation on the buffer. Lines 11 – 18 in Listing 6.5 show how the put method is implemented as described above.

The get method is implemented in the opposite way. As shown from lines 22 – 28, the consumer semaphore is arranged to call its acquire() method before being allowed to perform the get operation. After the get operation is performed, the release() method is called on the producer semaphore so that the producer will be allowed to fill the buffer again.

In addition, you may notice that the consumer semaphore is initialized with zero permits as shown at line 6. This is to help guarantee that the consumer will not start consuming the buffer before the producer starts filling the buffer. You might wonder if a semaphore has zero permits to start with, how could a consumer ever get a permit later. In fact, a semaphore is coded not to give out a permit if it has zero permits. However, it does not prevent a permit to be released back to the semaphore. The initial number of permits is not necessarily a constant. When a semaphore is created, the number of permits assigned is only an initial number and it can be reduced or increased later.

This is how the Buffer class is guarded with two semaphores. Next, we discuss the driver class, following Listing 6.5.

Listing 6.5 Buffer.java guarded by semaphores

```
1    package jcp.ch6.synchronizers;
2
3    import java.util.concurrent.Semaphore;
4
5    public class Buffer {
6       final Semaphore semaCon = new Semaphore(0);
7       final Semaphore semaProd = new Semaphore(1);
8       int buffer;
9
10      public void put(int n) {
11         try {
12            semaProd.acquire();
13         } catch (InterruptedException ie) {
14            System.out.println("Interrupted");
15         }
16         this.buffer = n % 100;
17         System.out.println("buffer put: " + buffer);
18         semaCon.release();
19      }
20
21      public void get() {
22         try {
23            semaCon.acquire();
24         } catch (InterruptedException ie) {
25            System.out.println("Interrupted");
26         }
27         System.out.println("buffer get: " + buffer);
```

```
28      semaProd.release();
29   }
30 }
```

Listing 6.6 shows the driver class for testing the `Buffer` class guarded by those two semaphores described in the previous section. Since the consumer and producer semaphores are built into the `Buffer` class, we do not see semaphores here. After the buffer object is created and handed to the producer and consumer objects through their constructors, the producer will keep filling the buffer while the consumer will keep consuming the buffer.

Executing the `SemaphoreDemo2` program on my Eclipse IDE yielded the following output:

```
......
buffer put: 0
buffer get: 0
buffer put: 1
buffer get: 1
buffer put: 2
buffer get: 2
buffer put: 3
buffer get: 3
buffer put: 4
buffer get: 4
buffer put: 5
buffer get: 5
......
```

As you see, each `put` operation is followed by a `get` operation. This concludes our coverage of the `Semaphore` class. Next, we discuss the `CyclicBarrier` class.

Listing 6.6 SemaphoreDemo2.java

```
1    package jcp.ch6.synchronizers;
2
3    public class SemaphoreDemo2 {
4      public static void main(String args[]) {
5        Buffer buffer = new Buffer();
6        new Producer(buffer);
7        new Consumer(buffer);
8      }
9    }
10
11   class Consumer implements Runnable {
12     private Buffer buffer;
13     Consumer(Buffer buffer) {
14       this.buffer = buffer;
15       new Thread(this, "Consumer").start();
16     }
17
18     public void run() {
```

```
19      while (true) {
20          buffer.get();
21      }
22    }
23  }
24
25  class Producer implements Runnable {
26    private Buffer buffer;
27    Producer(Buffer buffer) {
28        this.buffer = buffer;
29        new Thread(this, "Producer").start();
30    }
31
32    public void run() {
33        int i = 0;
34        while (true) {
35            buffer.put(i++);
36        }
37    }
38  }
```

6.2 CYCLICBARRIER

The CyclicBarrier class is designed to set up a barrier at a pre-determined execution point for a fixed number for threads to reach, before the tasks beyond the barrier can be executed. Next, let's look at how the CyclicBarrier class is implemented in Java.

6.2.1 CyclicBarrier Implementation

Listing 6.7 shows partially how the CyclicBarrier class is implemented in Java. At first, a private static class named Generation is defined from lines 5 – 7, with only one field and no method: broken initialized to false. This class is designed to represent each use of the barrier, which is the core concept for the CyclicBarrier class. The generation changes whenever the barrier is tripped or reset. Because a barrier is cyclic, there can be many generations, but only one of them can be active at a time and all others either tripped or broken.

Next, notice the following fields for the CyclicBarrier class:

- **lock**: The lock typed ReentrantLock for guarding the barrier entry
- **trip**: A Condition object to wait on until the barrier is tripped
- **parties**: The number of parties to synchronize
- **barrierCommand**: The action of Runnable to perform when the barrier is tripped
- **generation**: The current generation that is active
- **count**: Number of parties still waiting. Counts down from parties to 0 on each generation. It is reset to parties on each new generation or when broken

Next, let's look at some of the methods for the CyclicBarrier class that are relevant for us to understand how the CyclicBarrier class works. They are described as below:

- **nextGeneration()**: Called when the barrier is tripped. It signals all waiting threads, resets `count` to `parties`, and creates a new `generation`.
- **breakBarrier()**: Sets the current barrier generation as broken, resets `count` to `parties`, and signals all waiting threads.
- **doWait (boolean timed, long nanos)**: Implements various policies for waiting, for example, when a generation is broken or when the thread is interrupted or when the barrier is tripped.
- **CyclicBarrier(int parties)**: The first constructor that takes a parameter for the number of parties to synchronize.
- **CyclicBarrier(int parties, Runnable barrierAction)**: The second constructor that has one extra parameter for specifying what action to perform after the barrier.
- **await()**: When called, waits until all parties have invoked await on this barrier. Its main logic is hidden in the `doWait()` method. If the current thread is not the last to arrive then it is disabled until the last thread arrives.
- **await(long timeout, TimeUnit unit)**: The version of the `await` method that accepts a timeout parameter.
- **isBroken()**: Checks the `broken` field of the `generation` object. Note how the lock is used to guard the operation of checking the broken field of the generation object.
- **reset()**: Lines 70 -71 show what this method does: It breaks the barrier and creates a new generation.

Next, let's use an example to show how the `CyclicBarrier` class is used.

Listing 6.7 CyclicBarrier.java (partial)

```
1   package java.util.concurrent;
2   import java.util.concurrent.locks.*;
3
4   public class CyclicBarrier {
5       private static class Generation {
6           boolean broken = false;
7       }
8       private final ReentrantLock lock = new ReentrantLock();
9       private final Condition trip = lock.newCondition();
10      private final int parties;
11      private final Runnable barrierCommand;
12      private Generation generation = new Generation();
13      private int count;
14
15      private void nextGeneration() {
16          trip.signalAll();
17          count = parties;
18          generation = new Generation();
19      }
20
21      private void breakBarrier() {
22          generation.broken = true;
23          count = parties;
24          trip.signalAll();
25      }
```

```
26
27      private int dowait(boolean timed, long nanos)
28          throws InterruptedException, BrokenBarrierException,
29                  TimeoutException {
30          // body omitted
31      }
32
33      public CyclicBarrier(int parties) {
34          this(parties, null);
35      }
36
37      public CyclicBarrier(int parties, Runnable barrierAction) {
38          if (parties <= 0) throw new IllegalArgumentException();
39          this.parties = parties;
40          this.count = parties;
41          this.barrierCommand = barrierAction;
42      }
43
44      public int await() throws InterruptedException, BrokenBarrierException
    {
45          try {
46              return dowait(false, 0L);
47          } catch (TimeoutException toe) {
48              throw new Error(toe); // cannot happen;
49          }
50      }
51
52      public int await(long timeout, TimeUnit unit)
53          // body omitted
54      }
55
56      public boolean isBroken() {
57          final ReentrantLock lock = this.lock;
58          lock.lock();
59          try {
60              return generation.broken;
61          } finally {
62              lock.unlock();
63          }
64      }
65
66      public void reset() {
67          final ReentrantLock lock = this.lock;
68          lock.lock();
69          try {
70              breakBarrier();   // break the current generation
71              nextGeneration(); // start a new generation
72          } finally {
73              lock.unlock();
74          }
75      }
76
```

```
77      // other methods omitted
78  }
```

6.2.2 An Example of Using a CyclicBarrier

The general procedure for using a CyclicBarrier synchronizer is as follows:

- First, create a CyclicBarrier object with the specified number of threads to be synchronized. If you have some action to be performed by all threads after all threads have reached the barrier, pass a new instance of that action class to each thread as well.
- Next, pass the CyclicBarrier object to each thread and have each thread call the CyclicBarrier object's await() method to wait for all other threads to reach the barrier.
- Once the specified number of threads have reached the barrier, the await() call invoked by each thread will return and execution will continue. If the CyclicBarrier object was created with an action thread specified, execution will continue with that action thread.

Next, we use an example to demonstrate how the above procedure is used for a CyclicBarrier object to synchronize a number of threads to wait before executing an action.

Listing 6.8 shows the action thread class named BarrierAction. It implements the Runnable interface and has a run() method that does only one thing: printing a message of "reached the barrier."

Listing 6.8 BarrierAction.java

```
1   package jcp.ch6.synchronizers;
2
3   public class BarrierAction implements Runnable {
4     public void run() {
5        // action to perform when threads reach the barrier:
6        System.out.println ("reached the barrier");
7     }
8   }
```

Next, Listing 6.9 shows the driver class and the thread class named MyThread to be synchronized. It is coded as follows:

- In the driver class, line 10 creates a CyclicBarrier object with 3 threads and the designated action specified.
- Line 18 in the driver class passes the CyclicBarrier object to the three instances of the MyThread class, which are started by the ExecutorService.
- Now in the run() method of the MyThread class, line 40 represents the task that each thread is supposed to carry out before exiting the run() method. This is where each thread should call the CyclicBarrier object's await() method, as shown in the try-catch block there (lines 41 – 47). After all threads reach this point, execution will continue. Since an action class is specified when the CyclicBarrier object was created, the action specified in the BarrierAction class will be executed.

Executing this program on my Eclipse IDE yielded the following result:

```
This is thread 1
This is thread 2
This is thread 0
reached the barrier
```

A `CyclicBarrier` object will release all waiting threads when each time all of them have called the `await()` method. A `CyclicBarrier` object is not disposed and can be re-used. To show that this is the case, you can create twice the POOL_SIZE of threads by doubling the iteration of the `for`-loop specified at line 17 from `i < POOL_SIZE` to `i < 2 * POOL_SZIE` and re-run the example. The result should show that the barrier was tripped twice, as shown from the following output obtained in my environment. This proves that the `CyclicBarrier` object is re-usable or cyclic.

```
This is thread 0
This is thread 2
This is thread 1
reached the barrier
This is thread 3
This is thread 5
This is thread 4
reached the barrier
```

This concludes our coverage of the `CyclicBarrier` class. Next, we discuss the `CountDownLatch` class.

Listing 6.9 CyclicBarrierDemo.java

```java
1   package jcp.ch6.synchronizers;
2
3   import java.util.concurrent.BrokenBarrierException;
4   import java.util.concurrent.CyclicBarrier;
5   import java.util.concurrent.ExecutorService;
6   import java.util.concurrent.Executors;
7
8   public class CyclicBarrierDemo {
9     public static void main(String[] args) throws InterruptedException {
10        CyclicBarrier cyclicBarrier = new CyclicBarrier(3, new
             BarrierAction());
11        int POOL_SIZE = 3;
12        // 1. Create a newFixedThreadPool using the Executors utility class
13        ExecutorService executorService = Executors
14            .newFixedThreadPool(POOL_SIZE);
15
16        // 2. launch 3 counters
17        for (int i = 0; i < POOL_SIZE; i++) {
18          executorService.execute(new MyThread(i, cyclicBarrier));
19        }
20
21        // 3. wait 5000 ms for all threads to complete
22        Thread.sleep(5000);
23
24        // 4. shut down executorService to avoid resource leak
```

```
25       executorService.shutdown();
26    }
27  }
28
29  // Thread class: Prints ID and calls await() method before proceeding
30  class MyThread extends Thread {
31     int id;
32     CyclicBarrier cyclicBarrier;
33
34     MyThread(int id, CyclicBarrier cyclicBarrier) {
35        this.id = id;
36        this.cyclicBarrier = cyclicBarrier;
37     }
38
39     public void run() {
40        System.out.println ("This is thread " + id);
41        try {
42           cyclicBarrier.await();
43        } catch (BrokenBarrierException bbe) {
44           System.out.println("BrokenBarrierException: " + bbe);
45        } catch (InterruptedException ie) {
46           System.out.println("InterruptedException: " + ie);
47        }
48     }
49  }
```

6.3   COUNTDOWNLATCH

The CountDownLatch class is designed to set up a count of the number of events to happen, before the latch can be opened. Let's look at how this class is implemented next.

6.3.1 CountDownLatch Implementation

Listing 6.10 shows how the CountDownLatch class is implemented in Java. Similar to the Semaphore class, it first defines a Sync class that extends the AbstractQueuedSynchronizer class. The Sync class uses the AQS's state to represent count, as is shown by its constructor (lines 8–10) and the getCount() method (lines 12–14). In addition, it has a tryAcquireShared(int acquires) method for checking the synchronization state and tryReleaseShared(int releases) method for decrementing count if count is larger than zero or otherwise signaling that count has reached zero. These two methods have the acquires and releases parameters but they are not used.

Next, the CountDownLatch class has a field of sync, which, nevertheless, is not associated with *fairness* as is the case with the Semaphore. The CountDownLatch class's constructor simply passes count to the Sync class's constructor. Its two await methods are also simple: one is parameter-less, and the other has a timeout parameter. Its key method, countDown(), is a wrapper of the Sync class's releaseShared (int releases) method with releases set to 1 as shown at line 48. Therefore, every time the countdown() method is called, count is decremented.

Next, we use an example to demonstrate the use of the CountDownLatch class.

Listing 6.10 CountDownLatch.java

```
1   package java.util.concurrent;
2   import java.util.concurrent.locks.*;
3   import java.util.concurrent.atomic.*;
4
5   public class CountDownLatch {
6       private static final class Sync extends AbstractQueuedSynchronizer {
7
8           Sync(int count) {
9               setState(count);
10          }
11
12          int getCount() {
13              return getState();
14          }
15
16          protected int tryAcquireShared(int acquires) {
17              return (getState() == 0) ? 1 : -1;
18          }
19
20          protected boolean tryReleaseShared(int releases) {
21              for (;;) {
22                  int c = getState();
23                  if (c == 0)
24                      return false;
25                  int nextc = c-1;
26                  if (compareAndSetState(c, nextc))
27                      return nextc == 0;
28              }
29          }
30      }
31
32      private final Sync sync;
33      public CountDownLatch(int count) {
34          if (count < 0) throw new IllegalArgumentException("count < 0");
35          this.sync = new Sync(count);
36      }
37
38      public void await() throws InterruptedException {
39          sync.acquireSharedInterruptibly(1);
40      }
41
42      public boolean await(long timeout, TimeUnit unit)
43          throws InterruptedException {
44          return sync.tryAcquireSharedNanos(1, unit.toNanos(timeout));
45      }
46
47      public void countDown() {
```

```
48            sync.releaseShared(1);
49        }
50
51        // other methods omitted
52  }
```

6.3.2 An Example of Using a CountDownLatch

Listing 6.11 shows an example of using the CountDownLatch. The driver class creates a countdown latch with an event count of 3. Then, it passes the latch to an instance of the LatchThread. It calls the await() method of the latch (line 17) to wait for the latch thread to count down and return when countdown reaches zero.

Executing the CountDownLatchDemo program on my Eclipse IDE yielded the following output:

```
LatchThread counting down: 0
LatchThread counting down: 1
LatchThread counting down: 2
done
```

As you see, this example uses only one latch thread. You might wonder what would happen if a latch is passed to multiple latch threads. This is discussed following Listing 6.11.

Listing 6.11 CountDownLatchDemo.java

```
1   package jcp.ch6.synchronizers;
2
3   import java.util.concurrent.CountDownLatch;
4
5   public class CountDownLatchDemo {
6     public static void main(String args[]) {
7
8         // 1. create the latch
9         int EVENT_COUNT = 3;
10        CountDownLatch latch = new CountDownLatch(EVENT_COUNT);
11
12        // 2. pass latch to the latch thread
13        new LatchThread(latch);
14
15        // 3. wait
16        try {
17           latch.await();
18        } catch (InterruptedException ie) {
19           System.out.println(ie);
20        }
21
22        // 4. done
23        System.out.println("done");
24     }
25  }
```

```
26
27  class LatchThread implements Runnable {
28    CountDownLatch latch;
29    long count;
30
31    LatchThread(CountDownLatch latch) {
32       this.latch = latch;
33       count = latch.getCount();
34       new Thread(this).start();
35    }
36
37    public void run() {
38       for (int i = 0; i < count; i++) {
39          System.out.println("LatchThread counting down: " + i);
40          latch.countDown();
41       }
42    }
43  }
```

Listing 6.12 shows a modified version of the previous CountDownLatchDemo program. Instead of passing the latch to one latch thread, this new version of demo passes one latch to two latch threads. Executing this demo program on my Eclipse IDE yielded the following outcome:

```
LatchThread 0 counting down: 0
LatchThread 0 counting down: 1
LatchThread 1 counting down: 0
LatchThread 0 counting down: 2
LatchThread 1 counting down: 1
done
LatchThread 1 counting down: 2
```

It is seen that the barrier was tripped after one latch thread counted down to zero while another thread was still counting down. Therefore, it is important to keep in mind that one countDownLatch applies to one thread only. Of course, you can create multiple countdown latches for multiple threads, as long as latches are not shared.

This concludes our coverage of the CountDownLatch synchronizer. We discuss the Exchanger synchronizer next.

Listing 6.12 CountDownLatchDemo2.java

```
1   package jcp.ch6.synchronizers;
2
3   import java.util.concurrent.CountDownLatch;
4   import java.util.concurrent.ExecutorService;
5   import java.util.concurrent.Executors;
6
7   public class CountDownLatchDemo2 {
8     public static void main(String args[]) {
9
10        // 1. create a latch
```

```
11      int EVENT_COUNT = 3;
12      CountDownLatch latch = new CountDownLatch(EVENT_COUNT);
13
14      // 2. Create a newFixedThreadPool using the Executors utility class
15      int POOL_SIZE = 2;
16      ExecutorService executorService = Executors
17          .newFixedThreadPool(POOL_SIZE);
18
19      // 3. launch 2 latch threads
20      for (int i = 0; i < POOL_SIZE; i++) {
21          executorService.execute(new LatchThread2(i, latch));
22      }
23
24      // 4. wait
25      try {
26          latch.await();
27      } catch (InterruptedException ie) {
28          System.out.println(ie);
29      }
30      System.out.println("done");
31
32      // 5. shut down executorService to avoid resource leak
33      executorService.shutdown();
34   }
35 }
36
37 class LatchThread2 implements Runnable {
38   int id;
39   CountDownLatch latch;
40   long count;
41
42   LatchThread2(int id, CountDownLatch latch) {
43      this.id = id;
44      this.latch = latch;
45      count = latch.getCount();
46   }
47
48   public void run() {
49      for (int i = 0; i < count; i++) {
50          System.out.println("LatchThread " + id + " counting down: " + i);
51          latch.countDown();
52      }
53   }
54 }
```

6.4 EXCHANGER

An Exchanger synchronizer allows two threads to pair up and exchange data with each other. An Exchanger may be viewed as a bidirectional form of a SynchronousQueue. In this section, we explore how Exchanger is implemented in Java and how it can be used to allow two threads to exchange data.

6.4.1 Exchanger Implementation

The Exchanger synchronizer perhaps is the simplest to use but most complex in implementation. Internally, the Exchanger class maintains a "slot," which is a reference to a Node, as shown in Listing 6.13. A node holds an item and a "hole" waiting to get filled in. If an incoming thread sees that the slot is null, it comapreAndSets a node there and waits for another thread to invoke exchange. The second "fulfilling" thread sees that the slot is non-full, and so compareAndSets it back to null, also exchanging items by CASing (compareAndSetting) the hole, plus waking up the occupying thread if it is blocked.

However, a single slot could easily become the bottleneck due to CAS contention when many threads use an exchanger. So, instead of having a single slot, an "arena" is introduced to act as a hash table with a dynamically varying number of slots for multiple threads to use to perform an exchange. Incoming threads are coded to pick slots based on a hash of their thread ids. If a thread successfully locks into a slot but no other thread arrives, it tries another, until arriving at the zero slot, which always exists. To make sure those slots function properly, the implementation carefully considers waiting, sizing, hashing, probing and padding, and so on. Such details are beyond the scope of this text. Refer to the source code if you are interested in them.

Listing 6.13 Node class embedded in Exchanger

```
1       private static final class Node extends AtomicReference<Object> {
2           public final Object item;
3           public volatile Thread waiter;
4           public Node(Object item) {
5               this.item = item;
6           }
7       }
```

Listing 6.14 shows partially the Exchanger class implemented in Java. Line 8 declares the Node class as shown in Listing 6.13. Line 12 declares the Slot class that extends the AtomicReference, which represents an object reference to a value field that may be updated atomically. Line 16 defines a Slot array named arena. Line 17 defines the doExchange method, which handles all the detailed work of exchanging data between two threads. Lines 20 – 28 define the createSlot method for a given slot index. The other two interesting methods, spinWait (lines 30 – 41) and await (lines 43 – 59) are explained as follows:

- **spinWait(Node node, Slot slot)**: Performs *spinWait* for non-null slot. Fails if spin elapses before the hole is filled.
- **await(Node node, Slot slot)**: Waits for and gets the hole filled in by another thread. If the slot is null, it does spin-wait, then checks interrupts, and eventually blocks.

The constructor and the exchange methods of the Exchanger class are explained as follows:

- **Exchanger()**: A no-arg constructor
- **exchange(V x)**: The public method for exchanging the data specified as the parameter passed in. It depends on the private method doExchange to complete exchanging data.

- **exchange(V x, long timeout, TimeUnit unit)**: Similar to the previous exchange(V x) method except that it takes a timeout parameter.

Next, we use an example to demonstrate the use of the Exchanger synchronizer.

Listing 6.14 Exchanger.java

```
1    package java.util.concurrent;
2    import java.util.concurrent.atomic.*;
3    import java.util.concurrent.locks.LockSupport;
4
5    public class Exchanger<V> {
6
7        // private CONSTANTS omitted
8        private static final class Node extends AtomicReference<Object> {
9            // (Listing 6.12)
10       }
11
12       private static final class Slot extends AtomicReference<Object> {
13           // Improve likelihood of isolation on <= 64 byte cache lines
14           long q0, q1, q2, q3, q4, q5, q6, q7, q8, q9, qa, qb, qc, qd, qe;
15       }
16       private volatile Slot[] arena = new Slot[CAPACITY];
17       private Object doExchange(Object item, boolean timed, long nanos) {
18           // body omitted
19       }
20       private void createSlot(int index) {
21           // Create slot outside of lock to narrow sync region
22           Slot newSlot = new Slot();
23           Slot[] a = arena;
24           synchronized (a) {
25               if (a[index] == null)
26                   a[index] = newSlot;
27           }
28       }
29
30       private static Object spinWait(Node node, Slot slot) {
31           int spins = SPINS;
32           for (;;) {
33               Object v = node.get();
34               if (v != null)
35                   return v;
36               else if (spins > 0)
37                   --spins;
38               else
39                   tryCancel(node, slot);
40           }
41       }
42
43       private static Object await(Node node, Slot slot) {
44           Thread w = Thread.currentThread();
```

```
45              int spins = SPINS;
46              for (;;) {
47                  Object v = node.get();
48                  if (v != null)
49                      return v;
50                  else if (spins > 0)              // Spin-wait phase
51                      --spins;
52                  else if (node.waiter == null)    // Set up to block next
53                      node.waiter = w;
54                  else if (w.isInterrupted())      // Abort on interrupt
55                      tryCancel(node, slot);
56                  else                             // Block
57                      LockSupport.park(node);
58              }
59          }
60          private Object awaitNanos(Node node, Slot slot, long nanos) {
61              // body omitted
62          }
63          public Exchanger() {
64          }
65          public V exchange(V x) throws InterruptedException {
66              if (!Thread.interrupted()) {
67                  Object v = doExchange((x == null) ? NULL_ITEM : x, false, 0);
68                  if (v == NULL_ITEM)
69                      return null;
70                  if (v != CANCEL)
71                      return (V)v;
72                  Thread.interrupted(); // Clear interrupt status on IE throw
73              }
74              throw new InterruptedException();
75          }
76          public V exchange(V x, long timeout, TimeUnit unit)
77              throws InterruptedException, TimeoutException {
78              // body omitted
79          }
80  }
```

6.4.2 An Example of Using an Exchanger

Listing 6.15 shows an example of using an Exchanger. In the driver program, we first create an Exchanger object at line 9 and then pass it to threads 1 (line 12) and 2 (line 13). The Thread1 and Thread2 classes are identical except their names. In each thread class, an Integer buffer is filled with a random integer number, which is used as the parameter for the exchange method, as shown at line 32 as below:

buffer = exchanger.exchange(buffer);

In the above statement, the buffer passed to the exchange method as the argument represents the data to send to the other party, while the buffer on the left side represents the data received from the other party.

Executing this demo program on my Eclipse IDE yielded the following output:

Thread 1 send: 306
Thread 2 send: 391
Thread 1 receive: 391
Thread 2 receive: 306

As you can see, Threads 1 and 2 sent numbers of "306" and "391," respectively, which were received by their respective parties as expected. In Listing 6.15, I commented out the while-loop in the run() method of each thread class to make it simpler to verify. It will still work if the while-loops were uncommented out.

You might wonder what would happen if an exchanger were used with three threads, instead of two threads. This is discussed following Listing 6.15.

Listing 6.15 ExchangerDemo.java

```
1    package jcp.ch6.synchronizers;
2
3    import java.util.Random;
4    import java.util.concurrent.Exchanger;
5
6    public class ExchangerDemo {
7      public static void main(String args[]) {
8        // 1. create an exchanger
9        Exchanger<Integer> exchanger = new Exchanger<Integer>();
10
11        // 2. create two threads for exchanging data
12        new Thread1(1, exchanger);
13        new Thread2(2, exchanger);
14      }
15    }
16
17    class Thread1 implements Runnable {
18      int id;
19      Exchanger<Integer> exchanger;
20
21      Thread1(int id, Exchanger<Integer> exchanger) {
22        this.id = id;
23        this.exchanger = exchanger;
24        new Thread(this).start();
25      }
26
27      public void run() {
28        try {
29          //while (true) {
30            Integer buffer = new Random().nextInt(999);
31            System.out.println("Thread " + id + " send: " + buffer);
32            buffer = exchanger.exchange(buffer);
33            System.out.println("Thread " + id + " receive: " + buffer);
34          //}
35        } catch (InterruptedException ie) {
36          System.out.println(ie);
```

```
37        }
38     }
39  }
40
41  class Thread2 implements Runnable {
42     int id;
43     Exchanger<Integer> exchanger;
44
45     Thread2(int id, Exchanger<Integer> exchanger) {
46        this.id = id;
47        this.exchanger = exchanger;
48        new Thread(this).start();
49     }
50
51     public void run() {
52        try {
53           //while (true) {
54              Integer buffer = new Random().nextInt(999);
55              System.out.println("Thread " + id + " send: " + buffer);
56              buffer = exchanger.exchange(buffer);
57              System.out.println("Thread " + id + " receive: " + buffer);
58           //}
59        } catch (InterruptedException ie) {
60           System.out.println(ie);
61        }
62     }
63  }
```

As we know, an Exchanger is supposed to be used by two threads to exchange data. What would happen if we use an Exchanger to exchange data among three threads? This experiment can be done easily by adding one more thread as shown at line 9 in Listing 6.16. As is shown in Figure 6.2, threads 1 and 2 exchanged data successfully; however, thread 3 sent a number but was hung because of no party to receive it.

Next, we discuss the Phaser synchronizer.

Listing 6.16 ExchangerDemo2.java

```
1   public class ExchangerDemo2 {
2      public static void main(String args[]) {
3         // 1. create an exchanger
4         Exchanger<Integer> exchanger = new Exchanger<Integer>();
5
6         // 2. create two threads for exchanging data
7         new ThreadA(1, exchanger);
8         new ThreadB(2, exchanger);
9         new ThreadC(3, exchanger);
10     }
11  }
```

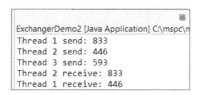

ExchangerDemo2 [Java Application] C:\mspc\n
Thread 1 send: 833
Thread 2 send: 446
Thread 3 send: 593
Thread 2 receive: 833
Thread 1 receive: 446

Figure 6.2 Exchanging data among three threads

6.5 PHASER

A `Phaser` is a reusable synchronization barrier, similar in functionality to `CyclicBarrier` and `CountDownLatch`, but requires each thread to register itself to participate in a particular phase. It was introduced in Java 7 and the implementation is fairly complicated. Therefore, let's change our approach a bit here. Instead of looking at the implementation at the source code level, we give an overview of its public methods first, and then present an example to demonstrate how it is used. So, let's start with an overview of the `Phaser` implementation first next.

6.5.1 An Overview of Phaser Implementation

Let's first look at how to construct a `Phaser` object. The `Phaser` synchronizer provides the following four constructors:

- `Phaser()`: Creates a new phaser with an initial phase number 0 but no initially registered parties and no parent.
- `Phaser(int parties)`: Creates a new phaser with an initial phase number 0 and the given number of registered unarrived parties but no parent.
- `Phaser(Phaser parent)`: Creates a new phaser with an initial phase number 0 and a parent but no registered unarrived parties.
- `Phaser(Phaser parent, int parties)`: Creates a new phaser with the given parent and number of registered unarrived parties.

Next, let's look at what public methods are available for the use of the phaser synchronizer. They are described as follows:

- `int register()`: Adds a new unarrived party to the phaser. Returns the arrival phase number to which this registration applied.
- `int arriveAndAwaitAdvance()`: Arrives at the phaser and awaits until all other parties have arrived. Returns the arrival phase number, or the (negative) current phase if terminated.
- `int arrive()`: Arrives at the phaser, but does not wait for others to arrive. It means that this method does not suspend execution of the calling method. The preceding `arriveAndWaitAdvance` method indicates the completion of a phase and then waits until all other registrants have also completed that phase.
- `int arriveAndDeregister()`: Arrives at the phaser and deregisters from it without waiting for others to arrive.

- int getPhase(): Returns the current phase number. The initial phase is always 0, then 1, 2, and so on.

Next, we present an example to show the use of the Phaser synchronizer.

6.5.2 An Example of Using a Phaser

This section provides an example of using the Phaser synchronizer. Listing 6.17 shows the PhaserDemo.java program, which consists of two classes: the driver and the ThreadN class. It works as follows:

- In the driver class, line 7 creates a Phaser that has only one party registered, namely the main thread.
- Lines 10 – 12 pass the phaser to three threads.
- Each thread registers itself to the phaser object in its constructor (line 37). This is very important, as otherwise, the threads executing various tasks in various phases will not be synchronized properly. You can try this out by commenting out line 37.
- Each thread calls the arriveAndAwaitAdvance method whenever a phase is complete, at which point, control returns back to the main thread or parent thread. However, after the last phase, each thread calls arriveAndDeregister method (line 62) before exiting the run() method.
- The main thread also calls the arriveAndAwaitAdvance method to synchronize all parties before moving to the next phase.
- The main thread calls the arriveAndDeregister method to deregister itself after all phases have completed.

Executing this PhaserDemo program yielded the following output in my environment:

```
C:\mspc\mydev\workspace\JCP\bin>java jcp.ch6.synchronizers.PhaserDemo
Initial phase ...
Thread 1 completed phase 0
Thread 3 completed phase 0
Thread 2 completed phase 0
Phaser completed phase 0
Thread 2 completed phase 1
Thread 3 completed phase 1
Thread 1 completed phase 1
Phaser completed phase 1
Thread 1 completed phase 2
Thread 2 completed phase 2
Thread 3 completed phase 2
Phaser completed phase 2
```

As you see, the three threads were orchestrated properly for executing each phase before moving to the next phase. This is how a phaser is supposed to work: synchronizing all participating parties to execute various tasks in phases.

This concludes our coverage of the Java synchronizers.

Listing 6.17 PhaserDemo.java

```
1   package jcp.ch6.synchronizers;
2
3   import java.util.concurrent.Phaser;
4
5   public class PhaserDemo {
6     public static void main(String args[]) {
7         Phaser phaser = new Phaser(1);
8         System.out.println("Initial phase ...");
9
10        new ThreadN(1, phaser);
11        new ThreadN(2, phaser);
12        new ThreadN(3, phaser);
13
14        int currPhase = phaser.getPhase();
15        phaser.arriveAndAwaitAdvance();
16        System.out.println("Phaser completed phase " + currPhase);
17
18        currPhase = phaser.getPhase();
19        phaser.arriveAndAwaitAdvance();
20        System.out.println("Phaser completed phase " + currPhase);
21
22        currPhase = phaser.getPhase();
23        phaser.arriveAndAwaitAdvance();
24        System.out.println("Phaser completed phase " + currPhase);
25
26        phaser.arriveAndDeregister();
27    }
28  }
29
30  class ThreadN implements Runnable {
31    int id;
32    Phaser phaser;
33
34    ThreadN(int id, Phaser phaser) {
35        this.id = id;
36        this.phaser = phaser;
37        phaser.register();
38        new Thread(this).start();
39    }
40
41    public void run() {
42
43        System.out.println("Thread " + id + " completed phase 0");
44        phaser.arriveAndAwaitAdvance();
45
46        try {
47            Thread.sleep(20);
48        } catch (InterruptedException ie) {
49            System.out.println(ie);
50        }
51
52        System.out.println("Thread " + id + " completed phase 1");
```

```
53        phaser.arriveAndAwaitAdvance();
54
55        try {
56           Thread.sleep(20);
57        } catch (InterruptedException ie) {
58           System.out.println(ie);
59        }
60
61        System.out.println("Thread " + id + " completed phase 2");
62        phaser.arriveAndDeregister();
63     }
64  }
```

6.6 SUMMARY

This chapter focused on the five synchronizers introduced in Java 5 and 7: Semaphore, CyclicBarrier, CountDownLatch, Exchanger, and Phaser. Each synchronizer solves a specific category of problems, and it's important to understand how each synchronizer should be used. We examined each synchronizer at the implementation level except the last synchronizer – Phaser. An example was presented for each synchronizer to help you understand how they work. See Table 6.1 for a summary of the five Java synchronizers introduced in this chapter. Pay attention to what methods are called to get the job done for each synchronizer.

The next chapter focuses on concurrent collections, which are ready-to-use data structures with proper synchronizations built-in.

Table 6.1 Five Java synchronizers

Synchronizer	Characteristics
Semaphore	Guards a number of permits. The acquire() and release() methods are used for incrementing and decrementing the number of permits, respectively. Access is granted only if the number of permits is larger than zero.
CyclicBarrier	Used to force a set of threads to call the await() method to wait at a predetermined barrier point until all threads have reached that point, upon which all threads can perform a pre-determined action. The barrier is called *cyclic* because it can be re-used after the waiting threads are released.
CountDownLatch	Keeps a count of a specified number of events initialized by the owning thread. The child threads call the countDown() method to decrement the number of events. The parent thread calls the await() method and blocks until the CountDownLatch object's internal counter reaches zero, after which the owning (waiting) thread is released and continues execution.
Exchanger	Designed for exchanging data between threads safely. Its method named exchange(V buffer) can be used by two threads to exchange data contained in the buffer.

Phaser	Allows multiple threads to perform various, different tasks that can be considered different *phases* of one job as the whole, such as in the scenario of workflows. A child thread must call the `register()` method to register itself to the phaser object. Both the parent and child threads call the `arriveAndAwaitAdvance()` method to synchronize each other. The child threads must also call the `arriveAndAwaitDeregister()` method before exiting.

6.7 EXERCISES

Exercise 6.1 Describe the concepts of semaphores, barriers and latches in general. Then, compare how they are used differently for Java concurrent programming.

Exercise 6.2 How do you enforce a semaphore to use fair or nonfair access policy?

Exercise 6.3 Is the number of *permits* capped once a semaphore is created?

Exercise 6.4 How many semaphores does a binary semaphore have, one or two?

Exercise 6.5 How do you pass a barrier action to a `CyclicBarrier`?

Exercise 6.6 Can you apply a `CountDownLatch` to more than one thread?

Exercise 6.7 Compare an `Exchanger` with a `SynchronousQueue` after completing the next chapter.

Exercise 6.8 Can you use an Exchanger with more than two threads?

Exercise 6.9 With a `Phaser` synchronizer, how do you enable a thread to participate a phase?

Exercise 6.10 Describe how you can break a complex workflow into several sub-workflows with a `Phaser`.

7   Synchronized Collections

Chapter 3 introduced many collection classes that implement various collection interfaces such as Set, List, Queue and Map. However, those classes do not have synchronization or concurrency support built-in. This chapter covers synchronized or concurrent collections available in the package of `java.util.concurrent`. Engineered for supporting concurrent operations, those concurrent collections include:

- ArrayBlocking, Synchronous, Delay, and PriorityBlocking Queues:

    ○ ArrayBlockingQueue
    ○ SynchronousQueue
    ○ DelayQueue
    ○ PriorityBlockingQueue

- Concurrent Maps, Queues and Set, including:

    ○ ConcurrentHashMap
    ○ ConcurrentLinkedQueue
    ○ ConcurrentLinkedDeque
    ○ ConcurrentSkipListMap
    ○ ConcurrentSkipListSet

- LinkedBlocking and Transfer Queues, including:

    ○ LinkedBlockingQueue
    ○ LinkedBlockingDeque
    ○ LinkedTransferQueue

- CopyOnWrite ArrayList and ArraySet, including:

    ○ CopyOnWriteArrayList
    ○ CopyOnWriteArraySet

Let's start with ArrayBlocking, Synchronous, Delay, and PriorityBlocking queues next.

7.1   ARRAYBLOCKING, SYNCHRONOUS, DELAY, AND PRIORITYBLOCKING QUEUES

This section covers the following synchronized queues:

- **ArrayBlockingQueue**: A bounded blocking queue backed by an array
- **SynchronousQueue**: A blocking queue in which each insert operation must wait for a corresponding remove operation by another thread, and vice versa
- **DelayQueue**: An unbounded blocking queue of elements typed `Delayed`, in which an element cannot be taken until its delay has expired.
- **PriorityBlockingQueue**: An unbounded blocking queue that uses the same ordering rules as class `PriorityQueue` and supplies blocking retrieval operations.

Figure 7.1 shows the lineage of the four classes we explore in this section. We once introduced the `AbstractQueue` class in §3.5.2. The `BlockingQueue` interface is implemented by all those four classes, so we introduce it next before we introduce those four classes.

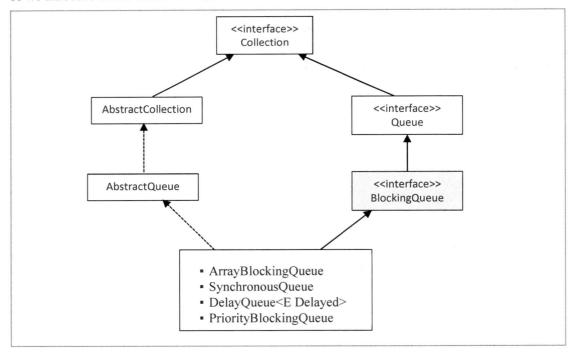

Figure 7.1 The lineage for the ArrayBlockingQueue, SynchronousQueue, DelayQueue and PriorityBlockingQueue

7.1.1 The BlockingQueue Interface

Unlike a regular queue, a BlockingQueue is a capacity-bounded Queue that blocks if the queue is empty or full until these conditions change. Blocking queues are used primarily for producer-consumer queues. However, as you see from Listing 7.1 that it's an interface, not a class, so it does not implement anything to impose *blocking* by itself. The blocking implementation lies with those classes that implement it, such as all those four classes we mentioned earlier. So, without further delay, let's move to discussing the ArrayBlockingQueue next.

Listing 7.1 BlockingQueue.java

```
1    package java.util.concurrent;
2
3    import java.util.Collection;
4    import java.util.Queue;
5
6    public interface BlockingQueue<E> extends Queue<E> {
7
8        boolean add(E e);
9        boolean remove(Object o);
10       boolean offer(E e);
11       boolean offer(E e, long timeout, TimeUnit unit)
12           throws InterruptedException;
13       E poll(long timeout, TimeUnit unit)
14           throws InterruptedException;
15
16       void put(E e) throws InterruptedException;
17       E take() throws InterruptedException;
18
19       int remainingCapacity();
20       public boolean contains(Object o);
21       int drainTo(Collection<? super E> c);
22       int drainTo(Collection<? super E> c, int maxElements);
23   }
```

7.1.2 ArrayBlockingQueue

An ArrayBlockingQueue is a bounded blocking queue backed by an array. It orders elements in FIFO (first-in-first-out) order. The head of the queue is the first element that entered the queue, while the tail of the queue is the element that entered the queue last. Since it promises the FIFO order, insert operations insert new elements at the tail of the queue, while retrieval operations retrieve elements at the head of the queue.

Listing 7.2 shows partially the ArrayBlockingQueue implementation. First, note the fields of items, takeIndex, putIndex, count, lock, notEmpty and notFull shown from lines 8 – 14. Given how far we have gone, there should be no explanation needed for these fields.

Of course, this class has internal methods to facilitate implementing the public methods. We have omitted most of them except a few, including the *insert* method shown from lines 18 – 23. As you see, internal methods do not use locks, but may use `Condition` objects to signal a condition change, such as line 22, which sends a signal whenever an item is inserted into the queue.

Lines 33 – 49 show the three forms of the `ArrayBlockingQueue` constructors as follows:

- `ArrayBlockingQueue(int capacity)`: Creates an `ArrayBlockingQueue` with the given (fixed) capacity and default access policy of non-fair access.
- `ArrayBlockingQueue(int capacity, boolean fair)`: Creates an `ArrayBlockingQueue` with the given (fixed) capacity and the access policy specified at line 41 when the lock is created.
- `ArrayBlockingQueue(int capacity, boolean fair, Collection<? extends E> c)`: Creates an `ArrayBlockingQueue` with the given (fixed) capacity, the specified access policy and an initial collection for populating the queue.

Lines 51 – 137 show some of the public methods for the `ArrayBlockingQueue`, such as add, offer, put, poll, take, peek, next, remove, contains, and so on. These methods are not very different from their non-concurrent counterparts, except that they are synchronized with explicit locks. You can pick a few, walk through the implementation, and understand how locks are used for intended operations.

Next, we present an example to demonstrate the use of the `ArrayBlockingQueue` concurrent collection, following Listing 7.2.

Listing 7.2 ArrayBlockingQueue.java (partial)

```
1   package java.util.concurrent;
2   import java.util.concurrent.locks.*;
3   import java.util.*;
4
5   public class ArrayBlockingQueue<E> extends AbstractQueue<E>
6           implements BlockingQueue<E>, java.io.Serializable {
7
8       final Object[] items; /** The queued items */
9       int takeIndex;
10      int putIndex;
11      int count; /** Number of elements in the queue */
12      final ReentrantLock lock; /** Main lock guarding all access */
13      private final Condition notEmpty; /** Condition for waiting takes */
14      private final Condition notFull; /** Condition for waiting puts */
15
16      // Internal helper methods (omitted)
17
18      private void insert(E x) {
19          items[putIndex] = x;
20          putIndex = inc(putIndex);
21          ++count;
22          notEmpty.signal();
23      }
24
25      private E extract() {
26          // body omitted
27      }
```

```
28
29      void removeAt(int i) {
30          // body omitted
31      }
32
33      public ArrayBlockingQueue(int capacity) {
34          this(capacity, false);
35      }
36
37      public ArrayBlockingQueue(int capacity, boolean fair) {
38          if (capacity <= 0)
39              throw new IllegalArgumentException();
40          this.items = new Object[capacity];
41          lock = new ReentrantLock(fair);
42          notEmpty = lock.newCondition();
43          notFull =  lock.newCondition();
44      }
45
46      public ArrayBlockingQueue(int capacity, boolean fair,
47                                Collection<? extends E> c) {
48          // body omitted
49      }
50
51      public boolean add(E e) {
52          return super.add(e);
53      }
54
55      public boolean offer(E e) {
56          checkNotNull(e);
57          final ReentrantLock lock = this.lock;
58          lock.lock();
59          try {
60              if (count == items.length)
61                  return false;
62              else {
63                  insert(e);
64                  return true;
65              }
66          } finally {
67              lock.unlock();
68          }
69      }
70
71      public void put(E e) throws InterruptedException {
72          checkNotNull(e);
73          final ReentrantLock lock = this.lock;
74          lock.lockInterruptibly();
75          try {
76              while (count == items.length)
77                  notFull.await();
78              insert(e);
79          } finally {
```

```
80                  lock.unlock();
81            }
82      }
83
84      public boolean offer(E e, long timeout, TimeUnit unit)
85            throws InterruptedException {
86            // body omitted
87      }
88
89      public E poll() {
90            final ReentrantLock lock = this.lock;
91            lock.lock();
92            try {
93                  return (count == 0) ? null : extract();
94            } finally {
95                  lock.unlock();
96            }
97      }
98
99      public E take() throws InterruptedException {
100           final ReentrantLock lock = this.lock;
101           lock.lockInterruptibly();
102           try {
103                 while (count == 0)
104                       notEmpty.await();
105                 return extract();
106           } finally {
107                 lock.unlock();
108           }
109     }
110
111     public E poll(long timeout, TimeUnit unit) throws InterruptedException
        {
112           // body omitted
113     }
114
115     public E peek() {
116           // body omitted
117     }
118
119     public boolean remove(Object o) {
120           // body omitted
121     }
122
123     public boolean contains(Object o) {
124           // body omitted
125     }
126
127     public boolean hasNext() {
128               return remaining > 0;
129       }
130
```

```
131     public E next() {
132         // body omitted
133     }
134
135     public void remove() {
136         // body omitted
137   }
138 }
```

Listing 7.3 shows the ArrayBlockingQueueDemo.java program to illustrate the use of the ArrayBlockingQueue synchronized collection for a producer-consumer scenario. Line 8 shows the arrayBlockingQueue object created with a capacity of 8 and fair access policy of FIFO (LIFO is the unfair access policy). Then, lines 9 and 10 pass the arrayBlockingQueue object to a new instance of Producer and a new instance of Consumer, respectively. The Consumer and Producer classes are coded similarly except that the Consumer class calls take() method of the arrayBlockingQueue object, while the Producer class calls the put() method of the arrayBlockingQueue object with a new Integer object every time.

Executing this program on my Eclipse IDE yielded the following output:

```
......
producer put 51746
producer put 51747
producer put 51748
producer put 51749
producer put 51750
producer put 51751
producer put 51752
producer put 51753
producer put 51754
producer put 51755
consumer got 51747
consumer got 51748
consumer got 51749
consumer got 51750
consumer got 51751
consumer got 51752
consumer got 51753
consumer got 51754
consumer got 51755
consumer got 51756
producer put 51756
......
```

As you see, the capacity of the ArrayBlockingQueue is set to 8, but there are 10 producer output lines followed by 10 consumer output lines. This is because the ArrayBlockingQueue is a synchronized collection, while the methods of the Consumer and Producer classes are not necessarily synchronized and the output lines from the Consumer and Producer objects are not necessarily aligned as they should have. Our purpose here is to demonstrate that the ArrayBlockingQueue is indeed a synchronized collection, which is evidenced by the absence of out-of-order items from either side of the Consumer and Producer.

This concludes our introduction to the ArrayBlockingQueue concurrent collection. We discuss the SynchronousQueue concurrent collection next.

Listing 7.3 ArrayBlockingQueueDemo.java

```
1   package jcp.ch7.synchedcollections;
2
3   import java.util.concurrent.ArrayBlockingQueue;
4
5   public class ArrayBlockingQueueDemo {
6     public static void main(String args[]) {
7
8         ArrayBlockingQueue<Integer> arrayBlockingQueue = new
              ArrayBlockingQueue<Integer> (8, true);
9         new Producer(arrayBlockingQueue);
10        new Consumer(arrayBlockingQueue);
11    }
12  }
13
14  class Consumer implements Runnable {
15    private ArrayBlockingQueue<Integer> arrayBlockingQueue;
16
17    Consumer(ArrayBlockingQueue<Integer> arrayBlockingQueue) {
18      this.arrayBlockingQueue = arrayBlockingQueue;
19      new Thread(this, "Consumer").start();
20    }
21
22    public void run() {
23      while (true) {
24        try {
25          int number = (Integer) arrayBlockingQueue.take();
26          System.out.println("consumer got " + number);
27        } catch (InterruptedException ie) {
28          System.out.println("consumer interrupted");
29        }
30      }
31    }
32  }
33
34  class Producer implements Runnable {
35    ArrayBlockingQueue<Integer> arrayBlockingQueue;
36
37    Producer(ArrayBlockingQueue<Integer> arrayBlockingQueue) {
38      this.arrayBlockingQueue = arrayBlockingQueue;
39      new Thread(this, "Producer").start();
40    }
41
42    public void run() {
```

```
43        int i = 0;
44
45        while (true) {
46           try {
47              arrayBlockingQueue.put(new Integer(i));
48              System.out.println("producer put " + i);
49              i++;
50           } catch (InterruptedException ie) {
51              System.out.println("producer interrupted");
52           }
53        }
54     }
55  }
```

7.1.3 SynchronousQueue

In §6.4, when discussing the Exchanger synchronizer, we mentioned that an Exchanger may be viewed as a bidirectional form of a SynchronousQueue. Indeed, a SynchronousQueue may act like a uni-directional channel through which an object running in one thread can sync up with an object running in another thread and hand it some information, event, or task. It is a blocking queue that can only contain a single element internally. The term "*blocking*" means that a thread performing the *put* operation to insert an element into the queue is blocked until another thread performs the *take* operation to take that element from the queue. Likewise, if a thread tries to take an element out of the queue but no element is currently present, that thread is blocked until a thread puts an element into the queue.

The internal implementation of the class starts with an embedded Transferer class as simple as shown below:

```
1      abstract static class Transferer {
2          abstract Object transfer(Object e, boolean timed, long nanos);
3      }
```

This Transferer class has only one method named transfer, which takes an Object e as its first parameter. It performs a put or take operation, based on the state of the object e. If e is not null, it's the object to be handed over to the consumer. If null, on the other hand, the Transferer object requests the transfer method to return an item offered by the producer. The other two parameters for the *transfer* method control *timeout*. Therefore, as you see, calling this class a queue is a bit of an overstatement. Rather, it's more of a *rendezvous* point.

The Transferer class is extended by two sub-classes: TransferQueue and TransferStack, as shown in Figure 7.2. The TransferQueue class has a QNode class as its node class, which has a volatile Object item field among others. Similarly, the TransferStack class has an SNode class as its node class, which has an Object item field as well. In both cases, it's the item field that is *put* or *taken*. However, only one method named transfer is designed for both *put* and *taken* operations:

```
Object transfer(Object e, boolean timed, long nanos) {
   ...
}
```

In the above method, if e is not null, it is *put* into the queue. However, if e is null, the awaitFulfill method is called for the producer to fill the queue as shown below:

```
// TransferQueue version
Object awaitFulfill(QNode s, Object e, boolean timed, long nanos) {
    ...
}
```

or

```
// TransferStack version
Object awaitFulfill(SNode s, Object e, boolean timed, long nanos) {
    ...
}
```

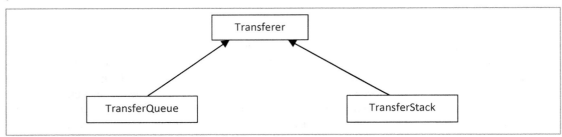

Figure 7.2 The Transferer class sub-classed by TransferQueue and TransferStack

The SynchronousQueue class has a transferer field, as shown in Listing 7.4, which is used to perform actual put and take operations. Additional details about the SynchronousQueue class are as follows:

- **Constructors**: The no-arg version (lines 11 – 13) creates a SynchronousQueue with non-fair access policy, while the parameterized version (lines 15 – 17) allows a choice of TransferQueue (FIFO – *fair*) or TransferStack (LIFO – *nonfair*).
- **put()**: Delegates to the transferer.transfer method (line 21) with the object to be put passed-in
- **take()**: Delegates to the transferer.transfer method (line 28) with null passed in

Next, we use an example to demonstrate the use of SynchronousQueue, following Listing 7.4.

Listing 7.4 SynchronousQueue.java (partial)

```
1    package java.util.concurrent;
2    import java.util.concurrent.locks.*;
3    import java.util.concurrent.atomic.*;
4    import java.util.*;
5
6    public class SynchronousQueue<E> extends AbstractQueue<E>
7        implements BlockingQueue<E>, java.io.Serializable {
8
9        private transient volatile Transferer transferer;
10
```

```
11      public SynchronousQueue() {
12          this(false);
13      }
14
15      public SynchronousQueue(boolean fair) {
16          transferer = fair ? new TransferQueue() : new TransferStack();
17      }
18
19      public void put(E o) throws InterruptedException {
20          if (o == null) throw new NullPointerException();
21          if (transferer.transfer(o, false, 0) == null) {
22              Thread.interrupted();
23              throw new InterruptedException();
24          }
25      }
26
27      public E take() throws InterruptedException {
28          Object e = transferer.transfer(null, false, 0);
29          if (e != null)
30              return (E)e;
31          Thread.interrupted();
32          throw new InterruptedException();
33      }
34
35      // all other methods omitted
36  }
```

Listing 7.5 shows the SynchronousQueueDemo.java program that consists of a driver (lines 5 – 18), a *Consumer* named Consumer2 (lines 20 – 39), and a *Producer* named producer2 (lines 41 – 63). It works as follows:

- In the driver program a SynchronousQueue object is created at line 8. Then, this object is passed to the producer (line 9) and consumer (line 16), respectively. Since the start() method is called in the Consumer and Producer's constructors, the producer and consumer threads will be started up after these calls.

- The syncrhonousQueue.take() method is called at line 31 for the consumer, while the syncrhonousQueue.put(new Integer(i)) method is called at line 54 for the producer. These methods help serialize the put and take operations between a consumer and a producer.

Note that we added Thread.sleep (2000) statements in various places in Listing 7.5 so that when we execute this demo, the output will be aligned as they should have been. These statements are not needed in real applications. Executing this demo program yielded the following output as expected:

```
consumer got 0
producer put 0
producer put 1
consumer got 1
consumer got 2
producer put 2
producer put 3
consumer got 3
```

producer put 4
consumer got 4
consumer got 5
producer put 5
......

This concludes our coverage of the SyncrhonousQueue concurrent collection. Next, we discuss the DelayQueue concurrent collection.

Listing 7.5 SynchronousQueueDemo.java

```
1   package jcp.ch7.synchedcollections;
2
3   import java.util.concurrent.SynchronousQueue;
4
5   public class SynchronousQueueDemo {
6     public static void main(String args[]) {
7
8        SynchronousQueue<Integer> syncrhonousQueue = new
           SynchronousQueue<Integer>();
9        new Producer2(syncrhonousQueue);
10       try {
11          Thread.sleep(2000);
12       } catch (InterruptedException e) {
13          // TODO Auto-generated catch block
14          e.printStackTrace();
15       }
16       new Consumer2(syncrhonousQueue);
17     }
18  }
19
20  class Consumer2 implements Runnable {
21    private SynchronousQueue<Integer> syncrhonousQueue;
22
23    Consumer2(SynchronousQueue<Integer> syncrhonousQueue) {
24       this.syncrhonousQueue = syncrhonousQueue;
25       new Thread(this, "Consumer").start();
26    }
27
28    public void run() {
29       while (true) {
30          try {
31             int number = (Integer) syncrhonousQueue.take();
32             System.out.println("consumer got " + number);
33             Thread.sleep(2000);
34          } catch (InterruptedException ie) {
35             System.out.println("consumer interrupted");
36          }
37       }
38    }
39  }
```

```
40
41  class Producer2 implements Runnable {
42      SynchronousQueue<Integer> syncrhonousQueue;
43
44      Producer2(SynchronousQueue<Integer> syncrhonousQueue) {
45          this.syncrhonousQueue = syncrhonousQueue;
46          new Thread(this, "Producer").start();
47      }
48
49      public void run() {
50          int i = 0;
51
52          while (true) {
53              try {
54                  syncrhonousQueue.put(new Integer(i));
55                  System.out.println("producer put " + i);
56                  Thread.sleep(2000);
57                  i++;
58              } catch (InterruptedException ie) {
59                  System.out.println("producer interrupted");
60              }
61          }
62      }
63  }
```

7.1.4 DelayQueue

The DelayQueue concurrent collection represents an unbounded blocking queue of elements typed Delayed. It differs from other queues that an element can only be taken when its delay has expired; thus, the head of the queue exists only if there are expired elements.

Since each element in a DelayQueue has an age, the DelayQueue fits well into the leader-follower pattern, which helps minimize unnecessary timed waiting, as when a thread becomes the leader, it waits only for the next delay to elapse, but other threads await indefinitely. The leader thread signals some other thread before returning from calls to take() or poll(...), unless some other thread becomes leader in the interim. So waiting threads must be prepared to acquire and lose leadership while waiting.

Listing 7.6 shows partially the implementation of the DelayQueue in Java. As you see, it has the following fields:

- lock: A reentrant lock for implementing synchronization
- q: A priority queue, which stores elements with delays
- leader: A leader thread, as it's always necessary to designate a leader based on the seniority of the elements
- available: A Condition variable for signaling the availability of expired members

The other implementation details include:

- Constructors: A no-arg constructor (line 13) and a parameterized constructor with a given collection (lines 14 – 16).

- offer(E e): Inserts the delayed element into the queue (lines 18 – 31). Note that when a new element is inserted into the queue as the head, the current leader is invalidated by setting it to null and the Condition object available's signal method is called to indicate that a newer element becomes available as the head of the queue and a new thread may need to become the leader. (Note that the add and put methods call this offer method for the same operation.)
- take(): The method for removing the head element of the queue (lines 45 – 76). The for-loop (lines 49 – 70) implements various wait conditions, such as when the first element is null (line 51), or when the first node has not expired (line 57), in which cases the Condition object available's await() method must be called. Finally, lines 72 – 73 show that when a leader has left and the queue still has elements left in the queue, the Condition object available's signal method must be called so that a new leader can be elected.

Actually, the DelayQueue is one of the simplest concurrent collections that require very minimum explanation. Next, we present an example to demonstrate the use of the DelayQueue, following Listing 7.6.

Listing 7.6 DelayQueue.java (partial)

```
1   package java.util.concurrent;
2   import java.util.concurrent.locks.*;
3   import java.util.*;
4
5   public class DelayQueue<E extends Delayed> extends AbstractQueue<E>
6       implements BlockingQueue<E> {
7
8       private transient final ReentrantLock lock = new ReentrantLock();
9       private final PriorityQueue<E> q = new PriorityQueue<E>();
10      private Thread leader = null;
11      private final Condition available = lock.newCondition();
12
13      public DelayQueue() {}
14      public DelayQueue(Collection<? extends E> c) {
15          this.addAll(c);
16      }
17
18      public boolean offer(E e) {
19          final ReentrantLock lock = this.lock;
20          lock.lock();
21          try {
22              q.offer(e);
23              if (q.peek() == e) {
24                  leader = null;
25                  available.signal();
26              }
27              return true;
28          } finally {
29              lock.unlock();
30          }
31      }
```

```
32
33      public boolean add(E e) {
34          return offer(e);
35      }
36
37      public void put(E e) {
38          offer(e);
39      }
40
41      public E poll() {
42          // body omitted
43      }
44
45      public E take() throws InterruptedException {
46          final ReentrantLock lock = this.lock;
47          lock.lockInterruptibly();
48          try {
49              for (;;) {
50                  E first = q.peek();
51                  if (first == null)
52                      available.await();
53                  else {
54                      long delay = first.getDelay(TimeUnit.NANOSECONDS);
55                      if (delay <= 0)
56                          return q.poll();
57                      else if (leader != null)
58                          available.await();
59                      else {
60                          Thread thisThread = Thread.currentThread();
61                          leader = thisThread;
62                          try {
63                              available.awaitNanos(delay);
64                          } finally {
65                              if (leader == thisThread)
66                                  leader = null;
67                          }
68                      }
69                  }
70              }
71          } finally {
72              if (leader == null && q.peek() != null)
73                  available.signal();
74              lock.unlock();
75          }
76      }
77
78      // all other methods are omitted
79  }
```

Listing 7.7 shows the DelayQueueDemo.java program. It consists of the following four classes:

- The `DelayObject` class: Implements the `Delayed` interface as required by the `DelayQueue` class. The class has only two fields: an `id` field and a `startTime` field. The constructor takes two parameters: `id` and `delay`, with `delay` representing the amount of time to be delayed, which is added to the current time for an instance of the class to be created. The `getDelay` method returns the amount of delay remaining at the time when the method is called, while the `compareTo` method is used for determining the priority or age of each `DelayObject` instance.
- The `DelayQueueProducer` class: Responsible for calling the `put(object)` method (line 52) to insert `DelayObject`s into the queue. Note that the `Random` class is used to create both random delays and ids for the `DelayObject`s to be inserted into the queue. The `Random` class is instantiated at line 44 and called twice: once at line 48 for creating random delays of less than 2000 milliseconds, and once at line 49 for creating an `id` for the `DelayObject`, both using the `nextInt(...)` method of the `Random` class. The `Random.nextInt()` method creates both negative and positive integers, because of which we use the parameterized `nextInt(...)` method instead.
- The `DelayQueueConsumer` class: Responsible for consuming the `DelayObject`s by calling the `DelayQueue`'s `take()` method, as shown at line 72.
- The `DelayQueueDemo` class: As simple as usual that it creates the blocking queue of `DelayQueue` in question, instantiates a `DelayQueueProducer` instance and a `DelayQueueConsumer` instance to start up the producer and consumer.

Next, we discuss the output of executing this program, following Listing 7.7.

Listing 7.7 DelayQueueDemo.java

```
1    package jcp.ch7.synchedcollections;
2
3    import java.util.Random;
4    import java.util.concurrent.BlockingQueue;
5    import java.util.concurrent.DelayQueue;
6    import java.util.concurrent.Delayed;
7    import java.util.concurrent.TimeUnit;
8
9    class DelayObject implements Delayed {
10     private Integer id;
11     private long startTime;
12
13     public DelayObject(Integer id, long delay) {
14       this.id = id;
15       this.startTime = System.currentTimeMillis() + delay;
16     }
17
18     public long getDelay(TimeUnit unit) {
19       long diff = startTime - System.currentTimeMillis();
20       return unit.convert(diff, TimeUnit.MILLISECONDS);
21     }
22
23     public int compareTo(Delayed obj) {
24       long objStartTime = ((DelayObject) obj).startTime;
25       if (this.startTime == objStartTime) return 0;
```

```
26          return (this.startTime < objStartTime) ? -1 : 1;
27      }
28
29      public String toString() {
30          return "DelayObject: id = " + id + ", delay = " +
                getDelay(TimeUnit.MILLISECONDS);
31      }
32  }
33
34  class DelayQueueProducer implements Runnable {
35      BlockingQueue<DelayObject> queue;
36
37      DelayQueueProducer (BlockingQueue<DelayObject> queue) {
38          this.queue = queue;
39          new Thread(this, "DelayQueueProducer").start();
40      }
41
42      public void run() {
43
44          Random random = new Random();
45          for (int i = 0; i < 10; i++) {
46              try {
47                  // 1. create a delayed object
48                  int delay = random.nextInt(10000);
49                  DelayObject object = new DelayObject(new
                        Integer(random.nextInt(Integer.MAX_VALUE)), delay);
50
51                  // 2. put delayed object into queue
52                  queue.put(object);
53                  System.out.println("producer put " + object.toString());
54              } catch (InterruptedException ie) {
55                  System.out.println("producer interrupted");
56              }
57          }
58      }
59  }
60
61  class DelayQueueConsumer implements Runnable {
62      BlockingQueue<DelayObject> queue;
63
64      DelayQueueConsumer (BlockingQueue<DelayObject> queue) {
65          this.queue = queue;
66          new Thread(this, "DelayQueueConsumer").start();
67      }
68
69      public void run() {
70          for (int i = 0; i < 10; i++) {
71              try {
72                  DelayObject delayObject = queue.take();
73                  System.out.println("consumer get " + delayObject.toString());
74              } catch (InterruptedException ie) {
75                  System.out.println("consumer interrupted");
```

```
76            }
77         }
78      }
79  }
80
81  public class DelayQueueDemo {
82    public static void main(String args[]) {
83
84        // 1. create a delay queue
85        DelayQueue<DelayObject> delayQueue = new DelayQueue<DelayObject>();
86
87        // 2. pass delay queue to producer and consumer
88        new DelayQueueProducer(delayQueue);
89        new DelayQueueConsumer(delayQueue);
90    }
91  }
```

Executing the above DelayQueueDemo program yielded the following output:

```
producer put DelayObject: id = 345604845, delay = 1222
producer put DelayObject: id = 185436596, delay = 1041
producer put DelayObject: id = 1581970626, delay = 2844
producer put DelayObject: id = 1319691989, delay = 4620
producer put DelayObject: id = 453111722, delay = 1158
producer put DelayObject: id = 562687654, delay = 6456
producer put DelayObject: id = 1263067978, delay = 8812
producer put DelayObject: id = 536129984, delay = 1427
producer put DelayObject: id = 1832280720, delay = 5242
producer put DelayObject: id = 1480877603, delay = 1428
consumer get DelayObject: id = 185436596, delay = -1
consumer get DelayObject: id = 453111722, delay = -1
consumer get DelayObject: id = 345604845, delay = -1
consumer get DelayObject: id = 536129984, delay = -1
consumer get DelayObject: id = 1480877603, delay = 0
consumer get DelayObject: id = 1581970626, delay = 0
consumer get DelayObject: id = 1319691989, delay = -1
consumer get DelayObject: id = 1832280720, delay = -1
consumer get DelayObject: id = 562687654, delay = 0
consumer get DelayObject: id = 1263067978, delay = 0
```

Note that the DelayObjects were consumed in the order of least amount of delay, with the object with id=185436596 first, and the object with id=453111722 second, and so on. In addition, by the time the objects were consumed, their delays had expired, with zero or negative delays.

This concludes our discussion on the DelayQueue concurrent collection. Next, we discuss the PriorityBlockingQueue concurrent collection.

7.1.5 PriorityBlockingQueue

Section 3.5.3 introduced PriorityQueue. The PriorityBlockingQueue is an unbounded *blocking* queue that uses the same ordering rules as PriorityQueue, but supplies blocking retrieval operations. However, *unbounded* is only a theoretical concept. Eventually, attempted additions to an unbounded queue may fail due to resource exhaustion, causing OutOfMemoryError.

Next, let's look at how PriorityBlockingQueue adds synchronization to the unsynchronized version of PriorityQueue.

Listing 7.8 shows partially the implementation of PriorityBlockingQueue. Lines 12 and 13 show the ReentrantLock named lock and Condition object named notEmpty. The offer(E e) method uses the reentrant lock to guard the critical section of the method, while the notEmpty condition object is used to signal waiting threads that the queue has become not empty. The poll() and take() methods retrieve and remove the head of this queue, but the poll() method does not wait while the take() method waits when the queue is empty, as indicated from lines 65 – 66, where the notEmpty.await() statement is placed. The poll() method calls the dequeue() method, which is called only when the thread has acquired the lock.

Next, we present an example to demonstrate the use of PriorityBlockingQueue, following Listing 7.8.

Listing 7.8 PriorityBlockingQueue.java (partial)

```
1    public class PriorityBlockingQueue<E> extends AbstractQueue<E>
2        implements BlockingQueue<E>, java.io.Serializable {
3
4        public PriorityBlockingQueue(int initialCapacity) {
5            this(initialCapacity, null);
6        }
7
8        public PriorityBlockingQueue(int initialCapacity,
9                                     Comparator<? super E> comparator) {
10           if (initialCapacity < 1)
11               throw new IllegalArgumentException();
12           this.lock = new ReentrantLock();
13           this.notEmpty = lock.newCondition();
14           this.comparator = comparator;
15           this.queue = new Object[initialCapacity];
16       }
17       // many private methods omitted here
18
19       public boolean add(E e) {
20           return offer(e);
21       }
22
23       public void put(E e) {
24           offer(e); // never need to block
25       }
26
27       public boolean offer(E e) {
28           if (e == null)
29               throw new NullPointerException();
```

```
30          final ReentrantLock lock = this.lock;
31          lock.lock();
32          int n, cap;
33          Object[] array;
34          while ((n = size) >= (cap = (array = queue).length))
35              tryGrow(array, cap);
36          try {
37              Comparator<? super E> cmp = comparator;
38              if (cmp == null)
39                  siftUpComparable(n, e, array);
40              else
41                  siftUpUsingComparator(n, e, array, cmp);
42              size = n + 1;
43              notEmpty.signal();
44          } finally {
45              lock.unlock();
46          }
47          return true;
48      }
49
50      public E poll() {
51          final ReentrantLock lock = this.lock;
52          lock.lock();
53          try {
54              return dequeue();
55          } finally {
56              lock.unlock();
57          }
58      }
59
60      public E take() throws InterruptedException {
61          final ReentrantLock lock = this.lock;
62          lock.lockInterruptibly();
63          E result;
64          try {
65              while ( (result = dequeue()) == null)
66                  notEmpty.await();
67          } finally {
68              lock.unlock();
69          }
70          return result;
71      }
```

Listing 7.9 shows the PriorityBlockingQueueDemo.java program. The Scheduler class simulates scheduling priority-based tasks using the PriorityBlockingQueue synchronized collection. Priorities are simulated at line 21, using the random.nextInt(100) call to limit the values of priorities to below 100.

The driver class, named PriorityBlockingQueueDemo, starts with creating a PriorityBlockingQueue object at line 29. Lines 37 – 39 show that three instances of schedulers are launched using an ExecutorService object, with the PriorityBlockingQueue object passed to each of the three schedulers. The statements defined from lines 41 – 45 allow the main thread to sleep five seconds before shutting down the ExecutorService thread pool. The for-loop defined from lines 50 – 62 illustrates how to use the methods of size(), peek() and poll() to get the size of the queue, peek the highest priority element and get and remove the highest priority element, respectively. The output of running this program, as shown below, verifies how those methods are used:

```
current pbq = [1, 9, 19, 55, 48, 51, 40, 93, 77, 95, 67, 55, 51, 60, 70] (size = 15)
after peek: 1, pq = [1, 9, 19, 55, 48, 51, 40, 93, 77, 95, 67, 55, 51, 60, 70] (size = 15)
after poll: 1, pq = [9, 48, 19, 55, 67, 51, 40, 93, 77, 95, 70, 55, 51, 60] (size = 14)

current pbq = [9, 48, 19, 55, 67, 51, 40, 93, 77, 95, 70, 55, 51, 60] (size = 14)
after peek: 9, pq = [9, 48, 19, 55, 67, 51, 40, 93, 77, 95, 70, 55, 51, 60] (size = 14)
after poll: 9, pq = [19, 48, 40, 55, 67, 51, 60, 93, 77, 95, 70, 55, 51] (size = 13)

current pbq = [19, 48, 40, 55, 67, 51, 60, 93, 77, 95, 70, 55, 51] (size = 13)
after peek: 19, pq = [19, 48, 40, 55, 67, 51, 60, 93, 77, 95, 70, 55, 51] (size = 13)
after poll: 19, pq = [40, 48, 51, 55, 67, 51, 60, 93, 77, 95, 70, 55] (size = 12)
```

As you see, the head element always represents the highest priority task.

This concludes our discussion on the PriorityBlockingQueue concurrent collection. Next, we discuss the ConcurrentHashMap concurrent collection.

Listing 7.9 PriorityBlockingQueueDemo.java

```
1    package jcp.ch7.synchedcollections;
2
3    import java.util.Random;
4    import java.util.concurrent.ExecutorService;
5    import java.util.concurrent.Executors;
6    import java.util.concurrent.PriorityBlockingQueue;
7
8    class Scheduler extends Thread {
9      int id;
10     Random random;
11     PriorityBlockingQueue<Integer> priorityBlockingQueue;
12
13     Scheduler(int id, PriorityBlockingQueue<Integer> priorityBlockingQueue)
     {
14       this.id = id;
15       this.random = new Random();
16       this.priorityBlockingQueue = priorityBlockingQueue;
17     }
18
19     public void run() {
20       for (int i = 0; i < 5; i++) {
21         priorityBlockingQueue.add(random.nextInt(100));
22       }
23     }
24   }
```

```
25
26  public class PriorityBlockingQueueDemo {
27
28    public static void main(String[] args) {
29      PriorityBlockingQueue<Integer> pbq = new
            PriorityBlockingQueue<Integer>();
30
31      int POOL_SIZE = 3;
32      // 1. Create a newFixedThreadPool using the Executors utility class
33      ExecutorService executorService = Executors
34          .newFixedThreadPool(POOL_SIZE);
35
36      // 2. launch schedulers
37      for (int i = 0; i < POOL_SIZE; i++) {
38        executorService.execute(new Scheduler(i, pbq));
39      }
40
41      try {
42        Thread.sleep(5000);
43      } catch (InterruptedException e) {
44        e.printStackTrace();
45      }
46
47      // 3. shut down executorService to avoid resource leak
48      executorService.shutdown();
49
50      for (int i = 0; i < 3; i++) {
51        // 4. check queue and size
52        System.out.println("current pbq = " + pbq + " (size = "
53            + pbq.size() + ")");
54
55        // 5. peek the highest priority
56        System.out.println("after peek: " + pbq.peek() + ", pq = " + pbq
57            + " (size = " + pbq.size() + ")");
58
59        // 6. return highest priority and remove it from the queue
60        System.out.println("after poll: " + pbq.poll() + ", pq = " + pbq
61            + " (size = " + pbq.size() + ")\n");
62      }
63    }
64  }
```

7.2 CONCURRENT MAPS, QUEUES AND SET

This section covers the concurrent collections with their class names prefixed with "*concurrent*," including ConcurrentHashMap, ConcurrentLinkedQueue, ConcurrentLinkedDeque, ConcurrentSkipListMap, and ConcurrentSkipListSet. Let's start with the ConcurrentHashMap class first, as this probably is the most commonly used concurrent collection of all.

7.2.1 ConcurrentHashMap

A ConcurrentHashMap is more similar to a Hashtable than to its unsynchronized counterpart HashMap introduced in §3.7.2. It obeys the same functional specification as a Hashtable, and includes versions of methods corresponding to each method of Hashtable. However, its implementation is drastically different, as elaborated below.

First, the core of a ConcurrentHashMap is a HashEntry data structure, which is shown in Listing 7.10. In addition to the fields of hash, key, and value, it has a field of next of the same type, making it a self-referencing data structure. Note the setNext method at line 14, which calls the UNSAFE.putOrederedObject method. UNSAFE.putOrderedObject is typically used for producing ultra-low latency code by allowing use of non-blocking code with guaranteed writes. Such writes will not be re-ordered by instruction reordering, with its faster store-store barrier property, rather than the slower store-load barrier (which is used when doing a volatile write), preserved. This is a good performance practice that it does not stall the bus, but with a side-effect that the writes may not immediately be visible to other threads (or even the current thread) within a few nanoseconds.

Listing 7.10 The HashEntry class embedded in the ConcurrentHashMap class

```
1    static final class HashEntry<K,V> {
2            final int hash;
3            final K key;
4            volatile V value;
5            volatile HashEntry<K,V> next;
6
7            HashEntry(int hash, K key, V value, HashEntry<K,V> next) {
8                this.hash = hash;
9                this.key = key;
10               this.value = value;
11               this.next = next;
12           }
13
14           final void setNext(HashEntry<K,V> n) {
15               UNSAFE.putOrderedObject(this, nextOffset, n);
16           }
17
18           // Unsafe mechanics
19           static final sun.misc.Unsafe UNSAFE;
20           static final long nextOffset;
21           static {
22             try {
23                 UNSAFE = sun.misc.Unsafe.getUnsafe();
24                 Class k = HashEntry.class;
25                 nextOffset = UNSAFE.objectFieldOffset
26                     (k.getDeclaredField("next"));
27             } catch (Exception e) {
28                 throw new Error(e);
29             }
30         }
31     }
```

The next crucial embedded class for the ConcurrentHashMap is the Segment class, as shown in Listing 7.11. As you see from its constructor defined from lines 2– 6, it has a HashEntry table as an array named table. Furthermore, this Segment class is synchronized as evidenced by: (1) it extends ReentrantLock (line 1); and (2) its methods use locks to guard critical code sections, such as shown at lines 10 and 47 for the put method. Without showing its source code, the scanAndLockForPut method called at line 10 scans for a node containing a given key while trying to acquire a lock, creating and returning one if not found. Upon return, this method guarantees that lock is held.

Listing 7.11 The Segment class embedded in the ConcurrentHashMap class

```
1   static final class Segment<K,V> extends ReentrantLock implements
    Serializable {
2       Segment(float lf, int threshold, HashEntry<K,V>[] tab) {
3           this.loadFactor = lf;
4           this.threshold = threshold;
5           this.table = tab;
6       }
7
8       final V put(K key, int hash, V value, boolean onlyIfAbsent) {
9           HashEntry<K,V> node = tryLock() ? null :
10              scanAndLockForPut(key, hash, value);
11          V oldValue;
12          try {
13              HashEntry<K,V>[] tab = table;
14              int index = (tab.length - 1) & hash;
15              HashEntry<K,V> first = entryAt(tab, index);
16              for (HashEntry<K,V> e = first;;) {
17                  if (e != null) {
18                      K k;
19                      if ((k = e.key) == key ||
20                          (e.hash == hash && key.equals(k))) {
21                          oldValue = e.value;
22                          if (!onlyIfAbsent) {
23                              e.value = value;
24                              ++modCount;
25                          }
26                          break;
27                      }
28                      e = e.next;
29                  }
30                  else {
31                      if (node != null)
32                          node.setNext(first);
33                      else
34                          node= new HashEntry<K,V>(hash, key, value, first);
35                      int c = count + 1;
36                      if (c > threshold && tab.length < MAXIMUM_CAPACITY)
37                          rehash(node);
38                      else
39                          setEntryAt(tab, index, node);
```

```
40                        ++modCount;
41                        count = c;
42                        oldValue = null;
43                        break;
44                    }
45                }
46            } finally {
47                unlock();
48            }
49            return oldValue;
50        }
51    // other fields and methods omitted
52 }
```

Having introduced the HashEntry class and the Segment class, it's much easier now to explain how ConcurrentHashMap class is implemented. As shown in Listing 7.12, a ConcurrentHashMap essentially is a Segment array, as defined at line 3. Lines 4 – 35 show one of its constructors parameterized with three fields: initialCapacity, loadFactor, and concurrencyLevel. Bulk of this constructor code is to figure out the best matching number of segments, before initializing the segments field from lines 31 – 34. To some extent, this constructor shows how a ConcurrentHashMap is implemented internally.

Furthermore, the put method defined from lines 37 – 48 shows that no locks are used in implementing the public methods of the ConcurrentHashMap class, since those methods operate on *Segments*, each of which is synchronized already. Whenever an operation is invoked, the ensureSegment method as shown at line 46 is called to return the segment for the given index, which will also create and record it in the segment table via compareAndSet (CAS) if not already present.

Even though all operations are thread-safe, retrieval operations with the ConcurrentHashMap class do not entail locking; thus, there is no support for locking the entire segment table. Retrieval operations generally do not block and may even overlap with update operations. Retrievals reflect the results of the most recently completed update operations holding upon their onset.

Next, we use an example to demonstrate the use of the ConcurrentHashMap class, following Listing 7.12.

Listing 7.12 ConcurrentHashMap.java (partial)

```
1  public class ConcurrentHashMap<K, V> extends AbstractMap<K, V>
2          implements ConcurrentMap<K, V>, Serializable {
3      final Segment<K,V>[] segments;
4      public ConcurrentHashMap(int initialCapacity,
5                          float loadFactor, int concurrencyLevel) {
6          if (!(loadFactor > 0) || initialCapacity < 0 ||
               concurrencyLevel <= 0)
7              throw new IllegalArgumentException();
8          if (concurrencyLevel > MAX_SEGMENTS)
9              concurrencyLevel = MAX_SEGMENTS;
10         // Find power-of-two sizes best matching arguments
11         int sshift = 0;
12         int ssize = 1;
```

```
13          while (ssize < concurrencyLevel) {
14              ++sshift;
15              ssize <<= 1;
16          }
17          this.segmentShift = 32 - sshift;
18          this.segmentMask = ssize - 1;
19          if (initialCapacity > MAXIMUM_CAPACITY)
20              initialCapacity = MAXIMUM_CAPACITY;
21          int c = initialCapacity / ssize;
22          if (c * ssize < initialCapacity)
23              ++c;
24          int cap = MIN_SEGMENT_TABLE_CAPACITY;
25          while (cap < c)
26              cap <<= 1;
27          // create segments and segments[0]
28          Segment<K,V> s0 =
29              new Segment<K,V>(loadFactor, (int)(cap * loadFactor),
30                          (HashEntry<K,V>[])new HashEntry[cap]);
31          Segment<K,V>[] ss = (Segment<K,V>[])new Segment[ssize];
32          // ordered write of segments[0]
33          UNSAFE.putOrderedObject(ss, SBASE, s0);
34          this.segments = ss;
35      }
36
37      public V put(K key, V value) {
38          Segment<K,V> s;
39          if (value == null)
40              throw new NullPointerException();
41          int hash = hash(key);
42          int j = (hash >>> segmentShift) & segmentMask;
43          // nonvolatile; recheck in ensureSegment
44          if ((s = (Segment<K,V>)UNSAFE.getObject
45              (segments, (j << SSHIFT) + SBASE)) == null)
46              s = ensureSegment(j);
47          return s.put(key, hash, value, false);
48      }
49  // other fields and methods omitted
50 }
```

Listing 7.13 shows the ConcurrentHashMapDemo.java program. The Mapper thread's run method illustrates the use of the put and get operations for the ConcurrentHashMap collection. We made some arbitrary choices here, for example, the loop max, output control, and so on, for illustrative purposes. Our focuses here are the ConcurrentHashMap's put method (line 27) and get method (line 32).

The driver class creates a ConcurrentHashMap object at line 46 to start with, with an initialCapacity, loadFactor and concurrencyLevel specified. The rest of it follows the standard procedure that it creates a fixed executor service thread pool, launches the mapper threads, shuts down the thread pool, waits until all threads are done, and finally prints out the size of the ConcurrentHashMap.

Next, we discuss the output of running this demo program, following Listing 7.13.

Listing 7.13 ConcurrentHashMapDemo.java

```
1   package jcp.ch7.synchedcollections;
2
3   import java.util.Random;
4   import java.util.concurrent.ConcurrentHashMap;
5   import java.util.concurrent.ExecutorService;
6   import java.util.concurrent.Executors;
7   import java.util.concurrent.TimeUnit;
8
9   class Mapper extends Thread {
10    int id;
11    Random random;
12    ConcurrentHashMap<Integer, String> concurrentHashMap;
13
14    Mapper(int id, ConcurrentHashMap<Integer, String> concurrentHashMap) {
15        this.id = id;
16        this.random = new Random();
17        this.concurrentHashMap = concurrentHashMap;
18    }
19
20    public void run() {
21        int IMAX = 10000;
22        for (int i = 0; i < IMAX; i++) {
23            Integer key = random.nextInt(IMAX);
24            String value = id + "_" + key;
25            boolean output = (i % (IMAX / 10)) == 0;
26            if ((id % 4) == 0) {
27                concurrentHashMap.put(key, value);
28                if (output)
29                    System.out.println ("Thread " + id + " put: " + key + "->"
30                        + value);
31            } else {
32                String val = concurrentHashMap.get(key);
33                if (output)
34                    System.out.println ("Thread " + id + " get: " + key + "->"
35                        + val);
36            }
37        }
38    }
39  }
40
41  public class ConcurrentHashMapDemo {
42
43    public static void main(String[] args) {
44
45        int POOL_SIZE = 8;
46        ConcurrentHashMap<Integer, String> concurrentHashMap =
47            new ConcurrentHashMap<Integer, String> (20000, 0.75f,
48                POOL_SIZE);
49
```

```
50     // 1. Create a newFixedThreadPool using the Executors utility class
51     ExecutorService executorService = Executors
52          .newFixedThreadPool(POOL_SIZE);
53
54     // 2. launch mappers
55     for (int i = 0; i < POOL_SIZE; i++) {
56        executorService.execute(new Mapper(i, concurrentHashMap));
57     }
58
59     // 3. shut down executorService to avoid resource leak
60     executorService.shutdown();
61
62     // 4. wait until all threads are done
63     try {
64        executorService.awaitTermination(Integer.MAX_VALUE,
65          TimeUnit.SECONDS);
66     } catch (InterruptedException e) {
67        e.printStackTrace();
68     }
69     System.out.println ("size = " + concurrentHashMap.size());
70   }
71 }
```

Listing 7.14 shows the output of executing this demo program on my Eclipse IDE. You can verify that threads 0 and 4 always called the put method, while all other threads called the get method, which returned null in most cases. I'd like to mention that we did not enumerate all the methods for the ConcurrentHashMap class here, as the ConcurrentHashMap class and its views and iterators implement all of the optional methods of the Map and Iterator interfaces, which were introduced in previous chapters. Finally, like a Hashtable but unlike a HashMap, the ConcurrentHashMap class does not allow null to be used as a key or value, but it returns null if the key does not exist.

Listing 7.14 Output of running the ConcurrentHashMapDemo program

```
Thread 6 get: 590->null
Thread 0 put: 2550->0_2550
Thread 1 get: 637->null
Thread 7 get: 6992->null
Thread 2 get: 4462->null
Thread 4 put: 3830->4_3830
Thread 3 get: 2337->null
Thread 5 get: 7352->null
Thread 6 get: 4346->null
Thread 5 get: 3433->4_3433
......
Thread 0 put: 3419->0_3419
Thread 4 put: 552->4_552
Thread 0 put: 8803->0_8803
Thread 4 put: 8626->4_8626
size = 8696
```

Note: Sizing a ConcurrentHashMap **for optimal concurrency and capacity**. Ideally, one should choose a concurrency value to accommodate as many threads as will ever concurrently modify the Segment table. Using a significantly higher value than needed can waste space and time, while using a significantly lower value can lead to thread contention. On the other hand, if you know that only n threads ($n \geq 1$) will modify and all others will read only, setting concurrency to n is appropriate. In addition, resizing the Segment table is costly in general. Therefore, whenever possible, provide an accurate initial capacity in relevant constructors to prevent resizing as much as possible.

7.2.2 ConcurrentLinkedQueue

In §3.4.5, we introduced LinkedList, which is an unsynchronized, doubly-linked list collection. The ConcurrentLinkedQueue class, on the other hand, is an unbounded, thread-safe, non-blocking FIFO (first-in-first-out) queue based on linked nodes. Since it's essentially a FIFO queue, new elements are inserted at the tail of the queue, while the queue retrieval operations obtain elements at the head of the queue. This becomes obvious, given how the Node class is defined as shown in Listing 7.15. As you see, the Node class has only two fields: item and next, with next pointing to the next node. It heavily depends on the operations of sun.misc.UNSAFE to achieve atomicity, such as:

- UNSAFE.putObject(this, itemOffset, item): Atomically sets the item field of this node to item passed into the constructor.
- UNSAFE.compareAndSwapObject(this, itemOffset, cmp, val): Used in the casItem method to atomically set this node's item to val if it is equal to cmp. (In other contexts, cmp and val are named expect and update, respectively, which are more explicit.)
- UNSAFE.putOrderedObject(this, nextOffset, val): Used in the lazySetNext method to atomically set this node's next field to val, eventually, if not immediately.
- UNSAFE.compareAndSwapObject(this, nextOffset, cmp, val): Used in the casNext method to atomically set this node's next field to val, if the current value is equal to the expected value represented by cmp.

Perhaps the most important implication here is that each node of a ConcurrentLinkedQueue is operated upon atomically at the node level so that the public methods of the ConcurrentLinkedQueue class can be implemented lock-free and wait-free, as we will see next.

Listing 7.15 Node class embedded in ConcurrentLinkedQueue

```
1        private static class Node<E> {
2            volatile E item;
3            volatile Node<E> next;
4
5            Node(E item) {
6                UNSAFE.putObject(this, itemOffset, item);
7            }
8
9            boolean casItem(E cmp, E val) {
```

```
10              return UNSAFE.compareAndSwapObject(this, itemOffset, cmp,
11                  val);
12          }
13
14          void lazySetNext(Node<E> val) {
15              UNSAFE.putOrderedObject(this, nextOffset, val);
16          }
17
18          boolean casNext(Node<E> cmp, Node<E> val) {
19              return UNSAFE.compareAndSwapObject(this, nextOffset, cmp,
20                  val);
21          }
22
23          // Unsafe mechanics
24
25          private static final sun.misc.Unsafe UNSAFE;
26          private static final long itemOffset;
27          private static final long nextOffset;
28
29          static {
30              try {
31                  UNSAFE = sun.misc.Unsafe.getUnsafe();
32                  Class k = Node.class;
33                  itemOffset = UNSAFE.objectFieldOffset
34                      (k.getDeclaredField("item"));
35                  nextOffset = UNSAFE.objectFieldOffset
36                      (k.getDeclaredField("next"));
37              } catch (Exception e) {
38                  throw new Error(e);
39              }
40          }
41      }
```

Listing 7.16 shows partially the implementation of the ConcurrentLinkedQueue class. First, note its two fields of head and tail, shown at lines 3 and 4, respectively. Its no-arg constructor sets both head and tail to a null-element node, as shown from lines 6 – 8. Its two private methods, casTail and casHead, as shown from lines 10 – 16, use the UNSAFE.compareAndSwapObject method to atomically set the head node and tail node, respectively. Its updateHead method uses the casHead method and lazySetNext method to atomically update the head node, as shown from lines 18 – 21. Finally, its offer and poll methods use those atomic methods to perform designated operations on the node intended, respectively. These representative methods show how synchronization is achieved with the ConcurrentLinkedQueue class. The ConcurrentLinkedQueue class and its iterator implement all of the optional methods of the Queue and Iterator interfaces, similar to the offer and poll methods in terms of accomplishing synchronization.

Next, we use an example to illustrate the use of the ConcurrentLinkedQueue concurrent collection, following Listing 7.16.

Listing 7.16 ConcurrentLinkedQueue.java (partial)

```
1    public class ConcurrentLinkedQueue<E> extends AbstractQueue<E>
2            implements Queue<E>, java.io.Serializable {
3        private transient volatile Node<E> head;
4        private transient volatile Node<E> tail;
5
6        public ConcurrentLinkedQueue() {
7            head = tail = new Node<E>(null);
8        }
9
10       private boolean casTail(Node<E> cmp, Node<E> val) {
11           return UNSAFE.compareAndSwapObject(this, tailOffset, cmp, val);
12       }
13
14       private boolean casHead(Node<E> cmp, Node<E> val) {
15           return UNSAFE.compareAndSwapObject(this, headOffset, cmp, val);
16       }
17
18       final void updateHead(Node<E> h, Node<E> p) {
19           if (h != p && casHead(h, p))
20               h.lazySetNext(h);
21       }
22
23       public boolean offer(E e) {
24           checkNotNull(e);
25           final Node<E> newNode = new Node<E>(e);
26
27           for (Node<E> t = tail, p = t;;) {
28               Node<E> q = p.next;
29               if (q == null) {
30                   if (p.casNext(null, newNode)) {
31                       if (p != t) // hop two nodes at a time
32                           casTail(t, newNode);  // Failure is OK.
33                       return true;
34                   }
35               }
36               else if (p == q)
37                   p = (t != (t = tail)) ? t : head;
38               else
39                   p = (p != t && t != (t = tail)) ? t : q;
40           }
41       }
42
43       public E poll() {
44           restartFromHead:
45           for (;;) {
46               for (Node<E> h = head, p = h, q;;) {
47                   E item = p.item;
48
49                   if (item != null && p.casItem(item, null)) {
50                       if (p != h) // hop two nodes at a time
51                           updateHead(h, ((q = p.next) != null) ? q : p);
52                       return item;
```

```
53                    }
54                    else if ((q = p.next) == null) {
55                        updateHead(h, p);
56                        return null;
57                    }
58                    else if (p == q)
59                        continue restartFromHead;
60                    else
61                        p = q;
62                }
63            }
64        }
65    // other methods omitted
66  }
```

Listing 7.17 shows the ConcurrentLinkedQueueDemo.java program. The class WorkerThread is both a producer and a consumer, depending on its id, *even* for producers and *odd* for consumers, as shown in the run method (lines 21 – 36). Line 27 shows that a producer calls the add method to add an item to the queue, while line 31 shows that a consumer calls the poll method to retrieve and remove an item from the queue.

The driver program for this demo (lines 39 –71) follows the standard procedure as shown below:

1. Creating a concurrent linked queue
2. Creating a newFixedThreadPool using the ExecutorService interface
3. Launching worker threads
4. Shutting down the executorService object to avoid potential resource leak
5. Waiting for all threads to finish before terminating the thread pool

Next, we discuss the result of executing this demo program, following Listing 7.17.

Listing 7.17 ConcurrentLinkedQueueDemo.java

```
1   package jcp.ch7.synchedcollections;
2
3   import java.util.Random;
4   import java.util.concurrent.ConcurrentLinkedQueue;
5   import java.util.concurrent.ExecutorService;
6   import java.util.concurrent.Executors;
7   import java.util.concurrent.TimeUnit;
8
9   class WorkerThread extends Thread {
10    int id;
11    Random random;
12    ConcurrentLinkedQueue<String> concurrentLinkedQueue;
13
14    WorkerThread(int id, ConcurrentLinkedQueue<String>
15        concurrentLinkedQueue) {
16      this.id = id;
17      this.random = new Random();
18      this.concurrentLinkedQueue = concurrentLinkedQueue;
```

```
19    }
20
21    public void run() {
22       int IMAX = 10000;
23       for (int i = 0; i < IMAX; i++) {
24          String item = id + "_" + random.nextInt(IMAX);
25          boolean output = (i % (IMAX / 10)) == 0;
26          if ((id % 2) == 0) {
27             concurrentLinkedQueue.add(item);
28             if (output)
29                System.out.println ("Thread " + id + " add: " + item);
30          } else {
31             String value = concurrentLinkedQueue.poll();
32             if (output)
33                System.out.println ("Thread " + id + " poll: " + value);
34          }
35       }
36    }
37 }
38
39 public class ConcurrentLinkedQueueDemo {
40
41    public static void main(String[] args) {
42
43       int POOL_SIZE = 8;
44
45       // 1. create a concurrent linked queue
46       ConcurrentLinkedQueue<String> concurrentLinkedQueue =
47          new ConcurrentLinkedQueue<String> ();
48
49       // 2. Create a newFixedThreadPool using the Executors utility class
50       ExecutorService executorService = Executors
51          .newFixedThreadPool(POOL_SIZE);
52
53       // 3. launch worker threads
54       for (int i = 0; i < POOL_SIZE; i++) {
55          executorService.execute(new WorkerThread(i,
56             concurrentLinkedQueue));
57       }
58
59       // 4. shut down executorService to avoid resource leak
60       executorService.shutdown();
61
62       // 5. wait until all threads are done
63       try {
64          executorService.awaitTermination(Integer.MAX_VALUE,
65             TimeUnit.SECONDS);
66       } catch (InterruptedException e) {
67          e.printStackTrace();
68       }
69       System.out.println ("size = " + concurrentLinkedQueue.size());
70    }
```

```
71  }
```

Executing this program on my Eclipse IDE yielded the result as shown in Listing 7.18. As you see, when the queue is empty, the poll method returns null.

This concludes our discussion on the ConcurrentLinkedQueue concurrent collection. We discuss the ConcurrentLinkedDeque concurrent collection next.

Listing 7.18 Result of executing the ConcurrentLinkedQueueDemo.java program

```
Thread 2 add: 2_9216
Thread 4 add: 4_1144
Thread 3 poll: 0_2009
Thread 1 poll: null
Thread 0 add: 0_2009
......
Thread 3 poll: 4_2645
Thread 5 poll: 4_1276
Thread 3 poll: 4_950
size = 530
```

7.2.3 ConcurrentLinkedDeque

In §3.5.1, we introduced an ArrayDeque class, which uses an array (E[] elements) with an indexed head and an indexed tail to simulate a doubly-linked, unsynchronized queue. The ConcurrentLinkedDeque class to be discussed here is an unbounded, lock-free, non-blocking, synchronized deque based on linked nodes. It supports concurrent insertion, removal, and access operations across multiple threads.

Similar to the ConcurrentLinkedQueue class, the ConcurrentLinkedDeque class has its own embedded Node class as shown in Listing 7.19 to represent its nodes. Compared with the Node class for the ConcurrentLinkedQueue class as shown in Listing 7.15, this Node class contains one more field of prev, and thus a few prev-related methods, such as lazySetPrev (lines 27 – 29) and casPrev (lines 31 – 34). Despite these minor differences, the underlying mechanism is the same: synchronization is achieved with various CAS-based operations from the UNSAFE class, as discussed previously.

Once again, the most important implication here is that each node of a ConcurrentLinkedDeque is operated upon atomically at the node level so that the public methods of the ConcurrentLinkedDeque class can be implemented lock-free and wait-free, as we will see next.

Listing 7.19 The Node class embedded in ConcurrentLinkedDeque class

```
1    static final class Node<E> {
2            volatile Node<E> prev;
3            volatile E item;
4            volatile Node<E> next;
5
6            Node() {
```

```
7          }
8
9          Node(E item) {
10             UNSAFE.putObject(this, itemOffset, item);
11         }
12
13         boolean casItem(E cmp, E val) {
14             return UNSAFE.compareAndSwapObject(this, itemOffset, cmp,
15                 val);
16         }
17
18         void lazySetNext(Node<E> val) {
19             UNSAFE.putOrderedObject(this, nextOffset, val);
20         }
21
22         boolean casNext(Node<E> cmp, Node<E> val) {
23             return UNSAFE.compareAndSwapObject(this, nextOffset, cmp,
24              val);
25         }
26
27         void lazySetPrev(Node<E> val) {
28             UNSAFE.putOrderedObject(this, prevOffset, val);
29         }
30
31         boolean casPrev(Node<E> cmp, Node<E> val) {
32             return UNSAFE.compareAndSwapObject(this, prevOffset, cmp,
33                 val);
34         }
35
36         // Unsafe mechanics
37
38         private static final sun.misc.Unsafe UNSAFE;
39         private static final long prevOffset;
40         private static final long itemOffset;
41         private static final long nextOffset;
42
43         static {
44             try {
45                 UNSAFE = sun.misc.Unsafe.getUnsafe();
46                 Class k = Node.class;
47                 prevOffset = UNSAFE.objectFieldOffset
48                     (k.getDeclaredField("prev"));
49                 itemOffset = UNSAFE.objectFieldOffset
50                     (k.getDeclaredField("item"));
51                 nextOffset = UNSAFE.objectFieldOffset
52                     (k.getDeclaredField("next"));
53             } catch (Exception e) {
54                 throw new Error(e);
55             }
56         }
57     }
```

Listing 7.20 shows partially the implementation of the ConcurrentLinkedDeque.java class. It is divided into parts and explained as follows:

- Lines 3–7: This part shows the fields of head, tail, and the no-arg constructor.
- Lines 9–15: This part shows the private casHead and casTail methods as wrappers of UNSAFE's compareAndSwapObject method, making the update operations on the head and tail of a ConcurrentLinkedDeque object atomic. These operations are external to the Node class.
- Lines 17–22: This part shows how some of the public methods, such as poll, remove, peek, element, push and pop, are implemented as wrappers of some other internal methods.
- Lines 24–58: This part shows how some of the public methods of the ConcurrentLinkedDeque class are implemented. Specifically, the offer and add methods are wrappers of the offerLast method, which itself is the wrapper of the linkLast method, which has a concrete implementation as shown in lines 36–58. This is a good example of how a public method of the ConcurrentLinkedDeque class is implemented using the CAS-based methods such as lazySetPrev, casNext, and casTail, which are all atomic as discussed previously.

Next, we use an example to demonstrate the use of the ConcurrentLinkedDeque concurrent collection, following Listing 7.20.

Listing 7.20 ConcurrentLinkedDeque.java (partial)

```
1   public class ConcurrentLinkedDeque<E> extends AbstractCollection<E>
2     implements Deque<E>, java.io.Serializable {
3       private transient volatile Node<E> head;
4       private transient volatile Node<E> tail;
5       public ConcurrentLinkedDeque() {
6           head = tail = new Node<E>(null);
7       }
8
9       private boolean casHead(Node<E> cmp, Node<E> val) {
10          return UNSAFE.compareAndSwapObject(this, headOffset, cmp, val);
11      }
12
13      private boolean casTail(Node<E> cmp, Node<E> val) {
14          return UNSAFE.compareAndSwapObject(this, tailOffset, cmp, val);
15      }
16
17      public E poll()          { return pollFirst(); }
18      public E remove()        { return removeFirst(); }
19      public E peek()          { return peekFirst(); }
20      public E element()       { return getFirst(); }
21      public void push(E e)    { addFirst(e); }
22      public E pop()           { return removeFirst(); }
23
24      public boolean offer(E e) {
25          return offerLast(e);
26      }
27      public boolean add(E e) {
28          return offerLast(e);
```

```
29          }
30
31          public boolean offerLast(E e) {
32              linkLast(e);
33              return true;
34          }
35
36          private void linkLast(E e) {
37              checkNotNull(e);
38              final Node<E> newNode = new Node<E>(e);
39
40              restartFromTail:
41              for (;;)
42                  for (Node<E> t = tail, p = t, q;;) {
43                      if ((q = p.next) != null &&
44                          (q = (p = q).next) != null)
45                          p = (t != (t = tail)) ? t : q;
46                      else if (p.prev == p) // NEXT_TERMINATOR
47                          continue restartFromTail;
48                      else {
49                          // p is last node
50                          newNode.lazySetPrev(p); // CAS piggyback
51                          if (p.casNext(null, newNode)) {
52                              if (p != t) // hop two nodes at a time
53                                  casTail(t, newNode);  // Failure is OK.
54                              return;
55                          }
56                      }
57                  }
58          }
59          // other methods omitted
60  }
```

Listing 7.21 shows the ConcurrentLinkedDequeDemo.java program. The class WorkerThread2 is both a producer and a consumer, depending on its id, *even* for producers and *odd* for consumers, as shown in the run method (lines 21–36). Line 27 shows that a producer calls the add method to add an item to the deque, while line 31 shows that a consumer calls the poll method to retrieve and remove an item from the deque.

The driver program for this demo (lines 39 – 71) follows the standard procedure as shown below:

1. Creating a concurrent linked deque
2. Creating a newFixedThreadPool using the ExecutorService interface
3. Launching worker threads
4. Shutting down the executorService object to avoid potential resource leak
5. Waiting for all threads to finish before terminating the thread pool

Next, we discuss the result of executing this demo program, following Listing 7.21.

Listing 7.21 ConcurrentLinkedDequeDemo.java

```java
1   package jcp.ch7.synchedcollections;
2
3   import java.util.Random;
4   import java.util.concurrent.ConcurrentLinkedDeque;
5   import java.util.concurrent.ExecutorService;
6   import java.util.concurrent.Executors;
7   import java.util.concurrent.TimeUnit;
8
9   class WorkerThread2 extends Thread {
10    int id;
11    Random random;
12    ConcurrentLinkedDeque<String> concurrentLinkedDeque;
13
14    WorkerThread2(int id, ConcurrentLinkedDeque<String>
15        concurrentLinkedDeque) {
16      this.id = id;
17      this.random = new Random();
18      this.concurrentLinkedDeque = concurrentLinkedDeque;
19    }
20
21    public void run() {
22      int IMAX = 10000;
23      for (int i = 0; i < IMAX; i++) {
24        String item = id + "_" + random.nextInt(IMAX);
25        boolean output = (i % (IMAX / 10)) == 0;
26        if ((id % 2) == 0) {
27          concurrentLinkedDeque.add(item);
28          if (output)
29            System.out.println ("Thread " + id + " add: " + item);
30        } else {
31          String value = concurrentLinkedDeque.poll();
32          if (output)
33            System.out.println ("Thread " + id + " poll: " + value);
34        }
35      }
36    }
37  }
38
39  public class ConcurrentLinkedDequeDemo {
40
41    public static void main(String[] args) {
42
43      int POOL_SIZE = 8;
44
45      // 1. create a concurrent linked deque
46      ConcurrentLinkedDeque<String> concurrentLinkedDeque =
47          new ConcurrentLinkedDeque<String> ();
48
49      // 2. create a newFixedThreadPool using the ExecutorService class
50      ExecutorService executorService = Executors
51          .newFixedThreadPool(POOL_SIZE);
52
```

```
53        // 3. launch worker threads
54        for (int i = 0; i < POOL_SIZE; i++) {
55           executorService.execute(new WorkerThread2(i,
56              concurrentLinkedDeque));
57        }
58
59        // 4. shut down executorService to avoid resource leak
60        executorService.shutdown();
61
62        // 5. wait until all threads are done
63        try {
64           executorService.awaitTermination(Integer.MAX_VALUE,
65              TimeUnit.SECONDS);
66        } catch (InterruptedException e) {
67           e.printStackTrace();
68        }
69        System.out.println ("size = " + concurrentLinkedDeque.size());
70    }
71 }
```

Executing this program on my Eclipse IDE yielded the result as shown in Listing 7.22. As you see, when the deque is empty, the poll method returns null.

This concludes our discussion on the ConcurrentLinkedDeque concurrent collection. We discuss the ConcurrentSkipListMap concurrent collection next.

Listing 7.22 Result of executing the ConcurrentLinkedDequeDemo.java program

```
Thread 0 add: 0_974
Thread 4 add: 4_4384
Thread 3 poll: 0_974
Thread 1 poll: null
......
Thread 7 poll: 2_6947
Thread 1 poll: 2_8745
Thread 3 poll: 0_4539
Thread 1 poll: 6_8571
size = 1651
```

7.2.4 ConcurrentSkipListMap

In §7.2.1, we introduced the ConcurrentHashMap concurrent collection, which is essentially a segment array, with each segment consisting of an array of HashEntry elements. Figure 7.3 shows the structure of a ConcurrentHashMap.

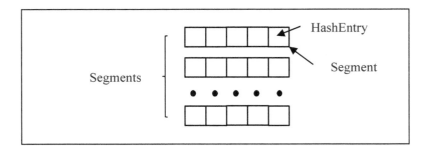

Figure 7.3 The structure of a ConcurrentHashMap

For a ConcurrentSkipListMap, we understand what it means by "*concurrent*" and "*map*," but what is a *skip list*? A skip list is a data structure that consists of layers of linked lists, as shown in Figure 7.4. In this example, there are four layers, with each layer getting sparser and sparser going upward. The bottom layer is the base layer, which is a sorted linked list. The upper layers are also sorted linked lists, but repeating fewer and fewer nodes than lower layers.

Now, suppose we would like to insert a node with a value of 60. Starting from layer 4, we know that 60 > 10; then moving down to layer 3, we know that 60 > 50; moving further down to layer 2, we know that 60 is between 50 and 90; finally at the base layer, 60 is located between 50 and 70, which is where 60 should be inserted. This is a specific example, but it shows how a skip list is used to support faster search for large, sorted linked lists.

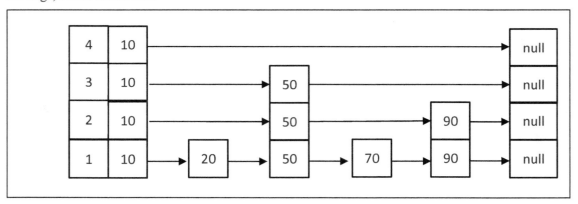

Figure 7.4 The structure of a skip list

Now, let's come back to the ConcurrentSkipListMap concurrent collection. First, Figure 7.5 shows the class hierarchy for the ConcurrentSkipListMap class. Given what we have covered in the previous chapters, this should be straightforward and needs no explanation.

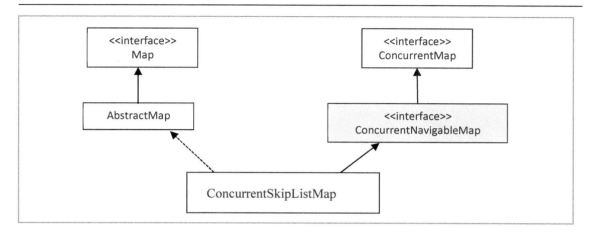

Figure 7.5 The class hierarchy for the ConcurrentSkipListMap class.

Since a ConcurrentSkipListMap is a map, there must be a node class that represents the nodes of the map. This Node class is shown in Listing 7.23. As you see, this is a Node class for maps, as indicated by its generic parameters of <K, V> at line 1. Next, it has three fields of key, value, and next, as shown from lines 2–4. Nodes hold keys and values, and are singly linked in sorted order. In addition, note the casValue and casNext methods as well as the UNSAFE mechanics shown in the remainder of this listing. This explains that atomic operations are performed at the node level, making the ConcurrentSkipListMap class a lock-free, non-blocking concurrent collection.

Listing 7.23 The Node class for the ConcurrentSkipListMap class

```
1    static final class Node<K,V> {
2            final K key;
3            volatile Object value;
4            volatile Node<K,V> next;
5
6            Node(K key, Object value, Node<K,V> next) {
7                this.key = key;
8                this.value = value;
9                this.next = next;
10           }
11
12           Node(Node<K,V> next) {
13               this.key = null;
14               this.value = this;
15               this.next = next;
16           }
17
18           boolean casValue(Object cmp, Object val) {
19               return UNSAFE.compareAndSwapObject(this, valueOffset, cmp,
20                   val);
21           }
```

```
22      boolean casNext(Node<K,V> cmp, Node<K,V> val) {
23          return UNSAFE.compareAndSwapObject(this, nextOffset, cmp,
24              val);
25      }
26
27   // other methods omitted
28
29      // UNSAFE mechanics
30
31      private static final sun.misc.Unsafe UNSAFE;
32      private static final long valueOffset;
33      private static final long nextOffset;
34
35      static {
36          try {
37              UNSAFE = sun.misc.Unsafe.getUnsafe();
38              Class k = Node.class;
39              valueOffset = UNSAFE.objectFieldOffset
40                  (k.getDeclaredField("value"));
41              nextOffset = UNSAFE.objectFieldOffset
42                  (k.getDeclaredField("next"));
43          } catch (Exception e) {
44              throw new Error(e);
45          }
46      }
47   }
```

Next, Listing 7.24 shows the Index<K, V> and HeadIndex<K, V> classes for the ConcurrentSkipListMap class. Index nodes represent the levels of the skip list, with fields of node, down, and right, as shown from lines 2–4. Besides, it has a casRight method, which is used by the link and unlink methods for managing the linked lists at various levels. The HeadIndex nodes heading each level keep track of their level with one extra field named level.

Listing 7.24 The Index<K, V> class and HeadIndex<K, V> class for the ConcurrentSkipListMap class

```
1   static class Index<K,V> {
2           final Node<K,V> node;
3           final Index<K,V> down;
4           volatile Index<K,V> right;
5
6           Index(Node<K,V> node, Index<K,V> down, Index<K,V> right) {
7               this.node = node;
8               this.down = down;
9               this.right = right;
10          }
11
12          final boolean casRight(Index<K,V> cmp, Index<K,V> val) {
13              return UNSAFE.compareAndSwapObject(this, rightOffset, cmp,
14                  val);
15          }
```

```
16
17        final boolean indexesDeletedNode() {
18            return node.value == null;
19        }
20
21        final boolean link(Index<K,V> succ, Index<K,V> newSucc) {
22            Node<K,V> n = node;
23            newSucc.right = succ;
24            return n.value != null && casRight(succ, newSucc);
25        }
26
27        final boolean unlink(Index<K,V> succ) {
28            return !indexesDeletedNode() && casRight(succ, succ.right);
29        }
30
31        // Unsafe mechanics
32        private static final sun.misc.Unsafe UNSAFE;
33        private static final long rightOffset;
34        static {
35            try {
36                UNSAFE = sun.misc.Unsafe.getUnsafe();
37                Class k = Index.class;
38                rightOffset = UNSAFE.objectFieldOffset
39                    (k.getDeclaredField("right"));
40            } catch (Exception e) {
41                throw new Error(e);
42            }
43        }
44    }
45
46    static final class HeadIndex<K,V> extends Index<K,V> {
47        final int level;
48        HeadIndex(Node<K,V> node, Index<K,V> down, Index<K,V> right,
49          int level) {
50            super(node, down, right);
51            this.level = level;
52        }
53    }
```

Listing 7.25 shows partially the ConcurrentSkipListMap.java program. Note its fields of keySet, entrySet, values, and descendingMap. The first three fields are common for all maps, while the last field of descendingMap essentially is a SubMap, which represents a subrange of mappings of its underlying map. Next, we have a casHead method, which is used to atomically update a head index node. Finally, the public put method is a wrapper of the private doPut method, which calls the atomic methods of casValue (line 44) and casNext (line 53) to implement the actual put logic. The purpose of showing this method is to give you a glimpse of how the ConcurrentSkipListMap is made a concurrent collection.

Next, we use an example to demonstrate the use of the ConcurrentSkipListMap concurrent collection, following Listing 7.25.

Listing 7.25 ConcurrentSkipListMap.java (partial)

```
1   public class ConcurrentSkipListMap<K,V> extends AbstractMap<K,V>
2       implements ConcurrentNavigableMap<K,V>, Cloneable,
3           java.io.Serializable {
4
5       private transient KeySet keySet;
6       private transient EntrySet entrySet;
7       private transient Values values;
8       private transient ConcurrentNavigableMap<K,V> descendingMap;
9
10      private boolean casHead(HeadIndex<K,V> cmp, HeadIndex<K,V> val) {
11          return UNSAFE.compareAndSwapObject(this, headOffset, cmp, val);
12      }
13
14      public V put(K key, V value) {
15          if (value == null)
16              throw new NullPointerException();
17          return doPut(key, value, false);
18      }
19
20      private V doPut(K kkey, V value, boolean onlyIfAbsent) {
21          Comparable<? super K> key = comparable(kkey);
22          for (;;) {
23              Node<K,V> b = findPredecessor(key);
24              Node<K,V> n = b.next;
25              for (;;) {
26                  if (n != null) {
27                      Node<K,V> f = n.next;
28                      if (n != b.next)                // inconsistent read
29                          break;
30                      Object v = n.value;
31                      if (v == null) {                // n is deleted
32                          n.helpDelete(b, f);
33                          break;
34                      }
35                      if (v == n || b.value == null) // b is deleted
36                          break;
37                      int c = key.compareTo(n.key);
38                      if (c > 0) {
39                          b = n;
40                          n = f;
41                          continue;
42                      }
43                      if (c == 0) {
44                          if (onlyIfAbsent || n.casValue(v, value))
45                              return (V)v;
46                          else
47                              break;
48                      }
49                      // else c < 0; fall through
50                  }
```

```
51
52                  Node<K,V> z = new Node<K,V>(kkey, value, n);
53                  if (!b.casNext(n, z))
54                      break;        // restart if lost race to append to b
55                  int level = randomLevel();
56                  if (level > 0)
57                      insertIndex(z, level);
58                  return null;
59              }
60          }
61      }
62      // other methods omitted
63  }
```

Listing 7.26 shows the ConcurrentSkipListMapDemo.java program. The SkipListMapper class has a field named concurrentSkipListMap of type ConcurrentSkipListMap. It then calls the put and get methods of the concurrentSkipListMap object to add map entries and get the value for a given key, respectively. The importance here is that the concurrentSkipListMap object is accessed concurrently by multiple threads.

The driver program for this demo (lines 45 – 135) follows the standard procedure as shown below:

1. Creating a concurrent skip list map object
2. Creating a newFixedThreadPool using the ExecutorService interface
3. Launching skip list mapper threads
4. Shutting down the executorService object to avoid potential resource leak
5. Waiting for all threads to finish before terminating the thread pool

The driver program also demonstrates how to access a ConcurrentSkipListMap using its navigable interface, such as the NavigableKeySet for retrieving the key set of the ConcurrentSkipListMap object as well as the ConcurrentNavigableMap interface for retrieving subMaps, headMaps and tailMaps, and so on. The procedure is the same that:

1. You first get the navigableKeySet from the map
2. Then you get the iterator from the navigableKeySet
3. Finally, you use the iterator to navigate through the key set

Next, we discuss the result of executing this demo program, following Listing 7.26.

Listing 7.26 ConcurrentSkipListMapDemo.java

```
1   package jcp.ch7.synchedcollections;
2
3   import java.util.Iterator;
4   import java.util.NavigableSet;
5   import java.util.Random;
6   import java.util.concurrent.ConcurrentNavigableMap;
7   import java.util.concurrent.ConcurrentSkipListMap;
8   import java.util.concurrent.ExecutorService;
9   import java.util.concurrent.Executors;
```

```
10  import java.util.concurrent.TimeUnit;
11
12  class SkipListMapper extends Thread {
13    int id;
14    Random random;
15    ConcurrentSkipListMap<Integer, String> concurrentSkipListHashMap;
16
17    SkipListMapper(int id, ConcurrentSkipListMap<Integer, String>
18       concurrentSkipListHashMap) {
19       this.id = id;
20       this.random = new Random();
21       this.concurrentSkipListHashMap = concurrentSkipListHashMap;
22    }
23
24    public void run() {
25       int IMAX = 10000;
26       for (int i = 0; i < IMAX; i++) {
27          Integer key = random.nextInt(IMAX);
28          String value = id + "_" + key;
29          boolean output = (i % (IMAX / 10)) == 0;
30          if ((id % 4) == 0) {
31             concurrentSkipListHashMap.put(key, value);
32             if (output)
33                System.out.println ("Thread " + id + " put: " + key + " - >"
34                   + value);
35          } else {
36             String val = concurrentSkipListHashMap.get(key);
37             if (output)
38                System.out.println ("Thread " + id + " get: " + key + " -> "
39                   + val);
40          }
41       }
42    }
43  }
44
45  public class ConcurrentSkipListMapDemo {
46
47    public static void main(String[] args) {
48
49       int POOL_SIZE = 8;
50       ConcurrentSkipListMap<Integer, String> concurrentSkipListMap =
51          new ConcurrentSkipListMap<Integer, String> ();
52
53       // 1. Create a newFixedThreadPool using the Executors utility class
54       ExecutorService executorService = Executors
55          .newFixedThreadPool(POOL_SIZE);
56
57       // 2. launch skip list mapper threads
58       for (int i = 0; i < POOL_SIZE; i++) {
59          executorService.execute(new SkipListMapper(i,
60             concurrentSkipListMap));
61       }
```

```java
62
63      // 3. shut down executorService to avoid resource leak
64      executorService.shutdown();
65
66      // 4. wait until all threads are done
67      try {
68         executorService.awaitTermination(Integer.MAX_VALUE,
69            TimeUnit.SECONDS);
70      } catch (InterruptedException e) {
71         e.printStackTrace();
72      }
73      System.out.println ("size = " + concurrentSkipListMap.size());
74
75      // 5. check ketSet, subMap, headMap and tailMap
76      System.out.println ("\ncall checkKeySet: ");
77      checkKeySet (concurrentSkipListMap);
78
79      System.out.println ("\ncall checkSubMap: ");
80      checkSubMap (concurrentSkipListMap);
81
82      System.out.println ("\ncall checkHeadMap: ");
83      checkHeadMap (concurrentSkipListMap);
84
85      System.out.println ("\ncall checkTailMap: ");
86      checkTailMap (concurrentSkipListMap);
87   }
88
89   public static void checkKeySet (ConcurrentSkipListMap<Integer, String>
90      concurrentSkipListMap) {
91
92      NavigableSet<Integer> navigableKeySet =
93         concurrentSkipListMap.keySet();
94      Iterator<Integer> iterator = navigableKeySet.iterator();
95      int i = 0;
96      while (i < 5 && iterator.hasNext()) {
97         Integer key = iterator.next();
98         String value = concurrentSkipListMap.get(key);
99         System.out.println("key = " + key + " value = " + value);
100        i++;
101     }
102  }
103
104  public static void checkSubMap (ConcurrentSkipListMap<Integer, String>
105      concurrentSkipListMap) {
106     ConcurrentNavigableMap<Integer, String> subMap =
107        concurrentSkipListMap.subMap(20, 50);
108     printMap (subMap);
109  }
110
111  public static void checkHeadMap (ConcurrentSkipListMap<Integer, String>
112      concurrentSkipListMap) {
113     ConcurrentNavigableMap<Integer,String> headMap =
```

```
114         concurrentSkipListMap.headMap(5);
115      printMap (headMap);
116   }
117
118   public static void checkTailMap (ConcurrentSkipListMap<Integer, String>
119         concurrentSkipListMap) {
120      ConcurrentNavigableMap<Integer,String> tailMap =
121         concurrentSkipListMap.tailMap(100);
122      printMap (tailMap);
123   }
124
125   public static void printMap (ConcurrentNavigableMap<Integer,String> map)
   {
126      NavigableSet<Integer> navigableKeySet = map.keySet();
127      Iterator<Integer> iterator = navigableKeySet.iterator();
128      int i = 0;
129      while (i < 5 && iterator.hasNext()) {
130         Integer key = iterator.next();
131         String value = map.get(key);
132         System.out.println("key = " + key + " value = " + value);
133         i++;
134      }
135   }
136 }
```

Executing this program on my Eclipse IDE yielded the result as shown in Listing 7.27. As you see, the object was indeed accessed concurrently by multiple threads, as each value has its first part representing the id of the thread that performed the action.

This concludes our discussion on the ConcurrentSkipListMap concurrent collection. We discuss the ConcurrentSkipListSet concurrent collection next.

Listing 7.27 Result of executing the ConcurrentSkipListMapDemo.java program

```
Thread 0 put: 987 - >0_987
Thread 6 get: 1346 -> null
......
Thread 4 put: 9743 - >4_9743
size = 8619

call checkKeySet:
key = 0 value = 0_0
key = 1 value = 0_1
key = 2 value = 4_2
key = 4 value = 0_4
key = 5 value = 0_5

call checkSubMap:
key = 20 value = 0_20
key = 23 value = 4_23
```

```
key = 24 value = 0_24
key = 25 value = 0_25
key = 26 value = 4_26

call checkHeadMap:
key = 0 value = 0_0
key = 1 value = 0_1
key = 2 value = 4_2
key = 4 value = 0_4

call checkTailMap:
key = 100 value = 0_100
key = 101 value = 0_101
key = 102 value = 4_102
key = 103 value = 0_103
key = 104 value = 4_104
```

☑ **Note**: **ConcurrentSkipListMap versus ConcurrentHashMap.** ConcurrentHashMap is more tunable than ConcurrentSkipListMap, since the former supports initialization with an initial capacity, a load factor, and a concurrency level, while the latter doesn't. ConcurrentHashMap is more commonly used than ConcurrentSkipListMap.

7.2.5 ConcurrentSkipListSet

While ConcurrentSkipListMap is the *concurrent* version of TreeMap, ConcurrentSkipListSet is the *concurrent* version of TreeSet. Like ConcurrentSkipListMap, ConcurrentSkipListSet provides navigability and thread-safety or concurrency. Furthermore, the implementation of ConcurrentSkipListSet is actually based on ConcurrentSkipListMap, as described below.

Listing 7.28 shows partially the implementation of the ConcurrentSkipListSet synchronized collection. Similar to the TreeSet class, it extends the AbstractSet class and implements the NavigableSet interface. Line 3 shows what is behind the implementation: a ConcurrentNavigableMap object named m. This m object is used to implement ConcurrentSkipListSet's constructors and methods, as follows:

- **Constructors**: Lines 4–22 show five different forms of constructors for the ConcurrentSkipListSet class. As you see, they are all based on ConcurrentSkipListMap.
- **clone()**: This method shows how a ConcurrentSkipListSet object is cloned. Once again, a new instance of ConcurrentSkipListMap is used to clone a ConcurrentSkipListSet object, as shown at line 28.
- **contains(Object o)**: This method is just a wrapper of the ConcurrentSkipListMap's containsKey method. On the other hand, this method shows that ConcurrentSkipListSet uses the key set of ConcurrentSkipListMap to implement a navigable, concurrent set.

- **add(E e)**: Similarly, this method is just a wrapper of the ConcurrentSkipListMap's putIfAbsent method. This method also shows that ConcurrentSkipListSet uses the key set of ConcurrentSkipListMap to implement a navigable, concurrent set.
- **first(), last(), pollFirst() and pollLast()**: Wrappers of proper methods of ConcurrentSkipListMap. Note the difference between first() and pollFirst() that first() returns the first element if the set is not empty or throws NoSuchElementException if the set is empty, while pollFirst() returns and removes the first element if the set is not empty or returns null if the set is empty.

Next, we use an example to demonstrate the use of the ConcurrentSkipListSet concurrent collection, following Listing 7.28.

Listing 7.28 ConcurrentSkipListSet.java (partial)

```
1    public class ConcurrentSkipListSet<E> extends AbstractSet<E>
2      implements NavigableSet<E>, Cloneable, java.io.Serializable {
3
4        private final ConcurrentNavigableMap<E,Object> m;
5
6        public ConcurrentSkipListSet() {
7            m = new ConcurrentSkipListMap<E,Object>();
8        }
9        public ConcurrentSkipListSet(Comparator<? super E> comparator) {
10            m = new ConcurrentSkipListMap<E,Object>(comparator);
11        }
12        public ConcurrentSkipListSet(Collection<? extends E> c) {
13            m = new ConcurrentSkipListMap<E,Object>();
14            addAll(c);
15        }
16        public ConcurrentSkipListSet(SortedSet<E> s) {
17            m = new ConcurrentSkipListMap<E,Object>(s.comparator());
18            addAll(s);
19        }
20        ConcurrentSkipListSet(ConcurrentNavigableMap<E,Object> m) {
21            this.m = m;
22        }
23
24        public ConcurrentSkipListSet<E> clone() {
25            ConcurrentSkipListSet<E> clone = null;
26            try {
27                clone = (ConcurrentSkipListSet<E>) super.clone();
28                clone.setMap(new ConcurrentSkipListMap(m));
29            } catch (CloneNotSupportedException e) {
30                throw new InternalError();
31            }
32
33            return clone;
34        }
35
36        public boolean contains(Object o) {
37            return m.containsKey(o);
```

```
38        }
39
40        public boolean add(E e) {
41              return m.putIfAbsent(e, Boolean.TRUE) == null;
42        }
43
44        public E first() {
45              return m.firstKey();
46        }
47
48        public E last() {
49              return m.lastKey();
50        }
51
52        public E pollFirst() {
53              Map.Entry<E,Object> e = m.pollFirstEntry();
54              return (e == null) ? null : e.getKey();
55        }
56
57        public E pollLast() {
58              Map.Entry<E,Object> e = m.pollLastEntry();
59              return (e == null) ? null : e.getKey();
60        }
61        // other methods omitted
62  }
```

Listing 7.29 shows the ConcurrentSkipListSetDemo.java program, adapted from the previous ConcurrentSkipListMapDemo.java program. The SkipListSetThread class has a field named concurrentSkipListSet of type ConcurrentSkipListSet. It calls the add and pollFirst methods of the concurrentSkipListSet object to add elements and retrieve/remove the first element, respectively. The importance here is that the concurrentSkipListSet object is accessed concurrently by multiple threads.

The driver program for this demo (lines 42 – 124) follows the standard procedure as shown below:

1. Creating a concurrent skip list set object
2. Creating a newFixedThreadPool using the ExecutorService interface
3. Launching skip list set threads
4. Shutting down the executorService object to avoid potential resource leak
5. Waiting for all threads to finish before terminating the thread pool

The driver program demonstrates how to access a ConcurrentSkipListSet using its Iterator for retrieving the elements of the ConcurrentSkipListSet object as well as the NavigableSet interface for retrieving subSets, headSets and tailSets, and so on. The procedure is the same that:

1. You first get the navigableSet from the set
2. Then you get the iterator from the navigableSet
3. Finally, you use the iterator to navigate through the set

Next, we discuss the result of executing this demo program, following Listing 7.29.

Listing 7.29 ConcurrentSkipListSetDemo.java

```
1    package jcp.ch7.synchedcollections;
2
3    import java.util.Iterator;
4    import java.util.NavigableSet;
5    import java.util.Random;
6    import java.util.concurrent.ConcurrentSkipListSet;
7    import java.util.concurrent.ExecutorService;
8    import java.util.concurrent.Executors;
9    import java.util.concurrent.TimeUnit;
10
11   class SkipListSetThread extends Thread {
12     int id;
13     Random random;
14     ConcurrentSkipListSet<Integer> concurrentSkipListSet;
15
16     SkipListSetThread(int id, ConcurrentSkipListSet<Integer>
17       concurrentSkipListSet) {
18       this.id = id;
19       this.random = new Random();
20       this.concurrentSkipListSet = concurrentSkipListSet;
21     }
22
23     public void run() {
24       int IMAX = 10000;
25       for (int i = 0; i < IMAX; i++) {
26         Integer element = random.nextInt(IMAX);
27         boolean output = (i % (IMAX / 10)) == 0;
28         if ((id % 4) == 0) {
29           concurrentSkipListSet.add(element);
30           if (output)
31             System.out.println ("Thread " + id + " add: " + element);
32         } else {
33           element = concurrentSkipListSet.pollFirst();
34           if (output)
35             System.out.println ("Thread " + id + " pollFirst: "
36               + element);
37         }
38       }
39     }
40   }
41
42   public class ConcurrentSkipListSetDemo {
43
44     public static void main(String[] args) {
45
46       int POOL_SIZE = 8;
47       ConcurrentSkipListSet<Integer> concurrentSkipListSet =
48           new ConcurrentSkipListSet<Integer> ();
49
50       // 1. Create a newFixedThreadPool using the Executors utility class
```

```
51    ExecutorService executorService = Executors
52       .newFixedThreadPool(POOL_SIZE);
53
54    // 2. launch skip list skip list set threads
55    for (int i = 0; i < POOL_SIZE; i++) {
56       executorService.execute(new SkipListSetThread(i,
57          concurrentSkipListSet));
58    }
59
60    // 3. shut down executorService to avoid resource leak
61    executorService.shutdown();
62
63    // 4. wait until all threads are done
64    try {
65       executorService.awaitTermination(Integer.MAX_VALUE,
66          TimeUnit.SECONDS);
67    } catch (InterruptedException e) {
68       e.printStackTrace();
69    }
70    System.out.println ("size = " + concurrentSkipListSet.size());
71
72    // 5. check iterator, subSet, headSet and tailSet
73    System.out.println ("\ncall checkIterator: ");
74    checkIterator (concurrentSkipListSet);
75
76    System.out.println ("\ncall checkSubSet: ");
77    checkSubSet (concurrentSkipListSet);
78
79    System.out.println ("\ncall checkHeadSet: ");
80    checkHeadSet (concurrentSkipListSet);
81
82    System.out.println ("\ncall checkTailSet: ");
83    checkTailSet (concurrentSkipListSet);
84  }
85
86  public static void checkIterator (ConcurrentSkipListSet<Integer>
87     concurrentSkipListSet) {
88
89     Iterator<Integer> iterator = concurrentSkipListSet.iterator();
90     int i = 0;
91     while (i < 5 && iterator.hasNext()) {
92        Integer element = iterator.next();
93        System.out.println("element = " + element);
94        i++;
95     }
96  }
97
98  public static void checkSubSet (ConcurrentSkipListSet<Integer>
99     concurrentSkipListSet) {
100    NavigableSet<Integer> subSet = concurrentSkipListSet.subSet(20, 50);
101    printSet (subSet);
102  }
```

```
103
104    public static void checkHeadSet (ConcurrentSkipListSet<Integer>
105       concurrentSkipListSet) {
106       NavigableSet<Integer> headSet = concurrentSkipListSet.headSet(5);
107       printSet (headSet);
108    }
109
110    public static void checkTailSet (ConcurrentSkipListSet<Integer>
111       concurrentSkipListSet) {
112       NavigableSet<Integer> tailSet = concurrentSkipListSet.tailSet(100);
113       printSet (tailSet);
114    }
115
116    public static void printSet (NavigableSet<Integer> set) {
117       Iterator<Integer> iterator = set.iterator();
118       int i = 0;
119       while (i < 5 && iterator.hasNext()) {
120          Integer element = iterator.next();
121          System.out.println("element = " + element);
122          i++;
123       }
124    }
125 }
```

Executing this program on my Eclipse IDE yielded the result as shown in Listing 7.30. As you see, the object was indeed accessed concurrently by multiple threads, as each main output line is prefixed with the thread id.

This concludes our discussion on the ConcurrentSkipListSet concurrent collection. We discuss the LinkedBlockingQueue concurrent collection next.

Listing 7.30 Result of executing the ConcurrentSkipListSetDemo.java program

```
Thread 6 pollFirst: null
Thread 1 pollFirst: 1145
Thread 4 add: 1145
Thread 7 pollFirst: null
......
Thread 0 add: 5110
Thread 4 add: 5208
size = 6873

call checkIterator:
element = 1
element = 2
element = 3
element = 4
element = 5

call checkSubSet:
```

element = 23
element = 24
element = 26
element = 27
element = 28

call checkHeadSet:
element = 1
element = 2
element = 3
element = 4

call checkTailSet:
element = 100
element = 101
element = 102
element = 104
element = 106

7.3   LinkedBlocking and Transfer Queues

In §3.4.5, we introduced LinkedList, which is characterized by its Node class that has an element and two pointers (next and prev) to point forward and backward to the same type of nodes to form a linked list. In §3.5, we introduced the ArrayDeque class and the PriorityQueue class. The ArrayDeque class has a field named elements of type E[] and two other fields of head and tail of type int. The PriorityQueue class has an Object[] queue field and a Comparator field for arranging the priority.

In this section, we cover three queue-related concurrent collections:

- LinkedBlockingQueue: This is an optionally-bounded, blocking FIFO queue based on linked nodes. The term optionally-bounded means that if not specified specifically, its capacity would be Integer.MAX_VALUE.
- LinkedBlockingDeque: This is an optionally-bounded blocking, deque based on linked nodes. Since it's a deque, the FIFO property does not apply.
- LinkedTransferQueue: This is an unbounded TransferQueue based on linked nodes. This queue orders elements in FIFO (first-in-first-out) with respect to any given producer.

Let's start with the LinkedBlockingQueue class first.

7.3.1 LinkedBlockingQueue

A LinkedBlockingQueue is a linked queue first. Therefore, it must have a Node class, which is shown in Listing 7.31 (lines 13–17). It has only an item field, a next pointer, and a parameterized constructor.

Next, to maintain the FIFO order, LinkedBlockingQueue needs to have a head node and a tail node so that it can perform retrieval operations at the head of the queue and insert operations at the tail of the queue. The `head` node and `tail` node of the `LinkedBlockingQueue` class are shown at lines 22 and 23, respectively.

To become a blocking queue, the `LinkedBlockingQueue` class needs to have locks and `Condition` objects for its `put` and `take` operations, as we learnt previously. This is why we have the `putLock`, `takeLock`, `notEmpty` and `notFull` condition objects from lines 25–28. Lines 30–48 show the `fullyLock()`, `fullyUnlock()`, `signalNotEmpty()` and `signalNotFull()` methods, which are helpful for facilitating lock and condition object related operations. In addition, note the private methods of `enqueue` (lines 60–64) and `dequeue` (lines 66–76), which are standard queuing operations.

Then, the constructors follow all embedded classes and private methods (if any), as shown from lines 78–104. The no-arg constructor defines an optionally-unbounded queue, while the other two parameterized constructors define bounded queues. Such details are not specific to this class, so we can just take them as they are.

The last part of Listing 7.31 shows how the two typical public methods, `take()` and `poll()`, are implemented with locks and condition objects described above. Given how much we have covered on locks, condition objects, queues, etc., you should be able to trace these two methods yourself if you want.

Next, we use an example to show the use of the `LinkedBlockingQueue` synchronized collection, following Listing 7.31.

Listing 7.31 LinkedBlockingQueue.java (partial)

```
1   package java.util.concurrent;
2
3   import java.util.concurrent.atomic.AtomicInteger;
4   import java.util.concurrent.locks.Condition;
5   import java.util.concurrent.locks.ReentrantLock;
6   import java.util.AbstractQueue;
7   import java.util.Collection;
8   import java.util.Iterator;
9   import java.util.NoSuchElementException;
10
11  public class LinkedBlockingQueue<E> extends AbstractQueue<E>
12          implements BlockingQueue<E>, java.io.Serializable {
13      static class Node<E> {
14          E item;
15          Node<E> next;
16          Node(E x) { item = x; }
17      }
18
19      private final int capacity;
20      private final AtomicInteger count = new AtomicInteger(0);
21
22      private transient Node<E> head;
23      private transient Node<E> last;
24
25      private final ReentrantLock putLock = new ReentrantLock();
26      private final ReentrantLock takeLock = new ReentrantLock();
```

```
27      private final Condition notEmpty = takeLock.newCondition();
28      private final Condition notFull = putLock.newCondition();
29
30      void fullyLock() {
31          putLock.lock();
32          takeLock.lock();
33      }
34
35      void fullyUnlock() {
36          takeLock.unlock();
37          putLock.unlock();
38      }
39
40      private void signalNotEmpty() {
41          final ReentrantLock takeLock = this.takeLock;
42          takeLock.lock();
43          try {
44              notEmpty.signal();
45          } finally {
46              takeLock.unlock();
47          }
48      }
49
50      private void signalNotFull() {
51          final ReentrantLock putLock = this.putLock;
52          putLock.lock();
53          try {
54              notFull.signal();
55          } finally {
56              putLock.unlock();
57          }
58      }
59
60      private void enqueue(Node<E> node) {
61          // assert putLock.isHeldByCurrentThread();
62          // assert last.next == null;
63          last = last.next = node;
64      }
65
66      private E dequeue() {
67          // assert takeLock.isHeldByCurrentThread();
68          // assert head.item == null;
69          Node<E> h = head;
70          Node<E> first = h.next;
71          h.next = h; // help GC
72          head = first;
73          E x = first.item;
74          first.item = null;
75          return x;
76      }
77
78      public LinkedBlockingQueue() {
```

```
 79              this(Integer.MAX_VALUE);
 80         }
 81         public LinkedBlockingQueue(int capacity) {
 82              if (capacity <= 0) throw new IllegalArgumentException();
 83              this.capacity = capacity;
 84              last = head = new Node<E>(null);
 85         }
 86         public LinkedBlockingQueue(Collection<? extends E> c) {
 87              this(Integer.MAX_VALUE);
 88              final ReentrantLock putLock = this.putLock;
 89              putLock.lock(); // Never contended, but necessary for visibility
 90              try {
 91                  int n = 0;
 92                  for (E e : c) {
 93                      if (e == null)
 94                          throw new NullPointerException();
 95                      if (n == capacity)
 96                          throw new IllegalStateException("Queue full");
 97                      enqueue(new Node<E>(e));
 98                      ++n;
 99                  }
100                  count.set(n);
101              } finally {
102                  putLock.unlock();
103              }
104         }
105
106         public E take() throws InterruptedException {
107              E x;
108              int c = -1;
109              final AtomicInteger count = this.count;
110              final ReentrantLock takeLock = this.takeLock;
111              takeLock.lockInterruptibly();
112              try {
113                  while (count.get() == 0) {
114                      notEmpty.await();
115                  }
116                  x = dequeue();
117                  c = count.getAndDecrement();
118                  if (c > 1)
119                      notEmpty.signal();
120              } finally {
121                  takeLock.unlock();
122              }
123              if (c == capacity)
124                  signalNotFull();
125              return x;
126         }
127
128         public E poll() {
129              final AtomicInteger count = this.count;
130              if (count.get() == 0)
```

```
131                  return null;
132              E x = null;
133              int c = -1;
134              final ReentrantLock takeLock = this.takeLock;
135              takeLock.lock();
136              try {
137                  if (count.get() > 0) {
138                      x = dequeue();
139                      c = count.getAndDecrement();
140                      if (c > 1)
141                          notEmpty.signal();
142                  }
143              } finally {
144                  takeLock.unlock();
145              }
146              if (c == capacity)
147                  signalNotFull();
148              return x;
149      }
150      // other methods omitted
151 }
```

Listing 7.32 shows the LinkedBlockingQueueDemo.java program. The LBQThread class has a field named linkedBlockingQueue of type LinkedBlockingQueue. It calls the add and poll methods of the linkedBlockingQueue object to add elements and retrieve/remove the element added to the queue earliest, respectively. The importance here is that the linkedBlockingQueue object is accessed concurrently by multiple threads.

The driver program for this demo (lines 39 – 69) follows the standard procedure as shown below:

1. Creating a linked blocking queue object
2. Creating a newFixedThreadPool using the ExecutorService interface
3. Launching linked blocking queue (LBQ) threads
4. Shutting down the executorService object to avoid potential resource leak
5. Waiting for all threads to finish before terminating the thread pool

Next, we discuss the result of executing this demo program, following Listing 7.32.

Listing 7.32 LinkedBlockingQueueDemo.java

```
1   package jcp.ch7.synchedcollections;
2
3   import java.util.Random;
4   import java.util.concurrent.ConcurrentLinkedQueue;
5   import java.util.concurrent.ExecutorService;
6   import java.util.concurrent.Executors;
7   import java.util.concurrent.LinkedBlockingQueue;
8   import java.util.concurrent.TimeUnit;
9
10  class LBQThread extends Thread {
11    int id;
```

```
12     Random random;
13     LinkedBlockingQueue<String> linkedBlockingQueue;
14
15     LBQThread(int id, LinkedBlockingQueue<String> linkedBlockingQueue) {
16        this.id = id;
17        this.random = new Random();
18        this.linkedBlockingQueue = linkedBlockingQueue;
19     }
20
21     public void run() {
22        int IMAX = 10000;
23        for (int i = 0; i < IMAX; i++) {
24           String item = id + "_" + random.nextInt(IMAX);
25           boolean output = (i % (IMAX / 10)) == 0;
26           if ((id % 2) == 0) {
27              linkedBlockingQueue.add(item);
28              if (output)
29                 System.out.println ("Thread " + id + " add: " + item);
30           } else {
31              String value = linkedBlockingQueue.poll();
32              if (output)
33                 System.out.println ("Thread " + id + " poll: " + value);
34           }
35        }
36     }
37  }
38
39  public class LinkedBlockingQueueDemo {
40
41     public static void main(String[] args) {
42
43        int POOL_SIZE = 8;
44
45        // 1. create a concurrent linked queue
46        LinkedBlockingQueue<String> linkedBlockingQueue =
47              new LinkedBlockingQueue<String> ();
48
49        // 2. create a newFixedThreadPool using the ExecutorService class
50        ExecutorService executorService = Executors
51              .newFixedThreadPool(POOL_SIZE);
52
53        // 3. launch worker threads
54        for (int i = 0; i < POOL_SIZE; i++) {
55           executorService.execute(new LBQThread(i, linkedBlockingQueue));
56        }
57
58        // 4. shut down executorService to avoid resource leak
59        executorService.shutdown();
60
61        // 5. wait until all threads are done
62        try {
63           executorService.awaitTermination(Integer.MAX_VALUE,
```

```
              TimeUnit.SECONDS);
64         } catch (InterruptedException e) {
65             e.printStackTrace();
66         }
67         System.out.println ("size = " + linkedBlockingQueue.size());
68     }
69 }
```

Executing this program on my Eclipse IDE yielded the result as shown in Listing 7.33. As you see, the object was indeed accessed concurrently by multiple threads, as each main output line is prefixed with the thread id.

This concludes our discussion on the LinkedBlockingQueue concurrent collection. We discuss the LinkedBlockingDeque concurrent collection next.

Listing 7.33 Result of executing the ConcurrentSkipListSetDemo.java program

```
Thread 1 poll: null
Thread 5 poll: 2_2369
Thread 4 add: 4_6760
Thread 6 add: 6_2584
Thread 3 poll: 0_3291
Thread 2 add: 2_2369
Thread 0 add: 0_3291
......
Thread 5 poll: 6_6663
Thread 1 poll: 0_2208
size = 39
```

7.3.2 LinkedBlockingDeque

In the preceding section, we introduced LinkedBlockingQueue, which is an optionally-bounded, blocking, FIFO queue based on linked nodes. LinkedBlockingDeque is an optionally-bounded blocking deque based on linked nodes. It is implemented as a simple doubly-linked list protected by a single lock and uses conditions to manage blocking. Next, we look at how it is implemented internally.

Since LinkedBlockingDeque is fundamentally a linked data structure, it must have a Node class, which is shown in Listing 7.34 (lines 15–22). It has an item field, a prev/next pointer pair, and a parameterized constructor for a given item. Note that the constructor parameterization does not include next and prev pointers.

LinkedBlockingDeque has the following fields:

- first/last: Pointing to the first/last node of the deque
- count: Number of items in the deque
- capacity: Maximum number of items in the deque
- lock: A reentrant lock for guarding all accesses
- notEmpty/notFull: Waiting condition for consumer/producer threads

LinkedBlockingDeque has the following three constructors:

- LinkedBlockingDeque(): The no-arg constructor that defaults to the maximum capacity of Integer.MAX_VALUE
- LinkedBlockingDeque(int capacity): The parameterized constructor with a given capacity
- LinkedBlockingDeque(Collection<? extends E> c): The parameterized constructor based on an existing collection. As is shown at line 50, the linkLast method is called to add elements of the existing collection at the last position each time.

In terms of methods, LinkedBlockingDeque has two sets of methods: one set simulating a Stack that follows the LIFO order, and the other set simulating a Queue that follows the FIFO order. The Stack-oriented method call-chains are:

push → addFirst → offerFirst → linkFirst
pop → removeFirst → pollFirst → unlinkFirst
element → getFirst
peek → peekFirst → getFirst
remove -> removeFirst

The Queue-oriented method call-chains for LinkedBlockingDeque are:

add → addLast → offerLast → linkLast
put → putLast -> linkLast
poll → pollFirst → unlinkFirst

Since we already have a LinkedBlockingQueue class that acts as a FIFO queue, we focus on understanding the Stack-behavior implementation for the LinkedBlockingDeque class here. Let's first look at the push method in the following sequence:

push → addFirst → offerFirst → linkFirst

The above chain is shown from lines 58–93 in Listing 7.34. As you see, the push and addFirst methods are just wrappers. The offerFirst method is where the lock is applied. The private method, linkFirst, does all the work at the bottom layer. The offer method creates a new node with the element intended. Then, it passes that new node to the linkFirst method, as defined from lines 79–93. The key to understanding the linkFirst logic is to consider f as the currentFirst, as shown below with f replaced by currentFirst:

```
1       private boolean linkFirst(Node<E> node) {
2           // assert lock.isHeldByCurrentThread();
3           if (count >= capacity)
4               return false;
5           Node<E> currentFirst = first;
6           node.next = currentFirst;
7           first = node;
8           if (last == null)
9               last = node;
10          else
11              currentFirst.prev = node;
12          ++count;
13          notEmpty.signal();
```

```
14          return true;
15      }
```

Let us now explain the implementation of the linkFirst method as shown above as follows:

- Lines 3 and 4 check the capacity.
- Line 5 creates a new reference to the first node.
- Line 6 sets the new node's next pointer pointing to the current first node, which is only half of the linking logic for this method.
- Line 7 makes the new node become the first node.
- Lines 8–11 designate the new node to be the last node if the last pointer is null. Otherwise, it sets current first node's prev pointer to the new node.
- Line 12 increments the count variable.
- Line 13 signals that the queue is not empty in case some consumer threads are waiting.

You can trace the above implementation logic by referring to Figure 7.7, following Listing 7.34.

Next, let's look at the pop method in the following sequence:

pop → removeFirst → pollFirst → unlinkFirst

The above chain is shown from lines 95–132 in Listing 7.34. As you see, the pop, removeFirst, and pollFirst methods are all wrappers, except that the pollFirst method is where the lock is applied. Similar to linkFirst, the private method, unlinkFirst, does all the work at the bottom layer to unlink the current first node so the node pointed to by the next pointer of the current first node will become the new first node. I suggest that you trace the logic of the unlink method yourself if you want.

Next, we use an example to demonstrate the use of the LinkedBlockingDeque concurrent collection, following Figure 7.6.

Listing 7.34 LinkedBlockingDeque.java (partial)

```java
1   package java.util.concurrent;
2
3   import java.util.AbstractQueue;
4   import java.util.Collection;
5   import java.util.Iterator;
6   import java.util.NoSuchElementException;
7   import java.util.concurrent.locks.Condition;
8   import java.util.concurrent.locks.ReentrantLock;
9
10  public class LinkedBlockingDeque<E>
11      extends AbstractQueue<E>
12      implements BlockingDeque<E>, java.io.Serializable {
13
14      /** Doubly-linked list node class */
15      static final class Node<E> {
16          E item;
17          Node<E> prev;
18          Node<E> next;
```

```java
19          Node(E x) {
20              item = x;
21          }
22      }
23
24      transient Node<E> first;
25      transient Node<E> last;
26      private transient int count;
27      private final int capacity;
28
29      final ReentrantLock lock = new ReentrantLock();
30      private final Condition notEmpty = lock.newCondition();
31      private final Condition notFull = lock.newCondition();
32
33      public LinkedBlockingDeque() {
34          this(Integer.MAX_VALUE);
35      }
36
37      public LinkedBlockingDeque(int capacity) {
38          if (capacity <= 0) throw new IllegalArgumentException();
39          this.capacity = capacity;
40      }
41
42      public LinkedBlockingDeque(Collection<? extends E> c) {
43          this(Integer.MAX_VALUE);
44          final ReentrantLock lock = this.lock;
45          lock.lock(); // Never contended, but necessary for visibility
46          try {
47              for (E e : c) {
48                  if (e == null)
49                      throw new NullPointerException();
50                  if (!linkLast(new Node<E>(e)))
51                      throw new IllegalStateException("Deque full");
52              }
53          } finally {
54              lock.unlock();
55          }
56      }
57
58      public void push(E e) {
59          addFirst(e);
60      }
61
62      public void addFirst(E e) {
63          if (!offerFirst(e))
64              throw new IllegalStateException("Deque full");
65      }
66
67      public boolean offerFirst(E e) {
68          if (e == null) throw new NullPointerException();
69          Node<E> node = new Node<E>(e);
70          final ReentrantLock lock = this.lock;
```

```
71              lock.lock();
72              try {
73                  return linkFirst(node);
74              } finally {
75                  lock.unlock();
76              }
77          }
78
79          private boolean linkFirst(Node<E> node) {
80              // assert lock.isHeldByCurrentThread();
81              if (count >= capacity)
82                  return false;
83              Node<E> f = first;
84              node.next = f;
85              first = node;
86              if (last == null)
87                  last = node;
88              else
89                  f.prev = node;
90              ++count;
91              notEmpty.signal();
92              return true;
93          }
94
95          public E pop() {
96              return removeFirst();
97          }
98
99          public E removeFirst() {
100             E x = pollFirst();
101             if (x == null) throw new NoSuchElementException();
102             return x;
103         }
104
105         public E pollFirst() {
106             final ReentrantLock lock = this.lock;
107             lock.lock();
108             try {
109                 return unlinkFirst();
110             } finally {
111                 lock.unlock();
112             }
113         }
114
115         private E unlinkFirst() {
116             // assert lock.isHeldByCurrentThread();
117             Node<E> f = first;
118             if (f == null)
119                 return null;
120             Node<E> n = f.next;
121             E item = f.item;
122             f.item = null;
```

```
123          f.next = f; // help GC
124          first = n;
125          if (n == null)
126              last = null;
127          else
128              n.prev = null;
129          --count;
130          notFull.signal();
131          return item;
132      }
133
134      // other methods omitted
135 }
```

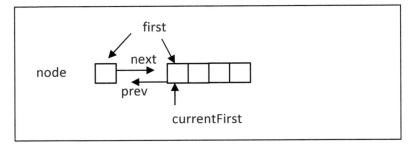

Figure 7.6 `linkFirst` logic

Listing 7.35 shows the LinkedBlockingDequeDemo.java program. The LBDThread class has a field named linkedBlockingDeque of type LinkedBlockingDeque. It calls the push and pop methods of the linkedBlockingDeque object to add elements and retrieve/remove the element added to the stack earlier, respectively. (Note that line 29 checks if the deque is empty before calling the pop method to avoid NoSuchElementExceptions.) The importance here is that the linkedBlockingDeque object is accessed concurrently by multiple threads.

The driver program for this demo (lines 38 – 69) follows the standard procedure as shown below:

1. Creating a linked blocking deque object
2. Creating a newFixedThreadPool using the ExecutorService interface
3. Launching linked blocking deque (LBD) threads
4. Shutting down the executorService object to avoid potential resource leak
5. Waiting for all threads to finish before terminating the thread pool

Next, we discuss the result of executing this demo program, following Listing 7.35.

Listing 7.35 LinkedBlockingDequeDemo.java

```
1   package jcp.ch7.synchedcollections;
2
3   import java.util.Random;
4   import java.util.concurrent.ExecutorService;
```

```
5   import java.util.concurrent.Executors;
6   import java.util.concurrent.LinkedBlockingDeque;
7   import java.util.concurrent.TimeUnit;
8
9   class LBDThread extends Thread {
10    int id;
11    Random random;
12    LinkedBlockingDeque<String> linkedBlockingDeque;
13
14    LBDThread(int id, LinkedBlockingDeque<String> linkedBlockingDeque) {
15      this.id = id;
16      this.random = new Random();
17      this.linkedBlockingDeque = linkedBlockingDeque;
18    }
19
20    public void run() {
21      int IMAX = 10000;
22      for (int i = 0; i < IMAX; i++) {
23        String item = id + "_" + random.nextInt(IMAX);
24        boolean output = (i % (IMAX / 10)) == 0;
25        if ((id % 2) == 0) {
26          linkedBlockingDeque.push(item);
27          if (output)
28            System.out.println ("Thread " + id + " push: " + item);
29        } else if (!linkedBlockingDeque.isEmpty()) {
30          String value = linkedBlockingDeque.pop();
31          if (output)
32            System.out.println ("Thread " + id + " pop: " + value);
33        }
34      }
35    }
36  }
37
38  public class LinkedBlockingDequeDemo {
39
40    public static void main(String[] args) {
41
42      int POOL_SIZE = 8;
43
44      // 1. create a concurrent linked queue
45      LinkedBlockingDeque<String> linkedBlockingDeque =
46          new LinkedBlockingDeque<String> ();
47
48      // 2. create a newFixedThreadPool using the ExecutorService class
49      ExecutorService executorService = Executors
50          .newFixedThreadPool(POOL_SIZE);
51
52      // 3. launch worker threads
53      for (int i = 0; i < POOL_SIZE; i++) {
54        executorService.execute(new LBDThread(i, linkedBlockingDeque));
55      }
56
```

```
57     // 4. shut down executorService to avoid resource leak
58     executorService.shutdown();
59
60     // 5. wait until all threads are done
61     try {
62        executorService.awaitTermination(Integer.MAX_VALUE,
63           TimeUnit.SECONDS);
64     } catch (InterruptedException e) {
65        e.printStackTrace();
66     }
67     System.out.println ("size = " + linkedBlockingDeque.size());
68   }
69 }
```

Executing this program on my Eclipse IDE yielded the result as shown in Listing 7.36. As you see, the object was indeed accessed concurrently by multiple threads, as each main output line is prefixed with the thread id.

This concludes our discussion on the LinkedBlockingDeque concurrent collection. We discuss the LinkedTransferQueue concurrent collection next.

Listing 7.36 Result of executing the ConcurrentSkipListSetDemo.java program

```
Thread 0 push: 0_2663
Thread 6 push: 6_2092
Thread 5 pop: 4_3242
......
Thread 7 pop: 0_6076
Thread 5 pop: 4_8037
size = 10
```

7.3.3 LinkedTransferQueue

In §7.1.3, we introduced SynchronousQueue, which is a blocking queue in which each *insert* operation must wait for a corresponding *remove* operation by another thread, and vice versa. As it is said, a synchronous queue does not have any internal capacity, not even a capacity of one. The LinkedTransferQueue is a real queue that even follows the FIFO order, with its head and tail fields as shown at lines 23 and 24 in Listing 7.37, respectively. The LinkedTransferQueue class has a private method named xfer as shown at line 26. This method is used by almost all other put/take-like methods, as it provides all alternatives with different combinations of parameters as follows:

- E e: The item for the node or null for take operation
- boolean haveData: true for put and false for take
- int how:

  ○ NOW: For untimed poll and tryTransfer
  ○ ASYNC: For add, put, and offer
  ○ SYNC: For take and transfer

　° TIMED: for timed `poll` and `tryTransfer`

- `long nanos`: Timeout in nanoseconds, used only if the mode (`how`) is TIMED

Next, let's look at two sets of public methods for the `LinkedTransferQueue` class as follows:

- `add(E e)`/`offer(E e)`/`put(E e)`: This set of methods is used for inserting data into the queue. The only difference is the return type that the `add` and `offer` methods return `true` while the `put` method has `void` type. These methods are shown from lines 30–42.
- `take()`/`poll()`/`transfer(E e)`/`tryTransfer(E e)`: This set of methods is used for retrieving/ removing or transferring elements to consumers. There are some subtle differences among those four methods as described below:

　° `take()`: Retrieves and removes the head of the queue, waiting if necessary until an element becomes available.
　° `poll()`: Retrieves and removes the head of the queue, or returns null if this queue is empty.
　° `transfer(E e)`: Transfers the element to a consumer, waiting if necessary to do so.
　° `tryTransfer(E e)`: Transfers the element to a waiting consumer immediately, if possible.

Therefore, as you see, `take` and `poll` operate on the head of the queue, while `transfer` and `tryTransfer` operate on the element specified as the argument of the methods. The method `take` may wait, while `poll` doesn't. Similarly, `transfer` may wait, while `tryTransfer` doesn't.

Next, we use an example to demonstrate the use of the `LinkedTransferQueue` concurrent collection, following Listing 7.37.

Listing 7.37 LinkedTransferQueue.java (partial)

```
1    package java.util.concurrent;
2
3    import java.util.AbstractQueue;
4    import java.util.Collection;
5    import java.util.Iterator;
6    import java.util.NoSuchElementException;
7    import java.util.Queue;
8    import java.util.concurrent.TimeUnit;
9    import java.util.concurrent.locks.LockSupport;
10
11   public class LinkedTransferQueue<E> extends AbstractQueue<E>
12       implements TransferQueue<E>, java.io.Serializable {
13
14       static final class Node {
15           final boolean isData;   // false if this is a request node
16           volatile Object item;   // initially non-null if isData
17           volatile Node next;
18           volatile Thread waiter; // null until waiting
19
20           // CAS methods for fields omitted
21       }
22
```

```
23      transient volatile Node head;
24      private transient volatile Node tail;
25
26      private E xfer(E e, boolean haveData, int how, long nanos) {
27          // body omitted
28      }
29
30      public boolean add(E e) {
31          xfer(e, true, ASYNC, 0);
32          return true;
33      }
34
35      public boolean offer(E e) {
36          xfer(e, true, ASYNC, 0);
37          return true;
38      }
39
40      public void put(E e) {
41          xfer(e, true, ASYNC, 0);
42      }
43
44      public E poll() {
45          return xfer(null, false, NOW, 0);
46      }
47
48      public E take() throws InterruptedException {
49          E e = xfer(null, false, SYNC, 0);
50          if (e != null)
51              return e;
52          Thread.interrupted();
53          throw new InterruptedException();
54      }
55
56      public void transfer(E e) throws InterruptedException {
57          if (xfer(e, true, SYNC, 0) != null) {
58              Thread.interrupted();
59              throw new InterruptedException();
60          }
61      }
62
63      public boolean tryTransfer(E e) {
64          return xfer(e, true, NOW, 0) == null;
65      }
66      // all other methods omitted
67  }
```

Listing 7.38 shows the LinkedTransferDemo.java program. The LTQThread class has a field named linkedTransferQueue of type LinkedTransferQueue. It calls the transfer method as a producer and calls the take method as a consumer to take objects from the producer.

The driver program for this demo (lines 48 – 78) follows the standard procedure as shown below:

1. Creating a linked transfer queue object
2. Creating a newFixedThreadPool using the ExecutorService interface
3. Launching linked transfer queue (LTQ) threads
4. Shutting down the executorService object to avoid potential resource leak
5. Waiting for all threads to finish before terminating the thread pool

Next, we discuss the result of executing this demo program, following Listing 7.38.

Listing 7.38 LinkedTransferQueueDemo.java

```
1    package jcp.ch7.synchedcollections;
2
3    import java.util.Random;
4    import java.util.concurrent.ExecutorService;
5    import java.util.concurrent.Executors;
6    import java.util.concurrent.LinkedBlockingDeque;
7    import java.util.concurrent.LinkedTransferQueue;
8    import java.util.concurrent.TimeUnit;
9
10   class LTQThread extends Thread {
11      int id;
12      Random random;
13      LinkedTransferQueue<String> linkedTransferQueue;
14
15      LTQThread(int id, LinkedTransferQueue<String> linkedTransferQueue) {
16         this.id = id;
17         this.random = new Random();
18         this.linkedTransferQueue = linkedTransferQueue;
19      }
20
21      public void run() {
22         int IMAX = 10000;
23         for (int i = 0; i < IMAX; i++) {
24            boolean output = (i % (IMAX / 10)) == 0;
25            if ((id % 2) == 0) {
26               try {
27                  String item = id + "_" + random.nextInt(IMAX);
28                  linkedTransferQueue.transfer(item);
29                  if (output)
30                     System.out.println ("Thread " + id + " transfer: " + item);
31               } catch (InterruptedException e) {
32                  e.printStackTrace();
33               }
34
35            } else {
36               try {
37                  String value = linkedTransferQueue.take();
38                  if (output)
39                     System.out.println ("Thread " + id + " take: " + value);
40               } catch (InterruptedException e) {
41                  e.printStackTrace();
```

```
42                }
43              }
44          }
45        }
46  }
47
48  public class LinkedTransferQueueDemo {
49
50    public static void main(String[] args) {
51
52        int POOL_SIZE = 8;
53
54        // 1. create a concurrent linked queue
55        LinkedTransferQueue<String> linkedTransferQueue =
56            new LinkedTransferQueue<String> ();
57
58        // 2. create a newFixedThreadPool using the ExecutorService class
59        ExecutorService executorService = Executors
60            .newFixedThreadPool(POOL_SIZE);
61
62        // 3. launch worker threads
63        for (int i = 0; i < POOL_SIZE; i++) {
64            executorService.execute(new LTQThread(i, linkedTransferQueue));
65        }
66
67        // 4. shut down executorService to avoid resource leak
68        executorService.shutdown();
69
70        // 5. wait until all threads are done
71        try {
72            executorService.awaitTermination(Integer.MAX_VALUE,
73                TimeUnit.SECONDS);
74        } catch (InterruptedException e) {
75            e.printStackTrace();
76        }
77        System.out.println ("size = " + linkedTransferQueue.size());
78    }
79  }
```

Executing this program on my Eclipse IDE yielded the result as shown in Listing 7.39. As you see, the object was indeed accessed concurrently by multiple threads, as each main output line is prefixed with the thread id.

This concludes our discussion on the LinkedTransferQueue concurrent collection. We discuss the CopyOnWrite ArrayList and ArraySet concurrent collections next.

Listing 7.39 Result of executing the ConcurrentSkipListSetDemo.java program

```
Thread 0 transfer: 0_3284
Thread 7 take: 6_6966
Thread 4 transfer: 4_4656
```

Thread 5 take: 4_4656

......

Thread 7 take: 2_8282

Thread 3 take: 0_9838

size = 0

7.4 CopyOnWrite ArrayList and ArraySet

CopyOnWrite (or COW) is a common performance optimization strategy in making a data structure available for multiple threads to access, which is particularly suitable when readers far outnumber writers. The idea is that when a thread needs to modify the shared data structure, it makes a private, local copy of it so that the underlying, shared data structure will not be affected.

In this section, we look at two CopyOnWrite concurrent collections: CopyOnWriteArrayList and CopyOnWriteArraySet. Let's start with the CopyOnWriteArrayList concurrent collection first next.

7.4.1 CopyOnWriteArrayList

The CopyOnWriteArrayList class is also an ArrayList but is thread-safe. It performs array traversal operations by using an iterator to create a snapshot of the underlying array list, with no remove, set and add (RSA) operations supported. It makes a fresh copy of the underlying array each time when a mutation, such as a remove, set or add, occurs, while read operations do not require synchronization.

Listing 7.40 shows partially the implementation of the CopyOnWriteArrayList class. As you see, it has two important fields: a reentrant lock named lock at line 4 for protecting all mutators as well as an Object[] named array at line 5, which is accessed only via getArray method (line 7) and setArray method (line 10).

The CopyOnWriteArrayList class has three constructors: a no-arg constructor that creates a zero-length Object array (lines 14–16), a constructor parameterized with an existing collection (lines 18–24), and a constructor parameterized with an existing element array (lines 26–29). Both parameterized constructors use Arrays.copyOf to copy the given array into a destination Object[].

Next, let's look at the iterator() and listIterator() methods of the CopyOnWriteArrayList class. As you see, both of the iterator() and listIterator() methods return a new instance of COWIterator, which implements the ListIterator interface, as shown from lines 39–69. The COWIterator class has the following two fields:

- Object[] snapshot: Represents a snapshot of the array (line 41)
- int cursor: Index of the element to be returned by a subsequent call to next (line 42)

The constructor of the COWIterator class is shown from lines 44–47. It has two parameters: Object[] elements and int initialCursor. This class has all public methods a ListIterator object should have, such as hasNext(), hasPrevious(), next(), previous(), nextIndex() and previousIndex(), except that it does not support remove, set and add operations as shown from lines 79–89.

Now, let's look at the remove(int index) method of the CopyOnWriteArrayList class, as shown from lines 92–113, to understand how CopyOnWriteArrayList works on the concept of CopyOnWrite. It is explained as follows:

- First, note that the entire operation is guarded with the reentrant lock of the CopyOnWriteArrayList object.
- Now pay attention to line 96. This line calls the getArray() method to return a copy of the array and assigns it to Object[] elements. The rest of the method operates on this object array of elements. The original array is not modified.
- Next, note the int numMoved variable, which represents how many elements to shift to the left.
- Whether the element to be removed is the last element (numMoved == 0) or not, the modified array is committed to the original array by calling setArray(newElements).

Note the use of System.arraycopy (...) call in the remove method discussed above. Its full signature is shown below:

```
public static void arraycopy(Object src, int srcPos,
                             Object dest, int destPos, int length)
```

This method copies an array from the specified source array (src), beginning at the specified position (srcPos), to the specified position of the destination array (desc), beginning at the specified position (descPos). The number of components to be copied is equal to the length argument.

Now it should be clear how the CopyOnWriteArrayList class works behind the scene: When an element needs to be mutated, a copy of the original is created and operated upon, which will be eventually committed back to the original array under the protection of the lock owned by the CopyOnWriteArrayList object. However, when a thread needs to traverse the entire array list or a sub list of it, use the iterator() method of the CopyOnWriteArrayList object to return a listIterator collection as a snapshot of the original array, which does not support mutations.

Next, we use an example to demonstrate the use of the CopyOnWriteArrayList concurrent collection, following Listing 7.40.

Listing 7.40 CopyOnWriteArrayList.java (partial)

```
1    public class CopyOnWriteArrayList<E>
2        implements List<E>, RandomAccess, Cloneable, java.io.Serializable {
3
4        transient final ReentrantLock lock = new ReentrantLock();
5        private volatile transient Object[] array;
6
7        final Object[] getArray() {
8            return array;
9        }
10       final void setArray(Object[] a) {
11           array = a;
12       }
13
14       public CopyOnWriteArrayList() {
```

```
15              setArray(new Object[0]);
16          }
17
18          public CopyOnWriteArrayList(Collection<? extends E> c) {
19              Object[] elements = c.toArray();
20              if (elements.getClass() != Object[].class)
21                  elements = Arrays.copyOf(elements, elements.length,
22                      Object[].class);
23              setArray(elements);
24          }
25
26          public CopyOnWriteArrayList(E[] toCopyIn) {
27              setArray(Arrays.copyOf(toCopyIn, toCopyIn.length,
28                Object[].class));
29          }
30
31          public Iterator<E> iterator() {
32              return new COWIterator<E>(getArray(), 0);
33          }
34
35          public ListIterator<E> listIterator() {
36              return new COWIterator<E>(getArray(), 0);
37          }
38
39          private static class COWIterator<E> implements ListIterator<E> {
40
41              private final Object[] snapshot;
42              private int cursor;
43
44              private COWIterator(Object[] elements, int initialCursor) {
45                  cursor = initialCursor;
46                  snapshot = elements;
47              }
48
49              public boolean hasNext() {
50                  return cursor < snapshot.length;
51              }
52
53              public boolean hasPrevious() {
54                  return cursor > 0;
55              }
56
57              @SuppressWarnings("unchecked")
58              public E next() {
59                  if (! hasNext())
60                      throw new NoSuchElementException();
61                  return (E) snapshot[cursor++];
62              }
63
64              @SuppressWarnings("unchecked")
65              public E previous() {
66                  if (! hasPrevious())
```

```
67                          throw new NoSuchElementException();
68                      return (E) snapshot[--cursor];
69                  }
70
71              public int nextIndex() {
72                  return cursor;
73              }
74
75              public int previousIndex() {
76                  return cursor-1;
77              }
78
79              public void remove() {
80                  throw new UnsupportedOperationException();
81              }
82
83              public void set(E e) {
84                  throw new UnsupportedOperationException();
85              }
86
87              public void add(E e) {
88                  throw new UnsupportedOperationException();
89              }
90          }
91
92      public E remove(int index) {
93          final ReentrantLock lock = this.lock;
94          lock.lock();
95          try {
96              Object[] elements = getArray();
97              int len = elements.length;
98              E oldValue = get(elements, index);
99              int numMoved = len - index - 1;
100             if (numMoved == 0)
101                 setArray(Arrays.copyOf(elements, len - 1));
102             else {
103                 Object[] newElements = new Object[len - 1];
104                 System.arraycopy(elements, 0, newElements, 0, index);
105                 System.arraycopy(elements, index + 1, newElements, index,
106                                 numMoved);
107                 setArray(newElements);
108             }
109             return oldValue;
110         } finally {
111             lock.unlock();
112         }
113     }
114     // all other methods omitted
115 }
```

Listing 7.41 shows the COWArrayListDemo.java program. The COWArrayListThread class has a field (line 12) named cowArrayList of type CopyOnWriteArrayList. It calls the add method (line 26) to add items to the cowArrayList object and calls the get method (line 32) to get items from the cowArrayList object. Note that line 29 checks that the cowArrayList object is not empty in order to avoid the exception of IllegalArgumentException: n must be positive that may occur when accessing the cowArrayList object.

The driver program for this demo (lines 40 – 71) follows the standard procedure as shown below:

1. Creating a COW array list
2. Creating a newFixedThreadPool using the ExecutorService interface
3. Launching COWArrayList threads
4. Shutting down the executorService object to avoid potential resource leak
5. Waiting for all threads to finish before terminating the thread pool

Next, we discuss the result of executing this demo program, following Listing 7.41.

Listing 7.41 COWArrayListDemo.java

```
1    package jcp.ch7.synchedcollections;
2
3    import java.util.Random;
4    import java.util.concurrent.CopyOnWriteArrayList;
5    import java.util.concurrent.ExecutorService;
6    import java.util.concurrent.Executors;
7    import java.util.concurrent.TimeUnit;
8
9    class COWArrayListThread extends Thread {
10     int id;
11     Random random;
12     CopyOnWriteArrayList<String> cowArrayList;
13
14     COWArrayListThread(int id, CopyOnWriteArrayList<String> cowArrayList) {
15       this.id = id;
16       this.random = new Random();
17       this.cowArrayList = cowArrayList;
18     }
19
20     public void run() {
21       int IMAX = 10000;
22       for (int i = 0; i < IMAX; i++) {
23         boolean output = (i % (IMAX / 10)) == 0;
24         if (id == 0) {
25           String item = id + "_" + i + "_" + random.nextInt(IMAX);
26           cowArrayList.add(item);
27           if (output)
28             System.out.println("Thread " + id + " add: " + item);
29         } else if(!cowArrayList.isEmpty()) {
30           int n = cowArrayList.size();
31           int index = random.nextInt(n);
32           String value = index + "_" + cowArrayList.get(index);
33           if (output)
34             System.out.println("Thread " + id + " get: " + value);
```

```
35            }
36        }
37    }
38 }
39
40 public class COWArrayListDemo {
41
42    public static void main(String[] args) {
43
44        int POOL_SIZE = 8;
45
46        // 1. create a COW array list
47        CopyOnWriteArrayList<String> cowArrayListThread =
48            new CopyOnWriteArrayList<String>();
49
50        // 2. create a newFixedThreadPool using the ExecutorService class
51        ExecutorService executorService = Executors
52            .newFixedThreadPool(POOL_SIZE);
53
54        // 3. launch COW array list threads
55        for (int i = 0; i < POOL_SIZE; i++) {
56            executorService.execute(new COWArrayListThread(i,
57                cowArrayListThread));
58        }
59
60        // 4. shut down executorService to avoid resource leak
61        executorService.shutdown();
62
63        // 5. wait until all threads are done
64        try {
65            executorService.awaitTermination(Integer.MAX_VALUE,
66                TimeUnit.SECONDS);
67        } catch (InterruptedException e) {
68            e.printStackTrace();
69        }
70        System.out.println("size = " + cowArrayListThread.size());
71    }
72 }
```

Executing this program on my Eclipse IDE yielded the result as shown in Listing 7.42. As you see, the object was indeed accessed concurrently by multiple threads, as each main output line is prefixed with the thread id.

This concludes our discussion on the CopyOnWriteArrayList concurrent collection. We discuss the CopyOnWriteArraySet concurrent collection next.

Listing 7.42 Result of executing the COWArrayListDemo.java program

```
Thread 0 add: 0_0_676
Thread 5 get: 0_0_0_676
Thread 4 get: 0_0_0_676
```

Thread 7 get: 42_0_42_2023
Thread 1 get: 51_0_51_8058

......
Thread 0 add: 0_7000_9978
Thread 0 add: 0_8000_1626
Thread 0 add: 0_9000_5339
size = 10000

7.4.2 CopyOnWriteArraySet

CopyOnWriteArraySet uses CopyOnWriteArrayList for all of its operations internally. Similar to CopyOnWriteArrayList, CopyOnWriteArraySet is best suited for scenarios where read-only operations outnumber mutative operations, since mutative operations (remove, set, add, etc.) usually entail copying the entire underlying array and are expensive. Iterators from CopyOnWriteArraySet rely on snapshots of the array at the time the iterators were constructed. Thus, traversal via iterators is fast and cannot encounter interference from other threads.

Listing 7.43 shows partially the implementation of CopyOnWriteArraySet. As you see, CopyOnWriteArraySet is just a wrapper of CopyOnWriteArrayList. In particular, note the use of addIfAbsent(E e) method at line 10 for the parameterized constructor and at line 14 for the add(E e) method, which guarantees that CopyOnWriteArraySet does not contain duplicate elements as required for a Set.

This concludes our coverage of all concurrent collections.

Listing 7.43 CopyOnWriteArraySet.java (partial)

```
1    public class CopyOnWriteArraySet<E> extends AbstractSet<E>
2            implements java.io.Serializable {
3
4        private final CopyOnWriteArrayList<E> al;
5        public CopyOnWriteArraySet() {
6            al = new CopyOnWriteArrayList<E>();
7        }
8        public CopyOnWriteArraySet(Collection<? extends E> c) {
9            al = new CopyOnWriteArrayList<E>();
10           al.addAllAbsent(c);
11       }
12
13       public boolean add(E e) {
14           return al.addIfAbsent(e);
15       }
16
17       public Iterator<E> iterator() {
18           return al.iterator();
19       }
20
21       public boolean remove(Object o) {
22           return al.remove(o);
```

```
23      }
24      // all methods omitted
25  }
```

7.5 SUMMARY

In this chapter, we covered all concurrent collections in the `java.util.concurrent` package, including `ArrayBlockingQueue`, `SynchronousQueue`, `DelayQueue`, `PriorityBlockingQueue`, `ConcurrentHashMap`, `ConcurrentLinkedQueue`, `ConcurrentLinkedDeque`, `ConcurrentSkipListMap`, `ConcurrentSkipListSet`, `LinkedBlockingQueue`, `LinkedBlockingDeque`, `LinkedTransferQueue`, `CopyOnWriteArrayList` and `CopyOnWriteArraySet`. In addition to getting a good understating of how they are implemented in Java, it's important to understand what real problems they can help solve. For this purpose, Table 7.1 summarizes all concurrent collections introduced in this chapter.

Table 7.1 Java concurrent collections

Synchronizer	Characteristics
ArrayBlockingQueue	A bounded, blocking, FIFO queue backed by an array.
SynchronousQueue	A blocking queue for transferring data from one thread to another like a uni-directional channel.
DelayQueue	An unbounded blocking queue of elements typed `Delayed`. The element whose delay expires first becomes the *leader*.
PriorityBlockingQueue	An unbounded blocking queue, similar to `PriorityQueue`, but supplies blocking retrieval operations.
ConcurrentHashMap	A combination of `HashEntry` and `Segment` data structures, with an array of segments, each of which is synchronized.
ConcurrentLinkedQueue	An unbounded, thread-safe, non-blocking FIFO queue based on linked nodes.
ConcurrentLinkedDeque	An unbounded, lock-free, non-blocking, synchronized deque based on linked nodes.
ConcurrentSkipListMap	A concurrent map based on the skip list data structure.
ConcurrentSkipListSet	A concurrent set based on the skip list data structure.
LinkedBlockingQueue	An optionally-bounded, blocking FIFO queue based on linked nodes.
LinkedBlockingDeque	An optionally-bounded, blocking deque based on linked nodes.
LinkedTransferQueue	A single-item, blocking queue for transferring data between two threads.
CopyOnWriteArrayList	A CopyOnWrite (COW) ArrayList.

CopyOnWriteArraySet	A wrapper of a CopyOnWriteArrayList for a COW set.

The next chapter focuses on understanding the use of the Fork-Join framework for parallel programming.

7.6 EXERCISES

Exercise 7.1 List the concurrent collections in the `java.util.concurrent` package that implement the `BlockingQueue` interface. Which ones support unbounded queues?

Exercise 7.2 How does the `ArrayBlockingQueue` support the FIFO access policy?

Exercise 7.3 What is the difference between the `offer` method and the `put` method for the `ArrayBlockingQueue` class? Similarly, what is the difference between the `poll` method and the `take` method for the `ArrayBlockingQueue` class?

Exercise 7.4 Compare the `ArrayBlockingQueue` implementation with the `SimpleBuffer` shown in Listing 1.13 and find a few major enhancements with the `ArrayBlockingQueue` implementation.

Exercise 7.5 Describe how a `SynchronousQueue` works.

Exercise 7.6 How can you create a queue-like (FIFO) or a stack-like (FILO) `SynchronousQueue`?

Exercise 7.7 What does the term "Delay" mean for a `DelayQueue`?

Exercise 7.8 How does a `DelayQueue` implement a leader-followers pattern naturally?

Exercise 7.9 Compare the `PriorityBlockingQueue` with the `PriorityQueue` and elaborate how synchronization is implemented in `PriorityBlockingQueue`.

Exercise 7.10 How does the `ConcurrentHashMap` mitigate the potential starvation locking risk?

Exercise 7.11 What factors may affect the performance of a `ConcurrentHashMap` most?

Exercise 7.12 Is a `ConcurrentLinkedQueue` just a concurrent version of a `LinkedList`? How come we do not have a `LinkedQueue` in the `java.util` package?

Exercise 7.13 Is a `ConcurrentLinkedDeque` just a concurrent version of an `ArrayDeque`? How come we do not have a `LinkedDeque` in the `java.util` package?

Exercise 7.14 How does a skip list data structure work?

Exercise 7.15 Compare the `ConcurrentSkipListMap` with the `ConcurrentHashMap` in terms of performance and scalability.

Exercise 7.16 How is the `ConcurrentSkipListSet` class implemented internally?

Exercise 7.17 Why is there a need for a `LinkedBlockingQueue` in addition to the `ConcurrentLinkedQueue`?

Exercise 7.18 Similarly, why is there a need for a `LinkedBlockingDeque` in addition to the `ConcurrentLinkedDeque`?

Exercise 7.19 What's the difference between a LinkedTransferQueue and a SynchronousQueue?

Exercise 7.20 What does the term CopyOnWrite (COW) mean in general? And what's the core concept behind COW?

Exercise 7.21 What do you need to consider when choosing CopyOnWriteArrayList or CopyOnWriteArraySet as your data structure for your project?

8 Parallel Programming Using the Fork-Join Framework

Multithreaded programming is about having multiple threads take turn to use CPU resource (either single CPU or multiple CPUs) executing tasks they are assigned to. Therefore, the concept of multithreaded programming applies even if the system has only one CPU. However, parallel programming is more about having a program run on a system that has two or more CPUs.

The Fork-Join Framework introduced in Java 7 is specifically designed for solving parallel programming challenges on the Java platform. It does not deprecate the multithreaded programming model we have covered in the previous chapters of this book, however. Instead, it enhances the traditional multithreaded programming model with two new features:

1. It simplifies the creation and use of multiple threads.
2. It automatically takes advantages of multiple CPUs and truly supports elastic scaling-up or scaling-down with a properly programmed application.

The Fork-Join parallel programming model is particularly suitable for solving large computing problems, such as sorting, transforming, or searching a large array. To solve such large computing problems, the divide-and-conquer strategy is used typically, namely, by breaking a larger problem into smaller pieces so that the smaller pieces can be run on multiple CPUs simultaneously. Then, the solution to the larger problem can be obtained by aggregating the partial results from those smaller sub-tasks executed on multiple CPUs.

In this chapter, we focus on understanding the Fork-Join framework contained in the `java.util.concurrent` package, available since JDK 7. We first look at how the main Fork-Join classes are designed and implemented in Java. Then, we use examples to demonstrate how those Fork-Join classes can be used to solve parallel programming problems.

The Fork-Join classes we cover include:

- `ForkJoinTask<V>`: An abstract class that defines a computing task
- `ForkJoinPool`: A pool for managing the execution of `ForkJoinTasks`
- `RecursiveAction`: A sub-class of `ForkJoinTask<V>` for computing tasks that do not return results

- `RecursiveTask<V>`: A sub-class of `ForkJoinTask<V>` for computing tasks that return results

Let's start with the `FokrJoinTask` class first next.

8.1   THE FORKJOINTASK<V> CLASS

The `ForkJoinTask<V>` class is an abstract base class for defining tasks that run within a `ForkJoinPool`. The type parameter `V` specifies the type of the result of the task. The reason it is named `ForkJoinTask`, rather than "ForkJoinThread," is that it is meant to represent lightweight abstraction of a *task*, rather than a thread of execution. However, this does not mean that `ForkJoinTask` is an independent entity and is not relevant to Java's `Thread` class, which is the foundation for multithreaded Java programming as we have explained in the previous chapters. In fact, there is a class in the Fork-Join framework named `ForkJoinWorkerThread`, as is explained below first.

8.1.1 The ForkJoinWorkerThread Class

Listing 8.1 shows partially the `ForkJoinWorkerThread` class, which extends the `Thread` class, as shown at line 1. Managed by `ForkJoinPools`, a `ForkJoinWorkerThread` performs a `ForkJoinTask`, in addition to bookkeeping in support of worker activation, suspension, lifecycle control, and so on. The `ForkJoinWorkerThread` class also implements the main mechanics for work-stealing, based on work-stealing queues, which are special forms of deque data structures that support only three of the four possible end-operations: *push*, *pop*, and deq (also known as *steal*). Here, the push and pop operations are called only from the owning thread, while the deq operation may be called from other threads.

Next, let us explore how the `ForkJoinWorkerThread` class is implemented. Some of the implementation details more relevant to our interests here include:

- Some interesting fields:
  - queue: The work-stealing queue array, with each queue item typed `ForkJoinTask` (line 2)
  - pool: The pool that contains `ForkJoinTasks` (line 3)
  - queueTop: The index of the next queue slot to push to or pop from (line 4)
  - queueBase: The index of the least valid queue slot, which is always the next position to steal from (line 5)

- The constructor: The only constructor parameterized with a `ForkJoinPool` object (lines 8–19). Note line 11 for registering the `FokJoinWorkerThread` to the pool and line 18 for setting the object as a daemon.
- The onStart method: Shown from lines 21–25, this method initializes the work-stealing queue array and sets up the random seed number for choosing a piece of work to steal.
- The onTermination method: Shown from lines 27–39, this method performs clean-ups such as setting the terminate status, canceling the task and de-registering the worker, and so on.
- The run method: Shown from lines 41–51, it calls the onStart and onTermination methods as described above. In addition, note line 45, which calls the work method of the pool. This method runs a top-level loop for worker threads that it may either execute a task or block for more work or return when the pool and/or worker terminate.

- The pushTask method: Shown from lines 53–65, this method pushes a task to the work queue by calling UNSAFE's putOrderedObject method, which partially explains why we don't see locks and condition objects used for this class.
- The deqTask method: Shown from lines 67–79, this method attempts to take a task from the base of the queue, which fails if empty or contended.
- The popTask method: Shown from lines 81–98, this method returns a popped task, or null if empty.
- The unpushTask(...) method: Shown from lines 100–110, this method is a specialized version of popTask to pop only if the topmost element is the given task.

In practice, we use the ForkJoinTask class to specify computing problems to be parallelized. This ForkJoinWorkerThread class is used internally for managing ForkJoinTasks. Therefore, let us move to the ForkJoinTask class next.

Listing 8.1 ForkJoinWorkerThread.java

```
1   public class ForkJoinWorkerThread extends Thread {
2       ForkJoinTask<?>[] queue;
3       final ForkJoinPool pool;
4       int queueTop;
5       volatile int queueBase;
6       // other fields omitted
7
8       protected ForkJoinWorkerThread(ForkJoinPool pool) {
9           super(pool.nextWorkerName());
10          this.pool = pool;
11          int k = pool.registerWorker(this);
12          poolIndex = k;
13          eventCount = ~k & SMASK; // clear wait count
14          locallyFifo = pool.locallyFifo;
15          Thread.UncaughtExceptionHandler ueh = pool.ueh;
16          if (ueh != null)
17              setUncaughtExceptionHandler(ueh);
18          setDaemon(true);
19      }
20
21      protected void onStart() {
22          queue = new ForkJoinTask<?>[INITIAL_QUEUE_CAPACITY];
23          int r = pool.workerSeedGenerator.nextInt();
24          seed = (r == 0) ? 1 : r; //  must be nonzero
25      }
26
27      protected void onTermination(Throwable exception) {
28          try {
29              terminate = true;
30              cancelTasks();
31              pool.deregisterWorker(this, exception);
32          } catch (Throwable ex) {        // Shouldn't ever happen
33              if (exception == null)      // but if so, at least rethrown
34                  exception = ex;
35          } finally {
```

```
36              if (exception != null)
37                  UNSAFE.throwException(exception);
38          }
39      }
40
41      public void run() {
42          Throwable exception = null;
43          try {
44              onStart();
45              pool.work(this);
46          } catch (Throwable ex) {
47              exception = ex;
48          } finally {
49              onTermination(exception);
50          }
51      }
52
53      final void pushTask(ForkJoinTask<?> t) {
54          ForkJoinTask<?>[] q; int s, m;
55          if ((q = queue) != null) {    // ignore if queue removed
56              long u = (((s = queueTop) & (m = q.length - 1)) << ASHIFT) +
57                  ABASE;
58              UNSAFE.putOrderedObject(q, u, t);
59              queueTop = s + 1;          // or use putOrderedInt
60              if ((s -= queueBase) <= 2)
61                  pool.signalWork();
62              else if (s == m)
63                  growQueue();
64          }
65      }
66
67      final ForkJoinTask<?> deqTask() {
68          ForkJoinTask<?> t; ForkJoinTask<?>[] q; int b, i;
69          if (queueTop != (b = queueBase) &&
70              (q = queue) != null && // must read q after b
71              (i = (q.length - 1) & b) >= 0 &&
72              (t = q[i]) != null && queueBase == b &&
73              UNSAFE.compareAndSwapObject(q, (i << ASHIFT) + ABASE, t,
74                  null)) {
75              queueBase = b + 1;
76              return t;
77          }
78          return null;
79      }
80
81      private ForkJoinTask<?> popTask() {
82          int m;
83          ForkJoinTask<?>[] q = queue;
84          if (q != null && (m = q.length - 1) >= 0) {
85              for (int s; (s = queueTop) != queueBase;) {
86                  int i = m & --s;
87                  long u = (i << ASHIFT) + ABASE; // raw offset
```

```
88              ForkJoinTask<?> t = q[i];
89              if (t == null)   // lost to stealer
90                  break;
91              if (UNSAFE.compareAndSwapObject(q, u, t, null)) {
92                  queueTop = s; // or putOrderedInt
93                  return t;
94              }
95          }
96      }
97      return null;
98  }
99
100     final boolean unpushTask(ForkJoinTask<?> t) {
101         ForkJoinTask<?>[] q;
102         int s;
103         if ((q = queue) != null && (s = queueTop) != queueBase &&
104             UNSAFE.compareAndSwapObject
105             (q, (((q.length - 1) & --s) << ASHIFT) + ABASE, t, null)) {
106             queueTop = s; // or putOrderedInt
107             return true;
108         }
109         return false;
110     }
111     // all other methods omitted
112 }
```

8.1.2 The ForkJoinTask Class

As stated earlier, a ForkJoinTask is a thread-like entity that is much lighter weight than a regular Java thread. A ForkJoinPool may contain a limited number of regular threads, which are then used to host much larger number of tasks and subtasks, represented by ForkJoinTasks. Thanks to the ForkJoinWorkerThread class discussed in the previous section, this process is transparent that the programmer only needs to deal with the ForkJoinTask and ForkJoinPool classes. Therefore, let us focus on understanding the ForkJoinTask class in this section.

Listing 8.2 shows partially the ForkJoinTask class implemented in Java. From a programming point of view, we are mostly interested in the following fork, join, invoke and invokeAll methods of the ForkJoinTask class:

- **ForkJoinTask<V> fork()** (lines 3–7): Arranges to asynchronously execute the task. As you see, it uses the ForkJoinWorkerThread's pushTask method described in the previous section to schedule the task.
- **V join()** (lines 9–14): Waits until the task is done and then returns the result of the computation. It calls the doJoin method, which is shown from lines 93–112. As you see, the doJoin method calls the ForkJoinWorkerThread's unpushTask and joinTask to accomplish what it's supposed to accomplish.
- **V invoke()** (lines 16– 21): This method is equivalent to calling fork and join in one call. It calls the doInvoke method as shown from lines 114–127 to accomplish what it's supposed to.

- **void invokeAll(ForkJoinTask<?> t1, ForkJoinTask<?> t2)** (lines 23–27): Invokes two tasks of t1 and t2. If one task throws an exception, the other task may be cancelled.
- **void invokeAll(ForkJoinTask<?>... tasks)** (lines 29–54): Invokes a variable number of tasks. If one task throws an exception, all other tasks may be cancelled.
- **<T extends ForkJoinTask<?>> Collection<T> invokeAll(Collection<T> tasks)** (lines 56–91): Invokes a number of tasks contained in a collection. Note calls to doInvoke at line 76 and doJoin at line 84. If one task throws an exception, all other tasks may be cancelled.

Next, we discuss the ForkJoinPool class, which manages ForkJoinTasks.

Listing 8.2 ForkJoinTask.java (partial)

```
1   public abstract class ForkJoinTask<V> implements Future<V>, Serializable {
2       // fields omitted
3       public final ForkJoinTask<V> fork() {
4           ((ForkJoinWorkerThread) Thread.currentThread())
5               .pushTask(this);
6           return this;
7       }
8
9       public final V join() {
10          if (doJoin() != NORMAL)
11              return reportResult();
12          else
13              return getRawResult();
14      }
15
16      public final V invoke() {
17          if (doInvoke() != NORMAL)
18              return reportResult();
19          else
20              return getRawResult();
21      }
22
23      public static void invokeAll(ForkJoinTask<?> t1, ForkJoinTask<?> t2) {
24          t2.fork();
25          t1.invoke();
26          t2.join();
27      }
28
29      public static void invokeAll(ForkJoinTask<?>... tasks) {
30          Throwable ex = null;
31          int last = tasks.length - 1;
32          for (int i = last; i >= 0; --i) {
33              ForkJoinTask<?> t = tasks[i];
34              if (t == null) {
35                  if (ex == null)
36                      ex = new NullPointerException();
37              }
38              else if (i != 0)
```

```
39                  t.fork();
40              else if (t.doInvoke() < NORMAL && ex == null)
41                  ex = t.getException();
42          }
43          for (int i = 1; i <= last; ++i) {
44              ForkJoinTask<?> t = tasks[i];
45              if (t != null) {
46                  if (ex != null)
47                      t.cancel(false);
48                  else if (t.doJoin() < NORMAL && ex == null)
49                      ex = t.getException();
50              }
51          }
52          if (ex != null)
53              UNSAFE.throwException(ex);
54      }
55
56      public static <T extends ForkJoinTask<?>> Collection<T>
57          invokeAll(Collection<T> tasks) {
58          if (!(tasks instanceof RandomAccess) || !(tasks instanceof
59            List<?>)) {
60              invokeAll(tasks.toArray(new ForkJoinTask<?>[tasks.size()]));
61              return tasks;
62          }
63          @SuppressWarnings("unchecked")
64          List<? extends ForkJoinTask<?>> ts =
65              (List<? extends ForkJoinTask<?>>) tasks;
66          Throwable ex = null;
67          int last = ts.size() - 1;
68          for (int i = last; i >= 0; --i) {
69              ForkJoinTask<?> t = ts.get(i);
70              if (t == null) {
71                  if (ex == null)
72                      ex = new NullPointerException();
73              }
74              else if (i != 0)
75                  t.fork();
76              else if (t.doInvoke() < NORMAL && ex == null)
77                  ex = t.getException();
78          }
79          for (int i = 1; i <= last; ++i) {
80              ForkJoinTask<?> t = ts.get(i);
81              if (t != null) {
82                  if (ex != null)
83                      t.cancel(false);
84                  else if (t.doJoin() < NORMAL && ex == null)
85                      ex = t.getException();
86              }
87          }
88          if (ex != null)
89              UNSAFE.throwException(ex);
90          return tasks;
```

```
91       }
92
93       private int doJoin() {
94           Thread t; ForkJoinWorkerThread w; int s; boolean completed;
95           if ((t = Thread.currentThread()) instanceof
96             ForkJoinWorkerThread) {
97               if ((s = status) < 0)
98                   return s;
99               if ((w = (ForkJoinWorkerThread)t).unpushTask(this)) {
100                  try {
101                      completed = exec();
102                  } catch (Throwable rex) {
103                      return setExceptionalCompletion(rex);
104                  }
105                  if (completed)
106                      return setCompletion(NORMAL);
107              }
108              return w.joinTask(this);
109          }
110          else
111              return externalAwaitDone();
112      }
113
114      private int doInvoke() {
115          int s; boolean completed;
116          if ((s = status) < 0)
117              return s;
118          try {
119              completed = exec();
120          } catch (Throwable rex) {
121              return setExceptionalCompletion(rex);
122          }
123          if (completed)
124              return setCompletion(NORMAL);
125          else
126              return doJoin();
127      }
128
129      // all other methods omitted
130 }
```

8.2   THE FORKJOINPOOL CLASS

ForkJoinPool is an ExecutorService for running ForkJoinTasks. In addition to managing and monitoring ForkJoinTasks, it also provides the entry point for submissions from non-ForkJoinTask clients. This section explores how the ForkJoinPool class is implemented in Java.

Listing 8.3 shows partially the implementation of the ForkJoinPool class in Java. First, let us look at its three constructors as follows:

- The fully-parameterized constructor (lines 4–35): This constructor takes the following four parameters:

   ◦ int parallelism: The parallelism level at which the tasks can be executed in parallel.
   ◦ ForkJoinWorkerThreadFactory factory: The factory for creating new threads using the constructor of the DefaultForkJoinWorkerThreadFactory class, as shown from lines 37–42, which implements the ForkJoinWorkerThreadFactory interface.
   ◦ Thread.UncaughtExceptionHandler handler: The handler for internal worker threads that terminate due to unrecoverable errors encountered while executing tasks.
   ◦ boolean asyncMode: If true, establishes local FIFO scheduling mode for forked tasks that are never joined. For applications in which worker threads only process event-style asynchronous tasks, use the default locally stack-based LIFO mode by setting it to false.
   In addition to the above parameters, also note the fields of workers, submissionQueue, submissionLock and terminate condition variable initialized in this constructor.

- The parallelism-parameterized constructor (lines 44–47): Uses default parameters for factory, handler and asyncMode except the parallelism parameter. Specifically, it uses defaultForkJoinWorkerThreadFactory, null handler, and LIFO mode for asyncMode.
- The no-arg constructor (lines 49–52): In addition to all other default parameters as stated above, the parameter of parallelism is set to the number of processors on the system the program is run. To some extent, this helps automatically scale an application on multi-CPU systems without having to hard-code a parameter like parallelism.

Next, let's look at the two execute methods for submitting FJ tasks and non-FJ tasks to be executed *asynchronously* as follows:

- void execute(ForkJoinTask<?> task): As shown from lines 54–58, this method executes the FJ-task passed in as the parameter for the method.
- void execute(Runnable task): As shown from lines 60–69, this method executes the task that implements the Runnable interface, which is a non-FJ task. It internally creates a FJ-task job, and then executes it.

Note that the above two execute methods call the forkOrSubmit method as shown from lines 71–81, which calls the pushTask method (line 78) if the task is a ForkJoinWorkerThread object or calls the addSubmission method (line 80) if not. The addSubmission method enqueues the given task in the submissionQueue, similar to ForkJoinWorkerThread.pushTask except that it is guarded with the submissionLock.

The two execute methods as described above have a return type of void, which means that they do not return result. The four submit methods are suitable for situations that require execution result to be returned, as described below:

- <T> ForkJoinTask<T> submit(ForkJoinTask<T> task): Similar to execute(ForkJoinTask<?> task) except that it returns a ForkJoinTask object for retrieving the execution result later.
- <T> ForkJoinTask<T> submit(Callable<T> task): Similar to submit(ForkJoinTask<T> task) except that it passes in a task that implements the Callable interface and returns a Future representing the pending results of the task. A reminder about Callable versus Runnable here: The

objects implement `Callable` interface or `Runnable` are potentially to be executed by another thread. However, unlike a `Callable`, a `Runnable` does not return a result and cannot throw a checked exception.

- `ForkJoinTask<?> submit(Runnable task)`: Similar to `submit(Callable<T> task)` except that it passes in a task that implements the `Runnable` interface and returns a `Future` representing the pending results of the task.
- `<T> ForkJoinTask<T> submit(Runnable task, T result)`: Similar to `submit(Runnable task)` except that the execution result will be available from the result object as well.

In addition to the `execute` and `submit` methods as described above, the `ForkJoinPool` class also has an `invoke` method and an `invokeAll` method for submitting tasks to be executed *asynchronously* as discussed below:

- `<T> T invoke(ForkJoinTask<T> task)`: Similar to `submit(ForkJoinTask<T> task)` except that it may call `task.invoke()` and `task.join()`, which may be executed immediately.
- `<T> List<Future<T>> invokeAll(Collection<? extends Callable<T>> tasks)`: Executes the given collections of tasks, and returns a list of `Future`s holding the status and results of the tasks when all tasks complete. Note that this method uses the `invokeAll` method of the `InvokeAll` class, which extends the `RecursiveAction` class.

Keep in mind that `execute` and `submit` calls are *asynchronous*, while `invoke` calls are *synchronous*.

◀**Note: Termination of a ForkJoinPool.** Since `ForkJoinPool` manages `ForkJoinWorkerThreads`, and each `ForkJoinWorkerThread` is a daemon as shown in Listing 8.1, there is no need to explicitly shutdown a `ForkJoinPool`. This is because a daemon thread is automatically terminated when all user threads have terminated. However, it is allowed to have a `ForkJoinPool` call its `shutdown()` method explicitly.

This concludes our discussion on the `ForkJoinPool` class. We discuss the `RecursiveAction` class next.

Listing 8.3 ForkJoinPool.java (partial)

```
1    public class ForkJoinPool extends AbstractExecutorService {
2
3        ForkJoinWorkerThread[] workers;
4        public ForkJoinPool(int parallelism,
5                            ForkJoinWorkerThreadFactory factory,
6                            Thread.UncaughtExceptionHandler handler,
7                            boolean asyncMode) {
8            checkPermission();
9            if (factory == null)
10               throw new NullPointerException();
11           if (parallelism <= 0 || parallelism > MAX_ID)
12               throw new IllegalArgumentException();
13           this.parallelism = parallelism;
14           this.factory = factory;
```

```
15        this.ueh = handler;
16        this.locallyFifo = asyncMode;
17        long np = (long)(-parallelism); // offset ctl counts
18        this.ctl = ((np << AC_SHIFT) & AC_MASK) | ((np << TC_SHIFT) &
19          TC_MASK);
20        this.submissionQueue = new
21          ForkJoinTask<?>[INITIAL_QUEUE_CAPACITY];
22        int n = parallelism << 1;
23        if (n >= MAX_ID)
24            n = MAX_ID;
25        else { // See Hackers Delight, sec 3.2, where n < (1 << 16)
26            n |= n >>> 1; n |= n >>> 2; n |= n >>> 4; n |= n >>> 8;
27        }
28        workers = new ForkJoinWorkerThread[n + 1];
29        this.submissionLock = new ReentrantLock();
30        this.termination = submissionLock.newCondition();
31        StringBuilder sb = new StringBuilder("ForkJoinPool-");
32        sb.append(poolNumberGenerator.incrementAndGet());
33        sb.append("-worker-");
34        this.workerNamePrefix = sb.toString();
35    }
36
37    static class DefaultForkJoinWorkerThreadFactory
38        implements ForkJoinWorkerThreadFactory {
39        public ForkJoinWorkerThread newThread(ForkJoinPool pool) {
40            return new ForkJoinWorkerThread(pool);
41        }
42    }
43
44    public ForkJoinPool(int parallelism) {
45        this(parallelism, defaultForkJoinWorkerThreadFactory, null,
46          false);
47    }
48
49    public ForkJoinPool() {
50        this(Runtime.getRuntime().availableProcessors(),
51            defaultForkJoinWorkerThreadFactory, null, false);
52    }
53
54    public void execute(ForkJoinTask<?> task) {
55        if (task == null)
56            throw new NullPointerException();
57        forkOrSubmit(task);
58    }
59
60    public void execute(Runnable task) {
61        if (task == null)
62            throw new NullPointerException();
63        ForkJoinTask<?> job;
64        if (task instanceof ForkJoinTask<?>) // avoid re-wrap
65            job = (ForkJoinTask<?>) task;
66        else
```

```
67              job = ForkJoinTask.adapt(task, null);
68          forkOrSubmit(job);
69      }
70
71      private <T> void forkOrSubmit(ForkJoinTask<T> task) {
72          ForkJoinWorkerThread w;
73          Thread t = Thread.currentThread();
74          if (shutdown)
75              throw new RejectedExecutionException();
76          if ((t instanceof ForkJoinWorkerThread) &&
77              (w = (ForkJoinWorkerThread)t).pool == this)
78              w.pushTask(task);
79          else
80              addSubmission(task);
81      }
82
83      private void addSubmission(ForkJoinTask<?> t) {
84          final ReentrantLock lock = this.submissionLock;
85          lock.lock();
86          try {
87              ForkJoinTask<?>[] q; int s, m;
88              if ((q = submissionQueue) != null) {
89                  long u = (((s = queueTop) &
90                    (m = q.length-1)) << ASHIFT)+ABASE;
91                  UNSAFE.putOrderedObject(q, u, t);
92                  queueTop = s + 1;
93                  if (s - queueBase == m)
94                      growSubmissionQueue();
95              }
96          } finally {
97              lock.unlock();
98          }
99          signalWork();
100     }
101
102     public <T> ForkJoinTask<T> submit(ForkJoinTask<T> task) {
103         if (task == null)
104             throw new NullPointerException();
105         forkOrSubmit(task);
106         return task;
107     }
108
109     public <T> ForkJoinTask<T> submit(Callable<T> task) {
110         if (task == null)
111             throw new NullPointerException();
112         ForkJoinTask<T> job = ForkJoinTask.adapt(task);
113         forkOrSubmit(job);
114         return job;
115     }
116
117     public ForkJoinTask<?> submit(Runnable task) {
118         if (task == null)
```

```
119                 throw new NullPointerException();
120            ForkJoinTask<?> job;
121            if (task instanceof ForkJoinTask<?>) // avoid re-wrap
122                job = (ForkJoinTask<?>) task;
123            else
124                job = ForkJoinTask.adapt(task, null);
125            forkOrSubmit(job);
126            return job;
127        }
128
129        public <T> ForkJoinTask<T> submit(Runnable task, T result) {
130            if (task == null)
131                throw new NullPointerException();
132            ForkJoinTask<T> job = ForkJoinTask.adapt(task, result);
133            forkOrSubmit(job);
134            return job;
135        }
136
137        public <T> T invoke(ForkJoinTask<T> task) {
138            Thread t = Thread.currentThread();
139            if (task == null)
140                throw new NullPointerException();
141            if (shutdown)
142                throw new RejectedExecutionException();
143            if ((t instanceof ForkJoinWorkerThread) &&
144                ((ForkJoinWorkerThread)t).pool == this)
145                return task.invoke();   // bypass submit if in same pool
146            else {
147                addSubmission(task);
148                return task.join();
149            }
150        }
151
152        public <T> List<Future<T>> invokeAll(Collection<? extends Callable<T>>
153          tasks) {
154            ArrayList<ForkJoinTask<T>> forkJoinTasks =
155                new ArrayList<ForkJoinTask<T>>(tasks.size());
156            for (Callable<T> task : tasks)
157                forkJoinTasks.add(ForkJoinTask.adapt(task));
158            invoke(new InvokeAll<T>(forkJoinTasks));
159
160            @SuppressWarnings({"unchecked", "rawtypes"})
161                List<Future<T>> futures = (List<Future<T>>) (List)
162                    forkJoinTasks;
163            return futures;
164        }
165
166        static final class InvokeAll<T> extends RecursiveAction {
167            final ArrayList<ForkJoinTask<T>> tasks;
168            InvokeAll(ArrayList<ForkJoinTask<T>> tasks) {this.tasks = tasks;}
169            public void compute() {
170                try { invokeAll(tasks); }
```

```
171                 catch (Exception ignore) {}
172         }
173     }
174     // other methods omitted
175 }
```

8.3   THE RECURSIVEACTION CLASS

In the preceding sections, we introduced three classes for the Fork-Join framework: ForkJoinWorkerThread, ForkJoinTask and ForkJoinPool. These are framework classes, though, and we have not mentioned how to define a computational task yet. The RecursiveAction class covered in this section and the RecursiveTask class to be covered in the next section fulfill that purpose.

Next, let's look at how the RecursiveAction class is defined first. We then use an example to demonstrate the use of the RecursiveAction class.

8.3.1 Definition of the RecursiveAction Class

Listing 8.4 shows the definition of the RecursiveAction class, which looks incredibly simple. Note the following details:

- It is an abstract class and extends ForkJoinTask.
- It has the following four methods:
  - void compute(): This method encapsulates the actual computational task and returns no result. Since it's an abstract method, it's left for the programmer to compose the actual class that defines a custom class by extending this RecursiveAction class. You will see such an example in the next section.
  - getRawResult() and setRawResult(): Since the return type of the compute() method is void, there is no result to get or set other than null. Therefore, these two classes are symbolic.
  - final boolean exec(): This method wraps the compute() method and returns true as shown from lines 8–11. In addition, since it is inherited from ForkJoinTask, it can serve as an entry point for a RecursiveAction object to be called by calling the invoke() method, which leads to the call chain of invoke() → doInvoke() → exec(), as shown in Listing 8.2.

As we mentioned, the RecursiveAction class is an abstract class, so the programmer is expected to extend it and implement the compute() method for the computational task intended. Next, we use an example to demonstrate the use of the RecursiveAction class.

Listing 8.4 RecursiveAction.java

```
1  public abstract class RecursiveAction extends ForkJoinTask<Void> {
2
3      private static final long serialVersionUID = 5232453952276485070L;
4
5      protected abstract void compute();
6      public final Void getRawResult() { return null; }
```

```
7     protected final void setRawResult(Void mustBeNull) { }
8     protected final boolean exec() {
9         compute();
10        return true;
11    }
12 }
```

8.3.2 An Example

This section presents a simple demo program adapted from the Java Doc for the RecursiveAction class. In general, this is the procedure to follow to code your task based on the RecursiveAction class to be executed by a ForkJoinPool:

1. Have your class extend the RecursiveAction class
2. Based on the context of the problem to be solved, declare proper fields and define proper constructor(s) to have all fields initialized properly
3. Consider setting a proper THRESHOLD constant to facilitate the divide-and-conquer strategy adopted in the compute() method
4. Carefully code your compute() method with a clear guideline about what to do prior to and after the threshold is reached. Add proper help methods if needed.

Listing 8.5 shows a RecursiveActionDemo program coded by following the above procedure. The context of the problem to solve is sorting a large long array. The idea is to keep dividing the array until the threshold is reached, at which point the sort action is performed on each segment of the array. At this point, I suggest that you trace this demo program shown from lines 8–46 and make sure you fully understand the procedure followed for coding it. The context may vary from application to application, but the procedure would be similar.

Now, let's look at the driver program shown from lines 48–82. Similarly, there is a procedure to follow in general when writing a driver for solving a problem using the Fork-Join framework, which is stated below:

1. Set up the context for using the Fork-Join framework, including preparing the necessary data structure, and so on.
2. Create a ForkJoinPool using either its default constructor or a parameterized constructor
3. Create the task object, which should extend either the RecursiveAction class or RecursiveTask class, depending on whether a result needs to be returned by each task thread.
4. Call a proper method on the ForkJoinPool object to invoke the task threads.

The driver class, RecursiveActionDemo, shows exactly how the above procedure is followed. In particular, note line 71 for how the forkJoinPool object, the invoke method and the task object work together in one statement to solve the problem of sorting a large long array.

Next, we discuss the result of running this demo program, following Listing 8.5.

Listing 8.5 RecursiveActionDemo.java

```
1   package jcp.ch8.fjframework;
```

```java
2
3   import java.util.Arrays;
4   import java.util.Random;
5   import java.util.concurrent.ForkJoinPool;
6   import java.util.concurrent.RecursiveAction;
7
8   class SortTask extends RecursiveAction {
9
10    final long[] array;
11    final int start;
12    final int end;
13    final int THRESHOLD = 2500000;
14
15    SortTask(long[] array, int start, int end) {
16       this.array = array;
17       this.start = start;
18       this.end = end;
19    }
20
21    SortTask(long[] array) {
22       this(array, 0, array.length);
23    }
24
25    protected void compute() {
26       if (end - start < THRESHOLD)
27          sortSequentially(start, end);
28       else {
29          int middle = (start + end) >>> 1;
30          invokeAll(new SortTask(array, start, middle),
31                    new SortTask(array, middle, end));
32          merge(start, middle, end);
33       }
34    }
35
36    void sortSequentially(int start, int end) {
37       Arrays.sort(array, start, end);
38    }
39
40    void merge(int start, int middle, int end) {
41       long[] buffer = Arrays.copyOfRange(array, start, middle);
42       for (int i = 0, j = start, k = middle; i < buffer.length; j++)
43          array[j] = (k == end || buffer[i] < array[k]) ? buffer[i++]
44                   : array[k++];
45    }
46  }
47
48  public class RecursiveActionDemo {
49    public static void main(String[] args) {
50
51       // 1. create a long array
52       int ARRAY_SIZE = 10000000;
53       long[] longArray = new long[ARRAY_SIZE];
```

```
54
55        Random random = new Random();
56        System.out.println ("A portion of the initial long array");
57        for (int i = 0; i < ARRAY_SIZE; i++) {
58           longArray[i] = Math.abs(random.nextLong());
59           if ((i % ARRAY_SIZE / 10) == 0) {
60              System.out.println ("i = " + i + " longArray[i] = " +
61                 longArray[i]);
62           }
63        }
64
65        // 2. create the FJ pool and task object
66        ForkJoinPool forkJoinPool = new ForkJoinPool();
67        SortTask task = new SortTask (longArray, 0, ARRAY_SIZE);
68
69        // 3. start the task
70        long startTime = System.currentTimeMillis();
71        forkJoinPool.invoke(task);
72        long endTime = System.currentTimeMillis();
73        System.out.println ("\nElapsed time (ms): " + (endTime - startTime));
74
75        // 4. check a portion of the sorted longArray
76        System.out.println ("\nA portion of the sorted long array");
77        for (int i = 0; i < 10; i++) {
78           System.out.println ("i = " + i + " longArray[i] = " +
79              longArray[i]);
80        }
81    }
82 }
```

Executing the above `RecursiveActionDemo` program on my system (an i7-based quad-core laptop) yielded the output as shown in Listing 8.6. This output was obtained with a `THRESHOLD` value of 2.5 million, as hard-coded at line 13 in Listing 8.5, which was arrived at by dividing the array size by the number of CPUs. I varied the `THRESHOLD` value around 2.5 million and obtained the following results:

THRESHOLD Value	ElapsedTime (ms) (two consecutive runs in a row for each case)
1M	389 404
2.5M	356 364
5M	406 416

As you see, although they did not vary significantly, the numbers indeed indicate that the `THRESHOLD` value of 2.5M yielded the best performance.

This concludes our coverage of the `RecursiveAction` class. Next, we discuss the `RecursiveTask` class.

Listing 8.6 Output of running the RecursiveActionDemo program

```
A portion of the initial long array
i = 0 longArray[i] = 1672770829440726409
i = 1 longArray[i] = 5612841400310070713
i = 2 longArray[i] = 6576392487584110737
```

```
i = 3 longArray[i] = 2039236894647299
i = 4 longArray[i] = 6643209362595247249
i = 5 longArray[i] = 6032658970147459987
i = 6 longArray[i] = 3166467477144675201
i = 7 longArray[i] = 4405331009211711841
i = 8 longArray[i] = 4958508611735935167
i = 9 longArray[i] = 1855246001507472810

Elapsed time (ms):  363

A portion of the sorted long array
i = 0 longArray[i] = 2144652411955
i = 1 longArray[i] = 2745157182700
i = 2 longArray[i] = 3186331203481
i = 3 longArray[i] = 3820285983950
i = 4 longArray[i] = 3942503943669
i = 5 longArray[i] = 4370127938981
i = 6 longArray[i] = 4439301856719
i = 7 longArray[i] = 10301382489777
i = 8 longArray[i] = 10496636754173
i = 9 longArray[i] = 11389290620118
```

8.4   THE RECURSIVETASK<V> CLASS

In the preceding section, we discussed the RecursiveAction class, which is designed for situations where no result needs to be returned. In this section, we discuss the RecursiveTask class, which is designed for situations where a result is expected.

Let's look at how the RecursiveTask class is defined first. We then use an example to demonstrate the use of the RecursiveTask class.

8.4.1 The Definition of the RecursiveTask Class

Listing 8.7 shows the definition of the RecursiveTask class, which looks very similar to the RecursiveAction class shown in Listing 8.4. Note the following details:

- It is an abstract class and extends ForkJoinTask.
- It has the following four methods:

  ○ V compute(): This method encapsulates the actual computational task and returns a result of type V. Since it's an abstract method, it's left for the programmer to compose the actual class that defines a custom class by extending this RecursiveTask class. You will see such an example in the next section.
  ○ V getRawResult() and void setRawResult(): Since the return type of the compute() method for this class is V, they are not dummy methods anymore as was the case with the RecursiveAction class. However, they do not need to be implemented in application code.

○ final boolean exec(): Similar to the RecursiveAction class, this method wraps the compute() method and returns true as shown from lines 13–16. In addition, since it is inherited from ForkJoinTask, it can serve as an entry point for a RecursiveTask object to be called by calling the invoke() method, which leads to the call chain of invoke() → doInvoke() → exec(), as shown in Listing 8.2.

Similar to the RecursiveAction class, the RecursiveTask class is an abstract class, and the programmer is expected to extend it and implement the compute() method for the computational task intended. However, keep in mind that the compute() method of the RecursiveTask class needs to return a properly typed result.

Next, we use an example to demonstrate the use of the RecursiveTask class, following Listing 8.7.

Listing 8.7 RecursiveTask.java

```
1   public abstract class RecursiveTask<V> extends ForkJoinTask<V> {
2       private static final long serialVersionUID = 5232453952276485270L;
3       V result;
4       protected abstract V compute();
5
6       public final V getRawResult() {
7           return result;
8       }
9
10      protected final void setRawResult(V value) {
11          result = value;
12      }
13      protected final boolean exec() {
14          result = compute();
15          return true;
16      }
17  }
```

8.4.2 An Example

This section presents a simple demo program adapted from the previous RecursiveActionDemo class. In general, this is the procedure to follow to code your task based on the RecursiveTask class to be executed by a ForkJoinPool:

1. Have your class extend the RecursiveTask class
2. Based on the context of the problem to be solved, declare proper fields and define proper constructor(s) to have all fields initialized properly
3. Consider setting a proper THRESHOLD constant to facilitate the divide-and-conquer strategy adopted in the compute() method
4. Carefully code your compute() method with a clear guideline about what to do prior to and after the threshold is reached. In addition, remember to return a result of the proper type.

Listing 8.8 shows a SumTask class coded by following the above procedure. The context of the problem is to sum up a large double array. The idea is to keep dividing the array until the threshold is reached, at which point the sum action is performed on each segment of the array. However, unlike the compute() method for the RecursiveAction class, when the threshold value is reached, the two sub-tasks are launched with the fork() method and the results are combined using the join() method. (Refer to lines 31–38 for such subtleties.) In addition, return a result that matches the type declared for the compute() method, as shown at line 41.

Now, let's look at the driver program shown from lines 45–75. Similarly, there is a procedure to follow in general when writing a driver for solving a problem using the Fork-Join framework, which is stated below:

1. Set up the context for using the Fork-Join framework, including preparing the necessary data structure, and so on.
2. Create a ForkJoinPool using either its default constructor or a parameterized constructor
3. Create the task object, which should extend either the RecursiveAction class or RecursiveTask class, depending on whether a result needs to be returned by each task thread.
4. Call a proper method on the ForkJoinPool object to invoke the task thread.

The driver class, RecursiveTaskDemo, shows exactly how the above procedure is followed. In particular, note line 68 for how the forkJoinPool object, the invoke method and the task object work together in one statement to solve the problem of summing up a large double array.

Next, we discuss the result of running this demo program, following Listing 8.8.

Listing 8.8 RecursiveTaskDemo.java

```
1    package jcp.ch8.fjframework;
2
3    import java.util.Random;
4    import java.util.concurrent.ForkJoinPool;
5    import java.util.concurrent.RecursiveTask;
6
7    class SumTask extends RecursiveTask<Double> {
8
9      final int THRESHOLD = 2500000;
10     final double[] array;
11     final int start;
12     final int end;
13
14     SumTask(double[] array, int start, int end) {
15        this.array = array;
16        this.start = start;
17        this.end = end;
18     }
19
20     SumTask(double[] array) {
21        this(array, 0, array.length);
22     }
23
```

```
24    protected Double compute() {
25        double sum = 0.0;
26        if (end - start < THRESHOLD)
27            for (int i = start; i < end; i++) {
28                sum += array[i];
29            }
30        else {
31            int middle = (start + end) >>> 1;
32            SumTask sumTask1 = new SumTask(array, start, middle);
33            SumTask sumTask2 = new SumTask(array, middle, end);
34
35            sumTask1.fork();
36            sumTask2.fork();
37
38            sum = sumTask1.join() + sumTask2.join();
39        }
40
41        return sum;
42    }
43 }
44
45 public class RecursiveTaskDemo {
46    public static void main(String[] args) {
47
48        // 1. create a double array
49        int ARRAY_SIZE = 10000000;
50        double[] doubleArray = new double[ARRAY_SIZE];
51
52        Random random = new Random();
53        System.out.println ("A portion of the initial double array");
54        for (int i = 0; i < ARRAY_SIZE; i++) {
55            doubleArray[i] = random.nextDouble();
56            if ((i % ARRAY_SIZE / 10) == 0) {
57                System.out.println ("doubleArray[" + i + "] = " +
58                    doubleArray[i]);
59            }
60        }
61
62        // 2. create the FJ pool and task object
63        ForkJoinPool forkJoinPool = new ForkJoinPool();
64        SumTask task = new SumTask (doubleArray, 0, ARRAY_SIZE);
65
66        // 3. start the task
67        long startTime = System.currentTimeMillis();
68        double totalSum = forkJoinPool.invoke(task);
69        long endTime = System.currentTimeMillis();
70        System.out.println ("\nElapsed time (ms): " + (endTime - startTime));
71
72        // 4. check the result
73        System.out.println ("\ntotalSum = " + totalSum);
74    }
75 }
```

Executing the above RecursiveTaskDemo program on my system (an i7-based quad-core laptop) yielded the output as shown in Listing 8.9. This output was obtained with a THRESHOLD value of 2.5M, as hard-coded at line 9 in Listing 8.8, which was arrived at by dividing the array size by the number of CPUs. As you see, summing up an array of the same size is much faster than sorting an array of the same size, roughly, a factor of 400–500 faster.

This concludes our coverage of the RecursiveTask class.

Listing 8.9 Output of running the RecursiveTaskDemo program

```
A portion of the initial double array
doubleArray[0] = 0.8736853842888901
doubleArray[1] = 0.8003042214769189
doubleArray[2] = 0.6990716220750619
doubleArray[3] = 0.3649106329099151
doubleArray[4] = 0.05007251996766493
doubleArray[5] = 0.7472237622655725
doubleArray[6] = 0.20837606077877002
doubleArray[7] = 0.020094971248944327
doubleArray[8] = 0.05101280426380017
doubleArray[9] = 0.8051657063065899

Elapsed time (ms): 9

totalSum = 4997794.876651249
```

8.5   FORKJOINPOOL'S ASYNCHRONOUS CALLS (EXECUTE AND SUBMIT)

Listings 8.5 and 8.8 demonstrate how ForkJoin tasks can be initiated by calling ForkJoinPool's invoke(task) method. As we mentioned earlier, the invoke method guarantees that the calling thread will wait until the initiated task has finished. However, if we replace invoke with execute or submit at line 71 in Listing 8.5, for example, the task will be initiated *asynchronously*, in which case, we will not see the result because the main thread will not wait for the result. You can replace invoke with execute or submit at line 71 in Listing 8.5 and re-run the program to confirm it.

ForkJoinPool has a method named isDone() to help check if an initiated asynchronous task is done. In the downloadable source code package for Chapter 8, you can find the AsynchronousDemo.java program, adapted from Listing 8.5 by making the changes shown in Listing 8.10. As you see, after replacing invoke(task) with execute(task) at line 24, we call the isDone() method in the while-loop shown from lines 28–36 to check the status of the task initiated every 100 milliseconds (line 31). Finally, the for-loop shown from lines 43-45 prints the last ten elements of the sorted array. Listing 8.11 shows the output, including the messages from line 29 as shown below:

```
System.out.println(forkJoinPool);
```

The messages output from the above statement contain detailed information about the progress of the task, such as *parallelism*, *size*, *active*, *running*, *steals*, *tasks*, *submissions*. To some extent, you can use an asynchronous call (execute(task) or submit(task)) in place of invoke(task) to know how a ForkJoin task is executed internally.

This concludes our coverage of the ForkJoin framework for parallel computing.

Listing 8.10 AsynchronousDemo.java

```
1   public class AsynchronousDemo {
2     public static void main(String[] args) {
3
4       // 1. create a long array
5       int ARRAY_SIZE = 10000000;
6       long[] longArray = new long[ARRAY_SIZE];
7
8       Random random = new Random();
9       System.out.println ("A portion of the initial long array");
10      for (int i = 0; i < ARRAY_SIZE; i++) {
11        longArray[i] = Math.abs(random.nextLong());
12        if ((i % ARRAY_SIZE / 10) == 0) {
13          System.out.println ("i = " + i + " longArray[i] = " +
                 longArray[i]);
14        }
15      }
16
17      // 2. create the FJ pool and task object
18      ForkJoinPool forkJoinPool = new ForkJoinPool();
19      SortTask2 task = new SortTask2 (longArray, 0, ARRAY_SIZE);
20
21      // 3. start the task
22      long startTime = System.currentTimeMillis();
23      //forkJoinPool.invoke(task);
24      forkJoinPool.execute(task);
25      //forkJoinPool.submit(task);
26
27      // 4. check status
28      while (!task.isDone()) {
29        System.out.println(forkJoinPool);
30        try {
31          Thread.sleep(100);
32        } catch (InterruptedException e) {
33          // TODO Auto-generated catch block
34          e.printStackTrace();
35        }
36      }
37
38      long endTime = System.currentTimeMillis();
39      System.out.println ("\nElapsed time (ms): " + (endTime - startTime));
40
41      // 5. check a portion of the sorted longArray
42      System.out.println ("\nA portion of the sorted long array");
43      for (int i = ARRAY_SIZE - 1; i > ARRAY_SIZE - 10; i--) {
```

```
44          System.out.println ("i = " + i + " longArray[i] = " +
                longArray[i]);
45      }
46   }
47 }
```

Listing 8.11 Output of running the AsynchronousDemo program

A portion of the initial long array
i = 0 longArray[i] = 53274746451512399
i = 1 longArray[i] = 2249939846275222626
i = 2 longArray[i] = 116668100834032860
i = 3 longArray[i] = 9158996984722015679
i = 4 longArray[i] = 8876655725510053294
i = 5 longArray[i] = 3445090836992357717
i = 6 longArray[i] = 1036682275048623459
i = 7 longArray[i] = 1202580474563541196
i = 8 longArray[i] = 8362704236561414215
i = 9 longArray[i] = 6666691009804381898
java.util.concurrent.ForkJoinPool@33909752[Running, parallelism = 8, size = 1, active = 1, running = 1, steals = 0, tasks = 0, submissions = 1]
java.util.concurrent.ForkJoinPool@33909752[Running, parallelism = 8, size = 8, active = 8, running = 8, steals = 0, tasks = 7, submissions = 0]
java.util.concurrent.ForkJoinPool@33909752[Running, parallelism = 8, size = 8, active = 7, running = 7, steals = 2, tasks = 1, submissions = 0]
java.util.concurrent.ForkJoinPool@33909752[Running, parallelism = 8, size = 8, active = 1, running = 1, steals = 9, tasks = 0, submissions = 0]

Elapsed time (ms): 408

A portion of the sorted long array
i = 9999999 longArray[i] = 9223371506187368642
i = 9999998 longArray[i] = 9223371392881087185
i = 9999997 longArray[i] = 9223371239678403162
i = 9999996 longArray[i] = 9223371089133380649
i = 9999995 longArray[i] = 9223370440829619812
i = 9999994 longArray[i] = 9223369448983817244
i = 9999993 longArray[i] = 9223367057347355184
i = 9999992 longArray[i] = 9223366079667392506
i = 9999991 longArray[i] = 9223365005899986108

8.6 SUMMARY

This chapter focused on helping you understand how the Fork-Join Framework is implemented internally and can be used in parallel programming. Figure 8.1 helps summarize all key classes of this framework. Some key points to keep in mind for using this framework include:

- The ForkJoinTask class has not only the fork() and join() methods but also the invoke() and invokeAll(...) methods to manage and execute *ForkJoin* tasks at the lower level. While fork() is asynchronous, invoke() is synchronous as it includes both fork() and join() in one method.
- The RecursiveAction and RecursiveTask are abstract classes for defining user tasks using the divide-and-conquer strategy. Since these two recursive classes extends the ForkJoinTask class, you call fork(), join() or invoke()/invokeAll(...) methods in the compute() method properly to achieved the intended result.
- The ForkJoinPool class does not deal with fork and join directly. Instead, it calls the invoke(task) method to get a task executed, which is essentially a synchronous call as it delegates to ForkJoinTask's invoke method that contains both fork() and join() calls. In addition, the ForkJoinPool class has two forms of methods of execute(...) and submit(...) for managing *ForkJoin* and *non-ForkJoin* tasks. The subtle differences among these three forms of methods include:

  ° The invoke method is *synchronous* while the execute and submit methods are *asynchronous*. This means that when you use the execute and submit methods, you need to keep the parent thread or main thread *alive* until the task has finished.
  ° The execute method does not take *Callables* and thus returns *void*, whereas the invoke method does not take *Runnables*, and thus can return a result.
  ° The submit method can take *ForkJoinTasks*, *Callables* and *Runnables*, and always return a result (status or computational result).

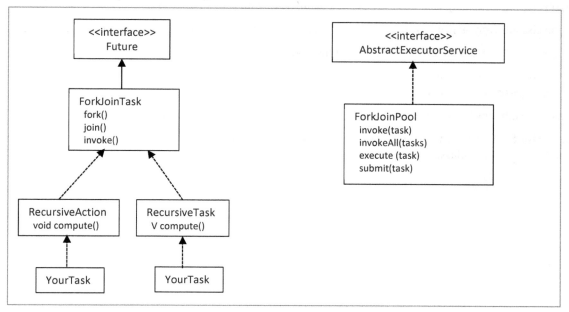

Figure 8.1 Class hierarchy summary for the ForkJoin framework

The Fork-Join Framework is a very compact framework, but offers tremendous flexibility and power for developing high-performance, scalable applications on the Java platform. The hardware technologies evolve fast, and so are the software technologies. You should constantly re-assess how you build modern software, especially for building high-performance, scalable enterprise applications, so that you can keep sharpening your programming skills.

If you have come so far, congratulations on your learnings and persistence! I hope that you have gotten a systematic training on Java concurrent programming, which should be valuable both for your current job and new jobs you look for at any point of your career. In the meanwhile, if you have any comments, please let me know so that future readers can benefit from your experience with my updates over time.

Thank you!

8.7   EXERCISES

Exercise 8.1 Describe what core classes are provided by the ForkJoin framework.

Exercise 8.2 Is a ForkJoin thread a regular Java thread?

Exercise 8.3 What methods does the ForkJoinTask class provide for executing ForkJoinTasks?

Exercise 8.4 Can a ForkJoinPool manage non-ForkJoin tasks?

Exercise 8.5 How do you specify the desired parallelism with a ForkJoinPool?

Exercise 8.6 Do you need to shut down a ForkJoinPool explicitly as we do with an ExecutorService?

Exercise 8.7 What's the difference between the RecursiveAction class and the RecursiveTask class?

Exercise 8.8 What procedure do you follow to implement the compute() method for a RecursiveAction class or a RecursiveTask class?

Exercise 8.9 How do you determine the optimal THRESHOLD for a ForkJoin computational task?

Exercise 8.10 Explain the differences among the three methods of invoke, execute and submit with the ForkJoinPool class.

Appendix A Algorithm Analysis

This appendix presents a brief overview of algorithm analysis, which is about analyzing the efficiency (either running time or space or both) of an algorithm with respect to the input size of a problem to be solved. First, an algorithm is an explicitly stated scheme for solving a problem, with no concern about which programming language will be used to implement it. This is an important skill to have both for becoming a high-caliber developer and for programming job interviews. Whether you once took an algorithm analysis class in college or not, this appendix gives you an overview of only what you need to know about algorithm analysis without having to go through all kinds of theorem-proof and derivation mathematical drudgeries.

Specifically, this appendix focuses on:

- The big-O notation
- Growth rate comparison
- Some guidelines for estimating running times
- Examples

Let's start with the big-O notation first next.

A.1 THE BIG-O NOTATION

Theoretically, it should be possible to count exactly how many operations an algorithm would take for a given problem input size n. However, such an "exact" approach can only give many disjoint data points, which provide little or no insight into the efficiency of an algorithm. Instead, what we are mostly interested in is a succinct formula that can represent the trend or the rate of growth as the problem input size increases. However, even such a humble goal is hard to achieve, so we have to compromise further.

In order to understand what we have to compromise or give up, let's start with the following four mathematical definitions:

1. **Big-O Definition**: $T(n) = O(f(n))$ if there exist two constants c and n_0 such that $T(n) \leq cf(n)$ for $n \geq n_0$. This definition says that the growth rate of $T(n)$ is no faster than $f(n)$. Thus, $f(n)$ represents the *upper bound* or *worst case* running times.

2. **Big-Ω Definition**: $T(n) = \Omega(g(n))$ if there exist two constants c and n_0 such that $T(n) \geq cg(n)$ for $n \geq n_0$. This definition says that the growth rate of $T(n)$ is no slower than $g(n)$. Thus, $g(n)$ represents the *lower bound* or *best case* running times.

3. **Big-Θ Definition**: $T(n) = \Theta(h(n))$ if and only if $T(n) = O(h(n))$ and $T(n) = \Omega(h(n))$. This definition says that $T(n)$ grows at the same rate of $h(n)$.

4. **Little-o Definition**: $T(n) = o(p(n))$ if $T(n) = O(p(n))$ and $T(n) \neq \Theta(p(n))$. This definition says that $T(n)$ grows slower than $p(n)$.

Apparently, definition 3 is hard to achieve and definition 4 is of little use as it only differs from definition 1 (big-O) by disallowing "*equal*." Thus, we are mostly interested in worst cases (big-O) and occasionally in best cases (big-Ω). In addition, note the two constants of c and n_0 introduced in definitions 1 and 2, which mean two important points to keep in mind:

- Constant c can be omitted, as we are only interested in growth rates. Thus, both $10n$ and $100n$ are considered $O(n)$, for example.
- Constant n_0 implies that we are only interested in very large problem input sizes.

☛**Note: A grain of salt**. Note that analytic big-O may result in over-estimates in reality such that the empirical average case can be significantly better than the worst case. In addition, even for the same algorithm, a clever, optimized implementation may outperform a quick-and-dirty, non-optimized implementation. One should be flexible with such factors when choosing an algorithm.

A.2 GROWTH RATE COMPARISON

Very often, we need to compare one growth rate with another. Table A.1 lists the sequence of typical growth rates from constant (best case) all the way to exponential (worst case), including: constant, logarithmic, log-squared, linear, linear-log, quadratic, cubic and exponential.

Table A.1 Sequence of typical growth rates in increasing order

Function	Big-O	Name
c	$O(1)$	Constant
$\log n$	$O(\log n)$	Logarithmic
$\log^2 n$	$O(\log^2 n)$	Log-squared
n	$O(n)$	Linear
$n \log n$	$O(n \log n)$	Linear-log
n^2	$O(n^2)$	Quadratic
n^3	$O(n^3)$	Cubic
2^n	$O(2^n)$	Exponential

Table A.2 shows some concrete numbers with n varied from 1 to 15, including $log(n)$, $log^2(n)$, n, $nlog(n)$, n^2, n^3 and 2^n . For better clarity, the data shown in Table A.2 is divided into two groups, which are shown graphically in Figures A.1 and A.2, respectively. We can now see that:

- *Log* and *log-squared* are about the same and the two are hardly distinguishable, as shown by the lower two curves in Figure A.1.
- *Linear* is worse than *n-log* before $n = 10$, but afterwards, *n-log* becomes worse than *linear*, as shown by the upper two curves in Figure A.1.
- *n-squared* and above are considered *bad* and should be avoided, as shown in Figure A.2.

Next, we look at some examples to see if we can correlate some algorithmic patterns with some of the growth rates we discussed here – without going through pages and pages of intricate mathematical calculations, which should be left for full-time mathematicians only.

Table A.2 Numerical examples for typical growth rates in increasing order

n	$\log n$	$\log^2 n$	n	$n\log n$	n^2	n^3	2^n
1	0	0	1	0	1	1	2
2	0.30103	0.090619	2	0.60206	4	8	4
3	0.477121	0.227645	3	1.431364	9	27	8
4	0.60206	0.362476	4	2.40824	16	64	16
5	0.69897	0.488559	5	3.49485	25	125	32
6	0.778151	0.605519	6	4.668908	36	216	64
7	0.845098	0.714191	7	5.915686	49	343	128
8	0.90309	0.815572	8	7.22472	64	512	256
9	0.954243	0.910579	9	8.588183	81	729	512
10	1	1	10	10	100	1000	1024
11	1.041393	1.084499	11	11.45532	121	1331	2048
12	1.079181	1.164632	12	12.95017	144	1728	4096
13	1.113943	1.24087	13	14.48126	169	2197	8192
14	1.146128	1.313609	14	16.04579	196	2744	16384
15	1.176091	1.383191	15	17.64137	225	3375	32768

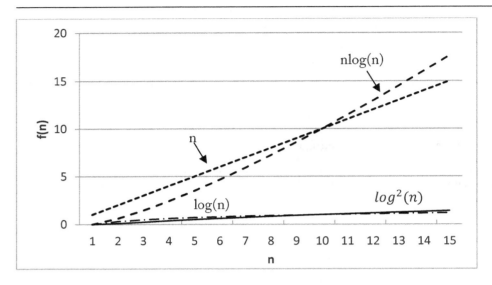

Figure A.1 Growth rate comparison among functions of $log(n)$, $log^2(n)$, n and $nlog(n)$

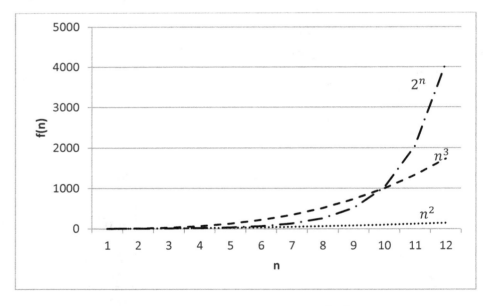

Figure A.2 Growth rate comparison among functions of n^2, n^3 and 2^n

A.3 RUNNING TIME ESTIMATES

Running time estimates mostly mean worst-case scenarios for some of the reasons given below:

- A worst-case estimate provides an upper bound. If the worst-case is acceptable, then it means no risk for the problem to be solved.
- The average-case is hard-to-obtain mathematically, or even hard to define in most cases.
- Sometimes, reading data may take significantly longer than solving the problem using a particular algorithm. Thus, a worst-case estimate is sufficient.

Here are some guidelines about arriving at worst-case running time estimates:

1. $O(1)$: If the operation accesses an element by indexing or hashing, then it's an $O(1)$ operation.
2. $O(n)$: If the operation resembles a linear traversal, such as a for-loop with the exit condition of the loop-variable's value < the problem size, then the operation is an $O(n)$ operation.
3. $O(\log(n))$: Operations performing binary-tree-like searches fall into this category.
4. $O(n\log(n))$: Most likely, the operation performs a binary-tree-like search first to locate the position for the operation to be performed and then requires part of the data structure to be shifted before the intended operation can be performed.
5. $O(n^2)$: Most likely a double, embedded for-loop with both loop variables confined by the problem input size. Note that an embedded for-loop with a constant max loop variable value is an $O(1)$ operation.
6. $O(n^3)$: Most likely a triple, embedded for-loop with all loop variables confined by the problem input size. Once again, an embedded for-loop with a constant max loop variable value is an $O(1)$ operation.

Next, we use examples to demonstrate how to arrive at running time estimates using the above simple guidelines. We present examples from the algorithm analysis point of view. (The examples are actually some of the typical job interview questions in the bay area, so feel free to adapt them to fit your purposes.)

The examples to be presented next include:

- Problem solving

  ○ Maximum sub-sequence sum problem
  ○ Array sub-array product problem
  ○ Two-sum-to-k problem

- Linked lists

  ○ Reverse a linked list
  ○ Detecting circularly linked list

- Hashtables

  ○ Hashing with linear probing
  ○ Hashing with separate chaining

- The binary search algorithm and binary search trees

  ○ Binary searching
  ○ Breadth-first traversal

- Sorting
  - Quick-sort
  - Merge-sort
- Intersection and Union
  - Intersection
  - Union
- LRUCache Implementations
  - Doubly-linked list based
  - LinkedHashMap based

Let us start with problem solving examples first next.

☞**Note**: The examples to be presented in the next few sections are also suitable for preparing for Java performance job programming interviews. In fact, all of them are from what the author experienced in the past few years first-hands. In general, programing problems differ from one to another, and it's hard to solve a programming task in a few minutes. However, to be positioned better to start with, it's helpful to know the following two questions upfront before jumping to writing code immediately:

1. What data structures are involved, arrays, lists, or maps?
2. What specific objects and associated fields and methods are involved and available?

If the answers to the above two questions are ambiguous, it means that you have the choice to choose your own, in which case, the collections covered in the main text of this book should be helpful. The last focus should be what algorithm you want to use to solve a given problem.

A.4 PROBLEM SOLVING EXAMPLES

The classical, well-known "*maximum subsequence sum problem*" demonstrates for-loop related running time estimates. It is defined as follows:

Given a negative and positive integer randomly mixed sequence of a_1, a_2, ..., a_n, find the subsequence of a_i ... a_j that yields the largest sum.

Figure A.3 illustrates the problem to be solved. We start with an algorithm of $O(n^3)$ for solving this problem first next.

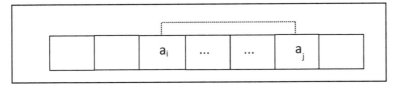

Figure A.3 The maximum subsequence sum problem

A.4.1 MAXIMUM SUBSEQUENCE SUM PROBLEM: $O(n^3)$

Given the problem described at the beginning of this section as shown in Figure A.3, we assume that the input would be an int array with size n and expected result would be represented by a variable like int maxSum as follows:

```
int[] a;
int n = a.length;
int maxSum = 0;
```

The most intuitive algorithm would be just to sum up each subsequence from a_i to a_j and compare it with maxSum and assign it to maxSum if it's larger than maxSum. Let's assume that the temporary sum is denoted as sum, we can describe this part of the algorithm as follows:

```
int sum = 0;
for (int k = i; k <= j; k++)
    sum += a[k];
if (sum > maxSum) {
    maxSum = sum;
}
```

Note that we have to initialize the variable sum prior to the for-loop. The running time for this for-loop would be $O(n)$, since it runs through the entire array.

Since we have two variables here, i and j, we need to wrap the above for-loop into two for-loops, as shown below:

```
for (int i = 0; i < n; i++ {
    for (int j = 0; j < n; j++ {
        int sum = 0;
        for (int k = i; k <= j; k++)
            sum += a[k];
        if (sum > maxSum) {
            maxSum = sum;
        }
    }
}
```

Combining all of the above, the maximum subsequence problem can be solved with the algorithm shown in Listing A.1. Apparently, since all three for-loops are embedded and the running time for each for-loop is $O(n)$, the total running time for the entire algorithm is $O(n^3)$. Such an algorithm is very inefficient as shown in Figure A.2. Next, we present an algorithm with a running time of $O(n^2)$.

Listing A.1 An $O(n^3)$ algorithm for solving the max subsequence sum problem

```
1    public class MaxSubSeq {
2       public static void main(String[] args) {
3
4          int[] a = { -5, 15, -1, 9, -2, -5, -8 };
5          int max = maxSubseqSum1(a);
```

```
6          System.out.println ("max sum = " + max);
7      }
8
9      public static int maxSubseqSum1(int[] a) {
10         int maxSum = 0;
11
12         int n = a.length;
13         for (int i = 0; i < n; i++)
14            for (int j = i; j < n; j++) {
15               int sum = 0;
16               for (int k = i; k <= j; k++)
17                  sum += a[k];
18               if (sum > maxSum) {
19                  maxSum = sum;
20               }
21            }
22
23         return maxSum;
24      }
25 }
```

A.4. 2 MAXIMUM SUBSEQUENCE SUM PROBLEM: O(n^2)

How can we improve the O(n^3) algorithm introduced in the previous section and come up with an O(n^2) algorithm for solving the maximum subsequence problem? Let's once again take an inside-out approach, namely, starting from the inner-most for-loop, as shown from lines 16 – 21 in Listing A.1.

Instead of calculating each subsequence for a given range from a_i ... a_j, for a given array element a_i, we can scan the remaining segment of a_i ... a_{n-1} so that when a new subsequence sum is found, we just assign it to the variable maxSum. This is feasible, as whenever a negative number decreases the temporary sum, the maxSum will not be replaced. So, the double for-loop essentially picks the maximum sum out of each iteration controlled by the outer-most for-loop. Listing A.2 shows this new algorithm. Apparently, this is an O(n^2) algorithm. Although this is significantly better than the previous O(n^3) algorithm, we can actually do better than this, namely, we can come up with an O(n) algorithm, an *online* algorithm, as described next.

Listing A.2 An O(n^2) algorithm for solving the max subsequence sum problem

```
1      public static int maxSubseqSum2(int[] a) {
2          int maxSum = 0;
3
4          int n = a.length;
5          for (int i = 0; i < n; i++) {
6             int sum = 0;
7             for (int j = i; j < n; j++) {
8                sum += a[j];
9                if (sum > maxSum) {
10                  maxSum = sum;
11               }
12            }
```

```
13        }
14
15        return maxSum;
16   }
```

A.4. 3 MAXIMUM SUBSEQUENCE SUM PROBLEM: O(N) (AN ONLINE ALGORITHM)

How can we improve the $O(n^2)$ algorithm introduced in the previous section and come up with an $O(n)$ algorithm for solving the maximum subsequence problem? It may not be possible to solve every problem with an $O(n)$ algorithm, but let's once again take an inside-out approach, namely, starting from the inner-most for-loop, as shown from lines 7 – 12 in Listing A.2.

Since the goal for this problem is to find the maximum subsequence sum, we can run through the entire array sequentially once by following the logic below:

- Whenever the temporary sum goes below zero, we can ignore the subsequence we have gone though so far by reinitializing temporary sum to zero.
- If the temporary sum still stays positive and is larger than the current maxSum, we assign the temporary sum to maxSum.

Listing A.3 illustrates this new algorithm with only one for-loop as shown from lines 6 – 13, where the variable j acts as the loop variable. Line 9 reinitializes the temporary sum variable to zero if sum < 0 while line 11 assigns a new temporary sum to maxSum variable if the temporary sum is larger than maxSum. This algorithm is called an *online* algorithm because of the following characteristics it possesses:

- It makes only one pass through the array without revisiting any element it already read and processed.
- Because it calculates the maximum of all elements processed so far, it works even for an infinite data stream. The previous two algorithms do not possess this property.

Next, we discuss the array sub-array product problem.

Listing A.3 An O(n) algorithm for solving the max subsequence sum problem

```
1    public static int maxSubseqSum3(int[] a) {
2         int maxSum = 0;
3         int sum = 0;
4
5         int n = a.length;
6         for (int j = 0; j < n; j++) {
7            sum += a[j];
8            if (sum < 0) {
9               sum = 0;
10           } else if (sum > maxSum) {
11              maxSum = sum;
12           }
13        }
14
```

```
15        return maxSum;
16    }
```

A.4. 4 ARRAY SUB-ARRAY PRODUCT PROBLEM

The array sub-array product problem is stated as follows:

Given an array int[] a with n elements, find the products of all $(n - 1)$ elements with one element excluded for each sub-array product. It is equivalent to calculating all p_i as follows:

$$p_i = \prod_{j=0}^{i-1} a_j \prod_{k=i+1}^{n-1} a_k$$

For example, for the sub-product excluding a_2, p_2 can be expressed as:

$$p_2 = a_0 a_1 \times a_3 \dots a_{n-1} \qquad (A.1)$$

Listing A.4 shows the method named products2, which takes the input array of a and stores all sub-products in array b. The two for-loops from lines 18–21 and from lines 25–28 calculate the first part and second part, respectively. Note that the variables firstPart and secondPart must be initialized and serve as the temporary place holders between arrays a and b. Since i is a variable, b[i - 1] in the second for-loop represents all sub-products from p_0 to p_{n-1}.

The running time is clearly O(n) as each for-loop performs n multiplications.

Next, we discuss the *two-sum-to-k* problem.

Listing A.4 ArraySubProducts.java

```java
1    package jcp.appendix.a.misc;
2
3    import java.util.ArrayList;
4    import java.util.Random;
5
6    public class ArraySubProducts {
7
8      public static void main(String[] args) {
9         //omitted
10     }
11
12     // approach from both ends
13     public static void products2(int[] a, int[] b) {
14        int n = a.length;
15
16        // first part
17        int firstPart = 1;
18        for (int i = 1; i < n; i++) {
19          firstPart *= a[i - 1];
20          b[i] = firstPart;
21        }
```

```
22
23        // second part
24        int secondPart = 1;
25        for (int i = n - 1; i > 0; i--) {
26            secondPart *= a[i];
27            b[i - 1] = b[i - 1] * secondPart;
28        }
29    }
30 }
```

A.4.5 TWO-SUM-TO-K PROBLEM

The *two-sum-to-k* problem is stated as follows:

Given a sorted array int[] a with *n* elements, find two elements whose sum is equal to a constant k. It is equivalent to fulfilling the following computation:

$$k = a_i + a_j \qquad (i < j) \quad (A.2)$$

Listing A.5 shows the method named linearSearch, which takes the input array of a and constant k to be matched. Since the array is already sorted, the algorithm starts with working on the left-most and right-most elements and decides which index pointer to move based on whether the sum is larger or smaller than the given constant as long as the condition ($i < j$) holds true.

The running time is clearly O(*n*) as the while-loop may need to traverse the entire array in the worst case.

Next, we discuss the linked list examples.

Listing A.5 TwoSumToK.java

```
1    package jcp.appendix.a.misc;
2
3    import java.util.Random;
4
5    public class TwoSumToK {
6
7      public static void main(String[] args) {
8      // omitted
9      }
10
11     // approach from both ends using two variables. condition: i < j
12     public static Boolean linearSearch (int[] a, int k) {
13       Boolean found = false;
14       int n = a.length;
15
16       int i = 0;
17       int j = n - 1;
18       int sum = 0;
19       while ( i < j ) {
20           System.out.println ("finding k = " + k + " at i = " +
```

```
                i + " j = " + j);
21          sum = a [i] + a [j];
22          if ( sum < k) {
23              i++;
24          } else if ( sum > k) {
25              j--;
26          } else {
27              System.out.println ("found k = " + k + " at i = " +
                    i + " j = " + j);
28              found = true;
29              break;
30          }
31      }
32      return found;
33  }
34 }
```

A.5 LINKED LIST EXAMPLES

With an array list, namely, a list implemented with an array, finding the *i*-th element takes constant time, since it's index-based. However, insertion and deletion are expensive, since such operations require shifting elements in one of the two directions (forward and backward) to make space for the new element for insertion or to claim space for the element to be deleted. Thus, insertion and deletion take O(n) running time, while building an entire array by n successive inserts would require quadratic time.

A linked list can help avoid linear cost of insertion and deletion operations associated with an array list. As it says, a linked list is a list of a series of linked nodes. Figure A.4 shows the general concept of a linked list that a series of nodes are linked together with the last node pointing to null, signifying the end of the list.

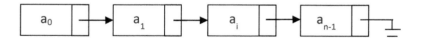

Figure A.4 A linked list

Listing A.6 shows how a list node is represented with a Java class. For simplicity, we use an int variable named data to represent the content of a node, as shown at line 4. The next field acts like a pointer that points to the next node of the same type – ListNode. This is what we meant by "*a linked list is a list of a series of linked nodes.*"

Next, we discuss how we can construct a singly linked list using the ListNode class shown in Listing A.6.

Listing A.6 ListNode.java

```
1   package jcp.appendix.a.linked.list;
2
```

```
3   public class ListNode {
4       private int data;
5       private ListNode next;
6
7       ListNode (int data) {
8           this.data = data;
9           this.next = null;
10      }
11      // getters and setters omitted here
12  }
```

Listing A.7 shows a sample implementation of a `SinglyLinkedList` class. It has two fields: `size` and `head`. Lines 7 – 10 show its no-arg constructor, while lines 12 – 16 show a parameterized constructor that allows a new linked list to be created with the `size` and the `head` from an existing linked list. In addition, it has two methods implemented: `insert` and `printList`, as described below:

- `insert`: Inserting a new node can be performed at the `head` or the `tail` of a singly linked list. Lines 20 – 39 show how the insert method is implemented. As you see, prepending at the head takes O(1) running time, while appending at the tail (commented out) takes O(n) running time as one has to traverse to the end of the list and then append the new node to the existing list. If we implement a `remove` method, same running time estimates apply as well, i.e., O(1) for removing at the head and O(n) for removing at the tail.
- `printList`: This is a typical linear traversal from head to tail, so it takes O(n) running time.

We could have stopped here for the singly linked list. However, I'd like to call out the exercise of reversing a linked list to the next section, as this is one of the most common interview questions and it's beneficial to review it here for all purposes.

Listing A.7 SinglyLinkedList.java

```
1   package jcp.appendix.a.linked.list;
2
3   public class SinglyLinkedList {
4       public int size;
5       public ListNode head;
6
7       public SinglyLinkedList() {
8           size = 0;
9           head = null;
10      }
11
12      public SinglyLinkedList(int size, ListNode head) {
13          super();
14          this.size = size;
15          this.head = head;
16      }
17
18      // getters and setters omitted to save space
19
20      public void insert (int data) {
```

```
21        ListNode node = new ListNode (data);
22        if (head == null) {
23           head = node;
24        } else {
25           // prepend:
26           node.setNext(head);
27           head = node;
28           // append
29           /*
30           ListNode currentNode = head;
31           while (currentNode.getNext() != null) {
32              currentNode = currentNode.getNext();
33           }
34           currentNode.setNext(node);
35           node.setNext(null);
36           */
37        }
38        size++;
39     }
40
41     public void printList () {
42        ListNode currentNode = head;
43        while (currentNode != null) {
44           System.out.println(currentNode.getData());
45           currentNode =currentNode.getNext();
46        }
47     }
48
49     public void reverse () {
50        ListNode current = head;
51        ListNode prev = null;
52        ListNode next = null;
53
54        while (current != null) {
55           next = current.getNext();
56           current.setNext(prev);
57           prev = current;
58           current = next;
59        }
60        head = prev;
61     }
62  }
```

A.5.1 REVERSING A LINKED LIST

When you are asked to write a piece of code for reversing a linked list, first, you have to realize immediately that the list is a singly linked list and has a head field. Next, you need a prev pointer and a next pointer to facilitate reversing the list represented by the head pointer. Then, for a given current node, which should be initialized to point to the head node to start with, the reversing operation can be accomplished by following the below procedure:

1. Buffer the next node of the current node before the next pointer is reversed
2. Point the next node of the current node to the prev node
3. Reset the prev node to point to the current node to advance the prev pointer one step forward
4. Reset the current node to point to the next node to advance the current pointer one step forward
5. The above four operations can be put into a while-loop until the current pointer points to null.
6. Finally, set the last node (which would be the prev node at the end of the while-loop) to be the new head of the reversed list.

Listing A.8 shows how the above procedure is implemented for reversing a linked list. You might want to trace it on your own a few times so that you will understand it fully without mechanically memorizing it. For our purpose here, this operation takes O(n) time, as it traverses the entire list linearly using a while-loop.

Next, we discuss another list-related example, which is about detecting a circularly linked list.

Listing A.8 Reversing a linked list

```
1    public void reverse () {
2        ListNode current = head;
3        ListNode prev = null;
4        ListNode next = null;
5
6        while (current != null) {
7            next = current.getNext();
8            current.setNext(prev);
9            prev = current;
10           current = next;
11       }
12       head = prev;
13   }
```

A.5.2 DETECTING A CIRCULARLY LINKED LIST

Apparently, a singly linked list with its last node pointing to null cannot be a circularly linked list. A double-ended linked list as shown in Listing A.9 can be potentially a circularly linked list, if its last node points back to a node in-between the first and the last nodes.

In contrast to the singly linked list shown in Listing A.7, which has only one pointer of head, a double-ended linked list as shown in Listing A.9 has two pointers of first and last, which point to the first and last nodes, respectively. As you see, the add/remove operations at the first and last nodes all have O(1) running time, while the get and fold operations require linear traversal, resulting in O(n) running time. Note that the fold operation is not a common operation for regular lists. It is here just for making a circularly linked list for our example of detecting a circularly linked list here, as discussed following Listing A.9.

Listing A.9 LinkedList.java

```
1    package jcp.appendix.a.linked.list;
2
3    public class LinkedList {
4      ListNode first;
5      ListNode last;
6      int size;
7
8      LinkedList () {
9        size = 0;
10       first = null;
11       last = null;
12     }
13
14     public void addFirst (int data) {
15       ListNode newNode = new ListNode (data);
16
17       if (size == 0) {
18         first = last = newNode;
19       } else {
20         newNode.setNext(first);
21         first = newNode;
22       }
23
24       size++;
25     }
26     public void addLast (int data) {
27       ListNode newNode = new ListNode (data);
28       if (size == 0) {
29         first = last = newNode;
30       } else {
31         last.setNext(newNode);
32         last = newNode;
33       }
34
35       size++;
36     }
37
38     public int getFirst () {
39       return first.getData();
40     }
41
42     public int getLast () {
43       return last.getData();
44     }
45
46     public void removeFirst () {
47       if (first != null) {
48         ListNode temp = first;
49         first = first.getNext ();
50         temp = null;
51         size--;
52       }
```

```
53     }
54     public void removeLast () {
55        if (last != null) {
56           ListNode node = first;
57           while (node.getNext () != last) {
58              node = node.getNext ();
59           }
60           last = node;
61           last.setNext (null);
62           size--;
63        }
64     }
65
66     public int get (int position) {
67        if (position >= 0 && position < size) {
68           ListNode node = first;
69
70           for (int i = 0; i < position; i++) {
71              node = node.getNext ();
72           }
73           return node.getData ();
74        } else {
75           System.out.println("out of range");
76           return -1;
77        }
78     }
79
80     public void fold (int position) {
81        // find the node at this position
82        ListNode node = first;
83        for (int i = 0; i < position; i++) {
84           node = node.getNext ();
85        }
86        last.setNext (node);
87     }
88 }
```

To emphasize more, a circularly linked list differs from a linearly linked list that: (1) every *node* in a circularly linked list has a next node that is not null; and (2) a circularly linked list provides a pointer that points to the head of the list for external access. The example to be presented here has two questions to answer: (1) whether a linked list is a circularly linked list, and (2) how to find the entry point for a circularly linked list.

To facilitate the discussion, Figure A.5 shows an example of a circularly linked list. As you see, the first part is linear, while the second part forms a circle. For convenience, the next pointer is omitted with each node, and only the data item associated with each node is displayed.

Now, let us do some simple math to find out whether the list contains a circularly linked list. First, we assume that:

1.   There are *m* nodes prior to the entry point to the circularly linked list.

2. The loop size is l for the circular part of the list.
3. We can set up a *slow* pointer and a *fast* pointer that the slow pointer moves one step forward while the fast pointer moves two setps forward. We further assume that the slow point will catch up the fast pointer after k nodes from the entry point to the circularly linked list if it exists.

Based on the above assumptions, we can state that the slow pointer needs to move (m + k) steps to meet the fast pointer at the meeting point that is k nodes after the entry point to the circularly linked list. Since the fast pointer moves twice faster, it would have moved 2*(m + k) steps to meet the slow pointer at the expected meeting point. Since the fast pointer moves faster, the differenec between the numbers of nodes that the fast pointer and slow pointer passed through must be an integer number of the loop size at the meeting point, namely,

$$2(m + k) - (m + k) = nl \qquad (A.3)$$

, resulting to

$$k = nl - m \qquad (A.4)$$

Since the condition $k > 0$ must hold true, we have

$$n > m/l \qquad (A.5)$$

For the example circularly linked list shown in Figure A.5, m = 11, and l = 8, so n can be calculated by dividing 11 with 8. Since n must be an integer, we should round it up to 2. Thus, according to Eq. (A.4), k = 2 * 8 - 11 = 5, that is, the slow and fast pointers will meet at node 17, as shown in Figure A.5.

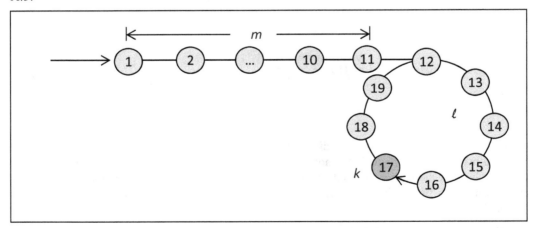

Figure A.5 A circularly linked list with 19 nodes

The next question is how we algorithmically find the entry point to the circularly linked list. Once again, we can find the answer from Eq. (A.4). If we add m to both sides of Eq. (A.4), the right-hand side would be nl, which means that the fast pointer would be at the entry point to the circularly linked list. This observation hints that if the slow pointer begins from the head node of the list and the fast pointer stays at the node at which they met, they would meet again at the entry point if they both move one step forward a time.

Given the above reasoning, we are ready to examine the `main` method and the `checkCircularLinkedList` method as shown in Listing A.10. The `main` method is simple: It creates a linearly linked list with 19 nodes (lines 8 – 10) and then folds it at position 11 (line 13, zero-index based) to make it a circularly linked list. Finally, it calls the `checkCircularLinkedList` method at line 20 to check whether the linked list created as above is a circularly linked list.

The `checkCircularLinkedList` method works as follows:

- Lines 35 – 36: Declare the slow and fast pointers and set both of them to the first node of the list.
- Lines 38 – 43: Move both pointers with the slow pointer one step a time and the fast pointer two steps a time. The breaking condition is that either the fast pointer becomes null or fast and slow pointers meet. If there is a circularly linked list and the slow and fast pointers meet eventually, the `while` loop ends with a `break` statement executed. So the `while` loop will end eventually whether there is a loop or not.
- Lines 46 – 52: If either the fast pointer or its next pointer is `null`, then we can conclude that there is no circularly linked list associated with the given list. Otherwise, the node at which the fast and slow pointers met would be output.
- Lines 55 – 61: This segment finds the entry point to the circularly linked list as we described above. It sets the slow pointer back to the first node of the list and then moves both slow and fast pointers at the same speed. When they meet, the `while` loop ends and the entry point is output.

Listing A.11 shows the output of running this example on my PC. Once again, our focus here is not about the implementation of the circularly linked list. Instead, the focus is on how to write a method to detect whether there is a circularly linked list in a given list.

Since a circularly linked list still is a linear list, the `checkCircularLinkedList` method takes O(n) running time.

You should study this example carefully so that you understand not only the code but also the simple math behind it.

This example concludes this section about reversing a singly linked lsit and detecting circularly linked lists. We discuss Hashtable examples in the next section.

Listing A.10 DetectCircularList.java

```
1    package jcp.appendix.a.linked.list;
2
3    public class DetectCircularList {
4
5       public static void main(String[] args) {
6          LinkedList list = new LinkedList ();
7
8          for (int i = 0; i < 19; i++) {
9             list.addLast(i + 1);
10         }
11
```

```
12        int position = 11;
13        list.fold (position);
14
15        System.out.println ("size = " + list.size);
16        System.out.println ("fold at " + position + " " + list.get (position));
17
18        printAll (list);
19
20        checkCircularLinkedList (list);
21
22    }
23
24    public static void printAll (LinkedList list) {
25        System.out.println ();
26
27        for (int i = 0; i < list.size; i++) {
28            System.out.println ("i = " + i + " " + list.get (i));
29        }
30
31    }
32
33    public static void checkCircularLinkedList (LinkedList list) {
34        // start at the same initial point
35        ListNode slow = list.first;
36        ListNode fast = list.first;
37
38        do {
39            slow = slow.getNext();
40            fast = fast.getNext ().getNext();
41            System.out.println ("slow fast: " + slow.getData() + " "
                    + fast.getData());
42            if (fast == null || slow == fast) break;
43        } while (true);
44
45        // no loop if fast or fast.next null
46        if (fast == null || fast.getNext() == null) {
47            System.out.println ("No circular list");
48            return;
49        } else {
50            System.out.println ("circular linked list meeting point: "
51                    + slow.getData());
52        }
53
54        // find entry point for circular linked list
55        slow = list.first;
56        while (slow != fast) {
57            slow = slow.getNext();
58            fast = fast.getNext ();
59        }
60        System.out.println ("circular linked list entry point: "
61                + slow.getData());
62    }
```

```
63  }
64  }
```

Listing A.11 Output of running the detecting circularly linked list example

size = 19
fold at 11 12

i = 0 1
i = 1 2
i = 2 3
i = 3 4
i = 4 5
i = 5 6
i = 6 7
i = 7 8
i = 8 9
i = 9 10
i = 10 11
i = 11 12
i = 12 13
i = 13 14
i = 14 15
i = 15 16
i = 16 17
i = 17 18
i = 18 19
slow fast: 2 3
slow fast: 3 5
slow fast: 4 7
slow fast: 5 9
slow fast: 6 11
slow fast: 7 13
slow fast: 8 15
slow fast: 9 17
slow fast: 10 19
slow fast: 11 13
slow fast: 12 15
slow fast: 13 17
slow fast: 14 19
slow fast: 15 13
slow fast: 16 15
slow fast: 17 17
circular linked list meeting point: 17
circular linked list entry point: 12

A.6 HASHTABLE EXAMPLES

A hash table is a data structure for storing key-value pairs. It is a commonly used mechanism for looking up frequently used data items fast. It can be used for caching data items in an in-memory table so that they can be looked up without going to the external disk when they are needed. I am sure you understand the memory hierarchy of a machine from register to CPU cache, to main memory, and to the external disk storage, as well as their performance ramifications, so we would not spend too much time to explain why we need efficient data structures such as hash tables.

A major issue that requires special attention is about how to deal with collisions when two different keys are hashed to the same hash code. A few most commonly used strategies include:

- *Linear probing*: Keep checking (hashCode + 1), (hashCode + 2), (hashCode + 3), ..., until a free slot is found.
- *Quadratic hashing*: Keep checking (hashCode + 1), (hashCode + 2^2), (hashCode + 3^2), ..., until a free slot is found.
- *Separate chaining*: Implement the hash table as an array of linked lists, where each table element is a pointer to a linked list – a chain – of items that the hash function has mapped to.

Next, we discuss the linear probing and separate chaining strategies for resolving hash table collisions.

A.6.1 LINEAR PROBING

As we mentioned, a hash table stores key-value pairs, and keys are required to be unique. Listing A.11 shows a simplified implementation of the hash table data structure based on linear probing. First, note a class named Entry defined from lines 3 – 19, which has two fields of key and value and a parameterized constructor, in addition to the getter and setter methods.

Next, note that lines 21 – 55 define a hash table data structure with a Java class named Hashtable. As is seen, it contains only two fields: TABLE_SIZE for the size of the hash table and an entry array (Entry[]) named table. Its get method retrieves an entry with a given key, while its put method stores an entry into the hash table. While the current element exists and the stored key is not equal to the hashed key, the next slot is probed with the following statement:

hash = (hash + 1) % TABLE_SIZE;

This is called linearly probing as we stated previously. Figure A.6 shows the concept of linear probing.

Lines 57 – 69 shows the main program for illustrating how a Hashtable can be created and used to store and retrieve key-value pairs using its put and get methods, respectively.

Next, we discuss separate chaining for resolving hash table collisions, following Figure A.6.

Listing A.11 HashTableDemo.java

```
1    package jcp.appendix.a.hashtable;
2
3    class Entry {
4      private int key;
5      private int value;
6
7      Entry(int key, int value) {
```

```
8          this.key = key;
9          this.value = value;
10      }
11
12      public int getKey() {
13          return key;
14      }
15
16      public int getValue() {
17          return value;
18      }
19  }
20
21  class Hashtable {
22      private final static int TABLE_SIZE = 512;
23
24      Entry[] table;
25
26      Hashtable() {
27          table = new Entry[TABLE_SIZE];
28          for (int i = 0; i < TABLE_SIZE; i++) {
29              table[i] = null;
30          }
31      }
32
33      public int get(int key) {
34          // 1. calculate hash
35          int hash = key % TABLE_SIZE;
36
37          // 2. find the key
38          while (table[hash] != null && table[hash].getKey() != key) {
39              hash = (hash + 1) % TABLE_SIZE;
40          }
41
42          // 3. return -1 if not found
43          return (table[hash] == null) ? -1 : table[hash].getValue();
44      }
45
46      public void put(int key, int value) {
47          int hash = key % TABLE_SIZE;
48
49          while (table[hash] != null && table[hash].getKey() != key) {
50              hash = (hash + 1) % TABLE_SIZE;
51          }
52          // either null or key exists (same key will be overwritten)
53          table[hash] = new Entry(key, value);
54      }
55  }
56
57  public class HashtableDemo {
58
59      public static void main(String[] args) {
```

```
60        Hashtable hashtable = new Hashtable();
61
62        hashtable.put(1, 100);
63        hashtable.put(2, 200);
64
65        System.out.println(hashtable.get(1));
66        System.out.println(hashtable.get(3));
67        System.out.println(hashtable.get(2));
68    }
69 }
```

table [0]	• →		hash entry
table [1]	• →		hash entry
...	• →		hash entry
table [n -1]	• →		hash entry

Figure A.6 A hash table data structure based on linear probing

A.6.2 SEPARATE CHAINING

Figure A.7 shows a hash table with each table element containing a linked list, which has no limit on how many nodes it can link to. Listing A.12 shows the implementation of a hash table based on separate chaining for resolving collisions, which is discussed next.

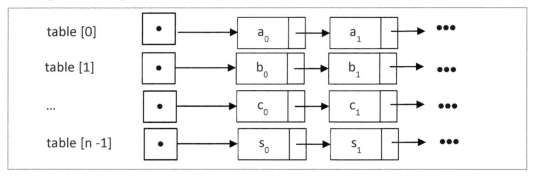

Figure A.7 A hash table data structure based on separate chaining

For the get method as shown from lines 29 – 45 in Listing A.12, it keeps checking whether the current entry is null, and if not, it continues checking whether the stored key equals the hashed key, until one of these two conditions turns out to be false. Then it returns either -1 to indicate that the entry for the given key does not exist or the value associated with the given key.

For the put method as shown from lines 49 – 70 in Listing A.12, it first checks if the current hashed slot is null. If null, it stores the entry there; if not, it keeps checking whether the next entry is null, and if not, it continues checking whether the next entry's stored key equals the hashed key, until one of these two conditions turns out to be false. Then it either sets the new entry or updates the value of the existing entry.

Lines 77 – 97 show the main program for testing LinkedHashTable as discussed above. It's simple, so we would not explain about it further.

Next, we discuss the running time of hashing, following Listing A.12.

Listing A.12 LinkedHashTableDemo.java

```
1   package jcp.appendix.a.hashtable;
2
3   class LinkedEntry {
4     private int key;
5     private int value;
6     private LinkedEntry next;
7
8     LinkedEntry(int key, int value) {
9        this.key = key;
10       this.value = value;
11       this.next = null;
12    }
13
14    // getters and setters omitted
15  }
16
17  class LinkedHashTable {
18    private final static int TABLE_SIZE = 64;
19
20    LinkedEntry[] table;
21
22    LinkedHashTable() {
23      table = new LinkedEntry[TABLE_SIZE];
24      for (int i = 0; i < TABLE_SIZE; i++) {
25        table[i] = null;
26      }
27    }
28
29    public int get(int key) {
30
31      int hash = key % TABLE_SIZE; // calculate hash
32
33      if (table[hash] == null) { // check if entry exists
34        return -1;
35      } else {
```

```
36          LinkedEntry entry = table[hash]; // current entry
37          while (entry != null && entry.getKey() != key) {
38              entry = entry.getNext();
39          }
40
41          if (entry == null) { // return -1 if not found
42              return -1;
43          } else {
44              return entry.getValue(); // key found
45          }
46      }
47  }
48
49  public void put(int key, int value) {
50      int hash = key % TABLE_SIZE;
51
52      LinkedEntry entry = new LinkedEntry(key, value);
53
54      if (table[hash] == null) { // first element
55          table[hash] = entry;
56      } else { // insert into the list
57          LinkedEntry currEntry = table[hash];
58
59          while (currEntry.getNext() != null
60                  && currEntry.getNext().getKey() != key) { // check next
61              currEntry = currEntry.getNext();
62          }
63
64          if (currEntry.getNext() == null) { // new entry does not exist
65              currEntry.setNext(entry);
66          } else { // entry exists. update the value
67              currEntry.setValue(value);
68          }
69      }
70  }
71
72  public void remove(int key) {
73      // implementation omitted
74  }
75 }
76
77 public class LinkedHashTableDemo {
78
79  public static void main(String[] args) {
80
81      LinkedHashTable linkedHashTable = new LinkedHashTable();
82      linkedHashTable.put(8, 80);
83      linkedHashTable.put(16, 160);
84      linkedHashTable.put(24, 240);
85
86      System.out.println(linkedHashTable.get(8));
87      System.out.println(linkedHashTable.get(16));
```

```
88        System.out.println(linkedHashTable.get(24));
89
90        linkedHashTable.remove(9);
91        linkedHashTable.remove(8);
92
93        System.out.println(linkedHashTable.get(8));
94        System.out.println(linkedHashTable.get(16));
95        System.out.println(linkedHashTable.get(24));
96    }
97 }
```

A.6.3 THE RUNNING TIME ESTIMATES OF HASHING

The running times of hashing based on linear probing and separate chaining can be characterized with a parameter named *load factor* as defined below:

```
α (load factor) = # of elements occupied / total capacity
```

In fact, formal algorithm analysis reveals that for linear probing as we demonstrated above, the average number of comparisons that a search requires is[1]

$$f(\alpha) = \frac{1}{2}\left(1 + \frac{1}{1-\alpha}\right) \; for \; a \; successful \; search \quad \text{(A.6a)}$$

and

$$f(\alpha) = \frac{1}{2}\left(1 + \frac{1}{(1-\alpha)^2}\right) \; for \; an \; unsuccessful \; search \quad \text{(A.6b)}$$

respectively. As you see, when the load factor approaches to 1 ($\alpha \to 1$), the # of comparisons required for both successful and unsuccessful searches would grow rapidly. (Unsuccessful searches are more costly, as they need to exhaust all searches until reaching the end of the hash table.) To put it into perspective, the average # of successful searches would increase to 1.17, 1.25, 1.5, 2.0, 2.5, 5.5, and 50.5 for $\alpha = 1/4, 1/2, 2/3, 3/4, 9/10$ and 0.99, respectively.

For separate chaining, Equations (A.6a) and (A.6b) become:

$$f(\alpha) = 1 + \frac{\alpha}{2} \; for \; a \; successful \; search \quad \text{(A.7a)}$$

and

$$f(\alpha) = \alpha \; for \; an \; unsuccessful \; search \quad \text{(A.7b)}$$

In contrast to linear probing, the number of comparisons grows linearly rather than exponentially with separate chaining. This is why separate chaining is more efficient than linear probing.

---

[1]D. E. Knuth, Searching and Sorting, vol. 3 of the Art of Computer Programming (Menlo Park, CA, Addison-Wesley, 1973).

This concludes our hash table examples. Next, we discuss running times for binary search and binary search trees.

A.7 BINARY SEARCH ALGORITHM AND BINARY SEARCH TREES

Binary search and binary search trees are not the same. Binary search refers to the algorithm that searches an item in a sorted data structure, while a binary search tree maintains a list of items in a binary tree data structure, which can have no more than two child nodes per parent node. Besides, for a given node (x) in a binary search tree, its key is larger than the key of its left child and smaller than the key of its right child.

This section discusses the running times of binary search and operations of a binary search tree. Let's start with the binary search algorithm next.

A.7.1 RUNNING TIMES OF A BINARY SEARCH ALGORITHM

A binary search algorithm works on a sorted data structure by taking a divide-and-conquer strategy to find a specific element in the data structure. Assuming that the underlying data structure is equivalent to a binary tree of level l with n nodes, then the following relation between l and n holds:

$$n = 2^{l-1} \qquad \text{(A.8a)}$$

or

$$l \propto \log(n) \qquad \text{(A.8b)}$$

Since a binary search takes at most l steps (the max number of levels), a binary search is an $O(log(n))$ operation. A binary update is also an $O(log(n))$ operation, as one has to find the element to be updated first before updating the element and the update operation is an $O(1)$ operation. However, a binary insert and a binary delete are $O(n)$ operations, because one has to shift the data structure to make space for the new element for insert or claim space for the element to be deleted.

Listing A.13 shows how a binary search algorithm works. The binarySearch method takes an integer array as input, in addition to the element to be found. It starts from both ends and keeps dividing the array using the middle index until the element is found or no element is found at the end.

Next, we discuss the binary search tree data structure.

Listing A.13 A binary search algorithm

```
1   public class BinarySearch {
2     public static void main(String[] args) {
3
4       int[] a = { 1, 15, 20, 29, 30, 40, 60 };
5       int index = binarySearch(a, 29);
6       System.out.println ("index = " + index);
7     }
8
9     public static int binarySearch(int[] a, int x) {
10
```

```
11        int start = 0;
12        int end = a.length - 1;
13        int middle = 0;
14
15         while (start <= end) {
16            middle = (start + end) >>>1;
17            if (a[middle] < x) {
18               start = middle + 1;
19            } else if (a[middle] > x) {
20               end = middle -1;
21            } else {
22               return middle;
23            }
24         }
25
26        return -1;
27    }
28 }
```

A.7.2 A BINARY SEARCH TREE

First, a binary search tree (BST) depends on a node as the basic element of a binary search tree. Listing A.14 shows a class named BSTNode, which has a field of int value for representing the content of the node and the left and right children of the node. With this BSTNode class and its various getters and setters, which are omitted to save space, we can discuss how to compose a binary search tree class next.

Listing A.14 BSTNode class (getters and setters are omitted)

```
1  class BSTNode {
2    int value;
3    BSTNode left, right;
4
5    public BSTNode () {
6      value = 0;
7      left = right = null;
8    }
9    public BSTNode (int value) {
10     this.value = value;
11     left = right = null;
12   }
13   public BSTNode(int value, BSTNode left, BSTNode right) {
14     this.value = value;
15     this.left = left;
16     this.right = right;
17   }
18   // getters and setters omitted
19 }
```

Listing A.15 shows the BST class that has only one field named root with a no-arg constructor. Its *insert*, *delete* and *search* methods are discussed as follows:

- **insert**: Lines 7 – 25 show the *insert* operation of the BST class, which has a public method paired up with a private method without exposing the root field. The private insert method inserts the new node at the root node if the tree is null or calls itself recursively using the left or right child, depending on whether the new node's value is smaller or larger than the value of its left child. At the end, it returns the new node inserted.
- **delete**: Lines 27 – 41 show the *delete* operation of the BST class, which has a public method paired up with a private method without exposing the root field. The public delete method first deals with the cases such as the tree is empty or the node with the given value does not exist. If the node with the given value does exist, it calls the private delete method to delete the node, whose implementation is too complicated and omitted here to save space.
- **search**: Lines 45 – 66 show the *search* operation of the BST class, which has a public method paired up with a private method without exposing the root field. The private search method uses the binary search algorithm to find the item specified by the given value. It also uses a pair of public/private countNodes methods to output information about the node found. You can find the countNodes methods from the source code of this class in the download for this text.

The running times for *insert*, *delete* and *search* operations are O(*log n*) *on average* if the binary tree can be maintained as a well-balanced tree, namely, its height satisfies Equation (A.8a). In worst cases, a binary search tree may end up with having left children only, which would result in a tree height of N, and thus running times of O(*n*) instead of O(*log n*) for the *insert*, *delete* and *search* operations. It is known that such worst cases could be avoided if the nodes are inserted in a random order, which is the case in general in practice.

Next, we discuss the running time for traversing a binary search tree.

Listing A.15 BST class

```
1   class BST {
2      private BSTNode root;
3      public BST () {
4         root = null;
5      }
6
7      public void insert (int value) {
8         root = insert (root, value);
9      }
10
11     // returns the new node inserted
12     // recursive
13     // allows inserting duplicate value
14     private BSTNode insert (BSTNode node, int value) {
15        if (node == null) {
16           node = new BSTNode (value);
17        } else {
18           if (value <= node.getValue()) { // "=" goes to left
19              node.left = insert (node.left, value);
20           } else {
21              node.right = insert (node.right, value);
```

```
22              }
23          }
24          return node;
25      }
26
27      public void delete (int value) {
28          if (isEmpty()) {
29              System.out.println ("tree empty");
30          } else if (search (value) == false) {
31              System.out.println ("value " + value + " does not exist");
32          } else {
33              root = delete (root, value);
34              System.out.println (value + " deleted");
35          }
36      }
37
38      private BSTNode delete (BSTNode root, int value) {
39          // implementation omitted
40          return root;
41      }
42
43      // returns BSTNode found rather than a boolean?
44      // recursive requires found in the while loop
45      public boolean search (int value) {
46          return search (root, value);
47      }
48
49      private boolean search (BSTNode node, int value) {
50          boolean found = false;
51          while ((node != null) && !found) { // keep searching if node not null
                                               // and not found
52              int nodeValue = node.getValue();
53              if (value < nodeValue) {
54                  node = node.getLeft ();
55              } else if (value > nodeValue) {
56                  node = node.getRight();
57              } else {
58                  found = true;
59                  System.out.println ("found value " + value + " who has " +
60                          (countNodes (node) - 1) + " children");
61                  break;
62              }
63              found = search (node, value); // recursive
64          }
65          return found;
66      }
67  }
```

A.7.3 TRAVERSING A BINARY SEARCH TREE

You can traverse a tree in general, including a binary search tree, using one of the following methods:

- **preOrder**: Follows the sequence of parent →left child → right child, namely, parent first
- **inOrder**: Follows the sequence of left child → parent → right child, namely, parent in the middle
- **postOrder**: Follows the sequence of left child → right child → parent, namely, parent last

Lines 7 – 40 show how above methods are implemented recursively. The running time for these traversal methods are O(*n*) for both average and worst cases.

Next, we discuss the breadth-first traversal for a binary tree.

Listing A.16 Methods for traversing a BST

```
1    class BST {
2      private BSTNode root;
3      public BST () {
4        root = null;
5      }
6
7      public void preOrder () {
8        preOrder (root);
9      }
10
11     private void preOrder (BSTNode node) {
12       if (node != null) {
13         System.out.print (node.getValue() + " ");
14         preOrder (node.getLeft());
15         preOrder (node.getRight());
16       }
17     }
18     // inorder and postorder are depth-first traversals
19     public void inOrder () {
20       inOrder (root);
21     }
22
23     private void inOrder (BSTNode node) {
24       if (node != null) {
25         inOrder (node.getLeft());
26         System.out.print (node.getValue() + " ");
27         inOrder (node.getRight());
28       }
29     }
30
31     public void postOrder () {
32       postOrder (root);
33     }
34     private void postOrder (BSTNode node) {
35       if (node != null) {
36         postOrder (node.getLeft());
37         postOrder (node.getRight());
38         System.out.print (node.getValue() + " ");
39       }
40     }
```

```
41  }
```

A.7.4 BREADTH-FIRST TRAVERSAL

We call out breadth first traversal as it's one of common programming interview questions. A breadth first traversal can be facilitated with a queue, as shown in Listing A.17. Initially, you add the root node to a queue such as a LinkedList as shown in §3.4.5, which is a doubly-linked list with both prev and next pointers. Then, you remove the node and returns the node removed, which is used to add its left child node and right child node in sequence as shown from lines 15 – 22. This procedure is repeated until the queue is empty.

Since breadth first traversal is also a linear traversal, its running time is O(n).

Next, we discuss an example of finding the common ancestor of two child nodes in a binary tree.

Listing A.17 breadthFirst traversal for a tree

```java
1    public void breadthFirst () {
2        Queue<BSTNode> q = new LinkedList<BSTNode> ();
3        BSTNode node;
4
5        if (root != null) {
6            q.add (root); // add to the end of the list
7
8            while (!q.isEmpty()) {
9                node = (BSTNode) q.remove(); // remove the head and print it
10               System.out.print (node.getValue() + " ");
11
12               // after the left is removed, right sibling will be the next
13               // because right sibling is added following the left sibling
14
15               if ( node != null ) {
16                   if (node.getLeft() != null) {
17                       q.add (node.getLeft());
18                   }
19                   if (node.getRight() != null) {
20                       q.add (node.getRight());
21                   }
22               }
23           }
24       }
25       System.out.println ();
26   }
```

A.7.5 FINDING THE CLOSEST COMMON ANCESTOR OF TWO CHILD NODES IN A BINARY TREE

Finding the closest common ancestor of two child nodes in a binary tree is another common programming interview question, so it is called out here for your reference. Listing A.18 shows how it can be done using a while-loop by keeping comparing the running node's value with the values of the two child nodes given. The loop stops if the running node's value is between the values of the two given child nodes, in which case, the running node is their immediate common ancestor.

Next, we discuss testing the breadth first method and finding the closest common ancestor of two child nodes in a binary tree, following Listing A.18.

Listing A.18 Finding the closest common ancestor of two child nodes in a binary tree

```
1      public BSTNode commonAncestor (BSTNode nodeX, BSTNode nodeY) {
2      int x = nodeX.getValue();
3      int y = nodeY.getValue();
4      BSTNode runningNode = root;
5
6      while (runningNode != null) {
7         int value = runningNode.getValue();
8         if (value > x && value > y) {
9            runningNode = runningNode.getLeft();
10        } else if (value < x && value < y) {
11           runningNode = runningNode.getRight();
12        } else {
13           return runningNode;
14        }
15     }
16     return null; // if empty tree
17  }
```

Listing A.19 shows the BSTDemo.java program. It inserts a sequence of nodes with values of {6, 2, 1, 4, 3, 5, 7}, from lines 6 – 12. Lines 14 – 16 print the binary search tree in preorder and breadth first orders. Lines 18 – 20 print the common ancestors for the pair of nodes {3, 5}, {3, 1} and {3, 7}, respectively. The following output shows the result:

pre-order: 6 2 1 4 3 5 7
breadth first: 6 2 7 1 4 3 5
commonAncestor 3 5: 4
commonAncestor 3 1: 2
commonAncestor 3 7: 6

You can check the above result against Figure A.8, which shows the binary tree created by this demo.

This concludes our presentation of the binary search algorithm and binary search trees. We present a few sorting examples next.

Listing A.19 BSTDemo.java

```
1   public class BSTDemo {
2
3      public static void main(String[] args) {
4
5         BST bst = new BST ();
6         bst.insert(6);
7         bst.insert(2);
```

```
8        bst.insert(1);
9        bst.insert(4);
10       bst.insert(3);
11       bst.insert(5);
12       bst.insert(7);
13
14       bst.preOrder();
15       System.out.println();
16       bst.breadthFirst();
17
18       System.out.println ("3 5:" + bst.commonAncestor(new BSTNode (3),
             new BSTNode (5)).getValue());
19       System.out.println ("3 1:" + bst.commonAncestor(new BSTNode (3),
             new BSTNode (1)).getValue());
20       System.out.println ("3 7:" + bst.commonAncestor(new BSTNode (3),
             new BSTNode (7)).getValue());
21   }
22 }
```

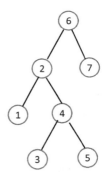

Figure A.8 A binary tree

A.8 SORTING EXAMPLES

Sorting is a common operation to perform in building software. Among many sorting algorithms, we pick two of them: quick sort and merge sort, which are not only very useful, but also appear as programming interview questions very often.

We start with the quick sort algorithm first next.

A.8.1 QUICK SORT

Quick sort consists of two important parts:

1. Partition an array around a pivot so that elements to the left of the pivot are smaller than the pivot and the elements to the right of the pivot are equal to or larger than the pivot. The elements flanking the pivot do not have to be sorted. Refer to the `partition` method shown in Listing A.20 about how partitioning is implemented.

2. Sort recursively around the `pivot` that is returned from the `partition` method shown in Listing A.20. Refer to the `quickSort` method there about how this method makes recursive calls.

The `QuickSortDemo.java` program also includes a test driver that you can try it out.

In terms of running times for quick sort, complicated mathematical analysis has proved that the average case and worst-case are $O(n * \log n)$ and $O(n^2)$, respectively. Quick sort is often used to sort large arrays. It is usually extremely fast in practice, despite its unimpressive, theoretical, quadratic worst-case running time.

Next, we discuss the merge sort algorithm.

Listing A.20 QuickSortDemo.java

```
1   package jcp.appendix.a.sorting;
2
3   import java.util.Collections;
4   import java.util.Random;
5   import java.util.ArrayList;
6
7   public class QuickSortDemo {
8
9     public static int partition(int[] a, int left, int right)
10    {
11          int i = left, j = right;
12          int tmp;
13          int pivot = a[(left + right) / 2]; // middle element as the pivot
14
15          while (i <= j) { //
16                while (a[i] < pivot)
17                      i++;        // left: found one not smaller than pivot
18                while (a[j] > pivot)
19                      j--;        // right: found one not larger than pivot
20                if (i <= j) {     // swap the above two
21                      tmp = a[i];
22                      a[i] = a[j];
23                      a[j] = tmp;
24                      i++;
25                      j--;
26                }
27          }; // loop as long as not done
28
29          return i;
30    }
31
32    public static void quickSort(int[] a, int left, int right) {
33          int pivot = partition(a, left, right);
34          if (left < pivot - 1)
35                quickSort(a, left, pivot - 1);
36          if (pivot < right)
37                quickSort(a, pivot, right);
```

```
38   }
39
40   public static void main(String[] args) {
41      // body omitted
42   }
43 }
```

A.8.2 MERGE SORT

Similar to the quicksort algorithm, the merge sort algorithm also operates on the principle of *divide-and-conquer*. However, it does not depend on the concept of a pivot like the quicksort algorithm. Instead, it keeps dividing a specified segment until only one item is left, which cannot be divided further. At that point, it starts to merge each pair of sorted segments until all sorted segments are merged into one. As such, the core logic of the merge sort algorithm is to merge two sorted segments.

Now, let us use the illustration shown in Figure A.9 to explain how the merge algorithm works. Given two segments that have already been sorted and a temp array for facilitating merging, the merge algorithm can be explained by using the symbols as shown in Figure A.9 as follows:

- **❶**: Since 2 on the left is smaller than 6 on the right, 2 is copied to the temp array first.
- **❷**: Since 5 on the left is smaller than 6 on the right, 5 is copied to the temp array next.
- **❸**: Since 6 on the right is smaller than 9 on the left, 6 is copied to the temp array.
- **❹**: Since 7 on the right is smaller than 9 on the left, 7 is copied to the temp array.
- **❺**: Since the right half has been exhausted, the remaining item 9 on the left is copied to the temp array. In this example, it happens that only one item is left. If more than one item were left, all remaining items would be copied to the temp array as a sorted sub-segment.

Listing A.21 shows the complete implementation of the merge sort algorithm in Java, including the merge method and the mergeSort method. These methods are explained as follows:

- **merge**: The signature of this method specifies the array to be sorted and the two sorted halves defined with three parameters of left, mid, and right. (The first range [left, mid] corresponds to the left sorted segment, while the range [mid + 1, right] corresponds to the right sorted segment.) Inside the method body, a tempArray is declared first. Then, the beginning and ending indices for both segments are defined. The while loop copies the items to the tempArray as described above in Figure A.9 until one of the segments is exhausted first. One of the first two of the three subsequent for loops copies the remaining items left over in one of the two segments to the temp array, while the last for loop copies all items in the temp array back to the original array.
- **mergeSort**: This method calls itself recursively to keep dividing each sub-segment from the middle and starts the merging process when the sub-segment's begin index named left becomes equal to its end index named right, which implies that the bottom has been reached.

The MergeSortDemo.java program also includes a test driver that you can try it out.

In terms of running times, merge sort always gives the same performance, regardless of the initial order of the array elements. Complicated mathematical analysis reveals that both the average case and worst-case are O($n * log\ n$).

Next, we discuss two set-related examples.

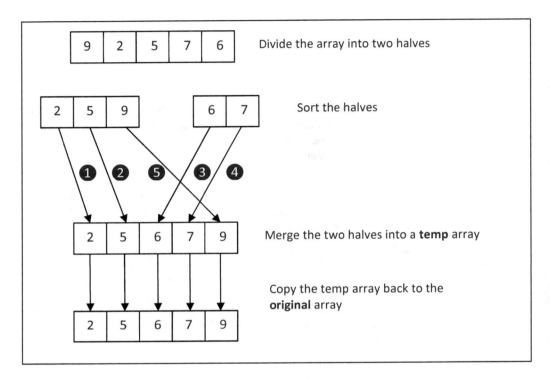

Figure A.9 The core logic of the merge sort algorithm

Listing A.21 MergeSortDemo.java

```
1   package jcp.appendix.a.sorting;
2
3   import java.util.Collections;
4   import java.util.Random;
5   import java.util.ArrayList;
6
7   public class MergeSortDemo {
8
9     public static void merge(int arr[], int left, int mid, int right)
10    {
11        int[] tempArray = new int [MAX_ARRAY_SIZE];
12        int left1 = left;
13        int right1 = mid;
14
15        int left2 = mid + 1;
16        int right2 = right;
17
```

```
18      int next = left1;
19
20      while ((left1 <= right1) && (left2 <= right2)) {
21         if (arr [left1] < arr [left2]) {
22            tempArray [next] = arr [left1];
23            ++left1;
24         } else {
25            tempArray [next] = arr [left2];
26            ++left2;
27         }
28         ++next;
29      }
30
31      // finish off the left half if any left using "next"
32      for (; left1 <= right1; ++left1, ++next) {
33         tempArray [next] = arr [left1];
34      }
35
36      // finish off the right half if any left
37      for (; left2 <= right2; ++left2, ++next) {
38         tempArray [next] = arr [left2];
39      }
40
41      // copy the result back to the original array
42      for (next = left; next <= right; ++next) {
43         arr [next] = tempArray [next];
44      }
45   }
46
47   public static void mergeSort(int arr[], int left, int right) {
48      if (left < right) {
49         int mid = (left + right) / 2;
50         mergeSort (arr, left, mid); // not mid - 1
51         mergeSort (arr, mid + 1, right);
52         merge (arr, left, mid, right);
53      }
54   }
55
56   public static final int MAX_ARRAY_SIZE = 10;
57   public static void main(String[] args) {
58
59      // body omitted
60   }
61 }
```

A.9 INTERSECTION AND UNION EXAMPLES

This section presents two algorithms that return the intersection and union of the two sorted integer arrays, respectively. As shown in Listing A.22, lines 8 – 29 show the getIntersection method, which merges the common elements into an ArrayList. Lines 32 – 60 show the getUnion method, which adds identical and different elements into a single ArrayList.

Since these two methods run the two sorted arrays in one run in a while-loop, the running times are O(n) accordingly.

Listing A.22 IntersectionAndUnion.java

```
1   package jcp.appendix.a.set;
2
3   import java.util.ArrayList;
4
5   public class IntersectionAndUnion {
6
7     // use merge since two arrays already sorted
8     public static ArrayList<Integer> getIntersection (int[] a, int[] b) {
9
10      int n = a.length;
11      int m = b.length;
12      ArrayList<Integer> c = new ArrayList<Integer> (n);
13
14      int i = 0;
15      int j = 0;
16
17      while ((i < n) && (j < m)) {
18        if (a[i] < b [j]) {
19          i++;
20        } else if (a[i] > b [j]) {
21          j++;
22        } else {
23          c.add (a [i]);
24          i++;
25          j++;
26        }
27      }
28      return c;
29    }
30
31    // use merge since two arrays already sorted
32    public static ArrayList<Integer> getUnion(int[] a, int[] b) {
33
34      int n = a.length;
35      int m = b.length;
36
37      ArrayList<Integer> c = new ArrayList<Integer> (n);
38      int i = 0;
39      int j = 0;
40
41      while ((i < n) && (j < m)) {
42        if (a[i] == b [j]) {
43          c.add (a [i++]);
44          j++;
45        } else {
46          c.add (a[i++]);
```

```
47              c.add (b[j++]);
48          }
49      }
50
51      // process leftovers
52      while (i < n) {
53          c.add (a[i++]);
54      }
55
56      while (j < m) {
57          c.add (a[j++]);
58      }
59      return c;
60  }
61
62  public static void main(String[] args) {
63      int[] a = { 1, 3, 5, 8, 18, 20 };
64      int[] b = { 2, 5, 6, 8, 15, 18 };
65
66      System.out.println ("Testing intersection:");
67      ArrayList<Integer> c = getIntersection(a, b);
68      for (Integer i: c) {
69          System.out.print (i.intValue() + " ");
70      }
71
72      System.out.println ("\nTesting union:");
73      ArrayList<Integer> u = getUnion (a, b);
74      for (Integer i: u) {
75          System.out.print (i.intValue() + " ");
76      }
77  }
78 }
```

This concludes our introduction to algorithm analysis. More running time estimates will be covered in the main text on an as-needed basis.

A.10 LRUCACHE IMPLEMENTATIONS

This section provides two *LRUCache* implementations: one based on a doubly-linked list data structure and the other based on the LinkedHashMap class provided in the java.util package, which is covered in §3.7.3. These implementations emphasize how the LRU (least recently used) policy can be implemented either from scratch or from a well-documented Java collection such as the LinkedHashMap class. If you use a framework like SpringSource, you can use a ConcurrentHashMap, Ehcache, Guava or GemFire and so on, as shown in Figure A.10 (http://docs.spring.io/spring/docs/current/spring-framework-reference/htmlsingle/).

35.6. Configuring the cache storage
35.6.1. JDK ConcurrentMap-based Cache
35.6.2. EhCache-based Cache
35.6.3. Guava Cache
35.6.4. GemFire-based Cache
35.6.5. JSR-107 Cache
35.6.6. Dealing with caches without a backing store

Figure A.10 Cache providers available from the spring framework

We start with the doubly-linked list based LRUCache implementation first next.

A.10.1 DOUBLY-LINKED LIST BASED

Listing A.23 shows the `LRUCacheDemo` program that consists of the following classes:

1. **Class Node**: This is the `Node` class that has the `key`, `value`, `prev` and `next` attributes. Since it's preferable to have both the `get` and `set` operations run in O(1) times, a singly-linked list cannot achieve the fastest possible *get/set* running time requirement.
2. **Class LRUCache**: This class uses a `HashMap` to implement the LRU cache. In addition to its `capacity` field, it has a `head` pointer and a `tail` pointer, which point to the head and the tail of the linked list, respectively. Whenever a node is accessed through the `get` method, it's removed and put to the head of the least, which maintains the desired access order. When a node is updated or inserted through the `set` method, it always makes sure that the updated node or the new node will be the new head node, maintaining the access order accordingly as well.
3. **Class LRUCacheDemo**: This is the test driver class for this LRUCache implementation. If you run this example, you should get an output similar to Listing A.24.

Next, we discuss the LRUCache implementation based on the `LinkedHashMap` class.

Listing A.23 LRUCacheDemo.java

```
package jcp.appendix.a.lcucache;

import java.util.HashMap;

class Node {
  int key;
  String value;
  Node prev;
  Node next;

  public Node(int key, String value) {
     this.key = key;
     this.value = value;
  }
}

class LRUCache {
  int capacity;
```

```
19    HashMap<Integer, Node> map = new HashMap<Integer, Node>();
20    Node head = null;
21    Node tail = null;
22
23    public LRUCache(int capacity) {
24       this.capacity = capacity;
25    }
26
27    public String get(int key) {
28       if (map.containsKey(key)) {
29          Node node = map.get(key);
30          remove(node);
31          setHead(node);
32          return node.value;
33       }
34
35       return "";
36    }
37
38    public void remove(Node node) {
39       if (node.prev != null) {
40          node.prev.next = node.next;
41       } else {
42          head = node.next;
43       }
44
45       if (node.next != null) {
46          node.next.prev = node.prev;
47       } else {
48          tail = node.prev;
49       }
50    }
51
52    public void setHead(Node node) {
53       node.next = head;
54       node.prev = null;
55
56       if (head != null) {
57          head.prev = node;
58       }
59
60       head = node;
61
62       if (tail == null) {
63          tail = head;
64       }
65    }
66
67    public void set(int key, String value) {
68       if (map.containsKey(key)) {
69          Node currentNode = map.get(key);
70          currentNode.value = value;
```

```
71              remove(currentNode);
72              setHead(currentNode);
73            } else {
74              Node newNode = new Node(key, value);
75              if (map.size() >= capacity) {
76                  map.remove(tail.key);
77                  remove(tail);
78                  setHead(newNode);
79              } else {
80                  setHead(newNode);
81              }
82              map.put(key, newNode);
83          }
84      }
85  }
86
87  public class LRUCacheDemo {
88
89      public static void main(String[] args) {
90          LRUCache cache = new LRUCache(9);
91
92          cache.set(1, "One");
93          cache.set(2, "Two");
94          cache.set(3, "Three");
95
96          System.out.println(cache.head.value + " ... " + cache.tail.value);
97
98          cache.get(2);
99          System.out.println(cache.head.value + " ... " + cache.tail.value);
100
101         cache.get(3);
102         System.out.println(cache.head.value + " ... " + cache.tail.value);
103
104         cache.get(1);
105         System.out.println(cache.head.value + " ... " + cache.tail.value);
106     }
107
108 }
```

Listing A.24 Output of running the LRUCache example

Three ... One
Two ... One
Three ... One
One ... Two

A.10.2 LINKEDHASHMAP BASED

Listing A.25 shows the Cache implementation by extending the LinkedHashMap class. As you have learnt in §3.7.3, a LinkedHashMap can either maintain the access order or insertion order. In our case, the access order corresponds to the desired LRU policy, which can be conveniently set in the constructor of the Cache class as shown at line 9. In addition, the removeEldestEntry is overridden by returning whether size is larger than capacity, as shown at line 14. You should refer to the original implementation of the LinkedHashMap if you want to know exactly how this method works.

Finally, running this example should produce an output similar to Listing A.26. Note that the first element is the least recently used entry and the last element is the most recently used entry.

This concludes our introduction to the LRUCache implementation examples.

Listing A.25 CacheDemo.java

```
1   package jcp.appendix.a.lcucache;
2   import java.util.LinkedHashMap;
3   import java.util.Map.Entry;
4
5   class Cache <K, V> extends LinkedHashMap<K, V>{
6     private int capacity;
7
8     public Cache (int capacity) {
9         super (capacity, 1.0f, true); // true access-order
                                        // false insertion-order
10        this.capacity = capacity;
11    }
12
13    protected boolean removeEldestEntry (Entry entry) {
14        return (size() > this.capacity);
15    }
16  }
17
18  public class CacheDemo {
19
20    public static void main(String[] args) {
21      Cache cache = new Cache (9);
22
23      cache.put(1, "One");
24      cache.put(2, "Two");
25      cache.put(3, "Three");
26
27      System.out.println (cache.toString());
28
29      cache.get(2);
30      System.out.println (cache.toString());
31
32      cache.get(3);
33      System.out.println (cache.toString());
34
35      cache.get(1);
36      System.out.println (cache.toString());
37    }
38
39  }
```

Listing A.26 Output of running the CacheDemo example

```
{1=One, 2=Two, 3=Three}
{1=One, 3=Three, 2=Two}
{1=One, 2=Two, 3=Three}
{2=Two, 3=Three, 1=One}
```

A.11 EXERCISES

Exercise A.1 *Maximum subsequence sum problem.* Given a negative and positive integer randomly mixed sequence of a_1, a_2, ..., a_n, find the subsequence of a_i ... a_j that yields the largest sum. Write a Java class method that solves this maximum subsequence sum problem.

Exercise A.2 *Array sub-array product problem.* Given an array int[] a with n elements, find the products of all $(n - 1)$ elements with one element excluded for each sub-array product. Write a Java class method that solves this array sub-array product problem.

Exercise A.3 *Two-sum-to-k problem.* Given a sorted array int[] a with n elements, find two elements whose sum is equal to a constant k. Write a Java class method that solves this two-sum-to-k problem.

Exercise A.4 Write a Java class method that reverses a singly linked list.

Exercise A.5 Write a Java class method that detects a circularly linked list.

Exercise A.6 Write a simple Hashtable class that implements linear probing for solving hashing collision problem.

Exercise A.7 Write a simple Hashtable class that implements separate chaining for solving hashing collision problem.

Exercise A.8 Write a Java class method to demonstrate how binary search algorithm works.

Exercise A.9 What are the average and worst-case running times for operations of a binary search tree?

Exercise A.10 Write a breadth-first traversal method for traversing a binary search tree implemented in a Java class.

Exercise A.11 Write a Java class method for finding the closest common ancestor of two nodes in a binary search tree.

Exercise A.12 Explain how you would implement the quick sort algorithm in Java.

Exercise A.13 Explain how you would implement the merge sort algorithm in Java.

Exercise A.14 Compare the quick sort algorithm with the merge sort algorithm in terms of their running times.

Exercise A.15 Given two sorted integer arrays, write a method in Java that returns the intersection of the two arrays.

Exercise A.16 Given two sorted integer arrays, write a method in Java that returns the union of the two arrays.

Appendix B The Bridge Exercise

For your reference, this appendix presents the author's implementation of the classical, multi-threaded programming exercise for multiple cars crossing a bridge. Please refer to section 1.10 for the problem description.

Listing B.1 Bridge.java

```
1   package bridge;
2   /**
3    * Author: Henry H Liu Date: 11/02/13
4    */
5   public class Bridge {
6
7      private static Bridge instance = null;
8      public static final int maxCars = 3;   // max # of cars permitted on the
                                               bridge
9      private static int[] numCarsCrossing; // # of cars on the bridge in a
                                             given direction
10     private static int[] numCarsCrossed;  // # of cars crossed the bridge in
                                             a given direction
11     private static int[] numCarsWaiting;  // # of cars waiting in a given
                                             direction
12
13     public static Bridge getInstance () {
14        // for better performance, do not synchronize the method
15        if (instance == null) {
16           synchronized (Bridge.class) {
17              instance = new Bridge();
18           }
19        }
20        return instance;
21     }
22
23     protected Bridge() {
24        numCarsCrossing = new int[2];
25        numCarsCrossing[0] = 0;
26        numCarsCrossing[1] = 0;
```

```
27
28       numCarsCrossed = new int[2];
29       numCarsCrossed[0] = 0;
30       numCarsCrossed[1] = 0;
31
32       numCarsWaiting = new int[2];
33       numCarsWaiting[0] = 0;
34       numCarsWaiting[1] = 0;
35     }
36     public synchronized static int getNumCarsCrossing(int dir) {
37         return numCarsCrossing [dir];
38     }
39     public synchronized static int getNumCarsCrossed(int dir) {
40         return numCarsCrossed [dir];
41     }
42     public synchronized static int getNumCarsWaiting(int dir) {
43         return numCarsWaiting [dir];
44     }
45
46     // to be called when a car exits the bridge
47     public synchronized static void setExit(int dir) {
48         numCarsCrossing[dir]--;
49         if (numCarsCrossed[dir] < maxCars) {
50           numCarsCrossed[dir]++;
51         } else {
52           numCarsCrossed[dir] = 0;
53         }
54     }
55
56     // to be called when a car starts to cross the bridge
57     public synchronized static boolean setCrossing(int dir) {
58         // check current direction if more than maxCars on the bridge
59         boolean success =  (numCarsCrossing[dir] < maxCars);
60         if (success) numCarsCrossing[dir]++;
61         if (success && numCarsWaiting[dir] > 0) {
62           numCarsWaiting[dir]--;
63           return true;
64         } else {
65           return false;
66         }
67     }
68
69     // to be called when a car arrives at the entarnce to the bridge
70     public synchronized static void setWaiting(int dir) {
71         numCarsWaiting[dir]++;
72     }
73
74     // to be called when max # of cars have crossed the bridge
75     public synchronized static void clearCrossed(int dir) {
76         numCarsCrossed[dir] = 0;
77     }
78
```

```
79   // to be called for checking whther a car can get on the brdige
80   public synchronized static boolean canGo(int direction) {
81      boolean okToGo = false;
82      int otherDirection = 1 - direction;
83      // on the other side: max cars have crossed or less than max cars
84      // crossed but no cars waiting => FAIRNESS imposed here
85      if ((getNumCarsCrossed(otherDirection) == maxCars)
86            || ((getNumCarsCrossed(otherDirection) > 0) && (
                  getNumCarsWaiting(otherDirection) == 0))) {
87         clearCrossed(otherDirection);
88         okToGo = true;
89         // on the other side, no cars on the bridge AND
90         // on this side: less than max cars crossed
91      } else if ((getNumCarsCrossing(otherDirection) +
                  getNumCarsCrossed(otherDirection)) == 0
92            && (getNumCarsCrossing(direction) +
                  getNumCarsCrossed(direction)) < maxCars) {
93         okToGo = true;
94         // other side empty
95      } else if ((getNumCarsCrossing(otherDirection)
96            + getNumCarsCrossed(otherDirection) +
                  getNumCarsWaiting(otherDirection)) == 0) {
97         okToGo = true;
98      }
99      if (okToGo) {
100        if (!setCrossing(direction)) {
101           okToGo = false;
102        }
103     }
104     return okToGo;
105  }
106
107  // to be called to check the # of cars "waiting" "crossing" "crossed"
   for each direction
108  public synchronized static String checkStatus() {
109     return " " + getNumCarsWaiting(0) + " " + getNumCarsCrossing(0)
110           + " " + getNumCarsCrossed(0) + " : "
111           + getNumCarsWaiting(1) + " " + getNumCarsCrossing(1)
112           + " " + getNumCarsCrossed(1);
113  }
114 }
```

Listing B.2 Car.java

```
1   package bridge;
2
3   /**
4    * Author: Henry H Liu Date: 11/02/13
5    */
6   public class Car extends Thread {
7      private String name;
```

```
8     private int direction;
9     private boolean crossed;
10
11    public Car(String name, int direction) {
12       super(name);
13       this.name = name;
14       this.direction = direction;
15       this.crossed = false;
16    }
17
18    public void run() {
19       while (!crossed) {
20          if (Bridge.canGo(direction)) {
21             go();
22          } else {
23             waiting(1000); // waiting an arbitrary period of 1000 ms
24          }
25       }
26    }
27
28    public void go() {
29       System.out.println(getCarName()
30             + " is crossing the bridge to direction " + direction + " "
31             + Bridge.checkStatus());
32
33       crossing(1500); // to simulate crossing bridge time
34       exitBridge();
35    }
36
37    public void crossing(long waitTime) {
38       try {
39          sleep(waitTime);
40       } catch (InterruptedException ie) {
41          System.out.println(getCarName() + " sleeping interrupted ...");
42       }
43    }
44
45    public void waiting(long waitTime) {
46       /*
47       System.out.println("\t" + getCarName()
48             + " is waiting to cross the bridge to direction " + direction
49             + " " + Bridge.checkStatus());
50       */
51       try {
52          sleep(waitTime);
53       } catch (InterruptedException ie) {
54          System.out.println(getCarName() + " sleeping interrupted ...");
55       }
56    }
57
58    public void exitBridge() {
59       Bridge.setExit(direction);
```

```
60        System.out.println("\t\t..." + getCarName()
61              + " crossed the bridge to direction " + direction + " "
62              + Bridge.checkStatus());
63        crossed = true;
64    }
65
66    public String getCarName() {
67        if (direction == 0) {
68            return name + " (->) ";
69        } else {
70            return name + " (<-) ";
71        }
72    }
73 }
```

Listing B.3 Driver.java

```
1    package bridge;
2
3    /**
4     * Author: Henry H Liu Date: 11/02/13
5     */
6    public class Driver {
7       private static int numCars;
8
9       public static void main(String[] args) throws InterruptedException {
10          if (args.length > 1) {
11              System.out.println("usage: java Driver numCars");
12              System.exit(-1);
13          } else if (args.length == 1) {
14              numCars = Integer.parseInt(args[0]);
15              System.out.println("total # of cars on both ends: " + numCars);
16          }
17
18          // prepare the bridge
19          Bridge.getInstance();
20
21          // make and start cars
22          for (int i = 0; i < numCars; i++) {
23              int direction = ((int) (Math.random() * numCars) % 2);
24              // int direction = i % 2;
25              String name = "car" + i;
26              Car car = new Car(name, direction);
27              Bridge.setWaiting(direction);
28              car.start();
29          }
30      }
31 }
```

Listing B.4 Sample test output

```
C:\mspc\misc\tests\bridge_problem>java Driver 30
total # of cars on both ends: 30
car0 (->)  is crossing the bridge to direction 0  1 1 0 : 1 0 0
car1 (->)  is crossing the bridge to direction 0  1 2 0 : 1 0 0
car3 (->)  is crossing the bridge to direction 0  3 3 0 : 2 0 0
        ...car1 (->)  crossed the bridge to direction 0  1 3 0 3 : 1 4 0 0
        ...car3 (->)  crossed the bridge to direction 0  1 3 0 3 : 1 4 0 0
        ...car0 (->)  crossed the bridge to direction 0  1 3 0 3 : 1 4 0 0
car6 (<-)  is crossing the bridge to direction 1  1 3 0 0 : 1 1 3 0
car2 (<-)  is crossing the bridge to direction 1  1 3 0 0 : 1 1 3 0
car8 (<-)  is crossing the bridge to direction 1  1 3 0 0 : 1 1 3 0
        ...car2 (<-)  crossed the bridge to direction 1  1 3 0 0 : 1 1 1 2
        ...car6 (<-)  crossed the bridge to direction 1  1 3 0 0 : 1 1 1 2
        ...car8 (<-)  crossed the bridge to direction 1  1 3 0 0 : 1 1 0 3
car4 (->)  is crossing the bridge to direction 0  1 0 3 0 : 1 1 0 0
car5 (->)  is crossing the bridge to direction 0  1 0 3 0 : 1 1 0 0
car7 (->)  is crossing the bridge to direction 0  1 0 3 0 : 1 1 0 0
        ...car4 (->)  crossed the bridge to direction 0  1 0 2 1 : 1 1 0 0
        ...car7 (->)  crossed the bridge to direction 0  1 0 0 3 : 1 1 0 0
        ...car5 (->)  crossed the bridge to direction 0  1 0 0 3 : 1 1 0 0
car18 (<-)  is crossing the bridge to direction 1  1 0 0 0 : 9 2 0
car12 (<-)  is crossing the bridge to direction 1  1 0 0 0 : 8 3 0
car14 (<-)  is crossing the bridge to direction 1  1 0 0 0 : 8 3 0
        ...car18 (<-)  crossed the bridge to direction 1  1 0 0 0 : 8 0 3
        ...car12 (<-)  crossed the bridge to direction 1  1 0 0 0 : 8 0 3
        ...car14 (<-)  crossed the bridge to direction 1  1 0 0 0 : 8 0 3
car10 (->)  is crossing the bridge to direction 0  8 2 0 : 8 0 0
car11 (->)  is crossing the bridge to direction 0  7 3 0 : 8 0 0
car16 (->)  is crossing the bridge to direction 0  7 3 0 : 8 0 0
        ...car16 (->)  crossed the bridge to direction 0  7 2 1 : 8 0 0
        ...car11 (->)  crossed the bridge to direction 0  7 0 3 : 8 0 0
        ...car10 (->)  crossed the bridge to direction 0  7 0 3 : 8 0 0
car17 (<-)  is crossing the bridge to direction 1  7 0 0 : 6 2 0
car13 (<-)  is crossing the bridge to direction 1  7 0 0 : 5 3 0
car9 (<-)  is crossing the bridge to direction 1  7 0 0 : 5 3 0
        ...car9 (<-)  crossed the bridge to direction 1  7 0 0 : 5 0 3
        ...car17 (<-)  crossed the bridge to direction 1  7 0 0 : 5 0 3
        ...car13 (<-)  crossed the bridge to direction 1  7 0 0 : 5 0 3
car20 (->)  is crossing the bridge to direction 0  5 2 0 : 5 0 0
car19 (->)  is crossing the bridge to direction 0  5 2 0 : 5 0 0
car24 (->)  is crossing the bridge to direction 0  4 3 0 : 5 0 0
        ...car19 (->)  crossed the bridge to direction 0  4 1 2 : 5 0 0
        ...car20 (->)  crossed the bridge to direction 0  4 1 2 : 5 0 0
        ...car24 (->)  crossed the bridge to direction 0  4 0 3 : 5 0 0
car15 (<-)  is crossing the bridge to direction 1  4 0 0 : 4 1 0
car29 (<-)  is crossing the bridge to direction 1  4 0 0 : 3 2 0
car26 (<-)  is crossing the bridge to direction 1  4 0 0 : 2 3 0
        ...car15 (<-)  crossed the bridge to direction 1  4 0 0 : 2 2 1
```

...car29 (<-) crossed the bridge to direction 1 4 0 0 : 2 0 3
...car26 (<-) crossed the bridge to direction 1 4 0 0 : 2 0 3
car25 (->) is crossing the bridge to direction 0 1 3 0 : 2 0 0
car27 (->) is crossing the bridge to direction 0 1 3 0 : 2 0 0
car21 (->) is crossing the bridge to direction 0 1 3 0 : 2 0 0
...car25 (->) crossed the bridge to direction 0 1 2 1 : 2 0 0
...car27 (->) crossed the bridge to direction 0 1 0 3 : 2 0 0
...car21 (->) crossed the bridge to direction 0 1 0 3 : 2 0 0
car22 (<-) is crossing the bridge to direction 1 1 0 0 : 0 2 0
car23 (<-) is crossing the bridge to direction 1 1 0 0 : 0 2 0
...car22 (<-) crossed the bridge to direction 1 1 0 0 : 0 1 1
...car23 (<-) crossed the bridge to direction 1 1 0 0 : 0 0 2
car28 (->) is crossing the bridge to direction 0 0 1 0 : 0 0 0
...car28 (->) crossed the bridge to direction 0 0 0 1 : 0 0 0

C:\mspc\misc\resume\bridge_problem>

Index

Other texts by the same author:

- Spring 4 for Developing Enterprise Applications: An End-to-End Approach
- A quantitative text on *Java Performance and Scalability*